LEARNING RESOURCES CTR/NEW ENGLAND TECH.
GEN   B398.K7 M64 1981
Moline, Jon,   Plato's theory of understa

3 0147 0000 7913 0

D1786458

B398 .K7 M64 1981
Moline, Jon, 1937-
Plato's theory of understanding

DATE DUE

FEB 0 3 1999

NOV 0 1 06

HIGHSMITH 45-220

Plato's Theory of Understanding

Plato's Theory of Understanding

Jon Moline

THE UNIVERSITY OF WISCONSIN PRESS

Published 1981

The University of Wisconsin Press
114 North Murray Street
Madison, Wisconsin 53715

The University of Wisconsin Press, Ltd.
1 Gower Street
London WC1E 6HA, England

Copyright © 1981
The Board of Regents of the University of Wisconsin System
All rights reserved

First printing

Printed in the United States of America

For LC CIP information see the colophon

ISBN 0-299-08660-7

Publication of this book has been made possible in part
by a grant from the Andrew W. Mellon Foundation

Contents

	Acknowledgments	vii
	Introduction	ix
1	Knowledge and Ἐπιστήμη	3
	Disparities between knowledge and Platonic ἐπιστήμη	7
	Non-Platonic Greek epistemic usage	12
	Euripides and the Socratic paradox	22
	Other Greek perspectives on the Socratic paradox	25
	Platonic ἐπιστήμη, excellence, and knowledge	27
2	Dialectic and Ἐπιστήμη	32
	Ἐπιστήμη, the dialectician, and the ability to give an account	33
	Dialectical testing and refutation	37
	The epistemic necessity of the ability to give an account	41
	The epistemic sufficiency of the ability to give an account	43
	The breakdown of Plato's confidence in the epistemic *sufficiency* of accounts	46
3	Ἐπιστήμη and the Psyche	52
	The parts of the psyche	53
	Faculties or agents?	57
	The activites of the parts	58
	The achievement of psychic harmony	62
	The psyche and the Socratic paradoxes	71
	Anthropomorphism, vicious regress, and the unity of the psyche	74
	Ἐπιστήμη as a relation of the psyche to an extrapsychic reality	78
4	Ἐπιστήμη and Forms in Early and Middle Dialogues	79
	The familiarity of forms	81
	The theory of forms as a philosophy of science	83
	Medicine and the forms as causes	84
	Early and middle Platonic forms as powers	88
	The separation of the forms	95
	Forms as noetic or intelligible objects	97
	The noetic "world"	100
	The "arguments for the existence of forms"	105

	Mixtures, ingredients, copies, and paradigms	109
	Forms, universals, and self-predication	112
	Individuals, forms, subjects, and predicates	115
	Conclusion	117
5	Ἐπιστήμη, Reality, and Truth	119
	Paradigms, copies, and approximations	121
	The paradigm/copy distinction as applied to accounts	123
	Destructive testing and the survival of the true or real	129
	Meaning, thinking, and reality	134
	Negation, falsity, and meaning	138
6	Eleaticism, Division, and Ἐπιστήμη in the Late Dialogues	141
	Did Plato abandon the power/mixture model?	143
	Sensible things as compounds of εἴδη and δυνάμεις in the late dialogues	149
	The challenge of extreme Eleaticism	155
	The ontological, dialectical, and epistemic significance of *Theaetetus* 200 ff.	157
	The ontological basis for dialectical account-giving in later dialogues	165
	The epistemological insufficiency of dialectical testing in the late dialogues	171
	Conclusion	178
	Notes	187
	Glossary of Greek Terms with Pronunciations	237
	Index	241

Acknowledgments

The interpretation of Plato offered in this book is the product of fifteen years of teaching Plato and Aristotle to graduate and undergraduate students at the University of Wisconsin, Madison, and, on a visiting appointment for one academic year, at the University of Texas in Austin. I am grateful to the Institute for Research in the Humanities and to the Graduate School Research Committee of the University of Wisconsin for making it possible to work on this book with the intensity required. I am grateful also to the National Humanities Center for help in preparing the typescript. To my wife, Sandra, and to my sons, Kevin and Eric, I owe a debt of gratitude for their patience at having a book written in their midst. Preliminary drafts of the manuscript over a period of years have been improved by the criticism and encouragement of colleagues and students too numerous to mention without risking unfair omissions. To these co-workers I again express thanks. I am conscious of special debts to Professor Friedrich Solmsen, Professor William H. Hay, and to the late Professor Julius Weinberg, to whose memory the work is gratefully dedicated. Part of Chapter 3 appeared in a somewhat different form as "Plato on the Complexity of the Psyche," *Archiv für Geschichte der Philosophie* (1978):1–26.

Introduction

The dialogues of Plato are perennially appealing, and not only to philosophers. They are still read with fascination by educators, pundits, political scientists, psychologists, sociologists, rhetoricians, bureaucrats, business people, and journalists. Plato showed an attractive concern with questions of enduring importance to the world of affairs: What traits in a person would justify our entrusting him or her with power over us? Can we ascertain reliably that a person has or lacks such traits, and if so, how? How can such traits be cultivated? Upon what do they depend for their sustenance? These are the questions which give epistemology and related disciplines their importance for thoughtful people who are not professional philosophers, and for some thoughtful people who are.

Such readers are attracted also by the Platonic zest for inquiry, discussion, and the examination of life that knows no disciplinary boundaries. Plato's dialogues depict a sustained attempt to develop and refine a powerful system that would unite in one coherent conception our politics, administration, education, athletic and military activity, economics, art, and science. Those who aspire to something more ambitious and more satisfying intellectually than a fragmented understanding of life's activities and concerns find the sustained attempt at integrity, range, and simplicity in Plato's dialogues exemplary.

From first to last Plato's dialogues have as their central integrating concept Plato's notion of ἐπιστήμη. This is usually interpreted as knowledge, but as I argue in Chapter 1, the term "knowledge" has become so debased in our day that it fails to convey adequately the power and range of Plato's notion. In this work I have tried to convey that power and range by considering ἐπιστήμη from a number of viewpoints. The principal unifying task of the work is its coordinated elucidation of ἐπιστήμη from these different but related viewpoints. This is an especially appropriate unifying theme for a work on Plato, for Plato himself uses the simile of "walking around and examining from all sides" the subject of one's inquiry.

Chapter 2 explores the dialectical tests which Plato believed all and only those who have ἐπιστήμη are capable of passing. It thus explores the overt linguistic behaviors he believed characteristic of those who are in the condition of ἐπιστήμη.

Chapter 3 examines Plato's conception of ἐπιστήμη as a condition of the psyche, a condition in which the psyche's parts are so adjusted that one whose psyche is in this condition will act rightly.

Chapter 4 recognizes that Plato regarded ἐπιστήμη as an understanding *of* certain objects, objects he often characterized as εἴδη, or forms. In this chapter these forms are interpreted and their role in sustaining the condition of ἐπιστήμη is clarified.

Chapter 5 is based upon the recognition that Plato regarded ἐπιστήμη also as an understanding of truth and reality. The chapter explores his quite unusual views on truth and reality, relating these to his views about meaning, and exploring some of the difficulties into which these views led him. It argues that Plato recognized and took account of these difficulties in dialogues of his later, "critical" period.

Chapter 6 explores additional difficulties posed for Plato's system by his adopting the view that dialectic involves a division of the objects of ἐπιστήμη. It advances the hypothesis that Plato's construal of dialectic as division had important implications not simply for his ontology, but for his views about epistemology and politics, which he had founded on an earlier and now quite untenable conception of dialectic. It thus helps explain Plato's having abandoned the political model of the *Republic* in favor of that of the *Laws*, and integrates the political developments of the *Laws* into a coherent picture of the epistemological and ontological views of the late, critical dialogues.

In the interpretation of ἐπιστήμη which this book offers it inadvertently challenges recent interpretive orthodoxy. An orthodoxy involves a paradigm of inquiry, a restriction of methods, and a use of assumptions which are seldom recognized as such and virtually never examined or defended. The orthodoxy in question here is a by-product of the verificationism which was so prominent in Anglo-American philosophy from the 1930s through the mid-1960s. Verificationism's paradigm of inquiry is the quest for certainty. Its methods are restricted to what are conceived to be ways of showing that a given proposition is certainly true. Moreover, adherents of this orthodoxy tend to assume that only others who accept what it involves are doing philosophy.

Within this broad orthodoxy certainty was sought in various ways. A few sought it in sense data. Others sought it in conceptual truths discovered by the analysis of meanings. The latter sort of philosopher cast an especially long shadow over the interpretation of Plato. If one is not willing to deny that Plato was doing philosophy, and if one's paradigm of the philosopher is the person engaged in the quest for certainty by analyzing the use of words and articulating the results of the analysis as verifiable conceptual truths, then one will interpret Plato as engaged (perhaps only half-heartedly or confusedly) in this same quest. And to the extent that

Introduction

what Plato articulated conflicts with the documented use of Greek terms (or even with the use of alleged synonyms in English) such an interpreter will tend to judge him a careless philosopher.

Owing to the work of such important contemporary philosophers as Karl Popper, Willard van Orman Quine, and Hilary Putnam, this recent orthodoxy in Anglo-American philosophy is waning.[1] As it wanes it becomes more and more obvious that its influence on interpreters of Plato has been largely unfortunate, for it has obscured some of Plato's more interesting philosophical aims, methods, assumptions, and contributions.

A defender of such an orthodoxy approaches Plato with a built-in bias against seeing any large-scale, wide-ranging argument involving many key concepts as being unified or even unifiable. What is such a defender likely to miss, or to misconstrue, in reading Plato? He or she is likely to ignore Plato's having called for our taking a synoptic view of seemingly disparate problems and areas of inquiry. It is not likely to register with such an interpreter that Plato apparently went to the trouble of coining the Greek word συνοπτικός, "synoptic," "seeing the whole together," "taking a comprehensive view," and that he did so in describing his methodology at *Republic* 537C. Such disparate problems and areas of inquiry as are involved in psychology and politics are likely to strike such an interpreter as self-contained, and as having little or no connection with problems of philosophical understanding or knowledge. The orthodox interpreter will favor reading Plato's treatment of each of these problems or areas of inquiry as self-contained and independent of one another, much as they would probably have been in the work of later verificationist philosophers. Such an interpreter is still temperamentally attuned to the canons of logical positivism even though he or she now knows them to be false.

This book presents an interpretation of Plato which reflects a different paradigm of inquiry and different methods and results. An interpretation of Plato is an hypothesis about what he meant. Like hypotheses in physics, interpretive hypotheses typically cannot be shown to be exactly true, but can at best be given every appropriate opportunity to show themselves inadequate (if not exactly false). These opportunities lie in an exploration of what such an hypothesis implies and in a careful comparison of these implications with the relevant data. These data will include chiefly the textual evidence provided by the dialogues themselves in their best Greek

---

1. See, e.g., the following essays: Karl Popper, "Science: Conjectures and Refutations," in *Conjectures and Refutations: The Growth of Scientific Knowledge*, 3rd ed. rev. (London, 1969), pp. 33–59; Willard van Orman Quine, "Two Dogmas of Empiricism," in *From a Logical Point of View* (Cambridge, Mass., 1951), pp. 20–46; Hilary Putnam, "Language and Philosophy" and "Philosophy of Language and the Rest of Philosophy," in *Mind, Language and Reality* (Cambridge, 1975), pp. 1–32, vii–xvii.

editions and by previous and contemporary Greek writings which might shed light on their meaning.

A better interpretation of Plato's work will be one which fits these data better than preceding ones. In this work I have set out to provide such an interpretation, recognizing that if it is better, it can be judged so only as a whole, and that it will of necessity owe much to the work of other interpreters, whose contribution is gratefully acknowledged. In an area of scholarship which is 2,400 years old, it would be a mistake to seek, expect, or claim novelty for anything save an interpretation regarded as a whole. Nothing which breaks radical new ground can be expected in such a well-plowed area. What is to be sought, rather, is the resolute avoidance of mistakes of interpretation. In the interpretation of Plato, as in physics or philosophy, a mistaken hypothesis may stimulate much fruitful inquiry. But our goal, like that of Plato's Socrates, is to "get through without making a mistake"; it is to avoid whatever mistakes we can by making our hypotheses fit and account for the data as best we can.

Fitting these data better involves at least two things—fitting the data more precisely, with less distortion or strain, and fitting and integrating *more* of the relevant data. In trying to work out a better interpretation of Plato's views, therefore, I have tried to respect both his temporal development as a philosopher who corrected himself and the topical seamlessness of his work. And I have tried to keep in mind the wide range of people who are now interested in better understanding the views of one of the most provocative and engaging of philosophers.

Respecting this topical seamlessness has required the use of tools not in favor in orthodox interpretations. One cannot suture incisions with a scalpel, and the tools of conceptual analysis, useful as they are, are the intellectual counterparts of scalpels. Those who recognize just how fragmented modern inquiry has become, with its specialties such as psychiatry, philosophy, and political science, will know that the intellectual counterparts of incisions are there to be sutured. Plato had a remarkably broad selection of intellectual tools, and to appreciate their use in his work one has to adopt similar tools as an interpreter. In this book such tools are brought to bear upon Plato's treatment of ἐπιστήμη.

The reader has been invited to approach ἐπιστήμη as one would a black box about which one wanted to understand all one could, asking, first, whether we have in our language a word for such a box; second, what sorts of sounds or other behaviors the box characteristically emits; third, how the box works internally to emit such sounds or behaviors; fourth, what external objects the box reacts to; fifth, what sort of view is involved in saying that the box draws its "truth," "reality," or "nourishment" from

Introduction

external sources; and sixth, how these external sources are structured on Plato's view, and what implications this structure has for his application of the notion of ἐπιστήμη to politics. In approaching ἐπιστήμη in this way one comes to see it as central to Plato's philosophical and practical concerns.

In a work of this scope two omissions call, perhaps, for specific comment. First, I have not attempted to address what has been called the Socratic question—the question of where, and how, one can discern in the dialogues which positive views are to be attributed to Socrates and which to Plato himself. Attempts to answer this question are in my judgment futile, for no data exist which might weaken the credibility of the many plausible, alternative answers which we can devise. Instead, I have interpreted the philosophical views presented sympathetically in the dialogues as Plato's own, recognizing that Socrates was probably responsible for some of these, though we have no way of telling which. The dialogues are Plato's own, and are best read as such.

Secondly, I have exercised considerable caution in appealing to Aristotle's remarks about Plato and Platonists. These remarks are valuable, and no interpreter can ignore the testimony of so brilliant a man who had such unexampled opportunity to become familiar with Plato's views. Where appropriate, I have relied without hesitation on Aristotle's remarks. But where is this appropriate? On this question I have taken a less optimistic line than many interpreters. Why?

Aristotle was a person of vastly different temperament and philosophical interests from Plato, and appears to have cared little for the chief subject of this book—epistemology. He had biases and limitations which his own work at *Rhetoric* 1378a has ironically equipped us to recognize as limiting the credibility of some of his remarks. Which remarks are these? They are his remarks concerning the Platonic forms, the objects of Platonic ἐπιστήμη. In all probability Aristotle never accepted the Platonic forms, as Düring and others have recognized.[2] More importantly, he may never have understood them. In the *Posterior Analytics*, which appears to

2. For powerful reasons to doubt that Aristotle ever accepted the Platonic theory of forms, see E. Frank, "The Fundamental Opposition of Plato and Aristotle," *American Journal of Philology* 61 (1940): 34–53, 166–85; and the following studies by I. Düring: "Aristotle and the Theory of Ideas," *Eranos* 37 (1938): 120–45; "Problems in Aristotle's *Protrepticus*," *Eranos* 52 (1954): 139–71; "Aristotle on Ultimate Principles from 'Nature and Reality,'" in I. Düring and G.E.L. Owen, eds., *Aristotle and Plato in the Mid-Fourth Century* (Göteborg, 1960), pp. 35–55, esp. pp. 53–55; and *Aristotle's Protrepticus*, Studia Graeca et Latina Gothoburgensia 12 (Göteborg, 1957), pp. 213 ff. See also K. von Fritz and E. Kapp, *Aristotle's "Constitution of Athens" and Related Texts* (New York, 1950), p. 34.

be among Aristotle's earliest Academic works, Aristotle remarked that "the forms may be dismissed; for they are mere twittering" (83a33–34). This hardly suggests a balanced assessment by a judicious critic who has, in all goodwill, made a serious effort to understand the point of view he is criticizing, an interpreter who is sufficiently unbiased on this matter to be trusted for hints as to how we may understand it. And this remark is not an isolated indication of possible bias. At *Metaphysics* 991a he remarks that if we say that forms are παραδείγματα, "paradigms" or "patterns", and that other things share or participate in them, we are simply using "empty phrases and poetical metaphors." The pre-Socratic medical background for the view he is so lightly dismissing here makes this dismissal seem very nearly outrageous. This background is explored in Chapter 4 below.

There is an additional reason for treating some of Aristotle's remarks about Plato's views with caution. Probably from the beginning of his philosophical career Aristotle looked at the world as "*logos*-structured," bifurcated into subjects and predicates correlated conveniently with the principal grammatical elements in the Indo-European language he happened to know. Plato never looked at the world in this way, as will be argued in Chapter 6, and Aristotelian and other interpretations of Plato which construe his views as if he did look at the world as having a subject-predicate structure are radically misleading. Indeed, more misunderstanding of Plato has flowed and continues to flow from this one ancient error than from all others combined.

Not only did Aristotle probably never accept the Platonic forms, it is also probable that he never assigned philosophical importance to the question-and-answer process of dialectic by which Plato held we come to understand the forms. At *Republic* 532D and 534E, Plato had placed dialectic above all other studies as the "coping stone" of his philosophy, and at *Philebus* 57E–59C he insisted that it was the truest and most accurate of studies. Even in Aristotle's *Topics*, which is widely regarded as an early work dating probably from his days in Plato's Academy, Aristotle evidently does not even consider dialectic to be philosophy (101a35–b4). And far from holding that it is the truest and most accurate of studies, Aristotle characterizes dialectic as beginning and ending with mere opinion (100a18–b23). As Friedrich Solmsen remarked, "His disagreement with Plato, even if never allowed to come into the open, would seem to be radical."[3]

---

3. Friedrich Solmsen, "Dialectic without the Forms," in G.E.L. Owen, ed., *Aristotle on Dialectic: The Topics* (Oxford, 1968), p. 55.

Introduction

Common prudence as well as a concern for fairness would suggest that we not place much weight on interpretations offered by one who, even in his youth, apparently held radically different and even hostile views. It seems more reasonable to read Aristotle in the light of what his teacher said, than to read Plato in the light of what his student said, even if we find Aristotle the more congenial of the two philosophers today. This seems not only reasonable but a prerequisite for fairness, given Aristotle's tendency to interpret his predecessors as striving more or less unsuccessfully to attain his level of philosophical perfection (see, e.g., *Metaphysics* 993a10–17). As Alisdair MacIntyre aptly put it, "We have to steer between the danger of a dead antiquarianism, which enjoys the illusion that we can approach the past without preconceptions, and that other danger, so apparent in such philosophical historians as Aristotle and Hegel, of believing that the whole point of the past was that it should culminate with us. History is neither a prison nor a museum, nor is it a set of materials for self-congratulation."[4]

This book is written so as to be accessible to all serious students and scholars interested in Plato's views, whether or not these students and scholars are trained in philosophy, classical literature, or Attic Greek. Greek words are translated where possible in their early occurrences at least, though they are not thereafter abandoned in favor of their translations, for it is necessary to keep reminding ourselves both that important nuances of the Greek are among the chief constraints upon interpretation and that misleading nuances of English translations are among the most formidable obstacles to the understanding of Plato's views. Where nuances are important, as in Chapters 1 and 5 especially, they are explained in some detail. Translations are mine except as indicated. In order to reduce their impatience at repeatedly seeing words they might not know how to pronounce, readers who do not know Attic Greek will find approximate pronunciations of important terms indicated in the Glossary.

It has been my intention to keep the main line of argument uncluttered. Notes are used to amplify points which various readers having specialized interests might want to see developed more fully than the main line of argument in the text requires.

Finally, I will ask the reader to attempt to set aside, if only temporarily, any preconceptions about Plato, or the Greeks, or even about what philosophy is, and to approach these as topics which can again be fresh and a source of that wonder in which the love of wisdom begins and is renewed.

---

4. Alisdair MacIntyre, *A Short History of Ethics* (New York, 1966), p. 4.

Plato's Theory of Understanding

1
Knowledge and Ἐπιστήμη

What account of knowledge did Plato give? Those who know the dialogues ought to be reminded of the all-too-familiar question, "Have you stopped beating your wife?" The question about Plato's account of knowledge is like the trite question about wife-beating in that it begs a prior question of some importance: Did Plato ever give an account of knowledge? Indeed, it begs a still deeper question: Did Plato even have a concept of knowledge?

Those who ask, "What was Plato's account of knowledge?" perhaps mean to elicit an account of Platonic ἐπιστήμη. But Platonic ἐπιστήμη is not knowledge.[1] And if it is not knowledge, his account of it is not an account of knowledge. In this chapter I argue that it is a mistake to construe Platonic ἐπιστήμη as knowledge. In subsequent ones I reinterpret Platonic ἐπιστήμη in the light of these arguments, examining his dialectical, psychological, semantic, and ontological treatments of ἐπιστήμη and its objects. My aim is to make contemporary assessment and appreciation of Plato's views on their philosophical merits easier than it would otherwise be, though this work is not directly concerned with those merits. It is concerned with the prior task of reinterpretation.

The principles underlying this reinterpretation of ἐπιστήμη are derived from a view of the tasks facing the translator, the interpreter, and the present-day student of an ancient philosopher, or of any philosopher who wrote in a language other than English as readers of Plato speak it now. For good or ill, translations furnish the terminology for the most widely read interpretations and commentaries. In their terms Plato will be understood or misunderstood by current readers. They will take Plato to be speaking their language as they find themselves speaking it, and any oddities that result are likely to be laid at the door of Plato himself. Attributing such oddities to Plato may be inaccurate. Whether it is or not will depend upon how well translators and interpreters have conveyed in English the force of what Plato said in Greek.

Conveying this force is far more difficult than has been widely appreciated, however. To speak or to write is to *accomplish* a number of disparate things, some intended, some perhaps not. Awareness of this fundamental fact on the part of Anglo-American philosophers has been encouraged by the pioneering work of J. L. Austin and furthered by more recent writers.[2] But too few have realized its significance for translation and interpretation.

Fortunately, some linguists and writers on translation have begun to realize its significance. E. A. Nida, in his presidential address to the Linguistic Society of America, argued that the translator should aim at functional equivalence.[3] There is not as yet an adequate theory of functional equivalence. But even without an adequate theory, the working intuition behind the notion of functional equivalence is clear enough: the translator's degree of success will depend upon the extent to which the translated text permits the readers for whom it is intended to understand how the original text was evidently designed to strike the readers for whom *it* was intended. One aims to convey the author's "linguistic intentions," though one recognizes that the author will have expressed these with the intended readers' capacities and likely reactions in mind.[4] To know all an author or speaker means by what he says requires knowing what he intends one to think; thus, conveying an author's meaning *involves* conveying the author's linguistic intentions.[5]

Effective writers tend to make upon their intended readers precisely the overall impression which they intend. This ought to be a truism. Such writers tend to convey to their readers their linguistic intentions. They are able to do so because they take into account their readers' foibles; they learn their readers' capacities and likely reactions, and express themselves accordingly. Translators and interpreters should attempt to do likewise.[6] In so doing we attempt to meet a standard of translation and interpretation. Even when there are extensive differences in knowledge and conceptual scheme between ancient and modern readers, modern readers can be led to understand, if not to adopt, the point of view of the intended ancient readers, and it must be the interpreter's task to facilitate this understanding and its application to texts.[7]

Knowledge and ἐπιστήμη

Those who teach the classics are usually well aware of how elusive any large measure of success is by the above standard. Nevertheless, the attempt to adhere to this standard serves to correct many avoidable errors. It is exceedingly unlikely, for example, that any ancient writer intended to convey to his readers the impression that he did not know how to speak his own language well enough to avoid confusions and absurdities. Let us suppose that on the basis of all we can learn about those readers and the likely determinants of their reactions to such a text we can ascertain that what the ancient writer actually wrote is unlikely to have conveyed to them this impression. If so, then a translator falls far short of the standard in allowing the translated text to convey it to modern readers.

This standard is often flouted. Even quite knowledgeable discussions of Plato's epistemology if phrased in terms derived from translations will lead many contemporaries who would like to understand his views to conclude that Plato was either less than competent or somewhat off his beam. He was neither. But such contemporaries may be pardoned for thinking otherwise. Many of them are philosophers or students of philosophy. They know no Greek, but they do know an absurdity when they encounter one. And they know that in their philosophical moments at least, they ordinarily conceive of knowing in ways which render the alleged Platonic account of it not merely alien but wrong in obvious and confused ways.

This is not to deny that there are partial Platonizers of Anglo-American thought scattered about. Nor is it to deny that the tradition of attempting to Platonize Anglo-American thought has had an effect in epistemology classrooms.[8] It is only to point out that if a student told most epistemology instructors what translators and interpreters have Plato telling us, such instructors would at best tell him that he lacked a sufficient command of English to do philosophy in this language or that his ear had been corrupted, possibly corrupted by reading too much Plato.

In saying this I am not suggesting that Plato's epistemology gives us a bad account of knowledge, though that would be the natural view for a philosopher now to take on conventional interpretations of it; indeed, a great many of my non–Greek-reading colleagues in epistemology do take it, though they are usually too kind to say so baldly. Rather, I am suggesting that in its most distinctive claims, it was no account of knowledge at all, and that we must free ourselves from the spell of translations and interpretations which suggest that it was before we can begin to understand Plato's epistemology aright.

In this chapter I wish to make possible the understanding of Plato's epistemology by first removing the thick layers of traditional detritus which now obscure it from contemporary view. In subsequent chapters I wish to describe in detail what has been excavated.

No extensive or novel claims about Plato's account of ἐπιστήμη, or about knowledge for that matter, will be needed to excavate Plato's concept. What is needed is an unblinking look at the differences between the distinctive Platonic concept of ἐπιστήμη and the concept of knowledge as employed by those who are the primary users of contemporary translations and interpretations of Plato. It will be sufficient to show two things:

1. As Plato employed the concept of ἐπιστήμη in distinctively philosophical passages, it differed in fundamental ways from the concept of knowledge as it is now employed. It does not correspond in its uses to the uses of "knowledge" and "know" among English translators' and interpreters' primary clientele.
2. As Greek writers other than Plato employed the concept of ἐπιστήμη, it could and very often did differ in the same fundamental ways from this concept of knowledge as now employed.

It will be necessary to establish both of these points. Merely to establish the first would only enhance the natural but erroneous view that Plato gave and employed a perverse and paradoxical account of knowledge, an account of a concept which it might be alleged that the early Greek reader had and employed, not as Plato prescribed, but more or less as we do.

But what is it for one concept to differ in fundamental ways from another? How do we count concepts? Doubtless for any type of thing, x, it is a matter of judgment just how deviant a specimen or token of x has to be before we can plausibly conclude that it is not a bad x but a mislabeled y. Concepts have terms as their vehicles, and they are differentiated on the basis of the disparate uses to which these terms are put. One concept can, of course, have two quite different terms as its alternate vehicles. But we can reasonably conclude that we have, not one concept, but two concepts marked by two different terms if we can discern that the contextual applications of the two terms differ markedly. Such marked differences would show in the consequences that followed from using such terms of their subjects, and in disparate relations of compatibility and incompatibility between using these terms of their subjects and using certain other terms.[9] It will be shown that knowledge and Platonic ἐπιστήμη differ in precisely such ways as these. Once we have shown this, it will be plain that no account of Platonic ἐπιστήμη could pass for even a bad account of knowledge. And once having made this plain, we can make a new beginning in understanding Plato's epistemology in its intimate connections with his other philosophical concerns.

This attention to terminology and its use is not intended to suggest that the issue at stake is primarily linguistic or even conceptual, however. It is certainly at least that, but it is also substantive and deep. In describing ἐπιστήμη Plato thought he was describing a condition of the psyche in which it apprehends reality in a special way and has its behavior automatically reordered. Plato held that this is the best possible condition for humans to strive for, and we must attempt to understand all this condition involves. But that will be impossible so long as we confuse this condition with the lesser one of knowledge. Why then is it a confusion to take Platonic ἐπιστήμη for knowledge?

Disparities between knowledge and Platonic ἐπιστήμη

There are two chief disparities between knowledge as conceived of by the interpreter's primary clientele and philosophical ἐπιστήμη as conceived of by Plato. The first has to do with the necessity of having a defense of the claims in which one's knowledge or ἐπιστήμη is expressed, and the second has to do with the conduct knowing or having ἐπιστήμη necessarily involves.

At *Phaedo* 76B Socrates asks a rhetorical question: ἀνὴρ ἐπιστάμενος περὶ ὧν ἐπίσταται ἔχοι ἂν δοῦναι λόγον ἢ οὔ; This has usually been rendered, "When a man knows anything, can he give an account of what he knows or not?" Simmias answers that he necessarily can. There are many such passages in the dialogues, and they illustrate a condition which Plato placed upon all ἐπιστήμη whatever.[10] On this condition, one who has ἐπιστήμη must be able to give an account. This condition is evinced at *Laches* 190C; *Alcibiades* I 108E–109A, 117A; *Gorgias* 465A, 510A; *Republic* 543C, 582A, D; *Symposium* 202A; *Phaedrus* 276A; *Phaedo* 76B; *Ion* 532B–C, 541E–542A; *Laws* 966A–B. Being able to give an account is a *consequence* of having ἐπιστήμη. Being able to give an account is no simple matter, as I shall argue fully in Chapter 2, but it plainly involved being able to articulate a defense upon demand in response to probing Socratic questioning.[11] One who proved unable to do this was invariably held to lack ἐπιστήμη. (See, e.g., *Meno* 84A.)

Would those who read Plato in English now regard one's having knowledge as having the same consequence? In our century there have been a few philosophers who would.[12] But consider the following comments by a contemporary philosopher:

Many women quite unreasonably jump to conclusions about their husbands, and we do not say that they knew what they say about their husbands to be true even when they happen to be right by accident. But what would we say of a woman who always made seemingly unreasonable but in fact quite accurate accusations about her husband? She takes one look at him and says "You've been up to something," and we find that he has indeed been losing too much at the races or kissing his secretary. We would not of course be prepared to say on the evidence of only one such occasion that she knew her husband had been up to something; but if it happened often enough, we would say that while we do not know how she knows this, somehow or other she does know it. It may be that we eventually explain her knowledge by the fact that there are some subtle indications of her husband's peccadilloes (the slight flush, the barely averted eye) in his face. But she may be quite unable to point to these. She acts, in fact, just like the unreasonable women, except that she is always right. And we would surely say, given all this information, that she knows on all these occasions, including the first.[13]

If we would say what Griffiths claims we would about this case, then we do not think it a necessary condition for all knowledge that the knower be able to defend his or her claim. We would be inclined to use "know" and "knowledge" on far less stringent grounds. A moment's thought will indicate that Griffiths *is* right. At the age of two my younger son knew that his name was Eric, and would have said so if asked. But he could not have defended the claim if pressed. And you now know whether or not your legs are crossed, even if you cannot refute the charge that you think so merely because you are either dreaming or the victim of some mad neurologist's machinations upon your brain. Nevertheless you know. Yet Plato would deny that you, my two-year-old, and the wife in Griffith's example have ἐπιστήμη. Consider Socrates' treatment of Anytus' claims about the vices of sophists in *Meno* 92B–C. Doubtless Socrates as Plato described him and Plato himself considered those claims perfectly true, but Socrates suggests that Anytus is perhaps a wizard since he says he knows what sophists are even though he concedes that neither he nor anyone close to him has any experience of them. Plainly, Socrates is represented in translations and commentaries as thinking that Anytus does not know what he is talking about, that his claim to know is spurious. This strikes many readers today as unfair of Socrates. In our age of multiple-choice and true-false examinations, Anytus would get more generous treatment: Anytus is right about the sophists, after all, as Socrates would be the first to agree. So why say he doesn't know? Few of us have any experience in measuring the distance to the sun, nor do many of us know anyone who has told us precisely how the distance is measured, but we nevertheless know that the distance is about 93 million miles.[14]

One might suspect that in requiring that one's alleged ἐπιστήμη be accountable, Plato was perhaps alluding only to what we might call "knowledge by description," not "knowledge by acquaintance."[15] It might be claimed that the only reason we say that a student knows something on the basis of a true-false or multiple-choice examination is that we wish to credit him with mere acquaintance with the right answers. It might be pointed out that even we might be inclined to demand solid reasons supporting a claim to knowledge by description on pain of denying that it is knowledge in that sense, as when a chemistry instructor requires that a

Disparities between knowledge and ἐπιστήμη

student show not merely the correct answer but the calculations by which he or she arrived at it. Thus, in the case of the distance to the sun, most of us can be said to know only in the sense that we are acquainted with a certain figure, not in the sense that we could adequately defend that figure in the face of technical objections.

The chief difficulty with this suspicion is one which Cross and Woozley appear to have sensed.[16] Plato does not distinguish ἐπιστήμη by description from ἐπιστήμη by acquaintance, and ἐπιστήμη as he describes it is not congruent with either sort of knowledge. Even in cases which strike us as cases of knowledge by description, he talks as if there were some *object* one had discerned and gained an acquaintance with; and in cases which strike us as cases of knowledge by acquaintance, he talks as if one could not possibly have gained such a knowledge without gaining the ability to give and defend an *account* or description.[17] He often describes a psyche's exposure to the forms in terms of seeing, coming into contact with, etc., which sounds to us like becoming acquainted with something, but he nevertheless denies that one has ἐπιστήμη in such cases if one cannot give and defend an account of what one has "seen."[18] Hence, one cannot claim that the differences between ἐπιστήμη and knowledge are the very differences we recognize between knowledge by description and knowledge by acquaintance.

If this were the only oddity in Plato's treatment of ἐπιστήμη, we might be inclined to think that ἐπιστήμη was simply a confused amalgam of what we call knowledge by acquaintance and knowledge by description.[19] But a second supremely divisive difference between knowledge and ἐπιστήμη blocks this inclination. This difference is suggested by the views commonly known as the Socratic paradoxes. According to these views as commonly rendered, no one does wrong willingly, and ἀρετή, "excellence" or "virtue," is knowledge. (For the first view see *Gorgias* 468C, 509E; *Protagoras* 345D–E; *Republic* 589D; *Laws* 860D–E. For the second, see *Gorgias* 460B–D; *Protagoras* 360B–D; *Republic* 340E, 342A–B, 351A–C; *Theaetetus* 176C.) An account of the psychological basis for these views will be given in Chapter 3. But even here a preliminary treatment is possible.

These views have often been treated obliquely as the embarrassment they are by interpreters whose inclination has been to represent Plato as a respectable modern theorist of knowledge. This has been facilitated perhaps by labeling such views paradoxical, since it is easy to think that what is paradoxical is in some way mysterious, unaccountable, or in any event so contrary to common sense as to be unworthy of serious scrutiny under the heading of epistemology. We are unlikely to give sympathetic scrutiny to views we believe paradoxical.

In an uncharacteristic lapse of sympathy Gregory Vlastos speaks of the allegedly Socratic view that virtue is knowledge as a "savage doctrine."[20] Vlastos calls Socrates a "heartless intellectual" (p. 8), and believes that there are plain facts which are incompatible with his view. He sees Socratic "knowledge" as a merely intellectual arrangement of information, yet accuses Socrates of confusing faith with such knowledge. Not even the few theorists of knowledge who sympathize with what they conceive to be Plato's view to the point of denying quite generally that one who is unable to give an account *knows* would be willing to venture the opinion that one who *does* know is thereby rendered virtuous. Nor would such theorists be willing to claim that all wrongdoing rests squarely upon ignorance.

Embarrassing or not, the view that ἀρετή, "excellence" or "virtue," is ἐπιστήμη cannot be ignored in any full attempt to understand what Plato thought ἐπιστήμη was, since they were willing to deny that one had ἐπιστήμη on no other evidence than a proven lack of ἀρετή, or virtue. (See, e.g., *Gorgias* 514D–520B.) This view is particularly relevant to the opinion that ἐπιστήμη was simply knowledge conceived of in a confused way. On closer examination the alleged confusions are points essential to the Platonic concept of ἐπιστήμη. Consider, for example, the *Protagoras*, where we find a passage commonly rendered about as follows:

Cowards . . ., and likewise the rash and the mad, feel fears or confidence which are discreditable, and can they exhibit discreditable fear or confidence from any other cause than ignorance? (No.) Well, then, is it cowardice or courage that makes a man a coward? (Cowardice.) Yet we have seen that it is ignorance of what is to be feared that makes them cowards; and if this ignorance makes them cowards, and you agree that what makes them cowards is cowardice, ignorance of what is and is not to be feared must be cowardice. (He nodded.) Well, courage is the opposite of cowardice. (He agreed.) And knowledge of what is and is not to be feared is the opposite of ignorance of these things. (He nodded again.) Which is cowardice. (Here he assented with great reluctance.) Therefore knowledge of what is and is not to be feared is courage.[21]

The term rendered "knowledge" here is not ἐπιστήμη but one of Plato's contextual equivalents, σοφία.[22] But the entire argument is absurd on its face if σοφία so rendered. We all know very well that knowledge does not have this sort of efficacy, and that attributing knowledge to someone does not imply that the knowledgeable person will act rightly. This is perhaps why Socrates' view is labeled paradoxical: it is contrary to common δόξα, or opinion, about knowledge. If so, "paradox" is perhaps too weak a word, for the offense is not against mere δόξα, or opinion. It is against what we know very well—first, the current meanings of the relevant English words, and second, the facts about knowledgeable rogues. The Platonic Socrates is represented as knowing a fine selection of such rogues. (See *Euthydemus* 281B–C; *Cleitophon* 407A; *Charmides* 171D–172A; *Alcibiades* I 117D–118A.) But as practically any seven-year-old knows, knowledge does not prevent a person's being a rogue. It does not rectify the acts of the knower. If it did, there would be no physicians who smoked cigarettes, no logicians who indulged in fallacious arguments, and no fat track coaches. It is not incredible perhaps that Socrates and Plato believed there is *some* psychic state which rectifies the acts of those who are in it. But it is more than a little incredible that grown men with some experience of the world could have believed this happy state was mere knowledge. Knowledge is what we are said to have on the basis of the examinations we pass in college and university courses; yet, as both students and instructors are well aware, this has little connection with action and still less with right action. Even knowing the difference between right and wrong requires, not total avoidance of wrongdoing, but only remorse at it, making reparations for it, and the like.[23] Is it any wonder, then, that Socrates and Plato often strike contemporary students and many of their instructors as simpletons or, at best, as "heartless intellectuals"?

But were they simpletons or heartless intellectuals? The interpreter is not obligated to find (and should be a bit suspicious of finding) some reading of their views which will render them true or even very congenial to us today.[24] But one is obligated to take into account the fact that they were considered to be great philosophers and great men by those in at least as good a position to understand them as anyone is now. And then as now, being a great philosopher or a great man was scarcely compatible with holding, on the most important matters of conduct, views which even the experiences of a child would show to be absurd. Yet by telling us that Plato and Socrates believed virtue to be the same thing as knowledge, translators and interpreters do in effect tell us that these philosophers held such views.

But given the differences between the applications of "knowledge" and ἐπιστήμη which we have already canvassed, and given that both Socrates and Plato did have a wide experience of the world, it would seem a more likely hypothesis that they were not talking about what we would now call "knowledge" or "knowing" at all.

Although this hypothesis seems more likely, we are not entitled to accept it unless it is consistent with the sort of evidence about his readers' capacities which Plato would presumably have taken account of in devising ways to convey to them his linguistic intentions. Would Socrates or Plato have been thought to be wrenching epistemic terms quite away from their normal meaning or abusing them by speaking in naive, absurd, or perverse ways? We can scarcely claim that present-day incredulity at the epistemological views translators and interpreters attribute to Socrates and Plato is inappropriate if those absurd views would have generated the same sort of incredulity in comparable Greek readers of Plato's age.

But would they have generated such incredulity for Greeks? There are two sorts of evidence on this. One consists in the available evidence concerning previous patterns of epistemic usage. The other consists in the actual recorded reactions of readers such as Aristotle. Consideration of these two sorts of evidence will form step two in the argument that ἐπιστήμη cannot rightly be viewed as the same thing as knowledge.

Non-Platonic Greek epistemic usage

Here we face two questions, questions corresponding to the two chief differences between knowledge and Platonic ἐπιστήμη which were pointed out in the previous section:

1. Did other Greeks associate the ability to give and defend a λόγος or account closely with ἐπιστήμη?
2. Did other Greeks conceive of ἐπιστήμη as rectifying the conduct of the one who possessed it?

The notion of a λόγος was an extremely vague one in pre-Socratic usage, and many of the occurrences of the term λόγος bear senses much looser than that attained in Socratic and Platonic dialectic. But as will be argued in Chapter 2, the giving of a λόγος in a Socratic or Platonic sense required one's answering a question and defending one's answer with careful elaboration in response to further questions.

Plainly, neither Socrates nor Plato invented the question, the answer, or, for that matter, incredulity about some answers. Nor did they invent the suspicion that one who could not answer a fair question and defend the answer was not in the most admirable possible epistemic state. In the late-fifth-century Hippocratic treatise *The Nature of Man* 1, the author comments: "It is right [δίκαιον] that a person who correctly claims to 'know' [γιγνώσκειν] about matters should maintain his account victorious always [αἰεὶ ἐπικρατέοντα τόν λόγον τοῦ ἑωυτοῦ] if he 'knows' what *is* and if he presents it correctly."[25] The writer immediately goes on to say that by their lack of understanding (ἀσυνεσίης) the glib-tongued overthrow themselves in the words of their very own accounts. They will be overthrown or refuted by what they say, but those who possess understanding will not, provided they present correctly what they understand.

Socrates and Plato would have omitted this last proviso and would have relied instead upon elaborate constraints upon the fair testing of an account, as will be discussed in detail in Chapter 2. But even in the effort to

Non-Platonic Greek epistemic usage

lay down such constraints, they had their antecedents, however loose. In the infamous dialogue between the hapless Melians and the representatives of imperial Athens in Thucydides, the Athenians propose at 5. 85 that the two parties engage in a close, point-by-point examination of their positions in an attempt to discern what would be the wisest course:

> Since our accounts [λόγοι] are not to be made before the assembly, your purpose being, as it seems, that the people may not hear from us once and for all, in an uninterrupted account, arguments which are seductive and untested (for we know that it is with this in mind that you bring us before a few), why don't you who sit here do something still safer? Take up each point, and don't you make a single speech, either, but conduct the inquiry by replying at once to any statement of ours that seems to be unsatisfactory.

In Thucydides as in the Hippocratic medical treatises there are surprisingly frequent references to testing, "torturing," and possibly refuting someone's claims, with suggestions that such a refuted view is scarcely a sign of ἐπιστήμη, but shows rather the opposite.[26] From Homer's Nestor to Xenophon, practical men among the Greeks had long engaged in the give-and-take of argument expecting to be challenged and to be viewed as less than σοφός, or wise, if they could not defend what they had said.[27] Xenophon, who was the paradigm of conventionality and hardly the sort to embrace paradoxes, depicts Socrates as having argued that a good cavalry commander must be good at λόγοι. Interpreters are tempted to render λόγοι here as "speeches," but Socrates was not simply praising rhetoric: he was praising the sort of didactic account through which people learn, he claimed, every good lesson they acquire. And he claimed that those who have the deepest ἐπιστήμη on the most important matters are those who are best at λόγοι.[28]

The line between the λόγος, or account, which, for example, taught the best cavalry tactics, and the λόγος which taught what was best in general was doubtless quite indistinct at first, as Socrates' own efforts to sharpen it in the early dialogues of Plato illustrate. (*Meno* 72A ff. provides perhaps the most familiar example.) But the view that on whatever topic one is speaking, one will speak well and not be refuted provided one has that power which was variously termed ἐπιστήμη, σοφία, φρόνησις, γνῶσις, or σύνεσις was scarcely paradoxical. Indeed, to deny it would evidently have been paradoxical. As Havelock has argued, Greek culture in Plato's day was still shaped largely by the norms and requirements of the oral communication which had been until very recently the sole form of cultural transmission.[29] In an oral culture no one *can* hide behind the printed word. That anyone could be thought σοφός on the basis of something written or on the basis of something said but not defended after the fashion of fair questioning and response was an innovation which as yet had no deep roots. Plato's contempt for this innovation shows clearly in the *Protagoras* at 347C–348A and in the *Theaetetus* at 161E–162A. (Cp. *Phaedrus* 278B–D.) This was not a century of inarticulate mystics withdrawn from public life and communication, but rather an age of direct democracy and involvement in the give-and-take of discussion in the assembly and the gymnasia. It was not a century of authorities who wrote or spoke without expecting to explain and defend their views. Ἐπιστήμη was to be voiced.

On the second point at issue, the connection between having ἐπιστήμη or σοφία and being moved to act, we have much evidence of pre-Platonic opinion. The earliest lies in the chief vehicle for the education of Greeks from preliteral times down to the time of Plato and beyond, the Homeric corpus. Children were required to commit to memory large segments of this, as Xenophon testifies in his *Symposium* 3. 6. And the memories thus formed would have been refreshed in adults by the performances of rhapsodes, who were important cultural figures in Socrates' time, as we know from Plato's own *Ion*. Homeric patterns of all sorts were employed and even recommended for general use in later prose writing by rhetoricians.[30] Thus Homeric uses of epistemic terms would have been influential and vivid in the minds of Plato's intended readers.

Those uses scarcely suggest that it would have seemed paradoxical to such readers to think that ἐπιστήμη or σοφία had expression in action. Sufficiently powerful evidence on the point at issue is provided by a family of peculiarities which are perhaps impossible to render into contemporary classroom English without sacrificing crucial connotations of the original. Consider the verb οἶδα, conventionally rendered "I know," and employed by Plato as a synonym for ἐπίσταμαι. (See, e.g., *Alcibiades* I 106C–E, 112C–E; *Cratylus* 435D.) Homer employed it with nouns and adjectives in the accusative neuter plural to ascribe to people what we can conceive of only as emotional states, states of moral character, and dispositions to act. Homeric personae were said, literally and nonsensically for us, to "know gratitude" (χάριν εἰδέναι) by way of saying that they felt grateful, to "know friendly things towards each other" (φίλα εἰδότες ἀλλήλοισιν) by way of saying that they felt well-disposed towards each other, to "know conscious things" (πεπνύμενα εἰδώς) by way of saying either that they were in possession of their faculties or perhaps that they were wise.[31] Achilles at *Iliad* 24. 41 was said to "know fierce things" (ἄγρια οἶδεν) by way of saying that he had a fierce disposition, and Polyphemus at *Odyssey* 9. 189 was said to "know lawless things" (ἀθεμίστια ᾔδη) by way of saying that he had a lawless character.

Scholars have borne mute witness to the fact that such locutions cannot be translated without sacrificing the connotations of the original by sacri-

Non-Platonic Greek epistemic usage

ficing them, no doubt reluctantly. They have translated these locutions via terms which no Greekless reader would guess were supposed to be getting across to us the force of a term translated as "know" elsewhere in the same work.[32] One cannot but sympathize with the plight of translators. They could do little else given that

1. Οἶδα is conventionally rendered "I know."
2. Since the time of Hume, if not earlier, and certainly since the time of Freud, knowing and the intellect in general have been contrasted with and practically divorced from action and motivation for action.[33] Knowing and being motivated are thought to lie in disparate categories. No one today would say of a football linebacker that he "knows fierce things" by way of indicating that he had a fierce disposition on the field. The term "know" carries almost no behavioral guarantees today. An Elizabethan might be said to have known his wife on a given occasion, but that use of "know" seems almost incredible to native speakers of English in our time, and both requires and gets explanatory footnotes.
3. Such contrasts as these in the range of application of two terms count heavily against their having the same meaning. This was recognized by Aristotle at *Topics* 152b25 ff., for example, and the recognition of the importance of such contrasts remains to this day the cornerstone of linguistics, as Lyons and others have recognized. Doubtless there are vestiges of a more potent conception of knowledge in English, especially in the richer English of scholars, but these are just vestiges. With Bacon, many of us still believe that knowledge is power, for instance, but we also hold the un-Platonic belief that having such power is consistent with misusing it. Such locutions are quaint traces of a way of looking at action which is now widely incomprehensible or widely disputable as literally absurd if expressed in terms of knowing. We may say of a person that he "knows no fear," but hearers will take the remark as figurative. A similar remark in Homer would not be figurative.

The foregoing evidence of early Greek indifference to our distinctions does not stand alone. It is reinforced by the Homeric occurrences of ἐπίσταμαι itself, the verb which Plato most often used to suggest a state coextensive with the highest excellence in action, but one conventionally rendered in English as "know." The writer of *Iliad* 2 described the Arcadians as ἐπιστάμενοι πολεμίζειν. He probably did not mean merely that they knew how to fight or that they were well-skilled in fighting, as the translations conventionally say, but that they were spoiling for a fight as well. (*Iliad* 2. 611.) Surely there is more than skill or know-how at stake when Idomeneus replies to Poseidon's taunts as he and his comrades are treating their wounds. Poseidon asks, "Where are all the Achaeans' threats against the Trojans now?" Idomeneus replies at 13.222–223, οὔ τις ἀνὴρ νῦν αἴτιος ὅσσον γιγνώσκω. πάντες γὰρ ἐπιστάμεθα πτολεμίζειν. This is usually rendered, darkly, "No man now is responsible whom I know of. For all are skilled in fighting." I say "darkly" because a claim to skill is plainly not sufficient to meet the implied charge that the Achaeans are responsible for not being out on the field of battle making good their threats. In the next line Idomeneus disclaims any fear in his men, but even skill and a lack of fear together would not stave off the implied charge. People who are skilled fighters and do not fear fighting nevertheless suffer defeats sometimes, particularly if their hearts are not in what they are doing. In order, then, to meet the implied charge, it strikes a modern reader that Idomeneus must be laying claim to a strong will or desire to fight as well. In fact he was laying claim to all that was humanly necessary to meet the charge when he said ἐπιστάμεθα πτολεμίζειν. The responsibility for the Achaeans' not making good their credible and heartfelt threats lies not with Idomeneus' men but with the gods who have meddled with the battle.

Similarly, when Aeneas spoke of his horses as ἐπιστάμενοι, he was not claiming, as Murray has it, that they were "well-skilled to course fleetly hither and thither over the plain."[34] He was almost certainly suggesting that they were eager to run fast and that they could be counted upon to do it now in evacuating a comrade from danger. A propensity one can count on is more than a skill, an eager readiness more than a mere ability. Ἐπίσταμαι, then, has connotations which strike us perhaps as conative.[35]

It also has connotations which strike us as emotional. Penelope (*Odyssey* 4. 730) discovers the secret departure of her son Telemachus on a hazardous voyage and scolds her handmaids for not awakening her. Her phrase, ἐπισταμέναι σάφα θυμῷ, charges them not merely with knowing full well what was going on but with cruelly liking it as well. She sees malice in their failure to warn her. The verb ἐπίσταμαι, like οἶδα, has cognitive, conative, and emotional connotations for modern readers as it is employed in Homer, connotations not reflected in translations which suggest mere skill, know-how, or knowledge.

This evidence is paralleled by similar evidence concerning one of Plato's alternative terms for ἐπιστήμη, νοῦς.[36] This term is often rendered "intellect" or "intelligence," but Homer employed it in ascribing to his personae what could again pass only for emotional states or states of character from our point of view. Agamemnon was said, literally and for us nonsensically, to rejoice in his "intellect" (χαῖρε νόῳ) by way of saying that he was delighted (*Odyssey* 8. 78), while Achilles was made to say that anger caused his "intellect" to swell (οἰδάνει . . . νόον) by way of saying that he was enraged (*Iliad* 9. 554). Likewise, Odysseus tells Eurymachos that he is running riot and that he has an ungentle "intellect" (καί τοι νόος ἐστὶν ἀπηνής) by way of saying that he has a cruel heart or temperament. Similar examples are not uncommon in Homer, as at *Odyssey* 18. 381 and *Iliad* 9. 554. Like the other terms for ἐπιστήμη, νοῦς does not have the exclusively cognitive, nonmotivational connotations of our term "knowledge."

Readers of an important Kurt von Fritz article may perhaps doubt these conclusions about νοῦς.[37] Professor von Fritz argued that there are "two basic meanings of the word νοεῖν: to realize a situation or to have an intention" (p. 85). The "original and fundamental concept," he claims, is "the realization of a situation," arguing that there are derived from it "a great many other concepts," "all of which are described by the same word" (p. 91).

One might think that because "realization" can sometimes mean merely "the action of forming a clear and distinct concept," the sort of realization of a situation which von Fritz had in mind is definitely not the undifferentiated cognitive-conative-emotional state which I claimed that νοῦς was. To realize something in this minimal sense is perhaps only to bring it vividly or clearly into consciousness, and that might seem a purely intellectual matter.

Yet it is not clear whether von Fritz had in mind such a minimal sense of "realization." At first he seems plainly to be arguing against such a view as this would represent when he disputes Boehme's claim that νοῦς and νοεῖν are *rein intellektuell* in meaning (pp. 80–88). If they are not purely intellectual in meaning, presumably they must be partially conative or emotional in meaning as well. Yet later in the article von Fritz seems to waver on this point, and in so doing he might appear to be in disagreement with the interpretation of νοῦς developed in the text as strongly as he appears to embrace something like it in rejecting Boehme's view. He propounds at least three distinct theses concerning the relation between νοῦς and the conative determination of behavior without giving any sign of sensing how importantly different and even incompatible they are: (1) "νόος implies both an intellectual element and an element of volition" (p. 82); (2) an intellectual element is inextricably connected with an element of volition in the concept of νόος (pp. 82, 86); (3) "whenever νόος and νοεῖν in Homer are used in the sense of plan or planning it is almost always in consequence of the realization of a dangerous situation" (p. 86). He adds: "Since, furthermore, in situations of this kind the plan and the intention to carry it out are psychologically identical, this would also explain νοεῖν in the sense of having an intention and so would, at the same time, show how the volitional element gradually creeps in" (p. 86).

There are serious difficulties here. A cause is not identical with its consequences. Its consequences are not a part of it. If x has to creep into y, x is not an inextricable part of y. The notion of a concept which von Fritz employs is so loose as to sometimes include but sometimes exclude the consequences of the operation of νοῦς, depending upon whether he is explicitly arguing against Boehme (in which case he includes them) or perhaps unwittingly agreeing with him (in which case he excludes them). Perhaps the difficulties here stem from von Fritz's not adhering systematically to his claim that there are a great many concepts of νοῦς, since having made that initial claim he thereafter speaks of "the" concept of νοῦς. Even if we interpreted the seeming inconsistencies in his argument in this way, however, there would still remain the unclarity as to which of these concepts was basic.

There are similar difficulties in von Fritz's treatment of the relation between νοῦς and emotion. He disputes Boehme's thesis that νοῦς is always put in contrast with emotion (p. 80), that there is no emotional element whatever in νοῦς, and that in fact it always appears as the very opposite of emotion. I think he is plainly right in disputing this thesis. But in his disputing it there is again a lack of clarity which robs his arguments of some of their force.

It is unclear whether he views the relation between νοῦς and emotion as one of implication, causation, or inclusion. For example, he remarks in regard to three Homeric passages that "in all three cases the verb is followed by a verb expressing violent emotion. In fact, this is the case in about one-fourth of all the passages in which the verb νοεῖν occurs in Homer. If one adds to these the cases in which the fact that νοεῖν causes a violent emotion does not need to be expressly stated because it follows immediately from the situation, one finds that more than half of the passages with νοεῖν imply violent emotion" (p. 84). Again, causation and implication are lumped together, with the perhaps anachronistic notion of a situation taking up the logical slack. It would seem preferable to conclude that emotion is included in the meaning of νοεῖν itself, and that such subsequent expressions or descriptions of emotion simply specify the particular form the emotion takes in that situation. This is not to say that the strange emotional element in the meaning of νοεῖν as we perceive it always seems prominent; it is not always played up, as one would expect given the flexibility which words have in different contexts. Yet it seems reasonable to conclude that it was always present nevertheless. Perhaps von Fritz himself would not disagree with this.

Even if we cannot translate such strange ways of talking in a way which preserves their connotations or conveys their range while still making

Non-Platonic Greek epistemic usage

sense to contemporary speakers of English, we had best attempt to discern their effect upon speakers and writers of Greek whose usage would have influenced Plato's early readers in their reaction to the Socratic paradox that ἀρετή is ἐπιστήμη. In view of the educational role played by the Greek poems, it is not surprising that such an effect is plainly visible in later Greek writers. The first of the curiosities mentioned above, χάριν εἰδέναι, became a standard expression employed with no evident sense of oddness by writers as varied in their backgrounds and interests as Herodotus, Lysias, Xenophon, Isocrates, and, significantly, Plato himself.[38]

Curious applications of the term νοῦς are likewise to be found in later writers such as Pindar, Aeschylus, Herodotus, and Plato himself.[39] Anaxagoras' νοῦς (fr. 12) was said to take command of the universe and to set in motion a vortex leading to the formation of an orderly cosmos. On the post-Humean view, reason or intellect is likely to be regarded as a slave of the passions, not as master of the cosmos. It is now quite ordinarily conceived of as being totally disparate from those passions, so that we would not be at all likely to use a single word to suggest first reason or a knowledgeable state and then the passions by which we probably regard it as being mastered. This would be like confusing the ego with the id, the moved with the mover, or the slave with the master. Anaxagoras' νοῦς, by contrast, was perhaps just a slight modification of Empedocles' Love and Strife.[40] Such pre-Platonic writers, like Homer before them, gave no sign of having seen a sharp distinction between οἶδα and νοῦς in those uses which to us seem to convey something purely intellectual and the same terms in those strange uses which to us must suggest something emotional, conative, or otherwise motivational.

In describing the way to ἀρετή, or virtue, Hesiod, in his *Works and Days* 293–94, says,

Οὗτος μὲν πανάριστος, ὃς αὐτὸς πάντα νοήσῃ
φρασσάμενος, τὰ κ' ἔπειτα καί ἐς τέλος ᾖσιν ἀμείνω.

That is, "He is best of all who understands all things having considered them himself, the things which will be better afterwards and at the end."

To be thus was, on the conventional Greek view, to be godlike in wisdom and virtue. Aeschylus describes an old Greek ideal when at *Suppliants* 598–99 he says of Zeus, "ancient in wisdom,"

πάρεστι δ' ἔργον ὡς ἔπος
σπεῦσαί τι τῶν βούλιος φέρει φρήν.

That is: "The deed overtakes as the word hastens whatever his counseling mind produces"; in other words, it is no more difficult for Zeus to do what he thinks best than to say what he thinks best. There is no disparity between what Zeus understands to be best and what he does. A similar thought is expressed at 101–3.

We should not be surprised, then, when we discover not just that pre-Socratic writers thought ἐπιστήμη a potent state motivationally but that some thought it movitated one to do the *right* thing. At various places in Thucydides' account of the Peloponnesian War one discerns the writer's tendency to attribute a leader's success to what he lumped together as ἀρετὴ καὶ ξύνεσις, commonly rendered "virtue and intelligence." He attributes the early diplomatic successes of the Spartan general Brasidas to these qualities, to the fact that he was plainly "in every respect a good man" (Thucydides 4. 81. 2; cp. 4. 54. 5). And Hermocrates of Syracuse at 4. 72. 2 is credited with having defeated the Athenian invaders because he was second to none in this same quality of ξύνεσις.[41] The term used here in conjunction again with ἀρετή, "virtue" or "excellence," ξύνεσις, is another of the terms Plato employed for the ἐπιστήμη he and Socrates equated with ἀρετή, or virtue, as at *Cratylus* 411A.

In philosophy and medicine the affinity for the allegedly paradoxical Socratic view was even stronger than in Thucydides. Thucydides had reported the remarks (or perhaps reconstructs the sentiments) of some who from time to time talked as if they did not accept the Socratic view. (See especially the account of Cleon's words at 3. 38. 1.) But Heraclitus had remarked: "Wisdom [σοφίη] is to speak the truth and to act it, listening to the voice of nature."[42] Again, σοφία is another of Plato's terms for ἐπιστήμη.

The allegedly Socratic "paradox" is evidently congenial to the atomist Democritus, who in fragment B181 remarked: "The man who acts rightly through understanding and knowledge [συνέσει τε καὶ ἐπιστήμηι] becomes at the same time brave and upright." In fragment B31 he is said to have remarked that medicine heals the ills of the body, while σοφίη relieves the psyche of passions.

In the Hippocratic treatise *On the Art*, chapter 11, dating from the age of the great sophists at the end of the fifth century B.C. and well before Plato began writing, we find the author contrasting δόξα or "opinion" with what the translator renders as "knowledge," and assigning to the latter precisely the efficacy Socrates did.[43] He remarks, in Jones's translation, "Even the attempted reports of their illnesses made to their attendants by sufferers from obscure diseases are the result of opinion rather than knowledge [δοξάζοντες μᾶλλον ἢ εἰδότες]. If indeed they understood their diseases [εἰ γὰρ ἠπίσταντο] they would never have fallen into them."

On evidence ranging from Homer to the Hippocratic corpus we have seen that (1) the categorical barrier recognized by the post-Humean and post-Freudian clientele of the interpreter of Plato between states which are cognitive and states which are motivationally potent was regularly ignored by influential Greek writers; and (2) remarks quite like the "Socratic paradox" that ἀρετή is ἐπιστήμη are to be found in Heraclitus, Democritus, and the Hippocratic writer, and the view they suggest would seem congenial to Thucydides and to Aeschylus.

It is important to realize precisely how much like Socrates' view these earlier opinions were. Earlier writers held not just that ἐπιστήμη is one among other *necessary* conditions for virtuous action; they held, with Socrates, that it is *sufficient* to produce such action. Such action, on their view, is a *consequence* of the agent's having ἐπιστήμη. If so, educated Greeks of Socrates' and even of Plato's day evidently would have thought the alleged Socratic paradox neither Socratic in origin nor a paradox in character.[44]

E. R. Dodds remarked that "the so-called Socratic paradoxes, that 'virtue is knowledge,' and that 'no one does wrong on purpose,' were no novelties, but an explicit generalized formulation of what had long been an ingrained habit of thought."[45] Dodds's interpretation of what this habit was seems to differ slightly from that offered here, however, since he terms it an "intellectualist approach to the explanation of behaviour." I do not doubt that in translation it strikes us as intellectualist, but I doubt very much that it could have struck those who first adopted or heard it as intellectualist. The intellect had not yet been distinguished from other faculties. The same terms are used for it as for conative and emotive faculties, which suggests strongly that the users of those terms drew no distinctions between them. As J. L. Austin remarked, "Our common stock of words embodies all the distinctions men have found worth drawing, and the connections they have found worth marking, in the lifetimes of many generations."[46] The same holds for the common stock of words of any other body of speakers or writers and for the generations antecedent to them. An important corollary is that if a people's common stock of words does not embody or mark a distinction, then this is evidence that they did not find it worth drawing or important to draw. That intellect, emotion, and conation were not distinct for early Greeks is clear not merely from the evidence about the uses of the term νοῦς already cited but from evidence on the uses of the term θυμός ("soul" or "spirit," the Liddell-Scott-Jones lexicon tells us). This term bore what appear to us to be highly intellectual meanings in some instances and highly emotive ones in others. (See, e.g., *Iliad* 1. 193, 2. 409, 4. 163, 16. 646, 15. 566.) But the way these uses strike us is a product of our relatively fragmented conceptual scheme, and is not indicative of the way they would have struck early Greeks.

That their conceptual scheme was not so fragmented or closely subdivided is evidenced by the single region of the body to which Greeks assigned what seem to us to be distinctly separate intellectual and emotional occurrences or states. That region they called the φρήν—probably the lungs[47]—had assigned to it bodily appetites (*Iliad* 11. 89 [hunger], 3. 442 [sex]), gladness (*Iliad* 13. 493), grief (*Iliad* 1. 362), pain (*Iliad* 8. 124), fear (*Iliad* 10. 10; Aeschylus, *Suppliants* 379), hatred (Aeschylus, *Eumenides* 986), madness (Aeschylus, *Seven Against Thebes* 484), inexorability (Aeschylus, *Prometheus Bound* 34), carelessness or superficiality (Aeschylus, *Agamemnon* 805), pride (*Iliad* 9. 514), hidden thoughts (*Iliad* 9. 313 ff.; Euripides, *Hippolytus* 612), imagination (Hesiod, *Works and Days* 455), persuasion (*Iliad* 7. 120, 16. 842), agreement (*Iliad* 9. 600; Plato, *Symposium* 199A), intention (*Iliad* 9. 434), suggestibility (*Iliad* 1. 55), musing to oneself (*Odyssey* 10. 438), the effect of wine upon one's wits (*Odyssey* 9. 362), those wits themselves (*Iliad* 16. 403; Sophocles, *Philoctetes* 865; Euripides, *Orestes* 1021, *Bacchae* 944, *Heraclidae* 709; Sophocles, *Antigone* 648; Aeschylus, *Agamemnon* 479; Pindar, *Olympian Ode* 7. 47), stupidity (*Iliad* 15. 724), "knowledge" (*Iliad* 22. 296; Plato, *Republic* 386D, quoting *Iliad* 23. 104, *Theaetetus* 154D), and refutation (Plato, *Theaetetus* 154D). Precisely the same indifference to our sharply felt distinction between cognition, conation, and emotion or between the powers or organs to which these are to be assigned can also be illustrated by an enumeration of the mixed bag of nouns and adjectives formed with the single prefix φρενο-. Since Dodds is familiar with all this evidence and more, and since he strenuously combats anachronism elsewhere in his book, I suspect that his phrase "intellectualist approach to the explanation of behaviour" is not to be stressed, and that he may have anticipated the point made here.

Despite the availability of such evidence as has been presented above, a number of modern scholars claim that there are conclusive reasons for thinking Socrates' view was paradoxical among his contemporaries. They claim that such reasons are provided by the plays and fragments of Euripides. Their position is very nearly standard now, and hence it demands consideration.

Euripides and the Socratic paradox

A number of modern scholars have claimed that Euripides wrote polemics against the Socratic view that ἀρετή is ἐπιστήμη in the *Hippolytus* and even in certain lost plays known to us only in fragments. Bruno Snell has argued that Medea's words at lines 1077–80 provided a thesis which led to Socrates' antithesis. This antithesis, Snell claims, provoked Euripides' rebuttal in the *Hippolytus* and in lost plays.[48] But as we have seen in the previous section, there is no reason to believe that Socrates was the originator of the view that ἀρετή is ἐπιστήμη. Hence there is no reason to think that he needed a Euripidean thesis to lead him to invent it, nor can any Euripidean attack on that view be construed simply as an attack on Socrates.

Nevertheless the view that the *Hippolytus* contained a polemic against Socrates has proven attractive to fine scholars such as Wilamowitz, Dodds, Winnington-Ingram, Lesky, and Lattimore.[49] This view, which I shall call the polemical interpretation of Euripides, has several variants. I have argued against all these variants in full detail elsewhere, and will not reproduce those arguments here.[50] This much will suffice: If the allegation that Euripides engaged in a polemic against the Socratic view that ἀρετή is ἐπιστήμη is to have any bearing whatever on the question of whether or not fourth- and fifth-century Greeks would have thought that view a paradox, then it can do so in only two possible ways:

1. It might be suggested that Euripides' polemic shows that Socrates' view was *already* paradoxical among Greeks even before Euripides wrote his plays; or
2. It might be suggested that Euripides' polemic influenced Athenians to reject Socrates' view, thereby causing it to become paradoxical subsequently.

Neither suggestion is well founded. Both fail to take account of what a polemic is. Plainly, the point of engaging in a polemic against someone's view would be to convince the audience to which the polemic is addressed that the view in question is incorrect. This being so, it is easily seen that the first suggestion above is incoherent. We are told that Socrates' view was paradoxical—i.e., that it went against prevailing opinion—*and* that Euripides engaged in a polemic against it in plays designed for the Athenian public—i.e., that he attempted to *change* public opinion against Socrates' view. If Socrates' view were indeed paradoxical, it would scarcely be necessary to polemize against it. Only a very unintelligent writer would waste a play in trying to convince people of what they already believed, if indeed they did believe it. And Euripides was anything but unintelligent. If he did polemize against Socrates' view, then we would be licensed to conclude that this view was widespread enough or attractive enough among the theater-going public to make it worth Euripides' effort to persuade them of its falsity.

The second suggestion fails on dramatic and rhetorical grounds which I shall not review fully here. In brief: Euripides is said to have employed Medea and Phaedra as his mouthpieces. Any playwright who wishes to convince a popular audience must use a credible character as a mouthpiece. To be credible, a character must not run afoul of the audience's prejudices and must not be contradicted by a more credible character. To my knowledge no one has ever claimed in writing that Medea was Euripides' mouthpiece in a *polemic*. Yet it has been claimed that she speaks for his view, which rhetorically comes to the same thing: he wanted his audience to believe her seemingly anti-Socratic words. But it is beyond belief that he would be so inept. Medea is by no stretch of the imagination a credible mouthpiece for convincing a popular Athenian theater audience of anything she says, since she is female, foreign, burdened by a long record of crimes against her family and state, utterly lacking in the crucial feminine virtue of σωφροσύνη, and perhaps even mad. Euripides could scarcely have made it less likely that any "philosophical" sentiments Medea expresses would be believed by a popular Athenian theater audience, given their attitudes.

Phaedra is not so blatantly unfit to be believed by Athenians as Medea, yet in her play some of the same factors present in the *Medea* work against the audience's acceptance of her seemingly anti-Socratic sentiments. Certainly, it does not help that she too is female and foreign, nor is it an advantage that she contemplates seducing her stepson and thereby proving treacherously unfaithful to her husband, an Athenian hero. Yet in lines 375 ff. she does claim to have thought many a night about her seemingly anti-Socratic view that plenty of people have ἐπιστήμη and yet fail to do the right thing owing to their being overcome by pleasure. In her case she cites the leisurely, luxurious, gossipy, self-indulgent life of the palace as being an obstacle to doing what she claims to know or understand is best.

For people who knew Socrates' simple way of life and his oft-repeated view that strenuous self-discipline was necessary both for ἀρετή and for ἐπιστήμη, Phaedra's many nights of thought would be a mockery. She would stand condemned out of her own mouth. See, for instance, Socrates' approving quotation of Hesiod and Epicharmus in Xenophon, *Memorabilia* 102. 56 and 2. 1. 20, and his advice to a friend on idleness, especially idleness among well-bred women, at 2. 7. 7–8. That such remarks, reminiscent of the so-called Protestant work-ethic, are not merely of moral significance but also of epistemic significance is shown by 2. 2. 20. Moreover, Phaedra plainly lacked an understanding of her own capabilities and limitations, which is incompatible with her having attained the self-understanding Socrates consistently urged people to pursue (see, e.g., 4. 2. 26). Finally, note the treatment of self-appraisals by the unwise at *Theaetetus* 176D. Phaedra could not possibly have possessed Socratic ἀρετή or ἐπιστήμη and in the very context in which she tells us in effect that she does possess it she unwittingly explains why she does not. Socrates' views are less the *target* of her words than the *explanation* of them. She cannot have reaped what she confesses she has never sown.

Worse, Phaedra's seemingly anti-Socratic lines are balanced by seemingly pro-Socratic lines spoken by the Nurse and by Hippolytus, each of whom is a more believable mouthpiece, from a conventional Athenian's point of view, than the treacherous Phaedra. (For the Nurse's lines see 698–701, and for Hippolytus's, see 1013 ff.) Hippolytus was a hero whose cult was still celebrated, and the Nurse, however inept, was a loyal, well-intentioned Athenian servant.[51] Euripides has his chorus at *Iphigenia in Aulis* 558 ff. sing that modesty is wisdom, and to do so in a way that seems to refer back to Phaedra.

Thus the *Medea* and *Hippolytus* provide no evidence that Socrates' view was paradoxical, or that these plays could have induced Athenians to regard it as paradoxical. This coheres with the evidence of the previous section that his view was not paradoxical, but was in fact reasonably congenial to a number of influential Greek writers and presumably to readers influenced by them.

To deny that Socrates' view was paradoxical, and even to affirm that he was not alone in holding something very like it, is not to claim that everyone in Athens agreed with him, however. We have evidence that opinion was divided on the efficacy of ἐπιστήμη for producing right action. Hence, even though Socrates' view was evidently not rejected widely enough to be paradoxical, it may well have been controversial. We turn now to evidence that it was.

Other Greek perspectives on the Socratic paradox

In Thucydides' account of an Athenian assembly-debate, the leader of the popular war-party, Cleon the tanner, is reported to have remarked as follows on a proposal to reconsider a vengeful motion already passed which would put to death all adult male Mytelenaeans who could be found and to enslave their women and children: "As for me, I have not changed my opinion, and I wonder at those who propose to debate again the question of the Mytelenaeans and thus interpose delay, which is in the interest of those who have done the wrong; for thus the edge of the victim's wrath is duller when he proceeds against the offender, whereas the vengeance that follows upon the very heels of the outrage exacts a punishment that more nearly matches the offense."[52] As A. W. Gomme noted, this remark suggests that if the Athenians are to do the right thing, they must yield immediately to rage rather than think out and discuss what it would be best to do.[53] Since thinking and discussion of this sort and the refusal to yield to immediate, blind passion were closely associated with Socratic and Platonic ἐπιστήμη, the remark hardly suggests sympathy for the Socratic view.

In the dialogue *Protagoras*, Plato describes Socrates as remarking that "the many," whom we know to have been under Cleon's seemingly anti-intellectual influence, did not share Socrates' view that ἐπιστήμη rectifies action even in the face of countervailing considerations of pleasure.⁵⁴ Socrates argues against popular psychological hedonism, claiming that it must admit that ἐπιστήμη can have greater influence than considerations of short-term pleasure if reasonable consideration of long-run pleasure and pain is as important as it claims.⁵⁵

Those who have taken Socrates' view to be paradoxical have laid considerable weight on this passage. Evidence pointing the same way may also be found in the *Meno* at 77B ff., where Meno balks initially at Socrates' view.

But what does this evidence indicate? Cleon the tanner, Meno the mercenary, and "the many" were pretty clearly not everybody in Socrates' eyes or in Plato's, as *Crito* 44C–D indicates. It was evidently a commonplace among the educated then as now that popular usage perverts the meanings of terms. At *Theaetetus* 168B–C, for example, Protagoras is imagined as saying to Socrates that most people pervert the ordinary meanings of names and words in haphazard ways and thereby cause much perplexity in one another.

The grounds on which Plato came to view ordinary usage of all sorts as a perversion are explored in Chapter 5 below.⁵⁶ But the weightiest testimony on whether the popular usage of epistemic terms was or was not a perversion and on whether the Platonic Socrates' use was or was not paradoxical is neither that of Plato himself nor that of the many, who could be expected not to understand Socrates' meaning. It is that of Aristotle.⁵⁷

In the *Nicomachean Ethics*, Aristotle comments on Socrates' apparent belief that ἀκρασία, or "weakness of will," as it is usually rendered, is not possible. Aristotle remarks at 1145b27 ff., οὗτος μὲν οὖν ὁ λόγος ἀμφισβητεῖ τοῖς φαινομένοις ἐναργῶς. This is perhaps the most widely misinterpreted passage in the *Nicomachean Ethics*. Rackham translates: "Now this theory is manifestly at variance with plain facts."⁵⁸ The difficulty is in ascertaining the meaning of τοῖς φαινομένοις, which Rackham renders as "plain facts," but which Aristotle often employs in various forms in a weaker sense to mean merely "things which appear to be so," with the emphasis on the "appear."⁵⁹ Whether it does mean "plain facts" or merely "things which appear to be so" here can be decided only on the basis of the context.

The context requires the weaker reading.⁶⁰ Aristotle concludes at 1147b14 ff. that we must agree with Socrates. Aristotle recognizes that ἐπιστήμη and its corresponding verb are sometimes used in a weaker sense than Socrates favored, though he is not just being even-handed and saying that in one sense Socrates is right, while in another his opponents are, since they are speaking of different states of mind. Rather, Aristotle calls Socrates' ἐπιστήμη ἡ κυρίως ἐπιστήμη, that is, ἐπιστήμη in the strict or correct sense. (In the other sense ἐπιστήμη is merely αἰσθητική, or sensory acquaintance.) The Socratic ἐπιστήμη he describes as differing from the weaker sort in that it is always present to the mind at the time of action, since it has been cultivated over a long period of time and has become deeply rooted (*Nicomachean Ethics* 6. 3. 8). One who has the weaker sort of ἐπιστήμη is said to be like a student who has just begun the study of a subject and can merely parrot certain maxims, or like the drunk who may talk as if he had ἐπιστήμη but has merely a sensory acquaintance with the maxims and can hence be dragged about by passion. Plato would have found nothing to disagree with here.

Aristotle's suggestion, then, amounts to this: Those who quarrel with Socrates about the efficacy of ἐπιστήμη are using it in a loose or vulgar sense. Or, to put it more concretely, they are not talking about the same thing he is. They are not attuned to the precise sense in which he is using it, a sense which, as we have seen, is a natural outgrowth of epistemic notions educated Greeks would have been familiar with. But Cleon the tanner, Meno the mercenary soldier, and "the many" were not educated Greeks. The astute reader of Plato's dialogues would have understood Socrates' view as Aristotle did, and would not have thought it paradoxical.

Platonic ἐπιστήμη, excellence, and knowledge

It is small comfort that educated Greeks would have understood Socratic and Platonic talk of ἀρετή as being the same thing as ἐπιστήμη if most of those who would like to understand it now are not educated Greeks but want to grasp such talk in English. If one tells such an audience to rest with the conventional view that ἐπιστήμη is knowledge, while adding that educated Greeks would not have found it odd, one is merely encouraging the ethnocentric view that educated Greeks were themselves oddly out of touch with reality. Yet this view would cohere neither with such Greeks' having had a rich experience with educated failures and frauds, nor with their linguistic sophistication, which permitted Aristotle to distinguish the popular, loose sense of ἐπιστήμη from the strict, more traditional Socratic and Platonic one. But how are we to construe what Socrates and those who agree with him were talking about in post-Humean, post-Freudian English of the sort readily intelligible today?

The chief problem facing us in this task is that Platonic ἐπιστήμη was plainly a state which was conceived of as if it had both articulate intellectual characteristics and powerful motivational ones, while many contemporary thinkers are so doubtful that there is any such state, especially one which can be named "knowledge," that their vocabularies at first sight seem bereft of any convenient term for it. Without such a term or at least a convenient phrase we shall have difficulty in getting speakers of contemporary English to develop a feel for Platonic ἐπιστήμη, and will lack such a feel ourselves insofar as we think in English.

We should not be content to tolerate this gross an inadequacy in the understanding of Socrates and Plato if it is avoidable or reducible. English may be unavoidably inadequate for a few of Homer's more exotic idioms, but happily those are not our immediate concern. Our concern is to help overcome a far-reaching obstacle to the appreciation of Plato's epistemology by speakers of English today. And that obstacle is the mistaken impression that Plato's epistemology contained paradoxes—mistaken because educated Greeks equipped to understand Plato would not have shared it.

Some translators and interpreters have made an effort to avoid giving this impression. Gould, for example, has construed ἐπιστήμη as Rylean "know-how" and also as a personal, subjective certainty.[61] But the alleged problem of ἀκρασία or "weakness of will" is precisely that many who *know how* to do the right nevertheless fail to. All automobile mechanics know full well how to change spark plugs and carry out instructions from motorists, but some of them merely clean old plugs and charge for new ones nevertheless.

"Wisdom" sounds like a more promising candidate, given that it captures the practical efficacy of ἐπιστήμη. Even now it is conceived of as a capacity for judging rightly in matters of life and conduct. But it captures the practical efficacy of ἐπιστήμη at the expense of sacrificing that end of the epistemic spectrum having to do with theoretical matters: it suggests no connection with the ability to give an account.[62] Our folklore has instilled in us the notion that one may be wise without being in the least capable of defending dialectically one's judgment. In the bifurcation of theory and practice begun by Aristotle, we have finally placed articulateness solely on the theoretical side, despite the abundance of counterexamples provided by wise and articulate teachers and practitioners in schools of medicine, nursing, automobile mechanics, and even "police science." This is symptomatic of the problem facing us in interpreting Platonic ἐπιστήμη. It is rather like that of taking a relatively large, soft object which passed through a large-grained screen unharmed and trying to find a large enough opening in our finer-grained screen through which it can pass without being cut up or reshaped in the process. Ἐπιστήμη showed itself in excellent action *and* in words, on Plato's view.

Still less appropriate than "wisdom" as a vehicle for carrying the force of Platonic ἐπιστήμη are Bluck's suggestions: "spiritual awareness" or "religious conviction" for ἐπιστήμη of the good, and "having an understanding of . . . teleological purpose" for other sorts of ἐπιστήμη.[63] The first sacrifices all connotations of articulateness and perhaps most connotations of practical efficacy as well, while the second suggests that the good is beyond the sort of articulate λόγος appropriate for other things, which in Plato's view it was not.

Another familiar notion serves better across the board, though still not in a wholly felicitous way.[64] This is our notion of understanding. The lexicon mentions "understanding" as a variant reading for ἐπιστήμη, and a few translators have used it occasionally, as they have also employed the verb "understand" to render ἐπίσταμαι. To my knowledge no interpreter of Plato has explored fully the implications of this line, though N. R. Murphy made a good beginning.[65] In exploring these implications further we must bear in mind three features of the notion of understanding which render it fairly well suited to convey roughly the force of Plato's ἐπιστήμη and ἐπίσταμαι.

First, the way we commonly employ it renders an accurate image of Plato's insistence that one who has ἐπιστήμη of something must be able to give an account of it which will hold up under questioning. I know a little about the workings of my automobile engine, but I certainly cannot give an adequate account of those workings because I do not understand them. This could be discerned by practically anyone with an eye for the consistency of answers in a sufficiently long chain. I might explain the car's fast idle by saying that the timing is too fast, only to explain the same phenomenon later by reference to an incorrect carburetor setting. Any claim that I understood such matters would be incompatible with my inability to give and defend a single, coherent account of them, just as a claim to Platonic ἐπιστήμη would be incompatible with an inability to give and defend a λόγος. One may, like the successful cook in Plato's *Gorgias*, occasionally tinker successfully with things, but successful tinkering is not a sufficient condition for being held to understand. We commonly contrast merely knowing with understanding in a way which points up clearly the more potent character of understanding. In view of the inarticulateness of much knowledge as now conceived, this more potent character is part of what is required to render the force of ἐπιστήμη.

This notion of understanding has a second important qualification: it suggests a second sort of potency guaranteed by ἐπιστήμη as Plato conceived of it but not by mere knowledge as now conceived of by the interpreter's clientele. Like the notion of wisdom, it is not uncommonly employed as if it spanned the yawning post-Humean, post-Freudian gap between reason and those passions or emotions which are thought to move and master us.⁶⁶ But unlike the notion of wisdom it does so without suggesting that one who has it is probably unable to give and defend an account of what is understood.

That understanding is treated as if it spanned this chasm is shown by a familiar tendency to explain insensitive or otherwise inappropriate actions by claiming that the agent did not understand his or her situation. The suggestion conveyed by such an explanation is that if the agent had understood the situation this would have led to the appropriate action. The same point is suggested by those who attempt to promote peace through international cultural and educational exchanges. These exchanges are touted as producing international understanding. And the belief underlying the attempt to produce international understanding is that if only hostile parties had a deeper understanding of one another, they would be disposed to treat one another better.

A third and related qualification of the notion of understanding is the aura of personal, human approval suggested when we speak of someone as "an understanding person." Plato certainly intended this in calling a person an ἐπιστήμων, but it is difficult to convey this suggestion by speaking of a person as "knowledgeable," as "knowing a lot," or as "well informed."

The beliefs illustrated by these uses of the term "understanding" may well appear false and perhaps naive to hard-boiled contemporaries. Indeed, there may not exist any phenomenon having a felicitous enough combination of properties to serve as a referent for the term. But that is irrelevant for our present purposes. From the point of view of pessimistic contemporaries my claim will then appear to be that we can grasp what Plato meant by ἐπιστήμη because speakers of contemporary English possess a concept equal in primitive naivete to that of Plato's ἐπιστήμη, and this despite the best efforts of Hume and Freud. I do not wish to put this deflationary an interpretation upon the situation, but if some readers find themselves doing so, I shall not object as an interpreter of Plato.⁶⁷

From the point of view of most contemporaries, however, or at least from that of a great many of those contemporaries who study and use translations and interpretations of Plato in the English language, the pessimism about the efficacy of knowledge to which I have referred does not as yet extend with much confidence to understanding. If so, the notion of understanding can for now serve as a tentative and imperfect vehicle for conveying to them part of Plato's epistemology without prejudicing judgment about its sanity in ways which would not parallel astute Greek reactions to it.⁶⁸ And that is what interpretation is, or ought to be, all about. Seen through the lens of our notion of understanding, Plato's epistemology and its connections with what are now regarded as disparate areas of inquiry—such as psychology, ethics, and political philosophy—cannot but seem richer and not so obviously wrong. One can then consider that epistemology on its merits. I think we owe at least that to Plato and to ourselves.

2
Dialectic and Ἐπιστήμη

In the previous chapter it was argued that it is a mistake to interpret Platonic ἐπιστήμη as knowledge since

1. "Knowledge" today is all too likely to suggest mere knowledge that something is the case.
2. Mere knowledge that something is the case is or is widely thought to be a purely intellectual or cognitive condition.
3. Purely intellectual or cognitive conditions are widely thought to have little or nothing to do with a person's fundamental motives and hence little or nothing to do with the fundamental control of behavior. Modern writers' assumption that one can know what is right or best and not do it is one important instance of this.
4. Platonic ἐπιστήμη was not described in the dialogues as a purely intellectual or cognitive condition, as the alleged Socratic paradox that ἀρετή, or excellence, is ἐπιστήμη, or understanding, illustrates. Ἐπιστήμη was described as motivationally potent.
5. Conceiving of that condition which was termed ἐπιστήμη, σοφία σύνεσις, or φρόνησις as if it were motivationally potent had a rich and influential history from Homer down to Plato, and would not have struck educated Greeks as paradoxical, though the many may well have misunderstood this conception, as Plato suggests. But Plato did not write for the many.

6. Neither Socrates as Plato describes him nor Plato himself intellectualized the explanation of behavior any more than they emotionalized the explanation of intellect. They simply had little use for distinctions between intellect and emotion.[1]
7. If we are to grasp the notion of ἐπιστήμη without anachronism, that is, as Plato and his educated readers evidently did, we cannot do so by relying upon an English word which is purely intellectual or cognitive in its current connotations. "Knowledge" is such a word, while "wisdom" and "understanding" are not, and are hence preferable as vehicles for conveying the force of Plato's σοφία, ἐπιστήμη, and equivalent terms, *though it may well be true that no English word conveys all and only this force*. Our object is not merely to supply a fitting English word, but rather to indicate *what* such a word must be fitted *to*, and why, for this will indicate some of the constraints upon the adequacy of an interpretation, and will be necessary in developing a more nearly adequate interpretation. Interpretations unduly influenced, whether wittingly or unwittingly, by the connotations of English words incautiously adopted as translations fail to satisfy these constraints, and are therefore inadequate.

Thus the previous chapter tells us more nearly what ἐπιστήμη *is not* than what it is. To explore what ἐπιστήμη *is*, having rid ourselves of the contemporary intellectualist bias attacked in Chapter 1, will require probing at several levels. It will require exploring ἐπιστήμη from several different points of view—dialectical, psychological, semantic, and ontological. In this chapter we shall explore ἐπιστήμη in its connections with dialectic, for it is in dialectical discussion that Plato evidently thought ἐπιστήμη and the lack of it show most vividly.

Ἐπιστήμη, the dialectician, and the ability to give an account

At *Republic* 534B–C Socrates is depicted as having the following exchange with Glaucon:

And do you not call the one who can give an account of the reality of each thing a dialectician? And to the extent that one is unable to give an account either to himself or to another you will not say that he has understanding [νοῦς] about this? —How could I say it, he said. —But isn't this true of the good also; he who is unable to distinguish the form of the good having cut it off from all others, who does not survive all tests as in a battle, exerting himself to test not in accordance with opinion but in accordance with reality, carrying through without tripping up in his account—such a person you will say does not understand [εἰδέναι] the good itself nor any other good at all; but if in some way he lays hold of some image of it, he lays hold of it by opinion [δόξῃ] not by understanding [ἐπιστήμη].

This passage is representative of many in the dialogues which suggest an intimate connection between being able to give a λόγος, or account, and having ἐπιστήμη. In order to understand the exact nature of this connection and its dialectical importance we shall have to understand the variety of things Plato evidently meant when he employed the term λόγος and the verb λέγω.

As always, however, one cannot understand what Plato meant without attempting to grasp his linguistic intentions. And these intentions would have been formed and expressed in a way which took account of his readers' capacities and propensities. These capacities and propensities, in turn, would have been shaped by the previous Greek uses of λόγος familiar to these readers; to express himself at all intelligibly Plato could not have departed very radically from such uses, and even detailed departures would have to be built carefully upon these uses.

As one would expect, given the educational role of the Homeric epics, the Homeric uses of the verb λέγω, from which λόγος is derived, were especially influential.[2] As has been widely recognized in Continental scholarship, the term's earliest uses are surprising in that many of them do not suggest speaking.[3] As Fournier has shown, the basic sense of λέγω was not "say" or "speak," but rather something like "gather," "collect," or "select."[4] At *Iliad* 7. 507 and 11. 755 it is used of gathering or selecting a particular person's bones from a common funeral pyre; at 12. 689 it is used of warriors selected or chosen, presumably, for their valor. At 21. 27 it is used when Achilles, temporarily weary of killing, selects twelve youths as prisoners.

The suggestion that one is selecting or gathering persists in uses of λέγω in which speaking is clearly involved. As Boeder has pointed out, λέγω is employed so as to suggest that the speaker is gathering up, selecting, and laying out for the hearer the separate parts of his subject.[5] To speak in this narrative way was to list, in effect, the multifarious things united loosely or "mixed" together. It was to select and present its parts, pieces, members, or constituents. (See, e.g., *Iliad* 9. 61 and 11. 706.) This was not to be done at random, but according to some plan, as Fournier emphasized, so that an element of calculation was suggested even in using λέγω of activities other than speaking or saying.[6] The bones of Patroclus or Hector are to be distinguished and separated from the rest; the best warriors are to be singled out and assembled to protect the ships; the youths are to be singled out to be taken back to camp as prisoners, while the others are to be killed immediately.

This suggests, then, that the object of λόγος was originally conceived as being complex and as needing a selecting or sorting out, even when that object was not talked about. This suggestion persists in cases in which λέγω is used of speaking, and has considerable ontological importance, explored further in Chapters 5 and 6. For now, however, it can be noted that what we would call describing a thing evidently struck early Greeks as selecting and laying out its constituents. A λόγος, then, might well resemble a catalog. The model and basis for such a catalog was presented in *Iliad* 2. 484 ff., where the poet invokes the Muses' help in saying who were the leaders of the Danaans. He claims to have heard only rumors and to know nothing at all, but the Muses are said to know because they were present. They can call to mind all the leaders and can communicate to him who they were. This is a model λόγος which follows in that it resembles a catalog of constituents and has its basis in recollected experience. Thus, Plato's later grounding of the ability to give a λόγος in recollection at *Meno* 81A–E and *Phaedo* 76B–C drew upon a familiar model, even as it applied that model in perhaps unfamiliar ways.

It is important to note, however, that the connotations of λέγω as selecting, gathering, or laying out do not necessarily suggest the view that what one gathers, selects, or lays out must be parts or pieces in any physical sense.[7] When Odysseus at *Odyssey* 8. 33 ff. is invited to say who he is by Antinoos, he must describe his house and lineage. It is expected that he will locate himself in a family tree, and locate the family itself in terms of its important relations with others. Even in the Muses' account of the leaders of the Danaans in *Iliad* 2, no mere recital of "parts" is expected; the "parts" or constituents themselves are charted genealogically. This, and not a mere nomenclature of physically contiguous constituents, is the early and all-important model for λέγω and for λόγος, a model which proved ontologically influential for Plato.[8]

Platonic dialectic, or διαλεκτική, was rooted in the notion of διαλέγεσθαι, which in Homer suggested a conversation aimed at making a decision on the basis of considering all the options and their consequences.[9] The decision to be reached in the epics had to do with future courses of action. In Plato's dialogues it had to do with what the participants were to say was the λόγος, or account, of something such as beauty or justice. Yet it was a decision nevertheless in that participants recognized a number of different things they might say; on the theory of recollection they were attempting dialectically to recollect what it was presumed they had previously apprehended and to lay it out in a λόγος, or account.

Although Plato employed the verb λέγω and the noun λόγος in very many different ways, all influenced by Homeric models, there can be no doubt that the philosophical center of gravity in his works is found in those applications in which a λόγος is an answer to a Socratic question—for example, Τί ἐστι τὸ καλόν; or "What is the beautiful?" as the question is posed at *Hippias Major* 286D. In attempting to understand these uses, we must differentiate them from another broad family of uses, for Plato applied the term λόγος in ways which fall into two main groups, one having to do with a range of *abilities* (δυνάμεις) possessed by a person, and the other having to do with various *manifestations* of such abilities. When λόγος refers to the best of these abilities it is usually rendered as "reason."

The abilities in question may be identified more accurately, however, in terms of what they allegedly enabled one possessing them to do. Thus, our principal interest in this chapter on dialectic will be in applications of the term λόγος to manifestations of these abilities, to the sorts of things Plato thought one might say in answer to a question of the Τί ἐστι *x*; or "What is *x*?" form.[10] These answers fell into three importantly different groups, and the term λόγος as applied to these three groups had different senses marking the different status its referent was conceived to have.

The initial answer—the Socratic account to be tested forthwith or used hypothetically without direct testing—was a λόγος in the first manifestation sense. See, e.g., *Gorgias* 463B; *Euthyphro* 11E; *Protagoras* 333C; *Republic* 338D, 354D (second occurrence); *Phaedrus* 265D. It was a declarative sentence or a group of such sentences which at the very least parsed. If it was examined forthwith in an attempt to test and if possible refute it, then the initial answer together with the answerer's elaboration and defense of it constituted a λόγος in a second manifestation sense. The term bears this sense at *Gorgias* 454C, 509E, 511B; *Euthyphro* 14D, 15C; and *Republic* 339D. It was Richard Robinson's failure to distinguish this second and expanded sense of λόγος from the first which led him to think that Plato believed one could deduce the denial of a claim from the claim itself with no help from additional premises.[11]

In the unlikely event that the answerer's elaboration and defense of the initial account in the face of sufficient testing was successful, Plato would evidently call the entire range of responses of the answerer a λόγος in a third manifestation sense. Plato demanded that an account which merits being called a λόγος in this third and best sense meet extraordinarily exacting criteria, to which we shall turn presently. This is the sense λόγος bears in his phrase λόγον διδόναι, "to give an account." It is the sense associated with ἐπιστήμη, "understanding." See, e.g., *Phaedo* 73A, *Republic* 582E (φρόνησις), and *Timaeus* 51E (νοῦς). This is the sense λόγος bears in the *Republic* passage quoted above. The epistemically interesting passages in the dialogues often contain uses of λόγος in this sense.

Merely having *an* answer, even an answer which someone else might be able to defend fully, is not sufficient on Plato's view to justify attributing understanding to the answerer. This is plain from *Meno* 81A in contrast with 86B–C and *Euthyphro* 5A–B in contrast with 4A. Ἐπιστήμη, or understanding, demands not merely that the one having it be able to give some answer or other, but that he be able to give an answer which *he* can defend fully. It is contrasted, not with the inability to say *anything*, but with the inability to *say* anything, anything which might constitute an account in his exacting third sense. Otherwise, we would have to take him as claiming in such passages as *Republic* 534C that those who have understanding or wisdom are never at a loss for words, being always able to say something which parses, even if something false. But given that the context is a discussion of the indispensable role of dialectic in developing and testing the guardians' views, which are to be the truest of all, he is using his term for "account" not in the first or second sense but in the exacting third. In this sense a λόγος is an impeccable dialectical performance, and the phrase λόγον διδόναι, "to give an account," suggests giving such a performance, not merely saying something which we might call true even though it is not in fact defended on the spot. Such a performance consisted in passing stringent tests. We turn now to those tests.

Dialectical testing and refutation

The key term for the understanding of Platonic testing of λόγοι, or accounts, is ἔλεγχος. A λόγος could not be a λόγος in the exacting third sense unless it could pass ἔλεγχος. But Plato used the term ἔλεγχος in several different ways. Socratic questioning was an ἔλεγχος in the sense of a fundamental *test* for incoherence; it probed for the possibility of ἔλεγχος in a second sense, that of a dialectical *refutation* based upon the exposure of incoherence. In probing for such incoherence, the questioner was to avoid ἔλεγχος in a third sense, that of a merely rhetorical or legal refutation.

This rhetorical or legal refutation differed from its dialectical counterpart in that it did not take just the answerer's uncoerced "vote" on a question, as Plato suggests at *Gorgias* 471D–472D and 474A–B. Rhetorical refutation could be achieved by laughing the answerer to scorn, attempting to frighten him out of his view, or appealing to the opinion of impressively numerous but dialectically irrelevant witnesses, as he notes at *Gorgias* 473D–E.

Such rhetorical refutation together with its positive counterpart—the instilling of a certain thought by persuasion—were epistemically important for Plato despite his censorious tone in describing them. Together, they figured in his argument that there is a clear distinction between δοξάζειν, or "thinking that . . . ," and ἐπίστασθαι, or "understanding that . . ." The person who merely thinks, believes, or opines that *p* can be gotten to think otherwise by rhetorical means, while the person who understands cannot. Hence, the two conditions have different origins (persuasion, as contrasted with learning) and are proof against different challenges. It seems likely that such considerations as those, not ontological ones concerning forms, were the original and decisive reasons for Plato's belief that ἐπιστήμη differs from ἀληθὴς δόξα, as *Meno* 98A ff., *Timaeus* 51D–E, and even *Republic* 477B indicate. He was sure that these were different δυνάμεις, or powers, before he was quite sure how to explain the ontological basis of that difference.

Dialectical refutation was considered to have been achieved when the broad, explicative λόγος offered in defense of the initial λόγος proved to contain sincere and fairly elicited admissions which contradicted the initial λόγος. (See, e.g., *Hippias Major* 286E; *Gorgias* 458A, 461A; *Phaedo* 85C–D.) The "structure" of dialectical testing up through the *Theaetetus* is that of a leisurely, relatively *un*structured search through the answerer's beliefs with an eye solely to their coherence. *Sophist* 230B–E describes this search in such terms. Considerations such as the range of the answerer's initial claims and their flying in the face of plain facts are relevant only insofar as they offer the questioner an opportunity to extract incoherent admissions. Incoherence is dialectic's cutting edge.

In practice, then, to give a λόγος which proved beyond dialectical refutation would be to give an account of the sort associated with the possession of ἐπιστήμη. It would be to state one's answer to a τί ἐστι question, submit oneself to a full and fair examination of that answer and any others which might strike the questioner as relevant, reply clearly and honestly to all questions, and emerge with one's claims all consistent and thus dialectically unrefuted at the end. At *Euthyphro* 11B Euthyphro complains that whatever account they give, it will not stay where they establish it, and Socrates at 13E indicates that "staying put" would be sufficient to satisfy him by remarking that he would rather have his accounts stay and be established as motionless than possess the skill of Daedalus and the wealth of Tantalus in addition. The crucial thing was to "survive without making a mistake." *Theaetetus* 146A speaks of "getting through without making a mistake," as if that would be quite enough to satisfy Socrates. As is remarked at *Phaedo* 85D, one is to adopt that account which is δυσεξελεγκτότατον, "hardest to refute." At *Phaedo* 100A it is suggested that we want the one which is ἐρρωμενέστατον, "strongest" or "healthiest." This is evidently the one which makes us contradict ourselves least, which would presumably be the one that made us contradict ourselves not at all (*Theaetetus* 200D).

Both the practical means of developing such a λόγος and the conditions

Dialectical testing and refutation 39

for its adequacy are illustrated by criticisms Platonic spokesmen direct against various accounts and various dialectical moves depicted in the dialogues. Together, these criticisms constitute a rough description of dialectic in practice, and if we generalize upon them carefully, they yield a set of requirements Plato evidently places upon dialectic. Their epistemic importance lies in the fact that on Plato's view the dialectic they guide is the sole means of attaining the highest ἐπιστήμη. This is indicated at *Republic* 533A; this view accounts for the preeminent place of dialectic in Plato's curriculum at 534E, and later at *Philebus* 58E–59C. The many failures and false dialectical starts in the early and middle dialogues are more instructive about Plato's working criteria for ἐπιστήμη than successes would have been, since the constraints upon any success achieved would not have emerged so clearly. I make no claim that the following list of constraints is complete, but offer it to show what a complex condition Plato must have thought he was testing for, and hence what a complex condition ἐπιστήμη must have been on his view. Consider first the constraints upon the answerer:

1. The answerer must agree to take up the role of answerer and must agree to answer whatever questions are put to him unless the sense of those questions is unclear (*Gorgias* 477B–C, 458D–E, 462B, 466B; *Protagoras* 329B, 333D, 335A–B, 336A–B, 348D–E, 348A–B; *Alcibiades* I 112D–113C; *Euthydemus* 295B–D).
2. The answerer must not stand in the way of taking up questions in the order likely to leave the fewest loose ends (*Protagoras* 361C; *Meno* 71A–B, 86D–87B, 100B; *Alcibiades* I 128E–129A; *Hippias Major* 304D–E; *Euthyphro* 6A–B; *Republic* 354C).
3. The answerer must say what he sincerely thinks even if he realizes that it contradicts what he said earlier (*Gorgias* 475D, 495A–B; *Protagoras* 331C, 360D–E; *Republic* 346A, 349A, 350C–E; *Meno* 83D).
4. The answerer must say what *he* thinks. Outside authorities are not relevant. Their views may be given only if the answerer takes full responsibility for their defense as his own (*Theaetetus* 166A, 171D; *Protagoras* 347C–348A; *Meno* 71C–D; *Philebus* 28E).
5. Answers must be succinct, not speeches or rhetorical performances (*Gorgias* 447B–C, 449B; *Protagoras* 329A–B, 334C–335A, 336A–D, 342D–343B; *Republic* 350E; *Theaetetus* 168E).
6. The answerer must express as clearly as possible what he means (*Gorgias* 451E, 462E, 463D–E, 489C–D, 489E; *Protagoras* 334E; *Euthyphro* 13A; *Euthydemus* 295B–D; *Charmides* 162B, 163D; *Republic* 338C–D).

7. The answerer must express his view as accurately as possible in order to give an account of precisely what he promises to give an account of, neither more nor less (*Gorgias* 454A; *Protagoras* 350B–351B; *Republic* 340E, 341B–C, 345D; *Theaetetus* 184C).
8. The answerer must accept dialectical refutation gracefully as a benefit and a purification (*Gorgias* 457E, 479B, 505C; *Euthydemus* 295A; *Sophist* 230B–E).

It is not necessary to add to this list of constraints that the answerer when asked Τί ἐστι x; must reply with an account of what makes all x's x, not an example or examples, as Allen, Burnet, Crombie, Geach, and other interpreters might suggest, for, as Alexander Nehamas has argued, Socrates' interlocutors do not in fact confuse universals with particulars or definitions with examples; rather, they give what are, in effect, various sufficient conditions for being x instead of the single necessary and sufficient condition Socrates supposes (perhaps wrongly) there must be.[12] For example, that one is prosecuting a religious wrong is sufficient to make one's act pious, but it is neither necessary for making one's act pious nor the only condition the satisfaction of which would make it pious. The answer Socrates wants is to capture all and only the necessary and sufficient conditions.

The questioner was also subject to strict constraints, being bound by such conditions as these:

9. The questioner may not put two questions in the guise of one (*Gorgias* 466C; *Euthydemus* 295B–D).
10. The questioner must ask questions with a view first to the orderly completion or safe delivery of the answerer's λόγος as he had conceived of it and then to the fair and sufficient testing of it (*Gorgias* 454C; *Protagoras* 360E–361A; *Theaetetus* 150B–151D, 157D, 163C, 146B–C, 151D, 191C).
11. The questioner must follow the answerer wherever he and the λόγος lead (*Euthyphro* 14C; *Republic* 349A).
12. Above all, the questioner is to point out which answers are inconsistent (*Gorgias* 461A; *Protagoras* 333A–B, 339D, 357B–358E, 360E–361A; *Euthydemus* 287B–C; *Theaetetus* 154E).

Both questioner and answerer were bound by other conditions:

13. Questioner and answerer must not fall into the habit of snatching at each other's words with a hasty guess as to the speaker's meaning, completing them in their own fashion and not as intended. Questioners in particular are to remember that they may not be grasping

The epistemic necessity 41

the intended meaning aright (*Gorgias* 454C, 458E; *Theaetetus* 166C, 166E, 168C, 177E).[13]
14. Neither questioner nor answerer may proceed κατὰ τὸ ὄνομα, or by making merely verbal distinctions and classifications. Conventional nomenclature is not to be the final arbiter in distinguishing and classifying. To trust such nomenclature as a dependable guide in dialectic is to turn dialectic into antilogic, or ἀντιλογική (*Republic* 454A–E).[14] One is to investigate rather κατ' εἴδη, or according to forms, recognizing that real affinities and distinctions may not be reflected in conventional language, but may require extraordinary usage and hence extraordinary claims.
15. Both questioner and answerer are to seek the truth, not debating points (*Gorgias* 457C–458B; *Philebus* 58D–E).

Together these conditions give one a sense of the sorts of constraints under which an account in the third sense was to be developed in dialogues down to the *Theaetetus*. From our own point of view the items in the list are extraordinarily miscellaneous, thus indicating that they could not possibly have been devised by any clear-headed person who wished to state how one can examine people to determine whether or not they have what we call knowledge. To meet Plato's conditions would require much more than knowledge, but this is as one would have expected from the previous chapter. The condition for which he is testing is more nearly a full understanding than knowledge.

In the next chapter we explore further this condition and the rationale behind these constraints. But our interest here lies in the way Plato *discerns* whether or not one is in this condition of ἐπιστήμη. We are now in a position to state dialectical conditions Plato seems to have regarded as necessary and sufficient to warrant attributing ἐπιστήμη to an answerer, even though we are scarcely in a position as yet to articulate all that the condition of ἐπιστήμη consisted in on Plato's view.

The epistemic necessity of the ability to give an account

Plato, like the Socrates he portrays, was plainly willing to deny that one had ἐπιστήμη if upon examination one proved unable to give an account of the preferred sort. This is now widely recognized.[15] As Diotima says at *Symposium* 202A, "You do not understand . . . that thinking the right thing without being able to give an account is neither understanding (for how could it be understanding without an account?) nor is it ignorance (for how can it be ignorance when it happens to hit upon what is so?).

Hence, thinking the right thing presumably comes between understanding and ignorance." At *Phaedo* 76B, without any argument whatever, Socrates gets the expected reply when he asks, "When a man understands, can he give an account of what he understands or not?" With the possible but controversial exception of the final pages in his *Theaetetus*, Plato consistently has his spokesmen and their respondents talk as if the ability to give and successfully defend an account were necessary for ἐπιστήμη. In this chapter I shall not discuss the connection or lack of it between ἐπιστήμη and the ability to give an account in this *Theaetetus* passage, since the important work of Cornford and his numerous critics requires that this be postponed until we have developed an account of Plato's forms in Chapter 4.[16] This is a small enough omission, however, since even those who claim that in the *Theaetetus* Plato refuted his earlier view that ἐπιστήμη requires the ability to give a λόγος concede that he nevertheless continued to hold this refuted view in subsequent dialogues.[17]

Thus, at *Timaeus* 51E Plato's spokesman declares that νοῦς (here equivalent to ἐπιστήμη) is always associated with ἀληθὴς λόγος, or a true account. The same necessary condition for ascribing ἐπιστήμη to a person is evinced as late as *Laws* 12, Plato's last book, and elsewhere in late dialogues: *Laws* 966B, 967E, 968C; *Phaedrus* 276A–278C; *Sophist* 230D–E (*Theaetetus* 202D, which may maintain the view, will be discussed in Chapter 5). Clinias at *Laws* 966B confidently gives the usual reply when the Athenian, having got his agreement to the view that the guardians of the law ought to understand in what respects the good and the fair are plural and in what respects they are one, asks: "Ought they to understand it but be unable to give an indication of it in an account?"

Thus, the necessary connection between the ability to give an account and the possession of ἐπιστήμη asserted at *Republic* 531E and in the passage at 534B–C quoted earlier in the chapter is maintained consistently in the dialogues with the sole possible exception of the *Theaetetus*. Plato rules out the possibility of inarticulate or "mystical" ἐπιστήμη of anything whatever, even the form of the good.[18] Though something like insight or mental vision may well have been involved in achieving ἐπιστήμη on Plato's view, there can be no doubt that such insight or vision is capable of expression, and that where there is no such capacity there is no such insight or vision.[19]

Not only does Plato hold that every object of ἐπιστήμη is necessarily an object of an adequate account; he also holds that everything good is at least potentially an object of ἐπιστήμη. This runs counter to mystical and skeptical views sometimes foisted upon Plato by interpreters of *Republic* 6 and *Epistle* 7.[20] On the unstated and quite untenable assumption that Plato must have thought Socrates was as wise as a person could become,

The epistemic sufficiency

Socrates' claim at *Republic* 505A that *we*—that is, he and Glaucon—do not adequately understand (οὐχ ἱκανῶς ἴσμεν) the good is construed as a claim that the good cannot be adequately understood by any person, and hence is beyond the reach of any adequate account. Yet it is clear from 506A–B and 534B–C that Plato is demanding of his guardians much more than Socrates says he can deliver. They must understand the good if they are to be worth much as guardians, and if they do understand it, they will be able to give an adequate account of it. That such guardians are not impossible on Plato's view is clear enough from 496B–497A and from 540A–E. Thus, an account of the good is possible.

Similarly, *Epistle 7*, even if it is genuine, provides no support for the view that Plato thought some things, the good perhaps among them, beyond the reach of λόγοι, or accounts.[21] At 341C–D he speaks of certain subjects as ῥητὸν γὰρ οὐδαμῶς, or "not at all expressible." But ῥητόν, like many English terms ending in *-ible* and *-able*, can bear either a capacity sense or a normative sense. It could suggest either the possibility of expressing oneself on these subjects or the advisability of it. The context indicates beyond question that Plato intends it in the latter sense. He argues at 341D–E that the best account on these subjects would be his own, but that it would not be good to offer it in writing, since that would have bad effects upon some readers. No clear-headed person bothers to justify refraining from the impossible. Plato has shown, then, that he regards these subjects, not as beyond our powers of expression, but simply as beyond the bounds of what ought to be expressed in writing.[22] Oral expression to appropriate students is not ruled out any more than it was in the similar passage at *Phaedrus* 274C–277A.[23]

The predominant view among recent commentators on Plato is that he did indeed regard the ability to give an account as necessary for ἐπιστήμη. Thus, the view argued in this section is not new. Yet it is, I think, new to many that in dialogues up through the *Republic* at least, Plato evidently thought he discerned an even more powerful connection between the attribution of ἐπιστήμη and the ability to give an account in the third sense. He evidently thought the ability to give such an account was sufficient to show that the one having it possessed ἐπιστήμη. We turn now to the evidence for his having thought this.

The epistemic sufficiency of the ability to give an account

The evidence that Plato believed the ability to give a λόγος of the best sort was sufficient to certify the possession of ἐπιστήμη is neither very direct nor very obvious, but it is, I think, powerful enough upon examination to warrant our concluding that he held the belief when he wrote the *Republic* and previous dialogues.

The prominence given to dialectical tests in the early and middle dialogues suggests that the ability to give a λόγος is not likely to be just one among a number of independently necessary and jointly sufficient conditions for the possession of ἐπιστήμη. They are given this prominence in the examination of answerers, an examination which seems to be directed at determining whether or not they have ἐπιστήμη. All Socrates and Plato could hope to achieve by wielding a merely necessary condition for the possession of ἐπιστήμη was to expose a lack of it. They could not hope to use a merely necessary condition to certify that a person possesses it. It is beside the point that Socrates does in fact expose this lack in his respondents. It is much more important that he seems entirely ready to concede that they possess ἐπιστήμη if their accounts will survive his tests.

Consider, for example, what Socrates is up to in the *Euthyphro*. Euthyphro at 4A–B claims to have advanced σοφία, or understanding, concerning matters of piety and impiety. Socrates at 5A–B enrolls as his pupil in hopes of having Euthyphro's wisdom rub off on him in the form of true opinion. So in order to learn from Euthyphro what piety is, Socrates sets out to question him at 5C–D. This expressed desire to acquire some pale shadow of Euthyphro's wisdom may seem ironic, as it does surely by 14D, after Euthyphro has floundered dialectically, yet just prior to this at 14B–C, Socrates indicated that Euthyphro was very close to an adequate account. Euthyphro had worked around to the view that piety consists in service to the gods, service of the sorts rendered by servants who do things which their masters are perfectly capable of doing for themselves. These services are helpful to the gods without suggesting any imperfection on their part. This much Socrates seems to accept, yet he wants to hear what the gods do that we help them with, and Euthyphro begs off. Socrates, with no hint of irony except in the first sentence, remarks: "It is clear that you are not eager to teach me. For now in fact you were close upon it but you turned back; and if you had answered this, I should already have been sufficiently taught about piety by you." Socrates seems genuinely ready to concede that Euthyphro possesses an understanding of piety if he can defend the view he has come around to by answering this one further question, which of course he cannot answer. He concedes then that Euthyphro was one answer away from giving us a sufficient account. But in the context of this dialogue, a sufficient account would be a sufficient reason to think he had ἐπιστήμη. That this might have been a difficult and involved answer is for our present purposes unimportant.[24] The crucial point is that answering would have been taken as sufficient.

A similar line of thinking is indicated at *Meno* 97C–98D. Whatever

The epistemic sufficiency

makes the difference between mere true opinion and understanding is sufficient for understanding. The sole dialectically relevant difference Socrates recognizes here between ὀρθὴ δόξα, or "thinking the right thing," and having ἐπιστήμη, or understanding, is that the latter is tied down, fixed, and dependable. What ties it down is αἰτίας λογισμός, or "reasoning out the cause," which is another name for recollection as accomplished by dialectical questioning and answering over a long period of time.[25] The ability to give a λόγος is thus sufficient to distinguish ἐπιστήμη from mere true opinion, as virtuous conduct is not.[26]

Had Plato not believed that the ability to give a sturdy λόγος in the best sense was *not merely necessary but also sufficient* for certifying the possession of ἐπιστήμη, the key arguments of the *Republic* concerning the distribution of power would not only be implausible from our point of view but would also be unwise in the extreme on Plato's own judgment. Plato does not wish to give any political power at all to people who lack ἐπιστήμη, as emerges at 473C–E and 414A. He proposes to give it all to his philosopher kings, who are to be the guardians of his state. At 428A–429A Plato indicates that they are to have ἐπιστήμη of the good, and of justice, moderation, and courage; they are to possess that εὐβουλία, or good counsel, by which the state will be preserved. Yet his reason for thinking that they possess this ἐπιστήμη is that they have passed certain dialectical tests. Elaborate behavioral tests, including an impeccable administrative and military record, are necessary before Plato will even allow such dialectical tests to be administered, yet the dialectical tests are plainly the ones which allow him to distinguish those military veterans who understand the good from those who do not. Passing such tests for them proves a *sufficient* condition for being admitted to absolute, unchecked power. Since Plato thought only those who possess ἐπιστήμη and the ἀρετή coextensive with it are to have such power, he must have thought that such dialectical tests allow one to cull out even the cleverest pretenders to wisdom, leaving as survivors only those who are truly wise and excellent. These tests are described at 506A–B and 531D–534E.

When he wrote the *Republic*, Plato evidently did not think he was merely describing ideals laid up in heaven and unsuitable for practical application (473A, 540D ff., 499D). At 472B ff. he indicates that he intended his political scheme to be applicable, if only in approximation. Nothing in it, he says at 499D, is incapable of realization. Presumably, then, nothing it presupposes or requires for its realization is impossible. And one of the things it presupposes is that dialectic provides a decision procedure for sorting those who have ἐπιστήμη into one class and those who do not into others.

Plato goes to great lengths to describe the nearly superhuman qualities of the guardians. He speaks at 413E and 503A of testing candidates for guardianship more thoroughly than gold which is repeatedly tried in the fire only to emerge pure and intact each time.[27] This metallurgical simile is suggestive in several ways. First, there is no suggestion in the *Republic* that the dialectical counterpart to the fire is lifelong, that the tests never come to a confident end short of death. Whether the tests he is describing are tests in the endurance of toils, fears, and pleasures, or tests of the ability to give an account without tripping up in defending it, Plato suggests that these are completable. Once candidates complete them, he has no reservations about putting unchecked dictatorial power in their hands, confident that they will use it rightly.

That such tests are completable on his view is clear from 413E–414A: "And the one who as a child, a youth, and a man is tested and comes forth unalloyed we must install as leader of the city and guardian." It is possible to "come forth" from these tests. They are not lifelong. That τέχνη or ἐπιστήμη rectifies conduct or proves to guarantee ἀρετή is clear from 340C ff., 341C–342B, 489C, 520E.

The high stakes he wagers on the outcome of these tests surely bespeak total confidence in their sufficiency to establish the possession of ἐπιστήμη and hence ἀρετή, or excellence. At *Republic* 425D Socrates remarks that it is not worthwhile to dictate to good and honorable men. At *Statesman* 297A–B he indicates that wise rulers do no wrong. He leaves no margin of error, and holds back no power which might rectify a mistaken choice of guardians.

The metallurgical simile is suggestive in a second way which perhaps helps explain why his use of it is so appropriate given the point he was evidently attempting to convey. Gold which has been repeatedly tried in the fire does not suddenly turn into 14 carat gold, 10 carat gold, or lead. It has been certified pure, and once certified in this way, it preserves its purity unless it is alloyed again. The psychic counterpart to this "alloying" is explored in the following chapter as is the corresponding process of purification. On Plato's view as expressed at *Timaeus* 41D our psyches are from their inception impure mixtures. But the impurities he speaks of removing by dialectic are false opinions and corresponding vices acquired after birth.[28]

The breakdown of Plato's confidence in the epistemic *sufficiency* of accounts

Plato's confidence that the ability to give a dialectically sturdy account is *necessary* for the possession of ἐπιστήμη evidently never came to an end. In *Epistle 7* at 342A–B, the author lists three necessary things from which ἐπιστήμη arises, one of these being an account. And in the sequel to the passage from *Laws* 12 quoted above, Plato's Athenian spokesman gets a positive response when he inquires (966B): "Do we hold the same account regarding all good things, that those who are to be real guardians of the laws must really understand what is the case about them, and be capable of explaining it in an account and conforming to it in deed?" This capability had been tested in every way Plato could imagine, from legally sanctioned opportunities for entrapment and an *in vino veritas* test to dialectical examination (*Laws* 647A–648C, 967E–968A, 968C). As Plato describes them in the *Laws*, the tests the guardians of the laws have to pass appear to be rather more rigorous and detailed than those which the candidates for guardianship were described as having to pass in the *Republic*. The use of wine, for example, was not envisioned as an officially sanctioned trap in the *Republic*, nor were candidates' families scrutinized, as they are in *Laws* 751A.

Despite the increased stringency of these tests, Plato is willing to wager less on their outcome. Far from confidently bestowing unchecked and sweeping powers on the guardians of the laws or indeed on anyone else, Plato at *Laws* 945B ff. envisions setting up a board of examiners to observe them and prosecute them for any wrongdoing they might engage in.[29] Such wrongdoing by thoroughly tested people was all but unthinkable in the *Republic*, but it is viewed as a live possibility in the *Laws*. Even the examiners themselves are subject to prosecution, though they are the people chosen as the best in the city and even as divine (*Laws* 946D, 947E). Plainly, a great change has come over the complicated web of Plato's views.

It is no easy task to locate precisely the character of that change. It is still less easy to trace confidently what led Plato to make just that change. Here I shall merely characterize the change. In the final section of Chapter 6 we shall be in a position to understand the reasons for it and the steps leading up to it in dialogues written between the *Republic* and the *Laws*. The rationale for being at all concerned with the change in a work on Plato's epistemology is that the root of the change proves to be epistemological and, even more deeply, ontological, and the change illustrates the practical political consequences which follow from taking epistemological and ontological views seriously, as Plato did.

Consider first a fairly common account of the character of the change which has come over Plato's views in *Laws* 12 and previous books. The common view is, I think, pretty much as follows: Plato had grown disillusioned with tyrannical power as a result of his experience in Syracuse. He had decided in his middle to late years that no man can exercise unchecked power without bringing himself and his city to grief.[30] Human nature, he had decided, was simply too weak to be entrusted with such license.[31] Hence, it seemed necessary to set up the board of examiners and to ensure that everyone in power was examined periodically by someone else no matter what tests for understanding and excellence they had passed previously. All of this was owing, then, to a prudent downgrading in Plato's estimate of human nature, a revision understandable in an older man.[32] He was, however, still a bit wistful about having guardians such as he had described in the *Republic*, and regarded the *Laws* as describing a state second best after the one described in the *Republic*, a state having made substantive compromises with quality for the sake of practicality.[33]

Such matters are extremely difficult to determine with confidence, but in my judgment this popular interpretation is subtly wrong on all counts. It has had distinguished defenders who surely have some textual evidence on their side, but on balance we had best reject it. For consider: Plato was plainly not inexperienced with former dialecticians' turning into rogues when he wrote the *Republic* or, for that matter, still earlier dialogues such as the *Charmides*.[34] Several fellow devotees of Socrates would be vividly in mind, and close relatives and perhaps former friends and associates were among them. Both Plato's uncle, Charmides, and his mother's cousin, Critias, were among the thirty collaborators set up by the Spartans after Athens surrendered to Lysander. Both died fighting the restoration of democracy in 404.

No living person gets rid of the appetitive and spirited parts of the psyche, on Plato's view. Hence, he well knew that each of us contains within himself forces which are by nature opposed to the right use of political power. It seems implausible, then, that additional political experience in what was by and large a quieter age politically than that preceding the *Republic* would have led to so vast a revision in his recommended distribution of power.

Such experiences with politicians could only have taught Plato what he well knew already. To become disillusioned one must formerly have been under the influence of what one later comes to see as an illusion. But when had Plato ever believed that *human* nature was capable of exercising unchecked power without bringing ruin upon its possessor and his fellows? Consider, for instance, his scathingly low estimate of what human nature had accomplished to date politically in the *Gorgias*, and his discouraging remarks to Alcibiades and to Callicles on the occasion of their expressed desire to go into politics (*Alcibiades* I 120A ff.; *Gorgias* 515A ff.). Plainly he had always believed that no nature was any good without a strong admixture of the divine, and that human beings even at their best can have no more than an admixture of it so long as they are alive (*Timaeus* 69C–72D; cp. *Republic* 492E–493A). There is no room here for disillusionment with human nature.

The breakdown of Plato's confidence 49

There is, however, room for an upward revision in Plato's estimate of what ordinary humans are capable of; and far from finding a disillusionment with them in the *Laws*, one finds such an upward revision, especially in *Laws* 12. His estimate of the extent to which divine nature is functional in ordinary human beings is far more optimistic than in *Republic*. See, for example, *Republic* 586A–B for a view of the multitude as so many cattle. His Athenian says at *Laws* 950B–C: "For it is not the case that the masses have failed to attain judgment about others (that these are evil and these good) by as much as they happen to have failed in attaining the substance of virtue, for something divine and shrewd is within the power even of the evil, so that very many even of the exceedingly evil distinguish well in accounts and opinions the better men and the worse." In the *Republic* the less heard from the masses about which people they regarded as good and which bad the better Plato would have liked it: note at 604E his contempt for the mob in the theater who cannot understand the intelligent and temperate. The masses, one will recall from *Republic* 493A ff., constitute the great noisy beast to which politicians and assorted sophists and rhetoricians are able to pander successfully just because the beast lacks the very discernment Plato now attributes to them in the *Laws*.

Plainly then, Plato's estimate of the masses' judgment has gone up dramatically, and this change of opinion is not an idle comment. He wagers considerable stakes on it by including what for him was a large measure of democratic power in the constitution of the state he describes in the *Laws*. This inclusion is often ascribed to an attempt to develop a "second-best" state, it being assumed that when he wrote the *Laws* Plato would have regarded the *Republic* as describing the best state and the *Laws* as describing the next best.[35] But this assumption is false. The best state described at *Laws* 710D–E is plainly not the *Republic*, since it has a separate lawgiver and monarch.[36] And on a principle stated in the *Republic* itself, the situation described in the *Laws* is better than that in the *Republic*. At *Republic* 590D he asks rhetorically whether "it is better for everyone to be governed by the divine and the understanding, *preferably indwelling and his own*, but in default of that imposed from without, in order that we all so far as possible may be akin and friendly because our government and guidance are the same?" Having recognized in the *Laws* that even for the masses a divine principle is "indwelling and their own," Plato accordingly assigns them a larger share of power than he did in the *Republic*. Thus his claim at *Laws* 713C—that human *nature* is not sufficient for assuming unchecked control of all human affairs without falling into hybris and injustice—has little political significance if human *beings*, even evil ones, have more than just human nature.[37] A great noisy beast would merit no particular say in the choice of its keeper, but the masses in the *Laws* at 693C and 694B are given a measure of participation and power, and are encouraged to develop freedom, friendliness, and even understanding.

The distribution of power in the *Laws* is as surprising at the other end as it is at the popular one. Plato is now as unwilling to trust completely people whom he has every good dialectical and behavioral reason to believe are of divine nature as he is willing to trust in part people whom he knows to be deficient in virtue. The extremes have been cut from his previous distribution of power. What is to be made of this?

Answers which attempt to make the *Laws* out to be Plato's vision of a state second only to the one described in the *Republic* rely on seeming Platonic doubts about how common candidates for unchecked guardianship are.[38] At *Laws* 875C Plato still recognizes that if there ever should arise a person competent by nature and by a divine endowment to exercise unchecked political power without being corrupted, such a person would have no need of any external check or ruler. In this passage Plato does seem to be in doubt as to just how reliable the supply of such people is. But by the time he writes *Laws* book 12 (945B–948C), he has ceased to believe in genetic droughts, although this is the very book where his mistrust of officials is most pronounced. He now declares at *Laws* 951B that there is an unfailing supply of divine natures, as many in bad states as in good ones. One need only search them out and put them in power. But in the search, I submit, lies his problem.

His testing procedure for officials is plainly aimed at discerning who has predominately divine nature and who does not. (See, for example, *Laws* 945C and 945E. The examiners must have "amazingly complete virtue.") As 946A and 946B–C indicate, this procedure certifies that the examiners are the best people in the state. If there is indeed an unfailing supply of divine natures and the process by which they are selected is reliable, plainly those selected must be of divine nature. And as *Laws* 961D–E shows, he still believes that those who possess νοῦς or ἐπιστήμη will save themselves and the state.

We have noted already how thorough his process of selecting those with ἐπιστήμη seems to be. It comes as something of a surprise, then, that at 947E Plato will gamble little on its outcome:[39] "But if any of these examiners, relying upon the fact of his election, shall demonstrate human nature after his election by becoming evil, the law shall enjoin on him who wishes to charge him, and the trial shall take place in the court in this way."[40] The reason for gambling so little on the outcome of his tests would seem to be that these tests for discerning which people have divine natures and which do not are insufficient on his view. Certainly he did not treat a person's nature as changing. Φύσις for Plato was always something one was born with and retained until death; see, for example, *Republic*

The breakdown of Plato's confidence 51

618B–E, where one's choice of φύσις, or nature, was irrevocable for life. (Note especially *Republic* 618D, where it is plain that one's φύσις is among the things one chooses when one makes the irrevocable choice of a life.) Plato now seems to believe, with Heraclitus (fr. B123), that nature loves to hide.

Plato's difficulty, then, would seem to be epistemological. He is now talking as if one did not have and could not get effectively applicable tests deploying necessary *and* sufficient conditions for having the sort of ἐπιστήμη coterminous with divine nature and virtue.

The roots of this problem are nowhere to be seen in the *Laws*, which is all but innocent of explicit epistemological, ontological, and psychological developments. If these roots are to be discerned at all, they must be discerned in the dialogues written between *Republic* and *Laws*. Not surprisingly, these are the very dialogues in which one sees dialectic taking on a new shape and having new immediate concerns. Yet it is not possible to understand sufficiently either the new shape of Platonic dialectic in dialogues later than the *Theaetetus* nor the modified epistemological and ontological views which dictated this new shape without understanding what provided a bridge between the old and the new—Plato's enduring conception of ἐπιστήμη as a psychic condition of a complex person having three or more psychic parts, only one of which has an affinity for reality. We turn first, then, to Plato's conception of the complex psyche and to his characterization of ἐπιστήμη as a condition of the psyche.

3
Ἐπιστήμη and the Psyche

The question, What is ἐπιστήμη? is susceptible to answers of several types, much as any "What is . . .?" question will be. One can well imagine a series of contexts in which the appropriate answer to "What is *that*?" might be "a wrong note," or "A-natural," or "the third note in measure 157," or "the tonic." One's interest in asking the question will determine which answer is the appropriate one in context.

Our interest in this study is in finding out as much as we can about Platonic ἐπιστήμη. We have found, not surprisingly, that it is whatever enables a person to survive certain dialectical tests, and that lack of it accounts for a person's inability to survive these tests. But surely there is much more to be said about it. To describe it dialectically might satisfy a behaviorist, but scarcely anyone else. We want to know precisely what condition in a person constitutes ἐπιστήμη and enables the person who has it to meet such tests, while accounting for the inability of those who are in any other condition to meet them. We want to know what condition of the psyche ἐπιστήμη is. In the *Republic* Plato tells us.

Plato frequently indicates that ἐπιστήμη is a condition of the psyche. At *Republic* 511D9, for example, he says that νόησις (which 534A1 shows to be another of his ways of denoting ἐπιστήμη) is one of four conditions of the psyche. What do we need to know in order to grasp precisely what this condition is?

Suppose you are told that a certain musical instrument (a violin, for example) is in tune; suppose also that you do not understand what it is for a violin to be in tune. What would you need to know in order to understand this? For one thing, you would need to know what a violin is—what parts it has, how these parts are adjusted, and which adjustment their being in tune consists in. Similarly, if ἐπιστήμη is a condition of the psyche, and even a condition involving its being in tune (as Plato indicates at *Republic* 443E9), we had best inquire about its parts and about the alternative relationships which may obtain among them.

The parts of the psyche

What were the parts of the psyche posited by Plato in the *Republic*? The question calls not simply for a list but for an account of the grounds on which Plato posited and distinguished such parts. It calls for an account of their nature and role in his system.

We are not lacking in attempts at such an account. These parts have been termed "faculties," "principles," "activities," "aspects," "instances," and "levels" of the psyche. Their nature and role have been characterized in ways influenced as much perhaps by the connotations of these terms as by the details of Plato's text. Yet scholars have long known better. Ritter, Taylor, and Graeser, to name only three, have plainly warned of the confusions that result from characterizing the parts Plato posits as if they were psychological divisions more familiar to us.[1]

Unhappily, to warn of possible confusions is not sufficient to deliver us from them, for they continue to be encouraged by familiar works of interpretation. Perhaps the most common of these confusions results from the suggestion that the parts of the psyche posited by Plato were faculties—"powers" or "capacities" on the order of those posited by Aristotle and modern psychologists.[2] It will be helpful in dispelling this and other such confusions to ask the question, What were the parts of the psyche posited by Plato? and to minimize the seductive influence of any later psychological terminology in answering it. The answer can then be applied to illuminate related themes in later dialogues, especially the *Phaedrus*. In particular, it can illuminate the way in which ἐπιστήμη on Plato's view comes about.

Any plausible account of what Plato thought the parts of the psyche were must be bound up with an account of his theory of justice. At *Republic* 386D–E and again at 435A–B Plato lays down the hypothesis that justice in the polis and justice in the individual are the same. In the latter passage he remarks: "So the just man will not differ at all in character from the just city, so far as the character of justice is concerned, but will be like it."³ This hypothesis dominates the dialogue.⁴ By 435A–B Plato has argued at length that justice in the polis is a restriction and specialization of function obtaining among distinct and potentially seditious classes of agents.⁵

The question Plato must explore from 435B on is whether or not the psyche, like the polis, actually contains distinct and usually seditious agents. The stakes riding on the answer are by this point high. Justice in the polis he makes out to be a certain relation among plausibily real and distinct *relata*. If the psyche does not contain equally real and distinct relata, justice there cannot be the same as justice in the polis, and Plato has wasted three and a half books. In effect, he recognizes these stakes at 434D6–7.

What Plato needs in order to show that he has not been exploring a blind alley must not be minimized. Nothing less than a structural and functional *isomorphism* between polis and psyche will do. It would be an understatement, then, to say that on Plato's view there must be an *analogy* between the polis and the psyche.⁶ The appearance of being one thing must prove as deceptive for the psyche as it did for the ordinary polis at 422E–423A. The psyche must upon examination prove to be literally complex, and literally reducible to parts which are independent of one another in the sense that they can stand in direct conflict as political factions do.

In his examination and argument Plato employs both formal and observational premises. At *Republic* 430E–431A he comments upon the phenomenon we call self-control:

The expression "self-control" is laughable, for the controller of self and the self that is weaker and is controlled is the same person. . . . But . . . the expression seems to want to indicate that in the psyche of the person himself there is a better and a worse part; whenever what is by nature the better part is in control of the worse, this is expressed by saying that the person is self-controlled or master of himself, and this is a term of praise. When, on the other hand, the smaller and better part, owing to poor upbringing or bad company, is over-powered by the larger and worse, this is made a reproach and is called being defeated by oneself, and a person in that situation is called uncontrolled.⁷

The view of self-control suggested here is one Plato continues to hold as late as the *Laws*.⁸ As stated here in the *Republic* it prepares the way for Plato's formal argument for regarding the psyche as literally complex and isomorphic to the polis. That argument proceeds in several steps, which we may paraphrase as follows:

1. It is plain that the same thing will not do or suffer opposites in relation to the same thing in the same respect and at the same time (436B5–C1). Such opposites would be assenting and dissenting,

The parts of the psyche   55

aiming at something and rejecting it, embracing and avoiding (437B1–3).⁹
2. Therefore, if perhaps one finds such opposites arising in oneself, one will not be "the same thing" but a plurality (436B7–C1).
3. One does find such opposites arising in oneself, since
   (a) often we observe that when appetites compel a person contrary to the "calculative" part (τὸν λογισμόν), he rebukes himself (449A9–B1);¹⁰
   (b) anger (τὴν ὀργήν) sometimes combats appetites (ταῖς ἐπιθυμίαις) as one alien thing does another (440A6–7);
   (c) the "spirited" part (τὸ θυμοειδές) is by nature the ally of the "calculative" *unless it is perverted by poor nurture* (441A2–4).¹¹

There is evidence, then, of "civil war in the psyche" (τῆς ψυχῆς στάσις, 440E5), a conflict requiring distinct and alien contestants. Evidence of such conflict may be observed not merely in oneself but in others. Thus, in Leontius' psyche there occurred a conflict between a part interested in viewing a pile of corpses and a part opposed to this as disgraceful (439E–440A).¹² This conflict was evinced in his behavior.

4. It follows, then, that the psyche is indeed complex and faction-ridden in precisely the way the polis had proved to be earlier (441C5–7). The psyche is isomorphic to the polis, for "the same kind of parts and the same number of parts are to be found in the *polis* and in the psyche of each of us" (441C6–7).
5. The psyche and the polis are isomorphic in their states or conditions, and in the origin of these: "It necessarily follows that the individual is wise in the same way, and in the same part of himself, as the city. . . . And the part which makes the individual brave is the same as that which makes the city brave, and in the same manner, and everything which makes for virtue is the same in both. . . . The city was just because each of the three classes in it was fulfilling its own task."¹³

Two parallel pieces of reduction take place in book 4. First, Plato reduces a polis to its parts and reduces characteristics of a polis to characteristics and relations of its parts. At 435E Socrates says: "It would be laughable if anyone thought that the appearance of spiritedness in a polis is not derived from the individuals in it, as with those in Thrace or Scythia or generally in the North." At 428E it is claimed that if a polis seems wise as a whole, this is owing to the ἐπιστήμη, or understanding, found in its smallest part, the class of guardians. It is that class which is influential when the polis is said to display wisdom. And this influence is clearly literal: the guardians cause certain wise things to be done and prevent the doing of unwise ones. Hence, Plato is not merely trafficking in points of informal logic.[14] The division into parts is likewise literal. The appearance that the polis as a whole is wise is deceptive, for it contains parts which lack wisdom, and if such parts had usurped the function of the wise part and had directed the behavior of the whole, the polis would have lacked wisdom.

Secondly, at 435E Socrates affirms that this same pattern of reductive argument is to be applied to the individual person.[15] Again, this neither is nor could be a loose analogy if Plato's arguments are to go through. It is to be taken as a piece of sober theorizing, and taken as literally as any piece of theorizing in the dialogues. There are many indications of this. For example, at 443B–D and 444B–C, with none of the hints or warnings with which Plato usually surrounds self-consciously figurative language, the cause of one's keeping oaths and refraining from various wrongs is said to lie in each part of the psyche's doing its own work, while the cause of one's doing wrong is said to lie in psychic civil war and the parts' interference with one another's proper work (see, e.g., 506B–E, esp. E5). At 436A Plato had laid it down as one of two hypotheses (the one later accepted) that the parts of the psyche are the entities responsible when we start or move. Again, at 439C–D overt conduct is said to mirror or be an image of inner activity. And in applying this theory later in the *Republic* to assess the happiness or misery of the tyrant and the causes of the tyrant's actions, Socrates is made to remark that the tyrant's external acts betray the miserable internal economy of the tyrant's psyche to the informed observer who is able to consider the entire psyche. The person who is a tyrant is so because he contains a tyrant, and it rules harshly over other, quite unwilling subjects even within the tyrant himself.[16] Plato suggests at 577A–B that he has grounded this view on the observation of tyrants in their unguarded moments, presumably those in which the miserable state of their oppressed parts and the fearful state of the oppressing one are evident.

There is no blinking the fact that Plato was attempting to account causally for persons' actions, not merely analyze concepts. One does not appeal to observations of tyrants in their unguarded moments to substantiate a piece of conceptual analysis. Plato is out to account causally not just for isolated actions but for the overall direction (or lack of it) in the life a person leads. This is evident at 581B–C, where Socrates is made to claim that there are three sorts of people and three corresponding sorts of lives. An individual is of one of these three sorts and leads the life he or she does because of the part of the psyche which *rules* the others in that individual's psyche. Talk of "rule" is plainly causal and explanatory in force; and given the isomorphism of polis and psyche that Plato posits and requires for his argument, we are to take it as straightforward, not metaphorical.[17]

Talk of the rule of one part over others and of the difficulty the best part has in achieving it in the face of efforts by the other parts to usurp its function underscores Plato's very ground for believing there are parts. The sole ground on which Plato distinguishes parts of the psyche is the psyche's susceptibility to internal conflict.[18] Susceptibility to internal conflict on this view shows that the psyche cannot be one entity.[19] The "cannot" here is logical: if x is both G and H, and anything which is H is not G, then it would follow that x both is G and is not G, which cannot be the case. If x nevertheless appears to be both G and not G, we must look for seams in x; x cannot conceivably be simple. Thus, if Leontius both wants to view corpses and despises corpse-viewing, and if x's despising corpse-viewing entails x's not wanting to view corpses, "Leontius" is the name of at least two entities deceptively packaged as one.

Faculties or agents?

We have noted that Plato divides human beings into classes in accordance with their predominant desires. He argues at *Republic* 485D–E and 486C that the desire that predominates in a person's life will correlate with that person's chief area of expertise or ability. As 475A ff. indicates, the kind of person one is depends upon one's predominant desire. One may have additional desires, however. Farmers, as we see at 374A–D, are able to form something they might call an army to defend the polis, and may even desire to do this, but they are likely to do a poor job of it and had best cater to appetite by growing food and leave defense to strong-spirited, practiced professional soldiers (375A9–B3). Function varies not precisely with capacity in any minimal sense of "capacity" but with competence. At 353A Plato indicates that a thing's function is shown by what it alone can do *or* by what it can do better than anything else. In his political thought, it is the second indication of function which is relevant. The auxiliaries have the protective function they do, not because craftsmen cannot wield weapons, but because the auxiliaries can perform this function better than anyone else. There would be no occasion for Plato's principle of specialization if citizens of diverse classes could not overlap at a minimal level in their capacities and their desires. The occasion for this principle is the widespread meddlesomeness in the ordinary polis. Plato sees clearly the distinction between minimal *capacity* and *competence*.[20]

Since Plato regards the psyche as isomorphic to a polis composed of people capable of meddlesomeness, it would be odd if he chose an entirely different principle of specialization for the parts of the psyche than the very principle he had invoked for the parts of the polis—the principle that one is to do what one is competent to do and leave other tasks to others.[21] Yet this odd shift in principles of specialization has been attributed to Plato by interpreters who characterize the parts of the psyche he posits as faculties. A faculty, by definition, is a capacity for the one thing its name would suggest.[22] "Appetite" on a facultist view would be a capacity for a certain sort of desire and nothing else; "Reason" would be simply and solely a capacity for reasoning. Thus a faculty's "specialization of function" would be the automatic and trivial result of its incapacity to do anything its name did not suggest.

Such triviality is not uncommonly charged against Plato's argument by interpreters and translators who speak of the parts of the psyche as if they were faculties.[23] But this will not fit the text. Talk of one faculty's usurping the function of another would be plainly absurd. Yet Plato at 440E5 speaks of τῆς ψυχῆς στάσις, a "civil war in the psyche," and at 443D3–6 describes the parts' meddlesome tendency to usurp the functions of other parts. Talk of usurpation or, indeed, of any other activity of a faculty would be doubly absurd once we realize that faculties are capacities, and capacities are not agents; they require agents to employ them, and usurpation is clearly the act of an agent.[24] Yet this talk of usurpation is essential to Plato's view of injustice.

Another insuperable textual obstacle to taking the parts as faculties is found in Plato's description of what it takes to inhibit such usurpation of function. At 442A–B and 586E5 he prescribes education and training to induce each part to perform its own function. Plainly, one does not have to induce what cannot by definition be otherwise.

The activities of the parts

Facultist mistakes stem from a failure to take seriously Plato's isomorphism of polis and psyche. At *Republic* 441C6–7 he claims that there are the same number *and* the same kind of parts in the psyche as in the polis. The parts of the polis were classes of people grouped together, not on the basis of their possessing one and only one capacity per group, but on the basis of the common predominant love or interest and common competence found in the group's members. With this isomorphism Plato commits himself to assigning to parts of the psyche usurpable functions and the modicum of versatility this presupposes.

Further evidence that Plato acts on this commitment may be found in the diverse names he gives to each part. To weigh this evidence fairly, however, we must for the time being refrain from taking any of these names as exhausting or limiting the capabilities of the part to which it is assigned. Given their history in faculty psychology and in interpretations influenced by it, the terms "Reason," "Spirit," and "Appetite" unfortunately do exhaust or limit the capacity of anything to which they are applied in our context. It will be prudent, then, to let the parts go incognito for a time, labeling them uncontroversially as A, B, and C, and noting the things Plato says and suggests about the desires, capacities, and activities of each in their names and descriptions.

One obstacle to doing this is the English definite article which occurs in mechanical renderings of such Platonic expressions as τὸ ἐπιθυμητικόν. We are often told this means "the desiderative" or "the appetitive." This translation is misleading, however, for the connotations of the English definite article differ substantially from those of Plato's neuter singular τό. Plato's τό was a standard Greek device for making a noun or piece of technical terminology out of anything to which it was prefixed. When so used, it does not suggest "the one and only," and thus provides no support for interpreters who treat a part of the psyche labeled τό ———— as the one and only thing in the psyche capable on Plato's view of ————. These parts, we must remind ourselves, are isomorphic to usurpers and busybodies.

Even usurpers and busybodies have overriding or predominant loves, however, and lesser desires over which these normally hold sway. One can be a lover of more than one thing. We should bear this in mind when Plato describes *each* part of the psyche—including the best—with multiple φίλο- compounds. Part A, dominant in his philosopher-kings, is termed τὸ φιλομαθές or "lover of learning," and τὸ φιλόσοφον, or "lover of wisdom," at 581B7. It is called τὸ λογιστικόν, or "calculative," at 439D5, and is accordingly assigned the role of taking counsel (442B7) and exercising forethought on behalf of the entire psyche (441E5). Part B, dominant in his auxiliaries, is called τὸ φιλόνικον, "lover of victory," and τὸ φιλότιμον, "lover of honor" (581B1–2). It is also called τὸ θυμοειδές, "spirited," as at 441A3. Part C, strongest in people suited to be craftsmen, is termed τὸ φιλοχρήματον, "lover of money" or "lover of possessions" (580E7), and τὸ φιλοκερδές, "lover of gain" (581A7). It is said to love food and drink (439D5–6), and is called τὸ ἐπιθυμητικόν, or "appetitive" (439D7).

What relation holds between the multiple "loves" attributed to each part? Plato evidently did not conceive of these as miscellaneous and unrelated. At 357B4–D2 he had pointed out that people value some things for their own sakes, others for their consequences, and still others for both. The parts of the psyche resemble people of various political classes in this respect as in most others. At 580E6 he calls part C τὸ φιλοχρήματον, or "lover of money," in the very sentence in which he is explaining that it loves money *because* it is most conducive to its ultimate end (ἀποτελοῦνται ἁι . . . ἐπιθυμίαι), the satisfaction of its appetites for food, drink, and sex. Its regard for money is instrumental, much as its regard for securing part A's superior logistical assistance is at 553C–D. It does not love thinking; it loves money and property as means to sensual gratification, and any regard it has for calculative ability is regard for this ability as a means to obtaining money and property. It is not indifferent to the *instrumental* value of thinking, and places some value on it, though it is not said to love it.

It seems reasonable to suppose that among the various loves assigned to part B at 581A, the love of honor is primary; and victory, good reputation, and rule are loved as means to this, though Plato is not explicit on this point.

If there is an ordering of means and ends in the various things loved by a given part, plainly there is nothing to prevent what is loved for its own sake by one part from being valued weakly as a means by another. At 441E5, part A is assigned the function of exercising forethought on behalf of the entire psyche. At 442C4–8 it is charged with understanding and seeking what will benefit each part and the whole they constitute. To be concerned for each part is to be concerned to quiet and satisfy each, as we see from 571D5–572B2. Thus, as 586D8 indicates, part A will actually prescribe or approve (ἐξηγῆται) certain pleasures of gain and victory. The parts need not disagree in their opinions about what is of value and what is allowable. In a just person they will not disagree (442D), even though their natural tendency is to disagree.

A common awareness of means/end relationships in *each* part suggests precisely the sort of versatility a *capacity* for usurpation presupposes. It suggests a minimal capacity we might call "cognitive" even in part C. Plato's distaste for demotic or popular senses of terms and for the ontological slum in which they have their use leads him to say that part C is senseless (ἀνοήτῳ, 605B9), but this must be taken in much the way one takes his claim that none of the *poleis* Greeks lived in deserved to be called a polis (422E2–423B2). Often he reminds us that on his view a term's primary denotation is an ideal paradigm and that things diverging widely from this scarcely deserve to have the term used of them. In the psyche the ideal ruler and administrator was part A, but we must not let Plato's zeal in claiming its comparative superiority over parts B and C in this function obscure the fact that he has endowed B and C with sufficient

The activities of the parts

ability to usurp the function, if only to botch it. If part C were senseless in the way a rock is, there would be no question of its usurping A's function. C is senseless more nearly in the way Cleon the Tanner was, and foolish (ἀλόγιστον, 439D7) as he was also.

That Plato assigns a minimal level of cognitive capacity to B and C is indicated in a number of ways other than their corresponding to political factions which have this capacity. At *Republic* 571C, part C is said to be capable of devising elaborate dream plots while part A sleeps. Thus, part C has the ability to imagine complex scenarios, and it is capable of ruling not simply in sleep but in the waking life of tyrants, on his view.

The parts are frequently depicted as being aware of one another. The story of Leontius at 439E–440A suggests that part B combats and rebukes part C on occasion. Both parts are depicted as being capable of obeying or following part A, which suggests that they are aware of it and in communication with it (586D5–7, E3).

What the parts are aware of in one another are not merely desires but opinions. The unleashing of part C at 571C is not simply the unleashing of many and dread appetites (573D6–8) but the emancipation of certain opinions which were formerly freed only in sleep (574D–E). That parts B and C hold opinions and hence may be said to "think" is borne out at 603D, where Plato speaks of us as having within ourselves contradictory opinions about the same thing at the same time. He is well aware of what this implies when taken together with his principle that the same thing cannot at the same time and in the same respect stand in opposite relations to a second thing. In fact, he reiterates at 604B his view that one may distinguish parts in cases of internal conflict.

This has surprising antecedents and implications. The practice of the elenctic Socratic dialectic in earlier dialogues and even in book 1 of the *Republic* itself had made it glaringly obvious that the same person can at the same time unwittingly hold two or more *opinions* which are in conflict on an issue.[25] But now Plato can explain how and why Socrates was able to find contradictory opinions in the same person. We each have inferior parts which tend to have inferior opinions. At 605C Plato speaks of a part which cannot distinguish the greater and lesser, but believes (ἡγουμένῳ) that the same things are now one, now the other. The opinions of a base part are also mentioned at 574D–E. Plato's stated goal is for all of the parts to agree in their opinions (442D3), for the person whose parts these are accordingly to be of one mind (603D).

Although the passage from 603 to 605 is more explicit than any in book 4, it makes no break with the views expressed in book 4, and is in fact anticipated there in its essentials.[26] When Plato at 437A stated his view that the same thing cannot at the same time and in the same respect be, do, or suffer opposites, he made it quite inclusive enough for later application to thoughts and opinions. And in fact he immediately suggests such an application at 437B, when he gives as his first example of a pair of opposites suggesting a division in the psyche τὸ ἐπινεύειν, "nodding assent" or "approving," and τὸ ἀνανεύειν, "nodding dissent" or "disapproving."

Part B is said not only to be capable of having opinions but also to be in need of intelligent communication either from the wisdom-loving part A within the person or perhaps from other persons' wisdom-loving parts. At 550B Plato speaks of bad communications in connection with the nurture of morally and politically inferior persons. As early as 410D he had claimed that τὸ θυμοειδές, which emerges as the "spirited" part B in book 4, will become brave if rightly trained, but brutal, harsh, and savage otherwise. He describes the training it needs as μουσική, or "music." But "music" includes λόγοι, or "accounts," as 376E–377A indicates. Plato holds that the honor-loving part B has need of stories, fables, and the like to tame its wilder tendencies. And at 441A2–4 he claims that it naturally heeds the instructions of the wisdom-loving part provided it has not been corrupted. If it heeds such instructions, stories, and fables, then it must be able to understand them, much as the soldiers to whom it corresponds are. If it can understand them, it is not devoid of sense.

This is not to say that parts B and C, left to their own devices, can think in such a way as to arrive at true opinions, on Plato's view, far less preserve any true opinion they may be given. They correspond, after all, to politicians, for whose opinions he had only contempt, as one will recall from 425E–426E. He had a similar contempt for the indigenous opinions of parts B and C, especially C.

The achievement of psychic harmony

If parts B and C dimly discern means to ends and have distinct opinions of their own, how is it possible for part A to dislodge their seditious opinions and achieve psychic harmony and justice? How can it rule over rivals which are neither weak nor witless?

Before addressing the question, *How* can it rule over rivals? it will be helpful if we address a prior question: *Why* should it want to rule over rivals? On familiar intellectualist interpretations of the "it" in question here—part A—we would not expect it to want anything at all, for it is a mere faculty for learning, inquiring, and calculating. Yet we have seen that part A cannot be such a faculty. Such intellectualist readings are

The achievement of psychic harmony

shown to be untenable by Plato's serious isomorphism of polis and psyche and by his describing each part—this one included—as a *lover*. He characterizes a lover of something as fanatically and insatiably bent upon enjoying what he or she loves. At 474B ff., he clarifies what he means by a philosopher, a lover of wisdom. And in so doing he clarifies what he means by the lover of wisdom within the psyche, part A. The lover of wisdom wants to learn and understand with a fervor Plato compares with that of a lover of wine or a paederast. One expects a lover of something to want to defeat or outwit whoever or whatever stands in the way of satisfying this love. The initial stories of psychological conflict in *Republic* 4 make it clear that for part A, the other parts can and often do stand in the way of its satisfying its love or loves. So it has every reason to want to influence them, if not rule over them.

On the face of it one might think it impossible for part A to rule over parts B and C. Plato pointedly calls C "the mass of the psyche" (442A6) and likens it to an immense, many-headed hydra caged with a small lion and a tiny human being (588B ff.). He tells us that it is the task of this tiny human being to tame and rule the beasts with which it is caged. But having depicted parts B and C as powerful beasts, he makes one wonder how on his view one might tame and rule them. Indeed, he makes one wonder whether justice in the psyche, so conceived, is possible at all. If one thinks justice in the polis is nevertheless possible, one must then ask whether justice in the polis and justice in the psyche *can* be the same, as Plato claimed, especially if justice in the polis must have its source in psychic justice.[27] Questions about *how* psychic justice can be achieved thus return to plague Plato's claim that justice in the polis is justice in the psyche writ large.

Plato's tale of the beasts was confessedly a simile, however, not a piece of psychological theorizing. On his actual theory, these parts are not beasts which the best part must master but more nearly bullies—large, selfish, and possibly overbearing people, as he indicates at 440E6–441C2. Since they correspond not to beasts but to people, they are being likened to persuadable agents. These parts hold opinions, and one opinion can be exchanged for another in the process of persuasion. We know that Plato's goal was unanimity between the parts (442D2). But does Plato go so far in his isomorphism of polis and psyche that he posits an internal, psychic counterpart to the process of persuasion?

He does. In the *Republic* itself Plato's model of a person's internal thought processes is unabashedly discursive. At 574D–E he speaks of a conflict in the tyrant's psyche between opinions accounted just and opinions normally restricted to expression in dreams.[28] Between the discrete opinion-holding agents in the psyche there can be bad communications, and one part may well cry out in protest at another (550B, 439E). In the psyche which overcomes such problems, one part tells soothing stories to another, calming, pacifying, and "charming" it into performing only its own function (441E–442A, 607B1–608B3).[29]

The view that thought is internal discourse is made still more explicit in the *Theaetetus* and *Sophist*. At *Theaetetus* 189E Plato characterizes a person's λόγος, or account, as the decisive utterance resulting from a conversation of the psyche with itself, a conversation complete with questions, answers, affirmations, and denials. Given that this is precisely what one would expect on the theory of the psyche as composed of agentlike parts, and given that Plato continues to hold that theory as late as *Timaeus* (69B–72D) and *Laws* (see n. 8 above), it is plain that on his view this internal conversation takes place between distinct parts of the psyche. Again, at *Sophist* 263E he suggests that the thought of a person and the account given by the person are the same, with only one important difference: thought is the silent internal dialogue of the psyche with itself, while an account is "the stream that flows from the psyche through the mouth."[30]

If such internal conversations as Plato posits can contain questions, answers, affirmations, and denials, it seems a small matter to add that some answers and affirmations might be persuasive, and others not. Again, this was anticipated in the *Republic*: Plato spoke of the gentleness and persuasiveness of the wisdom-loving part, and of the brutality and force to which the other parts tend (589B–D). The wisdom-loving part, A, is to study unity or harmony with an eye to what will help it achieve one crucial sort of harmony—harmony of belief between it and other parts of the psyche. At 442D2–3 Plato claims that all parts must believe together that the wisdom-loving part must rule. And the person in whom it does rule will bend all his or her efforts to studies which will help engender a condition of moderation (591B). What sorts of studies might these be? And how are they related to justice in the polis?

The answer is illuminated by a more informative and explicit passage matching *Republic* 591B, at *Phaedrus* 229E–230A. There, Socrates is made to remark that he has no time at all for investigating the truth about Boreas, the Centaurs, the Chimera, or the like:

For me there is no leisure at all for these things. The reason for this is that I am not yet able to understand myself in accordance with the Delphic inscription: so it appears to me ludicrous to investigate alien things when I do not understand that. Whence I am pleased to let these things go, and being persuaded by the customary view about them, . . . I investigate myself rather than these things—whether I happen to be a more complex beast than Typhon, or whether I am a

The achievement of psychic harmony

more domesticated and simpler animal who shares by nature in a certain divine portion and is not puffed up.

This passage suggests not merely the priorities of the wisdom-loving part at its best, but the principal source from which this part can gain additional influence over the other parts, as we shall see. This key study is self-study or literally psychology, the study of the psyche.[31] Even dialectical conversation on Socrates' view might be viewed as a form of self-study, for at *Phaedrus* 255D he suggests that others with whom we converse are like mirrors in which we can see ourselves reflected. Attention one might expend upon the study of mythology or even the trees and country places is better spent upon self-study, the examination of the psyche's complexities, Socrates suggests. Why?

The business of the wisdom-loving part is to guide the other parts by persuasion, to transplant into alien parts its own opinions or, more accurately, opinions corresponding in content to its ἐπιστήμη. It is not likely to succeed in doing this unless it recognizes the number and nature of those alien parts. Thus at *Phaedrus* 270C ff. Plato calls for a full study of these on the model of Hippocratic studies in medicine.[32] The focus of such studies will be the things each part does or endures, and what affects each in what ways. Above all, such studies will focus on the effects of different sorts of discourses on different parts of the psyche.

The function of discourse, Plato suggests at *Phaedrus* 271B, is to lead the psyche by persuasion. Presumably this is the function of those speeches of one part to another required by the sober dialectical passages in *Republic*, *Theaetetus*, and *Sophist* mentioned above, and by the myth of the charioteer and his horses in the *Phaedrus* itself (254C–D). As 271A suggests, the wisdom-loving part is to learn what each of the other parts is inclined toward. And it must understand that different parts, like different people, are moved by quite different sorts of appeals. The wisdom-loving part, like the wisdom-loving person ruled by this very part, must learn what each part loves and must construct discourses which are effective owing to their promising each part what it loves.[33] The prerequisites for self-mastery and the prerequisites for political mastery are precisely the same on Plato's view: an adequate, psychologically sophisticated rhetoric.

The political importance of this has long been recognized by commentators on the *Phaedrus*, but its psychological and moral importance have not, with the result that readers have often been quite uncertain why Plato would write a single dialogue dealing in succession with the seemingly miscellaneous and disparate topics of love, the psyche, and rhetoric.[34] But under the interpretation I am suggesting, the *Phaedrus*'s sequence of topics makes excellent sense. It makes more explicit the *Republic*'s notion that a person's constituent psychic parts may each be understood in terms of what it loves, and that each of these parts may be influenced by discourses offering it hope of attaining what it loves.

The *Phaedrus* provides evidence that in his discussion of rhetoric Plato is not talking simply about how to persuade plebians. He suggests that persuading plebeians begins at home, within one's own psyche. He evidently saw intrapersonal communication as more important than interpersonal communication, and as the basis for it, in fact, much as justice in the psyche was the basis for overt justice at *Republic* 443C ff. At *Phaedrus* 267A, for example, he claimed that the account, discourse, or speech written in the psyche itself is the most important of all, not the discourse the rhetorician writes out for others to read. At 278A7–B1 he noted that the most legitimate offspring of the genuine rhetorician will be the account or discourse written in his own psyche. This is not a recommendation that the rhetorician memorize speeches. Plato is recommending that the best part of the psyche lead the other parts by discourse, that it lead them to specialization of function and thereby to attunement to proper function and unity or harmony in belief and action. To implant an account in one's own psyche is for one part of the psyche to implant that account, not in itself, which is scarcely necessary, but in alien parts. The part which does the implanting is part A. Only when this implanting has been done is the possessor of this wisdom-loving part qualified to lead others by his craft. Like the true physician at *Gorgias* 514D ff., the true rhetorician must cure himself first. The cure consists in ridding oneself of internal dissent and faction, achieving the unanimity of belief held up as a goal at *Republic* 442D.

But this goal for the psyche is likened to health in the body at *Phaedrus* 270B7, thus reinforcing the impression made by *Gorgias* 479B9 and 486D, and *Republic* 444D–E, 476E2, 571D ff., 584E6, and 603B1. And Plato holds that this goal is attainable by verbal means—by the use of words so remarkable in their effect that he terms them ἐπῳδαί, "charms," and likens them to φάρμακα, or drugs.[35] Yvon Brès and Anthony Kenny have recognized and documented Plato's pioneering role in developing beyond metaphor a concept of mental health.[36] But Plato played a comparable role in developing, if not devising, a concept of psychotherapy by verbal means, as Lain-Entralgo has recognized.[37] Plato's Socrates (perhaps with mock modesty) concedes a debt to the Thracian physicians of Zalmoxis' school. At *Charmides* 157A he remarks that he learned from these physicians that "the treatment of the soul . . . is by means of certain charms, and these charms are words of the right sort: by the use of such words is temperance engendered in our souls, and as soon as it is engendered and present we may easily secure health to the head and the rest of

The achievement of psychic harmony

the body also."[38] Whether the concession of a debt here is serious or ironic, there is abundant evidence that Plato carries the notion of the treatment of the psyche very far, integrating it with his theory of the parts. This theory as he develops it is capable of accounting for the power of such Zalmoxian words or "charms."

Plato's theory of the power of words is modeled upon Greek theories of nutrition, according to which like feeds on like.[39] Previously we have seen that on Plato's view a λόγος, or account, proceeds *from* a particular part of the psyche. But it also proceeds in a sense *to* a particular part, which it then nourishes or feeds. At *Republic* 590E5–591A2 Plato notes that our aim in controlling children is to foster or treat the best part in them by means of the best part in ourselves, establishing a similar guardian in them, and only then leaving them free. His term θεραπεύσαντες has both nutritive and therapeutic connotations, as one would expect when it was used by one who evidently followed Hippocratic medical developments so closely.[40]

This nutritive and dietetic view of the treatment of the psyche is expressed in Plato's criticisms of actual poets, dramatists, sophists, and rhetoricians in the *Republic*. At 605B–C Plato criticizes the mimetic poet for pleasing an unreasonable part of the psyche. To please such a part, he suggests, is to feed it a hearty meal and thus to increase its strength and vitality relative to the other parts (606A–E, 585B4, 585D5–7, 589B7). Poetry and music which please the possession-loving part C he found psychologically, morally, and politically unhealthy, and he complains of them accordingly at 411A–412A, 404D–E, and 607A.

Plato's ground for recommending that traditional poetry and music be censored is not ascetic, if by "ascetic" one means to suggest an antipathy to any satisfaction of the possession-loving and honor-loving parts, for at 571E he does advise that these be neither starved nor overfed, and at 586E6–587A1 he notes that under the rule of the wisdom-loving part these parts will enjoy their own appropriate pleasures. The proposal that the poets be censored proceeds from Plato's view that they fail to understand that the possession-loving part is already quite large and overbearing, the mass of the psyche in each of us (442A; cp. *Laws* 689A–B). In their ignorance these poets stuff what needs a reducing diet. They overfeed it by describing in attractive terms their characters' excessive sensual gratification. And since these poets find it difficult to imitate a moderate and stable model, of which they are largely ignorant in any case, they starve the very part which on Plato's view needs feeding (605E–606A).

Yet it is possible and, on Plato's view, desirable to contrive poetry, music, and rhetoric which quiet and soothe the possession-loving and honor-loving parts and thus render them more easily satisfied and more nearly in tune with the wisdom-loving part (*Republic* 606B–607A). Indeed, it seems likely that the function of his own myths is to do just that to his readers, as *Gorgias* 493B–D suggests.[41] Note that they often deal with honors, victories, and ambrosial satisfactions, albeit in an afterlife. These are the very things which on his own view the wisdom-loving part of the psyche is least interested in. Such stories are addressed, then, not to the part which cares for truth and genuineness but to parts concerned with reputation, honor, and sensual gratification.

It may be a bit disconcerting to read Plato with the suspicion that he sometimes tried to appeal not merely to what he viewed as our wiser parts but to what he viewed as our unwise and gullible ones as well. It is perhaps slightly unsettling to think that he may be trying not merely to inform but to reform the reader. But on reflection, it would have been inappropriate for him to have done less than this if he held the views attributed to him in this study. To his credit, he usually employs appeals to honor and sensual appetite only after he has already tried to make his case in the straightforward dialectical way appropriate for an appeal to the wisdom-loving part. This is the case at *Phaedo* 114D, where he sums up the import of the beliefs he has been recounting since 108E, having already offered such arguments as he can to the same effect, though without such covert appeals to appetite as one sees at 113E ff. Similarly in the Myth of Er at *Republic* 619B–620E, the appeal is clearly to the possession-loving and honor-loving parts, which feel not only certain pleasures of indulgence but associated pains of deprivation and the threat of it; the threat posed to them here is evident.

At *Gorgias* 523A ff., the same sort of threat to the honor-loving and possession-loving parts may be recognized in the talk of a judgment after death, dungeons, stripes, and the like inflicted upon a naked psyche, talk admittedly offered to reinforce the more reasonable appeals made earlier. Compare, for example, 527B–E with 497D, where Socrates had argued that good things are not the same as pleasant ones, nor bad things the same as unpleasant ones; yet 527B–E dwells upon the pains, tortures, retributions, and the like allegedly awaiting the evil person after death. Socrates' concern, as he reminds us at 500C, is with that way of life which is best; and on his view such a way of life depends upon law and order in the psyche (504D), which requires the restraining of passions (505B), a process of restraint which, I submit, he himself embarks upon in this myth. As he had noted at 503D–E, in a passage which I take to apply to his own writing as he saw it, Plato remarks: "The good man, who is intent upon the best when he speaks, will surely not speak at random in whatever he says, but with a view to some object. He is just like any other craftsman who, having his own particular work in view, selects the things he applies to that work of his, not at random, but with the purpose of giving a certain form to whatever he is working upon."[42]

The form of most interest to Plato in such contexts is ἀρετή (*Republic* 445C6), which is health, good condition, or good order in the psyche (*Republic* 444D10–E1; *Gorgias* 504D–E). That good order is an arrangement of parts, as we have seen. Merely to make a straightforward dialectical case with no supplementary use of myths and charming stories would, on Plato's view, be to appeal solely to less than a third of one's hearer or reader—to a beleaguered fraction in love with wisdom already and in need of reinforcements in its attempt to unify or harmonize the psyche (*Republic* 527D–E). Stories which soothe and quiet parts B and C also increase the *relative* strength of part A, the wisdom-loving one. Stories which (perhaps deceptively) enlist the sympathy of part C in part A's projects also reinforce part A. (See, e.g., *Republic* 435A3; *Epistle 7*, 344B8; *Phaedrus* 247D–248B.)

In a good state such reinforcements would come from without in the form of carefully chosen myths, music, and poetry. In the poor states in which people actually live one may have to provide these for oneself. Indeed, Plato's positing an internal use of rhetoric and of "charms" in the *Phaedrus* as at *Republic* 608A provides a theoretic framework for this self-persuasive enterprise. And he had already described Socrates as engaged in what looks very like such an enterprise. One of the most striking passages occurs near the end of the *Phaedo*, where Socrates recounts an elaborate myth about an afterlife and much else. Upon completing it he remarks, at 114D–E, " Now it would not be fitting for a man of sense to maintain that all this is just as I have described it, but that this or something like it is true concerning our souls and their abodes, since the soul is shown to be immortal, I think he may properly and worthily venture to believe; for the venture is well worth-while; and he ought to repeat such things to himself as if they were magic charms, which is the reason why I have been lengthening out the story so long."[43] Note that Socrates recommends telling *oneself* such stories for the reassuring and calming effect they may have, and that immediately upon concluding this remark he calmly begins his final preparations to drink the hemlock and die. He has told a lengthy tale which he will not confidently claim is true, and has done so for the effect it has upon himself. The tale has been told, then, as an ἐπωδή, a "charm," answering both to Socrates' expressed eagerness to make himself believe that the psyche is immortal at 91A9–B1 and to the corresponding eagerness of Cebes and Simmias at 77E.[44] Significantly, his friends here do not wish to be regarded as themselves afraid of death, but as having perhaps a child *within* them who has such a fear. They regard Socrates as expert in charming away such fears, and suspect no one else can do it, but he tells them that they must *themselves* sing charms (ἐπᾴδειν, 77E8–9) to this child daily until they charm away the fear. This anticipates *Republic* 608A. *Laws* 665C carries this line of thought even further, making this self-treatment a civic duty.

If Socrates addresses tales to his own psyche, and advised Cebes and Simmias to do likewise, then he locates both the physician and the patient in the same psyche. On the interpretation of the *Republic*'s theory developed here, this is explicable. Much as the best part of one person's psyche can treat the best part in another's psyche (*Republic* 590E5 ff.), so the best part of a person's psyche can treat lesser, childish parts with which it cohabits if it has studied these parts and does not relax its guard (606A9). Such a person can "provide a λόγος for himself and others" (534B5).

The person who has done this successfully, on Plato's view, turns up under a variety of labels at *Phaedus* 266B, 269B, 271A–B, 271D–272B, 273D–274A, and 278A. This person is the dialectician, the psychically healthy person, the true statesman who knows what is best for the polis and how to get it, the psychologist, and the genuine rhetorician.[45] But this is also the virtuous or excellent person: to be ruled or led by a persuasively resourceful part which loves wisdom and harmonizes the other parts is to have no compelling motive for any conduct which is not virtuous or excellent.

It has been argued above that the parts of the psyche as Plato describes them overlap in a number of their capacities at a minimal level and that the very conceivability of one part's usurping the role of another turns on this. This is not to say that the parts overlap in all of their capacities even at a minimal level. Much as there are people who appear utterly devoid of certain capacities, thus making it appropriate to deny that they have them at all, so the parts are conceived of as having or lacking certain capacities. Part A, for example, is characterized as gentle, not forceful or violent, and it plainly lacks the capacity to overpower the other parts by brute strength, as part B might overpower the others in anger or part C in hunger, thirst, or sexual desire. If it utterly lacks sheer brute force, however, it is compensated for this by possessing a potential for deep psychological understanding of the other parts and a persuasive power predicated upon that understanding which parts B and C utterly lack. It is this understanding which, above all, is the wisdom of this part, a wisdom which, as Charles Kahn noted, "represents the dynamic causal principle for *bringing about* the other virtues, since it drains off psychic energy from the other desires. . . . Here philosophic wisdom appears as the sole and sufficient *cause* of the other virtues, and hence as the principle of their unity."[46] Contrast the rule of part B as reflected in the behavior of people whose psyches it rules: They do not persuade; they rely, rather, on harshness (549A1) and force in ruling (548B7). Those whose psyches are ruled by part C do not keep down evil desires by persuading themselves that they had better not indulge them, but keep them down, if at all, only out of fear for the loss of their possessions (554D2–3).

The psyche and the Socratic paradoxes

This interpretation of Plato's theory of the psyche is capable of shedding light on his continuing acceptance of the much misunderstood Socratic paradoxes. I have argued elsewhere that these are neither exclusively Socratic nor paradoxes, but we are now in a position to see why these views were so congenial to Plato.

Consider the claim that no one commits injustice willingly. In understanding this it is crucial to grasp the Platonic referent of "no one" and the exact technical use of his term ἕκων, imperfectly rendered as "willingly" or "voluntarily." The lasting core of a person's identity, on Plato's view, is the wisdom-loving part, which he conceives of as immortal, ineradicable, and stubbornly in love with wisdom, harmony, and the good. It cannot be wholly eradicated or suppressed by the other parts even in quite corrupt persons. The enfeebled, undernourished wisdom-loving part of even the ordinary person continues to love wisdom and harmony even if it does not understand how to attain them, and for this reason is "enslaved," not "corrupted," by the other parts. It is enslaved in that it does the bidding of a lesser part which rules the entire person. This would appear to be the basis for Plato's claim at *Laws* 950B–C that even in very corrupt people there is an element of the divine, and that even these people have some judgment.

The persistence and ineradicability of this divine and wisdom-loving part even in people dominated by their lower parts is, I submit, the final theoretical basis for Plato's frequently invoked distinction between what a person claims to want and what that person really wants, and also for the closely related view that despite appearances, when one acts wrongly, one is not doing what one really wants to do. The distinction is displayed most prominently perhaps at *Gorgias* 466D–468E before the complexity of the psyche is explicitly argued (though this complexity seems suggested by other *Gorgias* passages.)[47] What one really wants is what is wanted by one's most real part, he alleges; and this, he suggests at *Republic* 585D–E, is the wisdom-loving part, since it is immortal and presented at 611B–C as the lasting core of one's identity. What a *person* seems to want may be what is wanted simply by the person's overweening possession-loving part, and Plato is quite willing to discount such seeming wants if they are excessive. Action based upon the excessive wants of an inferior part is under compulsion and ἄκων, or "not voluntary," Plato suggests at *Republic* 603C.

Plato is wont to say paradoxical-sounding things when he is using ἄκων, or "involuntary," in his technical, part-related sense. He applies it to acts that thwart the true wishes of the best part of the psyche owing to coercion by another element and its own ignorance of how to avoid this.[48] A person who might strike us as acting willingly and wrongly will be said to be acting unwillingly, since such an act is not in accordance with his or her true wishes—that is, with the wishes of the person's immortal part. Since this part loves wisdom, its ignorance and any actions predicated upon its ignorance frustrate this love and are said to be involuntary or not what it wishes. What we call "doing injustice willingly" Plato calls at *Republic* 430E–431A and elsewhere "being weaker than oneself" or "being inferior to oneself." He clearly believed this was commonplace and hence, properly understood, is not denying a palpable fact, but rather reinterpreting its basis.

Being self-inferior, on Plato's view, is being ruled by one's possession-loving or honor-loving part, either of which would be acting willingly or pursuing what it wished in its actions. Given that part's domination over the person, an observer who did not share Plato's psychological view would gain the impression that the action was totally voluntary. But Plato invites us to look past the satisfaction of the dominant part to the condition of slavery suffered by the remaining parts (*Republic* 577A–578B, 579D–E). These parts have been coerced, not persuaded, since only the wisdom-loving part uses gentle means, as he indicates at 589B.

Clearly then, on Plato's view only harmonious, virtuous persons with the psychological understanding required to become that way act willingly, with all of their parts in tune. This is borne out at *Phaedrus* 256C, where Plato notes that the actions of those who are overpowered by their inferior parts are not approved by the entire mind. Only when acting in ways which are so approved can people be said to be doing what they really wish. And since all persons contain an ineradicable divine element which loves wisdom, only acts consistent with satisfying this love can be undertaken willingly.

Later controversy over ἀκρασία, or what has been termed "weakness of will," would on Plato's view be owing to a misunderstanding. If (*a*) one says that the will is the conative faculty, (*b*) one confuses a faculty with an "active element" or agent, and (*c*) one holds that conation is "*the* theoretical active element of consciousness showing itself in tendencies, impulses, desires and acts of volition," as Stout and Baldwin defined it, then Plato would have argued that (i) there is no such thing as *the* will but, rather, several "wills" per person, and (ii) the character of one of these wills—the possession-loving one—is best seen not in consciousness (if by this we mean waking life) but in dreams.[49] Plato assigned the highest value to the immortal "will," the wisdom-loving part, and given confusion *b* above, might be held to have viewed it as *the* will on the ground that he viewed acts not in accordance with it as ἄκων, "unwilling" or "involuntary," despite the fact that the psychic *parts* in the agent which cause such acts are acting willingly in that they are acting with their characteristic wishes.

If, however, the will is said to be what Hume seems to have held it to be (insofar as he was faithful to his own "bundle theory,") namely, our appetites or desires, then again, Plato would have divided these into several classes having distinct origins in the psyche, and again would have said that we have several distinct wills.[50]

If the sensual desires associated with the possession-loving part are said to constitute the will, then Plato would balk at the notion that acting willingly is a good thing. Richard Taylor, taking the notion of will in this way, has claimed: "The corruption of a man was for Plato precisely the dominance of the will, that is, of a man's appetites or desires, this being a deviation from what human nature ideally should be."[51] I prefer not to take the notion of will in this way, however, since Plato has no noun for "will," only adverbs rendered "willingly" or "voluntarily" and "unwillingly" or "involuntarily," and since he usually treats acting *un*willingly as a bad thing, not a good one.[52] If we insist on forcing something into the role of Platonic counterpart to the will, then this had best be an entity which on his view it is not good to inferfere with. This can only be the wisdom-loving part, not the possession-loving one, though we would do better to avoid the term "will" altogether in interpreting Plato's views.

The other "Socratic paradox" can also be illuminated by this interpretation of Plato's theory of the psyche. This is the view that ἀρετή, "excellence" or "virtue," is ἐπιστήμη, "understanding." Such ἐπιστήμη —as *Republic* 428B, 441C, and 442A–B show—is a condition of an *entire* psyche, which might be said to have philosophical virtue if and only if its best part possesses the science of εὐβουλία, "good counsel," a science which proves to be psychological and rhetorical. The knowledge or understanding attained by a small part which loves wisdom and harmony already and learns how to achieve them by persuading the other parts is thus the sufficient condition of that total psychic condition of harmony which Plato termed indifferently "virtue," "health," or "wisdom."

Anthropomorphism, vicious regress, and the unity of the psyche

That the parts of the psyche are so conceived that they overlap in certain capacities but not others only serves to make them all the more like the people to whom they correspond. This brings us, finally, to an almost inevitable reservation one must at least entertain about Plato's theory as interpreted here. In fact, if this reservation is thought seriously unflattering to Plato, and Plato is thought deserving of flattery, one may think the reservation damaging to the interpretation itself rather than to Plato's theory.[53]

The reservation has to do with likening anything whatever to a human being. It would be easy to caricature the theory as portrayed here as if it involved Plato in positing a committee of homunculi animating each person. Indeed, it is evident that a number of interpreters have been deterred from offering the sort of interpretation developed here, despite the textual evidence for it, because of the seeming absurdity of the view it attributes to Plato.[54] One can understand the reluctance to recognize in Plato's theory so sweeping an anthropomorphism. People are scarcely our current paradigms of constancy or intelligibility. The theory may appear to have gone so far in its anthropomorphism that it incorporates at a new level the very sorts of problems it was designed to illuminate. If we are curious, as Plato evidently was, as to why a tyrant lacks self-control, it will scarcely impress us to be told that this is owing to his being ruled within by a mini-tyrant who lacks self-control (575C5–D2). This internal agent may seem all too like the one whose foibles motivated the theory in the first place. The explanatory power of a theory positing such an agent within may seem to rank about as low as that of Anaxagoras' alleged view that everything is what it contains the most of, and that what it contains the most of is readily apparent in its sensible qualities.[55]

This sort of problem has been recognized in the literature before, but has not to my knowledge had an adequate treatment.[56] The dangers it poses are not confined to a seeming dearth of explanatory power. On the pattern of explanation Plato employs—namely, the pattern of explaining the action of a whole as the action of a part within a whole—one may wonder why, if at all, one cannot then ask about the action of that part, treating it in turn as a whole, and so embark upon a vicious infinite regress.[57] The more closely Plato assimilates parts of the psyche to people, the more he appears to risk this regress. Such a regress of parts-within-parts could make nonsense of Plato's theory as interpreted in this study.

The unity of the psyche

Too close an assimilation of parts of the psyche to the very people of whom they are parts would risk not simply a breakdown of explanatory power and a vicious infinite regress, but a third, though closely related problem. It risks leaving Plato no plausible way to account for the unity of the psyche. Not even a schizophrenic is literally two people loosely confined in one skin. Plato owes us an account of whatever the personlike parts share that makes them *one* psyche, an account which describes a deeper and more portentious sort of sharing than that of animals in a common cage or citizens persuaded or forced to live under a common government. Cages can be escaped without their being destroyed, and citizens can emigrate without bringing down the polis they leave. Yet Plato seems to regard the association of psychic parts in a body as permanent, in this life at least. (See *Republic* 441C, 611B–612A; *Phaedrus* 253C–D.)

The regress problem is the key to the other two. A regress of parts-within-parts could make nonsense of Plato's theory as interpreted here only if Plato were so engrossed in making the parts correspond to people that he made the parts subject to the same sorts of problems which motivated him to posit parts initially. These, it will be recalled, were problems of internal conflict, and the incoherence which can infect our descriptions of people if we do not understand this internal conflict. Did Plato describe any part of the psyche as being beset by the sorts of conflict suffered by a person such as Leontius?

It is important to recognize here that not just any internal conflict in a part will be sufficient to start an infinite (and hence vicious) regress. An infinite regress would require that the conflicts be between subparts isomorphic to the tripartite person, subparts which love wisdom for its own sake, honor for its own sake, and sensual gratification for its own sake, all of these subparts within the honor-loving part itself, for example. But there is not the slightest evidence that Plato regarded any of the parts of the psyche as isomorphic in structure to the entire tripartite psyche. There is evidence that he recognized conflicts within part C, and hence that he was committed to regarding at least that part as having subparts. But these conflicts are between subparts given to different sorts of sensual appetites, not the familiar conflicts between a sensual part, an honor-loving one, and a wisdom-loving one.[58]

It is still more important, however, to recall that Plato terms the parts of the psyche εἴδη, a term usually rendered "forms" elsewhere. The paradigmatic forms are not animate, as the parts of the psyche are, and by not translating εἶδος as "form" in its psychological use we prevent a certain confusion.[59] But we may also overlook an affinity Plato wished to acknowledge. One of the crucial characteristics of a paradigmatic form such as equality was its purity; it was to contain no tincture of anything incompatible with it (*Phaedo* 74B–C). The εἴδη τῆς ψυχῆς are "pure" in a related way, despite their being essentially active. They are, each of them, pure and constant in their priorities. And in this crucial respect they differ from the people to whom they correspond by as vast a margin as heat does from a fire.

At *Republic* 581B1, for example, the honor-loving part B is said to be wholly set upon (ὅλον ὡρμῆσθαι) ruling, winning, and good reputation. There is, as argued earlier, a means-end relationship even among these three things which part B is set upon, but Plato's point here appears to be that anything *other than* these three is never valued by this part save as a means to one or more of these. The lover of something loves all of it (475B5), cannot get enough of it (475C9), and welcomes it on any pretext (475A7). Plainly no *person*, no matter how fanatical or crazed, is likely to measure up to the Platonic description "lover of ———." A lover of ——— is a stereotype, a paradigm, an εἶδος, which a person can only approximate. A part of the psyche, on this view, is such an εἶδος, one which a person can only approximate. A part of the psyche, on this view, is a stereotypically constant lover of one sort of thing for its own sake, and of others merely as means to this, if at all.

No person containing a portion of several such stereotypical εἴδη set quite insatiably on disparate goals could easily measure up to any one of them fully. People, living in the realm of becoming (525B5), cannot easily rise out of it and ignore what any part demands. Unlike their psychic parts, people contain independent and inherently fractious parts. The parts of the psyche Plato posits, then, cannot mirror the exact sorts of factions and confusions about priorities to which people are prone. His isomorphism of polis and psyche cannot generate a vicious infinite regress, for the political agents in the psyche are from the beginning elevated into formlike stereotypes unwavering in their disparate aims.[60]

There remains the question about the explanatory power of the theory. The question runs well beyond the scope of this study and, indeed, beyond the scope of Platonic scholarship itself. One must defer here to philosophers of science competent enough or audacious enough to hazard a measure of explanatory power. One may well defer also to philosophers interested in assessing without prejudice the philosophical merits and demerits of anthropomorphism and paradigmatism.[61]

It is perhaps appropriate to remind ourselves that the term "Platonist" has two distinct senses: "one who studies and explicates the views of Plato," and "one who adheres to and defends the views of Plato." One can scarcely adhere to and defend intelligently what has not been adequately explicated; hence, the work of the Platonist in the first sense is prior to that of the Platonist in the second. I have attempted in this chapter to do

The unity of the psyche

only the first sort of work except where the philosophical defects seem to have loomed so large for so long and to so many that it is difficult to entertain the argument that Plato held views subject to them. To allow questions of the philosophical worth or defensibility of Plato's views to have any more extensive effect than this upon a work of interpretation is to risk proceeding on the unstated assumption that Plato's views—whatever they were—are known a priori to be philosophically defensible. But ideas of philosophical defensibility vary widely from place to place and time to time. Hence, to assume that Plato's views are known a priori to be philosophically defensible by current standards is tantamount to making Platonism into a variable-content religion, not a definite web of philosophical positions.[62] Among those called Platonists, as among the denizens of the polis Plato envisions, a certain specialization and restriction of function is wise. At the very least, we should keep as distinct as we can the tasks of interpretation and advocacy, realizing which one we are engaged in at the moment and not allowing the first task to be unduly affected by our desire to perform the second successfully.

Finally, there remains the third problem arising out of Plato's assimilation of parts of the psyche to people, the problem of accounting for the fact that even Leontius is one person with one psyche, not two or three. This problem does not loom so large once one realizes that the psychic parts are not people, but rather, stereotypes or paradigms which people approximate. In this light, the charge that Plato described the psyche as a committee of homunculi loses its force. Yet part of our third problem remains. Even if the parts are not people, their person-like independence stands in a certain tension with their being *parts* of one entity. Plato's political model for parts of the psyche can be perplexing if extended to the realization that dissatisfied citizens of a polis can emigrate without destroying it, and animals in a cage can sometimes escape without causing the decay of their common cage, while parts of the psyche evidently cannot leave the body without its dying (*Republic* 588B, 591C, 572B). It is appropriate, then, to ask what besides a body these parts share that makes of them one psyche, and confines them in this life to one body.

Plato's answer is suggested in his famous hydraulic simile at *Republic* 485D–E. The parts of the psyche are like channels or tubes into which the flow of a single stream is divided. The total flowage is a constant, so that what goes into one tube or channel is lost to the others (*Republic* 485D, borne out at 588E–589B). Both the *Republic* and the *Symposium* suggest that this single source-stream is *eros*, a primordial energy source powering not simply the stereotypically erotic activities but all human activities whatever.[63] Appropriately, perhaps, Freud remarked in more than one place that by "libido" he meant no more than Plato meant by *eros*.[64] The parts of the psyche are one psyche in that they are but different ways of channeling one finite, personal stream of energy or desire. And this one stream, on Plato's view, is correlated with one body, or *perhaps* with one body at a time in a lengthy series.[65]

Ἐπιστήμη as a relation of the psyche to an extrapsychic reality

This chapter has presented an answer to the question, What, on Plato's view, made it possible for a person to give and successfully defend an account in the face of fair and thorough questioning? The answer was that a certain condition of the psyche, ἐπιστήμη, made this possible, and that this condition was a condition of the psyche's parts, a condition in which each part is attuned to its proper function, which attunement preserves agreement or harmony between the parts. It was argued that this attunement is produced by persuasion, and that Plato advocates an intrapsychic rhetoric of self-persuasion or self-charm, a rhetoric conceived of as simultaneously therapeutic and just in its outcome. Plato conceives of this persuasion as possible, however, only because the best part of the psyche in its condition of ἐπιστήμη apprehends, feeds on, and is strengthened by an essentially extrapsychic reality. We turn next to that reality—the realm of forms.

4
Ἐπιστήμη and Forms in Early and Middle Dialogues

Plato consistently maintained in the early and middle dialogues at least that ἐπιστήμη is a relationship between two relata—the psyche and the εἴδη, or forms. We have now examined and interpreted what Plato has to say about the first of these relata. Since he holds that the health of the psyche, peace in and among nations, and the quality of human life in general depends on just this relationship, one would expect him to clarify the relationship further by illuminating the second of these relata, the forms. One way in which to do this systematically would be to pose and answer the question, What is a form?

Unfortunately, Plato neither poses nor directly answers this question. This omission is extraordinary. The question, Τί ἐστι εἶδος; or What is a form? sounds eminently Platonic, but it is not to be found in the dialogues of Plato. Since on his view an account is an attempt to provide an answer to just such a question, by his own standards there is in the dialogues no straightforward *attempt* to tell us what an εἶδος, or form, is. Given this omission and the dispersion of comments on forms throughout dialogues having disparate aims and subjects, it is not surprising that competent interpreters considering the same body of evidence disagree widely about what Platonic forms were.[1]

For the modern reader who has grasped Plato's dialectical method but finds his forms unfamiliar and difficult to grasp, this omission of an account ought to be surprising.² Forms strike us as needing clarification. Asking τί ἐστι questions and trying to answer them defensibly is depicted as Socrates' professed way of trying to clarify things, and it remains Plato's to the end. Plato's suggesting (at *Phaedo* 100B, e.g.) that forms are hypotheses or things assumed does not alter our expectation that he will clarify what they are. He himself warns us at *Phaedo* 101D and *Republic* 510B–511C that hypotheses must not go unexamined. Since we find this hypothesis unclear, we naturally expect Plato to examine it and clarify it for us if he is to live up to his own demands. He does ask for and offer straightforward answers concerning such miscellaneous trivia as mud or clay, fishing, and square roots.³ But he has an almost irritating way of writing as if we already understand what a form is and hence need no account of it.

These interpretative observations might strike one as bordering on the self-defeating, but they are crucial admissions if we are to react honestly to what we find in the text of Plato. We must suspend irritation and the premature judgment it invites and attempt seriously to ascertain why Plato said only what he did about forms. Plato is among the least presumptuous or inconsiderate of philosophical writers, and this partly explains the high level of interest which his works still sustain. He himself cautions against ignoring the reaction of the one with whom one wishes to communicate. As *Gorgias* 457C–458B illustrates, he evidently considered irritation a most unfortunate reaction to provoke, and as his diatribe against Protagoras in the *Theaetetus* illustrates, he found obscurantism even in written works an abomination. One wonders, then, why he wrote in such an obscure and irritating way by treating forms as readily understandable when they plainly are not.

If we could go no further than confessing the irritating inadequacy of the text, we would have to write off interpreting Plato's theory of forms as a bad job. Happily, though, we can go further than this. Once we begin to inquire why a philosopher who expressed a passion for clarity in communication might in good faith leave the reader in such a plight as modern ones customarily find themselves, we shall be on our way to remedying matters somewhat. Thus, what might seem an irritating stylistic vice in Plato's treatment of his forms will, when explained, provide a clue leading to important supplementary data on the origin of the theory of forms and on five of the most baffling features of the forms as usually represented today: their causal role, their "self-predicability," their "separation," their being objects of thought rather than unaided sensation, and their relations among themselves. Inquiring, then, why he wrote *as* he did will help illuminate why he wrote *what* he did about forms. Once this is clarified, the development of his theory of forms in relation to his conceptions of dialectic and ἐπιστήμη can be explained in more detail.

The familiarity of forms

Plato not only writes as if the reader already knows what a form is, but has Socrates treat a wide range of interlocutors as if they also know.[4] And strangely, the interlocutors, even the most disputatious ones, go along with this. In the *Phaedo*, for example, a seemingly heterogeneous group is gathered for Socrates' death. They are depicted at 65D, 74A, and 100B as acquiescing in the claim that these curious forms are things which "we" believe in or customarily assume. Socrates is not given to using the royal "we." Hence, the docility of his hearers surprises modern readers, given that he strikes us as asserting quite technical, theory-laden things, without giving an account of the underlying theory. This is doubly surprising since he encourages his interlocutors to question anything they find doubtful or unclear. But they do not balk at even the most technical-sounding uses of his unexplained but allegedly familiar notion of a form. Why?

This surprising docility cannot be explained on grounds of Plato's desire to depict Socrates' interlocutors as being polite towards a friend who was about to die. He depicts them as being honest enough or rude enough to press the doomed Socrates about his alleged proofs for the immortality of the psyche; hence, it would seem a relatively small matter in context to have one of them ask what these curious forms they are all supposed to believe in or assume *are*. But the interlocutors neglect to ask. One of them, Cebes, is even represented as being "the most obstinately incredulous of mortals," yet at 77A he accepts without question Socrates' notion of a form and does not protest when Socrates says that they all assume or believe in such things.

This ready acquiescence in talk of forms is common in Plato's dialogues. Even the young Phaedrus is expected to grasp what a form is when Socrates (at *Phaedrus* 247C–248C and 250E) introduces forms as the objects of understanding and of the Charioteer's passion. In the *Timaeus* also, as Taylor observed, some view about what a form is supposed to be "is assumed to be known and accepted by the Locrian astronomer Timaeus, and he, too, though no member of the familiar Socratic group, . . . represents it as something universally believed in by a community."[5] Even in the *Parmenides*, where at 129A–130B the elderly Parmenides is depicted as strenuously questioning various claims Socrates makes about forms, there is not the slightest indication that he does not know from the outset what Socrates is talking about. In that respect he is surely one up on modern readers and rather difficult for us to identify with for that reason. It is as if we had walked in on the middle of a conversation. Socrates' interlocutors appear to know something we do not.

Contemporary readers—especially, perhaps, philosophers—may find unfamiliar and perhaps uncomfortable the suspicion that their counterparts of 2,400 years ago had the advantage of them, and may be inclined to indulge suspicions rather less flattering to Plato. Those who are inclined to suspect the worst may surmise that Plato engaged in the rhetorical trick of treating his most doubtful claim as a piece of common sense, hoping to carry credulous readers along in a crowd of dialectical yes-men. But this is scarcely credible given that it would immediately be seen as not just inconsistent but hypocritical. Plato himself had depicted Socrates as combatting just such presumptuousness in various sophists and rhetoricians.[6] Indeed, he displayed a penchant for ending dialogues with the claim that nothing the participants had concluded was clear or certain since they had neglected to examine some crucial hypotheses they had all been using.[7] Having thus trained his readers to look out for questionable hypotheses, he could scarcely expect to have his forms escape their scrutiny and protest if indeed they believed them to be as unclear as we do now.

Readers who balk at this worst of suspicions and entertain instead the next-to-worst may surmise that Plato's inattention to what a form is was an oversight. But that seems unlikely given (1) the central role forms seem to play in his system and (2) his professed method, which demanded the straightforward examination of any central notion that was not clearly understood. Consider, for example, the way Socrates inquires about what λόγος might mean in Theaetetus' third definition of ἐπιστήμη, or understanding, at *Theaetetus* 202D ff. At *Laches* 187B and *Gorgias* 514E, Plato had Socrates condemn "learning pottery by making wine jars," that is, attempting the most difficult projects before mastering fundamentals. Is it at all plausible that he would overlook what his early readers would see as serious unclarity about what a form is in employing this fundamental notion to say what, for example, the form of beauty is? Plainly not.[8]

If we set aside these barren suspicions as to why Plato wrote about forms in the familiar way he did, we can inquire what honest basis he might have had for doing so. If we have in effect walked in on the middle of a conversation, we can attempt to surmise what the unheard portions contained. Where, then, might early Greek readers of the sort for whom Plato wrote have got the background beliefs concerning εἴδη, or forms, which Plato seems to presume, and what precisely were these beliefs? What light do they shed on what Plato actually does say about forms in the dialogues?

The theory of forms as a philosophy of science

Plato's basis for writing as if his readers could readily understand what a form is lay in their likely familiarity with Greek science, most especially with the oldest, most familiar, and philosophically most sophisticated science, medicine.[9] Medicine was the most advanced of the sciences, and its accomplishments were reflected even in the educationally ubiquitous Homeric poems. The poet thought it appropriate to give anatomically exact descriptions of the many wounds he describes in the course of his works, and to praise the expertise of physicians.[10]

Like the sophists, some physicians traveled from city to city. They treated patients for a fee, acquainted themselves with local disease-producing conditions, and most importantly for our purposes, lectured to a public having literally a vital interest in their work and in the theories behind it.[11]

Physicians and their admirers also wrote various treatises defending or explaining the art of medicine, and some of these explicitly relate medicine to the philosophy of the time of Melissus, Empedocles, and Anaxagoras. A number of the treatises in the Hippocratic corpus seem to be addressed to a wider audience than physicians. *Ancient Medicine* defends medicine against the incursions of philosophical hypotheses of the sort espoused by Empedocles, whom it mentions by name. *On the Art* takes issue in rhetorical style with those who say that there is no art or science of medicine, but that cures are owing to spontaneity or to luck. *The Sacred Disease* combats quackery and superstition about epilepsy. *Regimen* gives advice on diet and exercise (1. 2, 1. 32, 1. 35) which would be of interest primarily to laymen interested in avoiding illness and injury. *The Nature of Man* is of philosophical as well as medical interest, and mentions the views of Melissus. Such medical treatises were evidently popular, since Xenophon knew of them and at *Memorabilia* 4. 2. 10 depicted Socrates as saying they were numerous.

Even readers having an antipathy to physicians' public lectures could scarcely escape their private, bedside ones. As Plato himself tells us at *Laws* 720B–E, 722B–C, and 857C–E, the physician in treating a free citizen did not merely give prescriptions but gave an explanation or account as if he were trying not merely to cure the patient but also to turn the patient into another physician. This being so, medical theories of disease, nutriment, and regimen and the concepts employed in them would have been familiar to Plato's intended Greek readers. Since a number of these concepts are, as we shall see, very close to those in Plato's early and middle treatment of forms, it would not seem unnatural to such readers if

Plato depicted a wide range of interlocutors as responding to mention of forms as if they were familiar and unobjectionable, especially if he jogged readers' memories, as he frequently did, with references to medicine as the model art or science, the area in which understanding had most clearly been attained, or at least approached.[12]

Given such a background in his early readers, Plato could rely upon the familiarity of these medical notions in assessing and developing some of them critically. In doing so he would be proceeding much as a philosopher of science might today in assuming that the notion of explanation need not be defined and illustrated elaborately. Just as the philosopher of science can treat the notion of an explanation as common property available for his immediate use and extension with only a minimum of systemizing, so Plato could treat the notion of a form.

If we are to understand Plato's use of the notion of a form and his scanty remarks designed evidently to systemize it a bit, we must attempt to put ourselves in the position of early Greek readers and interlocutors familiar with the concepts of Greek medicine and with the penetration of such concepts into pre-Socratic philosophy. We must, in effect, try to hear the parts of the conversation we missed by being born when we were. Fortunately, enough of it appears to have been recorded. We turn now to this record.[13]

Medicine and the forms as causes

The chief pattern for Greek medical thought was set by Alcmaeon in the early fifth century.[14] He is said to have held that the majority of things having to do with human affairs come in twos. These things were conceived of as being opposing δυνάμεις, "powers" or "forces." But as the names of these "powers" or "forces" indicate, they were thought of as if they were an amalgam of things we would readily distinguish—qualities, and constituents of things which were thought to impart their qualities to the whole into which they were compounded. Moist and dry, cold and hot, bitter and sweet, are examples of such powers. Vlastos aptly remarks:

The original meaning of δύναμις, as Peck observes, is not "a substance that has power" but rather "a substance which *is* a power, which can assert itself, and by the simple act of asserting itself, by being too strong, stronger than the others, can cause trouble. Its strength must, therefore, be "taken away" and thus "moderated." And this is to be done not through repression by a superior but through counterpoise against an equal. This is the heart of the doctrine of *krasis*.[15]

This doctrine of κρᾶσις, or mixture, was to become the backbone of much medical practice. Health was thought to lie in an ἰσονομία, or equal balance, of powers, in a mixture so constituted that none of its constituent powers would be conspicuous and thereby attain "monarchy" over the others (Aetius 5. 30. 1). This mixture or equal balance was purely qualitative, as the names of the powers again suggest. If Alfred is hot, this view would suggest, not that there is something, hotness, which *he has*, but that there is evidently some power, the hot, which *has him*. It would suggest that he has been, as it were, infiltrated and captured by a power capable of fighting on many fronts at once—in his fireplace, on the sun, and so on. To fend off this excessive power ancient medicine would suggest sending reinforcements that would consist in shares of that power's opposite. As the writer of *On Breaths* 1 put it, "Opposites are cures for opposites. Medicine in fact is addition and subtraction, subtraction of what is in excess, addition of what is wanting."[16] Anaxagoras only applies this old line of thought when he declares in Fragment B12, Ὅτων πλεῖστα ἔνι, ταῦτα ἐνδηλότατα ἓν ἕκαστον ἔστι καὶ ἦν, that is, "Each individual thing most clearly is and was that of which it contains the most." In ἰσονομία, or equal balance, neither of the two opposites could suppress or obliterate each other. The healthy person is in a state of ἰσονομία, and hence would be perceived as neither especially hot nor especially cold.

No doubt this now strikes the contemporary philosophical reader as metaphorical, since if taken literally it seems to embody "category mistakes" we could commit only deliberately and figuratively. But there is no evidence that the relevant categories were recognized before Plato, if then, and much sober writing indicates that they were not. Such powers were simultaneously things, qualities, causes of qualities in compound things, and agents working against antithetical agents. As Cornford noted,

> In the fifth century "the hot" was conceived as an active "power" (δύναμις) residing in bodies and enabling them to act on our senses, and to cause affections (πάθη) in one another. A portion of "the hot" present in a body is the "power" which makes us feel hot and heats other, colder bodies. The names corresponding to (or falling under) the several powers will form a list of opposite qualities, arranged, as in the Phythagorean Table of Opposites, in two sets.[17]

On first consideration, one might suppose that these early physicians thought of a diseased patient very differently from the way we do today. We think of a patient as having a disease. On this early model of Alcmaeon and his followers, however, it would be more accurate to say that the disease has the patient, or, more accurately still, that the patient is merely one front in a war between opposites attacking each other, and that what we call the disease is simply the name we give to the characteristic sorts of incidental damage done to the scene of the battle.[18] The patient's dying of fever was conceived much as we would conceive of a tree's being destroyed by artillery fire in a war between two armies struggling for control of the ground on which it stands.

Upon further consideration, however, such a conception of the diseased patient does not differ radically from that held by physicians today. On their model, the patient may be merely one front in a war between viruses and antibodies, with what we call the disease being merely the environmental depradation occasioned by the battle going on in the patient's body. Physicians and laymen commonly speak of a patient as having been attacked by a given type of virus or bacterium, and we speak easily of antibodies in the blood stream as helping the patient to fight off the infection. Attacking and defending agents are characterized in terms of what they *do* in, to, or for the patient, by doing something to whatever they are combatting. Drugs are similarly characterized.

Only some philosophers, who in our century have been quick to indict anyone talking in such ways for the allegedly mortal intellectual offense of anthropomorphism, are really bothered by such talk or even inclined to regard it as metaphorical. Even in contemporary chemistry, various chemical agents are referred to as oxidizing agents, wetting agents, drying agents, surface-active agents, and the like. To my knowledge there is no evidence that working physicians or chemists find themselves misled by such language, as we might conclude that they did if they tried to converse with such entities.

Correspondingly, however, there is no evidence that early or even later Greek medical thinkers were misled by their conceiving of δυνάμεις as "quality-things" or agents doing characteristic sorts of things; as *Regimen* 1. 2–3, shows, they resorted to diet and exercise to control the mixture in which these agents were perceived to be out of balance with other, counterposed agents. Nor was it necessarily misleading when they discussed the "strength" of such agents. Even today drugs are regarded as "strong" if small doses do a lot in, to, or for the patient. And in chemistry, acids and bases are regarded as strong or weak, and such strength or weakness correlates not merely with a quantitative measurement of equivalents per liter but with a qualitative assessment of how remarkable an effect they are capable of having upon other substances. Vinegar is a weak acid and sulphuric acid a strong one for obvious reasons. Given the usefulness of such ways of talking even now, we should not be too quick to censure comparable and perhaps equally innocent ones in pre-Socratic scientific work, especially in the earliest such work.

There is no talk of εἴδη in Alcmaeon as yet, but the influential notion of a δύναμις, or power, which was later to be merged with the notion of an εἶδος, or form, was already operative. The merging of such powers with εἴδη, or forms, was made easy by two facts:

1. The powers operating in a patient were judged to be monarchical or else blended in equal balance on the basis of the way the patient felt, looked, or appeared.
2. The root meaning of the term for "form," εἶδος, was something like "shape" and, more generally, "appearance" or "look." The German *Gestalt* captures its ambiguity better than any term in English.[19]

Occurrences of εἶδος and ἰδέα bearing this root meaning are not uncommon in nonphilosophical Greek long before Plato. Herodotus (I. 199) describes the Babylonian custom that every woman born in the country must go once in her life to the Precinct of Mylitta and have intercourse with a stranger. He remarks, "Such of the women as are big and beautiful in εἰδέος are quickly released, but others who are shapeless [ἄμορφοι] have to remain there a long time, being unable to fulfill the law." It is clear what εἰδέος means here. Given the contrast with ἄμορφοι, "shapeless," it is certainly used of the figure of a person, and probably of the entire appearance, given the context. Similar uses of ἰδέα and εἶδος were fairly common, even in Plato's own writing.[20]

The earliest philosopher to develop very explicitly a connection between δυνάμεις, or powers, and εἴδη, or forms, was Empedocles.[21] As Vlastos noted, Empedocles "builds a universe to the specifications of Alcmaeon's formula of health."[22] That is, Empedocles (DK B23) generalized and extended the use of Alcmaeon's conception of a person as a blend of antithetical quality-things or powers manifested in the person's appearance. In all things, whether alive or not, these basic quality-things were blended so as to produce the apparent qualities compound things have, much as a few simple pigments could be blended by a skilled painter to produce manifold colors. Unlike his contemporary Anaxagoras, who appears to have conceived of every perceivable quality as being an irreducible power or quality-thing compounded into every mixture in which that quality is perceived, Empedocles was something of a reductionist and thought of some perceived qualities as being produced by a blend of a few basic quality-things.

The causal role of these quality-things or forms-powers is evident both from the medical tradition and from philosophers such as Empedocles and Anaxagoras. As Vlastos put it, "The hot is that which heats, the moist is that which moistens; each is an active tendency to change other things after its own fashion, unless checked, or balanced, by its opposite. Sensation itself is conceived as just such a change in the percipient. I perceive anything as hot so far and only so far as that thing heats me."[23] The identification of such quality-bearing causes with forms was made quite clearly in the Hippocratic treatise *On Breaths*.[24] The writer remarks that all diseases have a single ἰδέη καὶ αἰτίη, "form and cause," a rather more sparing view than one finds in most of the medical treatises but not an unusual one in its suggestion that form and cause come to the same thing.[25] In the Hippocratic treatise *On the Art*, for instance, the author affirms that nothing happens spontaneously but that everything has a cause, something through which (διά τι) it is as it is.[26] The physician is to investigate this. And a bit earlier in the same treatise (2) one finds the view that when the physician or indeed the practitioner of any art investigates, the investigation is by means of forms (διὰ τὰ εἴδεα). Fire is one of these (6), and it is said to operate (δημιουργεῖ) with great strength, more strength than other powers possess. This language and its medical background indicate that a cause was an agent bearing and communicating to environing objects its characteristic quality. Such a cause was a form or power, a quality-thing existing in larger and smaller detachments located in many places but nowhere confined.

Early and middle Platonic forms as powers

Socratic and Platonic dialectic proceeded by finding agreed premises—commonly accepted, uncontroversial hypotheses. Agreed premises were the strongest philosophical foundations Plato knew for an investigation. And what the Platonic Socrates and his interlocutors agree on without question as strongest (*Phaedo* 100A5) and safest (*Phaedo* 100D8) is the hypothesis that there are causally efficacious forms.

In the dialogues thought to belong to his early and middle periods Plato employs the model of forms described in previous sections of this chapter. He treated εἴδη as δυνάμεις, or powers, and conceived of these powers as quality-things or character-powers much as his medical predecessors had. This is why he was able to treat forms as "much discussed" (*Phaedo* 100B5) and to assume that they were familiar both to interlocutors of all sorts and to his intended readers. It is why Socrates can be made to say, quite truly, that in positing such entities, what he is saying is "nothing new" (*Phaedo* 100B1). Not only had he posited such entities in previous dialogues and previously in this one, as we shall discern shortly, but his predecessors in medicine had made such posits common property.

On this model of forms, forms exert causal influence upon the particulars in which portions of them are found. If the portion found in a particular is strong enough, it will dominate that particular and impart to it its own "look," its own characteristic qualities, without thereby obliterating qualities imparted to it by the presence of portions of other forms.

Plato expresses this dominance in military language. At *Phaedo* 104D and 105D, a form is said to occupy or take possession of (κατέχει) a particular. It compels (ἀναγκάζει) whatever it occupies to accept not only its own form but whatever form it "brings up" (ἐπιφέρει), much as an occupied territory has to accept reserves brought up by the forces occupying it.[27] Much as a patient in the medical tradition was conceived more nearly as being had or caught by a disease than as having or catching it, so Plato regards the portion of a form present in a particular as capturing and possessing it. A form already present in a particular is said to retreat or go away at the approach of its opposite (104D). This is no mere metaphor, for it is essential to Plato's argument. The point of this extended argument in its context is to show that the psyche is immortal. Psyche is treated as a form, which brings with it life, much as the number 3 brings with it oddness and fire, heat.[28] Our psyches are treated as portions or shares of the form psyche, and if death captures our bodies, our psyches go away, much as heat leaves freezing water.

Plato is much more interested in using the notion of a form or power—in doing philosophical work with it, so to speak—than in claiming falsely that it was his own invention. As John Burnet asked rhetorically quite a long time ago, when has anybody ever propounded his own new philosophical discovery by representing it as "perfectly familiar to . . . distinguished living contemporaries some years before he had thought of it himself?"[29] It is implausible on the face of it that the notion of a form was a Platonic invention.

At most we can credit Plato with having made the notion of form and its use systematic enough so that it might perhaps be appropriate to speak of him as the author of a "theory" of forms. He codified, clarified, extended, and refined the use of the notion of a form. He worked through some of the implications of using it. But above all, he used it. And he could be understood in so using it because it was one of the agreed premises of Greek thought that there were forms which had causal influence upon the environments in which portions of forms were placed.

Recent interpreters have repeatedly suggested that we must treat with great caution Plato's suggestion (in *Phaedo* 100B ff.) that a form is a cause, for his term αἰτία does not mean what our term "cause" does.[30] Such interpreters appear to assume that speakers of English who read translations and interpretations of Plato share some fairly precise common understanding of what "cause" means. But this assumption is questionable. There is no more unanimity among such speakers of English or even among recent English-speaking philosophers of science about what "cause" means than there was among classical writers about what αἰτία meant.³¹ Indeed, some philosophers of science have regarded the notion of cause as a relic of a bygone if not classical age, and as worthless.³² Others who are not ready to dispense with it regard recent advances in understanding it as largely illusory.³³ This disagreement yields a certain flexibility which still permits "cause" to be used intelligibly as αἰτία was used by Plato. Indeed, there is no other word so well suited to convey the meaning of αἰτία as Plato used it while avoiding misleading connotations of current philosophical logic.

Consider: we might now, in quite ordinary discourse, speak of the blue pigment stirred into a can of white paint as the cause of the paint's being blue. In speaking in such a way, we would be following Empedocles, who adopted this pigment-mixing model as paradigmatic for the role of earth, air, and the like in sensible things. And we would be following Plato also, for in the *Cratylus* at 424D ff. he appropriates Empedocles' mixture model. It is plain that he knew Empedocles' work.³⁴ In the *Lysis* Plato speaks of dyeing hair in terms suggestive of this same model. He does so in the context of deciding which things are "friendly" with which, a context in which the things in question are evidently the opposites of pre-Socratic medicine and philosophy.

Plato applies this pigment-mixing model over a very broad range of inquiry. In the *Lysis*, he treats health and disease as the model requires, and suggests that we treat good along these lines also. The difference between appearing F and being F evidently lies in whether or not enough F is present to obliterate all traces of non-F. Obviously, if sensible particulars are by nature mixtures of opposites, opposites ordinarily standing in some sort of ratio or balance, no sensible thing *is* F without qualification on this view. Only F is F without qualification, though sensible things may appear to be F if F predominates over the non-F also present in them. Such an F is an εἶδος, a form, a δύναμις or "character-power." And it is a cause of particulars' having its characteristic properties.

That such δυνάμεις or εἴδη are the bearers and imparters of qualities is signified in Plato's vivid use of a magnetism model in the *Ion* at 533D ff. The power of the poet is said to be acquired from the Muse and passed on to inspired hearers, much as what Euripides first called a magnet but most Greeks called Heraclean stone not only attracted iron rings but magnetized them so that they could attract other iron rings in turn. Such quality-things were causes in the same way that the heat of a burning torch held to a pile of straw is the cause of the straw's becoming hot and burning. They communicate their qualities to the things in which they are mixed.

This is hardly the only place in the dialogues in which forms are characterized as essentially active in the characteristic behaviors or powers of various individuals. At *Protagoras* 332D ff., Socrates talks as if a moderate action were performed not by the moderate person exactly but by (ὑπό) moderation itself. And *Republic* 609D–610A indicates that ὑπό signals a proximate cause.

Such ways of speaking were not merely figurative, as G. F. Else noted.[35] At *Republic* 351D–E justice is said to create harmony and injustice, discord by being or dwelling in a state. This "by" is not merely logical: it is causal. Thus, in asking Socrates to define justice, Glaucon says, "What does it *do* when a person has it in his psyche?" That is, what does it do when it has a person in its grip? What does the person do by virtue of having justice in him? At *Republic* 443B it is again remarked that justice is the power that *makes* people just. The "make" is causal. And at *Phaedo* 102–106, as Else again noticed, forms are conceived of as causing the things participating in them to have their characteristic qualities and behaviors.[36] Calling εἴδη "kinds," Else remarked: "This notion that the Kinds are active is frequently summed up in the word δύναμις. Thus in *Protagoras* 330A the virtues, and in *Republic* 346A the arts, are said to be distinct from each other because each has its own special power or function. But not only do the Kinds *have* powers, they *are* powers."[37]

This same view may be discerned at *Hippias Major* 296C2–3, where Plato takes the position that it is by power (δυνάμει) that those who are powerful are so (δύνανται οἱ δυνάμενοι). This is said in explaining people's *acts*, and is explicitly causal in its explanatory intent, as 296E14–15 shows: the beneficial (τὸ ὠφέλιμον) is that which *makes* or *creates* good (τὸ ποιοῦν ἀγαθόν), and what makes or creates (τὸ ποιοῦν) is none other than the cause (τὸ αἴτιον). Efforts to read such occurrences of ποιεῖν as logical rather than causal in force make an idle exercise of Plato's work and ignore the fact that in such contexts he is explicating, not human properties, but human actions and the forces behind those actions.

That this is the use to which Plato puts his talk of forms as δυνάμεις is especially clear from the *Protagoras* 332B–C. Having already set out the view that foolish behavior is due to folly and moderate behavior to moderation, he makes the point quite general at 332C1–3: if something is done in a certain way (εἴ τι δὴ ὡσαύτως πράττεται), it is done by the same (δύναμις understood), and whatever is done in an opposite way is done by the opposite (δύναμις understood). Thus, if we act temperately, this is to be conceived of as the effect of the temperance in us. This point, and not an idle one about logical properties, is what is conveyed when Plato says that it is *by* temperance or moderation that one is temperate or moderate.

Plato, in fact, defines and distinguishes δυνάμεις in terms of what they do or accomplish (ὃ ἀπεργάζεται) at *Republic* 477C, and attributes any power a person has to the workings of such a power in the person. In context he is discussing certain powers of the psyche. As *Republic* 620D shows, he still regards psyches as *mixed* with bodies. The psyche causes the movement of the body. It would not be far wrong, then, to say that Plato was something of a behaviorist in his conception of forms as δυνάμεις, or quality-things, communicating their own characteristic behavior to their participants. This talk of δυνάμεις is talk of εἴδη, or forms, since in 477C Plato characterizes δυνάμεις as realities; and on his view, the εἴδη, or forms, are the only ὄντα, or realities. He also refers to δυνάμεις as εἴδη at 477C4 and E2, where it would simply multiply senses beyond necessity and beyond the textual evidence to translate εἶδος as "class" rather than "form."

Plato evidently employs this model to explain every appearance presented to us by a sensible thing, even ones such as beauty (*Phaedo* 100C4) and largeness (*Phaedo* 102B). Beauty is a beautifying quality-thing and largeness an enlarging one.[38] If Simmias is larger than Socrates, this is owing to his having more largeness in him than Socrates does. His largeness enlarges him as heat would warm him. Plato has but one model on which he explains anything one says about a particular, a model on which the behavior of a particular is viewed as being more exactly the behavior of one of the δυνάμεις mixed into the particular as a constituent. As Socrates asks, rhetorically, at *Phaedo* 92E ff., "Do you think a harmony or any other composite can be in any condition other than that of the things of which it is compounded?" He receives the expected negative answer. What a compound is, does, or suffers, then, must be understood in terms of what its constituents are, do, or suffer. Its behaviors are their behaviors writ large.

Plato is careful to indicate that this model of forms as *dynamic* is not original with him. He explicitly attributes it to Hippocrates the physician at *Phaedrus* 270D ff., where it is said that in investigating the nature of a thing, we are to ask how many εἴδη, or forms, it has in it and ask its δύναμις. This is to be seen in τὸ τί ποιεῖν αὐτὸ πέφυκεν ἢ . . . τι παθεῖν, that is, in what each of the forms naturally does or suffers.[39]

It has been widely debated where if anywhere in the Hippocratic corpus as we presently know it Plato could have found such views.[40] But it seems fairly plain that *Regimen* 1 contains them most clearly, and also furnishes antecedents for many of Plato's nutritional metaphors.[41] At *Regimen* 1. 2, the physician states:

I maintain that he who aspires to treat correctly of human regimen must first acquire knowledge and discernment of the nature of man in general—knowledge of its primary constituents and discernment of the components by which it is controlled. For if he be ignorant of its primary constitution, he will be unable to gain knowledge of its effects; if he be ignorant of the controlling thing in the

Early and middle Platonic forms as powers

body, he will not be able to administer suitable treatment. These things therefore the author must know, and further, the power possessed severally by all the foods and drinks of our regimen.[42]

Both the terminology and the uses to which it is put here in giving causal explanations of a thing's behavior are close enough to Plato's own to make quite believable his attributing what we might mistakenly take to be his own unexplained philosophical production to some medical figure whom he calls Hippocrates.

Early readers familiar with ancient medicine, then, would not have found such forms or powers as Plato employs at all extraordinary. Appeal to such entities was a commonplace of scientific explanation as then conceived of in medicine. They were the qualitative constituents, or powers, postulated to account for the shared qualities of particular things. They were conceived of as furnishing these qualities.

Plato was careful, however, to distinguish the following: (1) bearing a quality and thus tending to furnish it to mixtures in which a share of the bearer is present, and (2) being a mover and thus tending to cause the mixture in which the mover is found to move. Although Plato terms both the entities which accomplish 1 and the entities which accomplish 2 εἴδη or ἰδέαι, he calls only the second ψυχή, "psyche," or νοῦς, "mind." Psyche is as much entitled to be called an εἶδος or ἰδέα as anything else apprehended (much as each part is at *Phaedrus* 33D, 270D, and *Republic* 439F, 440E, and 612A). He does not hesitate to call psyche an εἶδος without the slightest hint that he is using εἶδος in a different sense. See, for example, *Phaedrus* 246A, and *Phaedo* 105C–107A in the light of 104C–105B. At *Phaedo* 98B ff. he has Socrates indicate that air, ether, water, and the like—the paradigmatic δυνάμεις, "character-powers" or "quality-things," of his predecessors—were not causes of motion. What causes things to be placed as they are is νοῦς, his term here for the psyche at its best.

In the *Phaedrus* at 245C–D, psyche is said to be the only thing which moves itself, and is said to be the ἀρχὴ κινήσεως, the source or cause of motion in everything else. The influence of the old model is clear even here—psyche can cause other things to move because it is itself in motion. Water is wet and moistens whatever is next to it, but if it is made to change place, this must be owing to the influence of psyche.

As late as the *Timaeus* 46C–D, Plato maintains the distinction between causes, which must be endowed with the capacity to think, and the old quality-things—earth, air, fire, and water—which are συναιτίαι, or auxiliary causes. Yet these quality-things are still said to be responsible for their characteristic qualities, for at 53A–B they are said to have some traces of their nature even in a state of the universe devoid of the ordering effects of νοῦς.

Plato's having employed the fifth-century notion of a δύναμις, or quality-thing, makes understandable his otherwise perplexing tendency to use a number of terms in ways which may well strike a modern reader as shifting illicitly back and forth between reference to an entity, an ability of that entity, and the exercise or activity associated with that ability. At *Phaedo* 97C we are told that νοῦς arranges and causes all things. This suggests that νοῦς is a psychic agent. At 98C we are told that Socrates does whatever he does by means of or with νοῦς. This suggests that νοῦς is an ability, a tool which, far from being an agent, is used by an agent, Socrates. At 99B we are told that it would be extreme rashness in an account to say that Socrates does certain things νῷ or "by means of νοῦς," but not from the choice of what is best (οὐ τῇ τοῦ βελτίστου αἱρέσει—99B1). This makes νοῦς sound less like an ability than like its necessary manifestation in activity. Yet at 99B–C it is suggested that νοῦς is a δύναμις, or "ability," since νοῦς has already been said to be the cause of things' being placed as it is best for them to be, and this cause is now called a δύναμις.

The source of our perplexity at these seeming shifts in the use of Plato's term νοῦς is his adherence to the very notion of a δύναμις described earlier. A δύναμις is not a mere ability, but is rather a substance which is a power and can assert itself. Readers of Plato's Greek text will notice many other examples of his seeming indifference to our distinction between what a thing has dominating it "from within," what it is, and what it does. The source of the indifference lies in the ancient doctrine of κρᾶσις, ("mixture") of active constituent powers, which Plato accepts, develops, and exploits for his own philosophical purposes.

Plato's acceptance of the doctrine puts in a new perspective his claim at *Phaedo* 97D that the understanding of the best and the most excellent is also the understanding of the inferior. The inferior—that is, the sensible particular—is just a mixture of portions of the "best and most excellent," the various forms, some or all of which can be obscured by their opposites in particulars.[43]

There is some controversy about whether in the middle dialogues Plato thought all forms have opposites. With Alexander Nehamas and R. E. Allen, I would suggest that Plato did not think that each form has an opposite.[44] I would suggest this, not because Plato could not consistently have held this, as Nehamas argues, but because Plato mentions forms which do not have opposites (fire, bed, and snow, e.g.) in the *Phaedo* and in the *Republic*. Each of these may bring with it one of a pair of opposites,

The separation of the forms

the other of which it cannot therefore admit, as Plato suggests at *Phaedo* 103C–104D, but this does not detract from the point: a number of forms Plato mentions clearly have no opposite of their own.

The separation of the forms

If forms in the early and middle dialogues were primarily causes or powers, it might seem embarrassing that Plato goes to such lengths to insist on their separation from the theater in which they are alleged to be doing battle. What are we to make of his separation talk?

This facet of Plato's forms has been less understood than any other. To avoid such misunderstanding one must start again with Hippocratic thought and with Empedocles to discern the background which such talk had, and hence the connotations which Plato probably intended it to have for his early readers.

Consider, for example, Empedocles' Fragments B98, B71, and B35. Empedocles called fire, which was one of his four "roots" or "elements" of all things, an εἶδος, and also used the term εἶδος of things constructed or compounded of these four roots. These Empedoclean forms clearly have the causal role power had had in Alcmaeon's theory, which Empedocles extended. Human flesh and blood, on his view, are blends of the powerful roots or forms he calls earth, air, fire, and water; and illness is explained as owing to a disturbance in their balance. The four roots, which are to be balanced in health, have distinct qualities or behaviors which are given to the senses, though when properly blended these are very subtle and perhaps not easily distinguished, as we find indicated in B35 and B3. He can, however, conceive of these four quality-things or forms as "unmixed" and "apart" (Fragments B17, A30). Does Empedocles, then, contemplate a separate realm of pure forms?

Though Empedocles is fond of spatial metaphors, one must beware of taking these literally. As Vlastos notes, Empedocles declares that "love is 'equal in length and breadth.' But when he formally declares that the roots are equal, he immediately goes on to say that (1) they are of equal age, (2) each has its peculiar honor (τιμή), but (3) they rule in turn (Frag. B. 17. 27–29). Could we ask for more conclusive proof that not mere extension but 'power' (with its associated concept of 'honour') is uppermost?"[45] What Empedocles evidently had in mind in such talk of separateness was the qualitative distinctness in power that he saw each of the roots as having.

Empedocles' influence upon medicine was considerable. The author of *Ancient Medicine* mentions him by name and sets out to combat his med-

96   Ἐπιστήμη *and Forms in Early and Middle Dialogues*

ical influence. Empedocles himself seems to have been at least a medical quack and possibly a physician.[46] But there were physicians who professed to be baffled by his cosmic extension of Alcmaeon's views. And in their bafflement we can find a good clue to the understanding of Empedocles' talk of separate or distinct forms, one bearing upon Plato's similar talk.

The author of *Ancient Medicine* expresses outright hostility to Empedocles' hypothesizing separate forms, powers, or roots to account for the behaviors of familiar things. He admits that physicians who accept such hypothesizing rightly notice that there are various component qualities in people and in the food and drink we consume which are beneficial if blended so as to be almost unnoticeable as such—for example, saltiness, sweetness, bitterness, heat, and cold (*Ancient Medicine* 14). And he admits that when any one of these is "separated off and stands alone" (ἀποκριθῇ καὶ αὐτὸ ἐφ ἑωυτοῦ γένηται), then it is apparent (φανερόν), and it becomes harmful to the person. He concedes that such physicians are right in associating illness with unusual tastes in the mouth, unusual odors emanating from the patient, extraordinary excreta, fever, and so on, and equally right in associating the restoration of health with the administering of foods which will drive the offending quality back below the threshold of noticeability. But he insists (15) that this much was common ground in ancient medicine before the advent of Empedoclean hypotheses, and he is skeptical that there is any medical gain in talking of such forms as separate or absolute, since even those who do talk in such ways "have not discovered, I think, an absolute hot or cold, dry or moist [αὐτό τι ἐφ' ἑωυτοῦ θερμὸν ἢ ψυχρόν ἢ ξηρὸν ἢ ὑγρόν] that participates in no other form [μηδὲν ἄλλῳ εἴδει κοινωνέον]. But I think that they have at their disposal the same foods and the same drinks as we all use."

The author is protesting that we know of no medically prescribable substance which is hot-and-nothing-else. Food will be astringent or insipid, but also wet or dry, sweet or sour, and so on. *Everything* we discover is a complex mixture or blend of various opposites; hence, to speak of something which is not such a mixture or blend is to speak of something which is unknown in medical practice and hence medically irrelevant. The author even suggests (14) that if such a thing were discovered—something which was simply hot and lacked those other powers of wetness or dryness, sweetness or sourness—it would be too powerful, too strong a dose, for our constitutions to cope with.[47] Since we cope most easily with well-mixed, highly diluted compounds such as we ourselves are, any pure power would radically upset our internal ἰσονομία, or equilibrium.

The Empedoclean claim in question is that a power is *distinct* from other powers, not physically separate. The medical writer points out that even so, we have not discovered such a distinct power as a usable or prescribable item in a diet. The only sort of discovery the medical writer has in mind is discovery by the senses. In this respect the author of *Ancient Medicine* is an anomaly among those Hippocratic writers interested in philosophy, as we shall discuss in detail in the next section; but in one respect at least, he and Empedocles agree with Plato that whatever the relevant mode of discovery or apprehension involved, if a power or form is to be regarded as pure or unmixed, this is because it is *apprehended* as such, and not necessarily because it is located as such (*Ancient Medicine* 15). Plato agreed that we find no sensible foodstuff or drink to be constituted solely of a single form or power, but all are mixtures of such forms or powers. This would follow from his general characterization at *Republic* 478E ff. of sensible things as not "pure," but as beautiful and ugly, for example. Plato did not, however, think that the end of the matter, nor did all other medical writers prior to Plato. The author of the treatise *On the Art* (11) remarks that what escapes the eyesight is nevertheless mastered by the eye of the mind. It is by this "eye" that we achieve understanding. Understanding (ἐπιστήμη) is *of* what *is*. Among the things that *are* there are active δυνάμεις, or powers, Plato argues at *Republic* 477B–C.

Forms as noetic or intelligible objects

It may strike Plato's modern readers as a confusion that he could think one investigates causes by the mind, not by the senses. If his forms were primarily powers or causes, why would he claim that they were "intelligible" but not visible? Readers weaned on Baconian conceptions of scientific or causal explanation may find this alleged confusion particularly pernicious.[48] But in taking such a view Plato was following the best science of his day, a science still rooted in notions readily intelligible to ordinary Greeks.

Consider then how this science could have developed a notion of a cause, power, or agent which is apprehended by the mind as unmixed, though in its normal sphere of actions in the particular things about us it was admitted to be mixed with many other powers, even opposite ones, and perceived obscurely in such mixtures.

If the root meaning of the term εἶδος was "appearance," then Greeks who had memorized the story of the Trojan horse for their tutors as children would scarcely need a Plato to tell them that appearances could be deceiving, especially to one interested in the causal efficacy or power of the thing perceived. The terms εἶδος and ἰδέα could be and were used with a suggestion of superficiality and possible deceptiveness long before Plato found it useful to contrast the visible form with the intelligible form at *Republic* 510D. The writer of *Ancient Medicine* 7 seems to argue against Empedoclean influences in medicine on the unstated assumption that whatever is of any medical relevance is seen, smelled, tasted, or felt. Yet he employed the term εἶδος in a way suggestive of superficiality when he discussed the difference, if any, between curative medicine and preventative medicine. The ancient theory of κρᾶσις which he accepted suggested that both were concerned with health conceived as an equilibrium of powers in the body, so he asks, rhetorically, "How do these pursuits differ, save in εἶδος ?"

But what does one discern when one penetrates past such superficiality or deceptiveness in appearance? Arguments between serious investigators over how a thing looks to them may strike us now as arguments over how to classify the thing, especially if the investigators agree about the sensible appearance of the thing. Hence, we are perhaps inclined now to translate many occurrences of εἶδος and ἰδέα as "kind," "class," "sort," "style," or the like.[49] But we do so at our peril, for in so doing we fail to preserve their likely connotations for a Greek and fail to sense a deep undercurrent of realism in such talk. *We* can easily think of a kind or class as nothing but a product of the classifier's imagination, as, for example, the class of all persons in my office now who are over seven feet tall, which is identical with the null class. But for a Greek moving, hesitantly perhaps, away from a straightforwardly visual sense of εἶδος as the "look" of a thing to a sense of εἶδος as something less deceptive, the εἶδος in which he was interested would still be something real which was apprehended, if not by the senses exactly, then by the mind. If some Trojan captain had said of the Trojan horse, "Don't pull it inside the gates—it's a trap," and had been proven right by subsequent events, it would have been natural for a Greek to think that his successful classification of the object was just his apprehension of its εἶδος by the power of his mind.[50] The very etymology of εἶδος suggested a link with perception or apprehension of some sort, and this suggestion was not lost even when it was recognized that the sensible look of a thing could be fatally deceptive.[51] Not all εἴδη were sensed.

Long before Plato, Heraclitus had declared, "Bad witnesses are eyes and ears for people if they have barbarian psyches."[52] Medical writers interested in such subtle problems as an exact causal understanding of the difference between the power of malaria and that of other diseases with similar initial symptoms had reason to carry this line of thought much further.[53] In the Hippocratic treatise *On the Art* 11, the author remarked, "Without doubt no one who sees only with his eyes can understand anything of what has here been described."

The author of *On the Art* 10 did not as yet conceive of what escapes eyesight as differing in purity from what does not, evidently, since he mentioned as examples hidden bodily cavities in which disease develops. But the author of a very Anaxagorean contemporary work in the same corpus, *On Regimen* 1. 4, makes the problem not just the practical or technical one of seeing into the diseased patient's body without causing death in so doing but rather the deeper problem of what the eyes are equipped in principle to do. In explaining away a popular belief, he remarks of those who hold it: "They trust eyes rather than mind [ὀφθαλμοῖσι γὰρ πιστεύουσι μᾶλλον ἢ γνώμῃ], though these are not sufficient to distinguish even things that are seen. But by means of mind I relate these things in full."

Though the discovery of the εἶδος, or "look," of a thing was now to be by some sort of mental activity bound only loosely to the senses, it was still plainly concerned with powers or causes active in many cases. The Hippocratic writers distinguished εἴδη of air, water, climate, disease, physique, and so on.[54] Not all of these writers talked like inductive reasoners, either. One remarks that investigation is to proceed by λογισμός, or reasoning.[55] Several ask τί ἐστι or "What is . . .?" questions in an attempt to develop accounts (*Ancient Medicine* 20, 22).

There was no great leap, then, from earlier medical views to those of Plato in the early and middle dialogues. Even the view that accounts or claims were to survive testing if the one giving or making them was to be regarded as having understanding was not unprecedented. In *The Nature of Man*, which even in Hellenistic times Plato was thought to have relied upon (Galen 15. 9 ff.) the medical writer comments, "It is right [δίκαιον] that a person who correctly claims understanding about matters should maintain his account victorious always [αἰεὶ ἐπικρατέοντα τὸν λόγον τοῦ ἑωυτοῦ] if he understands what is and if he presents it correctly" (*The Nature of Man* 1). The tests against which claims would have to be defended evidently often consisted in attempts to discern counterexamples drawn from experience with phenomena covered by the account, much as they did in Platonic dialectic. Hot and cold, for example, had been viewed as completely distinct, antithetical powers holding great sway over human health and well-being, powers distinguishable by their distinct effects of burning or chilling us. But the author of *Ancient Medicine*, in 16, 17, and 18, cites frostbite symptoms to prove that excessive cold has the same power to cause painful burning sensations and tissue damage as excessive heat, and cites fever symptoms to prove that excessive heat has the same power to cause chills as excessive cold.

Not just Plato's theory of forms considered as an ontology but also important features of his epistemology as connected with forms can be viewed as an early philosophy of science presuming and drawing together some details of views that were widely scattered and perhaps not well integrated in the medical thought of the time. This is not to say that Plato confines his use of medical notions to the original problems on which physicians employed them, or that they went wholly unchanged in his novel uses of them. Like Empedocles extending the medical thought of Alcmaeon to problems of cosmology and to the constitution of both living and nonliving things, Plato extends Hippocratic medical notions to areas remote from the professional concerns of physicians—to ethics and politics, for instance. And he emphasizes that the old medical character-powers are *intelligible*. But once we have understood the medical origin and connotations of Plato's terminology, both the intelligibility of forms as separate or distinct powers and several other problematic features of them emerge in a clearer light. We turn now to these features.

The noetic "world"

Aside from the "separation" language mentioned earlier, there are two chief grounds upon which Plato is credited with having torpedoed his own view by assigning his causal forms or powers to a literally separate world or realm from that of their effects. The first of these is his explicit talk of his forms as being in a νοητὸς τόπος, or a noetic "realm," at *Republic* 508C. The second lies in his having characterized the constitution of the best city at *Republic* 592B as being perhaps a παράδειγμα . . . ἐν οὐρανῷ, a "paradigm in heaven." We shall consider these in turn.

The passage mentioning a noetic realm occurs in the *Republic*'s simile of the sun. Socrates remarks, in Cornford's translation, "Let me remind you of the distinction we drew earlier and have often drawn on other occasions, between the multiplicity of things that we call good or beautiful or whatever it may be and, on the other hand, Goodness itself or Beauty itself and so on. Corresponding to each of these sets of many things, we postulate a single Form or real essence, as we call it."[56] These many things, he adds at 507B–C, can be seen, but are not objects of thought (νοεῖσθαι δ' οὔ), while the forms are thought of, but not seen. Pretty clearly then, when he speaks at 508C of the good as standing in the noetic realm (ἐν τῷ νοητῷ τόπῳ) to νοῦς and its objects (τὰ νοούμενα), as the sun stands in the visible realm to vision and to things seen (τὰ ὁρώμενα), he is talking about a form of good. This form reigns sovereign over νοητοῦ γένου τε καὶ τόπου, "the noetic form or realm," and the sun, over τὸ δ' αὖ ὁρατοῦ, "the visible one." At 516B he again speaks of the sun as presiding over all things in the visible "realm." And at 532C he speaks of

The noetic "world"

dialectic as having the power to lead the best part of the psyche "up" to the good, as he had spoken of the way in which the clearest and most certain thing in the body (presumably the power of vision) was turned to what is brightest in the bodily and visible realm.

The first thing to be noted about this passage is a point we had occasion to remind ourselves of in a previous chapter. This passage is hedged about with some of the most powerful warnings and apologies in the Platonic dialogues. It is not meant as an expression of a literal account, on Plato's own insistence at 504A–507B.

This licenses and in effect invites one to investigate what figurative sense his talk of two τόποι, or realms, was intended to bear here. Plainly τόπος cannot be taken literally, since to do so would destroy the causal efficacy of the forms, as Plato knew (*Parmenides* 134D–E).

One finds additional reason to investigate what figurative sense τόπος might have had here in the fact that figurative uses of it were not uncommon. Plato's contemporary Isocrates (5. 109, 10. 38) used it to mean "topic" several times, and Aristotle used it at *Rhetoric* 1358a14, 1396b30, and 1397a7 to mean something like "commonplace move" when discussing the sorts of appeals that were fundamental elements in rhetorical practice. Aeschines (3. 216) also employed τόπος in a nonliteral sense, and Thucydides may have.

This evidence from other writers need not give us the precise sense of Plato's own figurative use of τόπος but offers at least some encouragement to look for such a sense in the confidence that doing so is not anachronistic. It is prudent to seek such encouragement, for although place and world metaphors are now common and natural in philosophy, they need not always have been so.[57] Yet it is no surprise that they were. If forms were antithetical causal powers it would be natural to conceive of these as holding different bits of turf, as it were, and forming themselves into families or blocs. It is natural to liken any ordering or compartmentalization into discrete types to a sorting into spatially separate places. Even now, philosophers speak of mapping, of logical maps or logical space, and of locating things in a conceptual scheme. One hears talk of nets and networks of concepts related like strands in webs or fabrics. I trust no one would accuse Quine of placing certain beliefs in another world simply because he characterizes them as rather distant from the sensory periphery of the web of belief.[58]

Similarly, in logic and elsewhere one hears talk of "possible worlds," where these are not planets in an alien galaxy but rather possible concatenations of situations or states or conditions. Crudely put, such a "world" is a condition or set of conditions fully described.[59]

With this in mind, consider then Plato's *Theaetetus* 176A–B, where he disambiguates a bit of τόπος-talk. Socrates remarks:

> It is impossible that evils should be done away with, Theodorus, for there must always be something opposed to the good [ὑπεναντίον γάρ τι τῷ ἀγαθῷ]; and they cannot have their place [ἱδρῦσθαι] in the gods [ἐν θεοῖς] but must inevitably hover about mortal nature and this region [τόνδε τὸν τόπον]. Therefore we ought to try to escape [φευγεῖν] from here to there [ἐνθένδε ἐκεῖσε] as quickly as we can; and to escape is to become like god, so far as this is possible [φυγὴ δὲ ὁμοίωσις θεῷ κατὰ τὸ δυνατόν], and to become like [god] is to become just and holy with understanding [ὁμοίωσις δὲ δίκαιον καὶ ὅσιον μετὰ φρονήσεως].

Clearly, Plato's place talk here is a metaphor for a situation, condition, or state of affairs, and his flight talk is a metaphor, not for space travel, but for what we would characterize as the attempt to come into a different situation, condition, or state of affairs while remaining, perhaps, exactly where one was before. He himself identifies the place sought with the condition or power of justice and holiness which he sought here, and the place fled with the condition or power of appetite. Even in the *Phaedo*, where Socrates speaks of departing εἰς βέλτιστον τόπον, "into the best place," this is plainly closely related to and perhaps identical with his talk of changing one's condition or state of being dominated by the body.

In the *Theaetetus* passage, as elsewhere, place language is proxy for condition language. The relevant condition is that of being dominated by and evincing a power, which is also perceived as a virtue. *Theaetetus* 177A makes this particularly clear. Although the *Theaetetus* is much later, even in the *Republic*, the intelligible place or realm would seem to be the *condition* of being dominated and illuminated by the good, a condition Socrates' own search, as described at *Republic* 592B, would suggest is to be at least approximated here and now, not literally in another world.

In the *Symposium* at 211B Plato's mouthpiece, Diotima, denies that beauty is to be found ἐν ζῴῳ ἢ ἐν γῇ ἢ ἐν οὐρανῷ ἢ ἐν τῷ ἄλλῳ, "in an animal, the earth, heaven, or anything else." The suggestion is plainly that such a form is not the sort of thing to be *confined to* or *contained within* any particular place.

If we adhere to a customary ontology of "moderate-sized dry goods" or, like G.E. Moore, regard a watch, book, or human hand as our paradigm for what may safely be thought to exist, we may be left incredulous at the notion of an alleged reality which is "located in many places but nowhere confined." Many of us have accepted without sufficient examination Aristotle's dogma that to exist in the universe is to exist in a place—that is, to be confined within the limits of some specifiable environing body (*Physics* 209a23–26, 210b23–31, 212a17–24, 212a30–b1, 212b14–22). Such

The noetic "world"

dogma can atrophy the interpretative imagination as it can the scientific, and far from being a prerequisite for intellectual discipline, it can be an obstacle to it. Gravity is certainly "real," though (*a*) it is not locatable in Aristotle's sense, if the universe is not a finite, closed body, and (*b*) it is in a perfectly intelligible sense everywhere, even though it is stronger near our sun than near Earth and is reportedly far stronger near a black hole than near our sun. It is simply a myth that we can sensibly count as real only those entities which are confined to a location specifiable in terms of an environing body.

Once we are disabused of this myth, we are well on our way to understanding why Plato might take the pre-Socratic theory of δυνάμεις, "powers," "forces," or "quality-things," as seriously as its authors did, and we can discern why he did not need to posit a spatially separate "world" for forms to be located in. Indeed, he could not have posited such a world consistently. Since the intelligible, on Plato's view, is not confined, to speak *literally* of an "intelligible world" would be a contradiction in terms. We should not force such a blatantly contradictory reading on the text if there is any viable alternative, and there is: Plato's mention of an "intelligible realm" is meant to serve an epistemic purpose, not a pseudogeographic one.

Even so, talk of "two worlds" dies hard. One may say, "Why should Plato have posited two separate ways of approaching *one* world?" If he posits two ways of approaching this world—through the senses and through the mind—and it looks very different when approached in these two ways, what warrant could there be for claiming it is only *one* world?

This question requires a careful response. First, the question contains literal uses of "world," and since the issue here is whether or not we should take Plato's uses literally, any answer to it would inadvertently concede the point at issue. Let us approach it instead in a different manner. In more nearly neutral terms, the question is whether the objects of sensory experience can be *numerically* identical with the objects of mental experience even if these are *qualitatively* not identical. And the answer is surely yes. Even sensory experience itself provides a parallel: if we judge the texture of a wall by sight, we may be misled by a clever application of paint, by color, by clever lighting tricks, or the like. We can judge texture definitively only by touch, which will not be misled by a clever application of paint, by color, or by clever lighting tricks, since it is oblivious to these. It would be absurd to deny that the texture we feel with our fingers is not numerically one and the same feature we see with our eyes. But it would not be absurd to deny that what is numerically one and the same feature of the wall can be apprehended by these two senses as if it were qualitatively not one and the same. A wall which looks rough may feel smooth, though there is only one wall; and one will conclude that, visual appearances to the contrary, it is smooth. If one were concerned about the inaccuracy that might result from relying solely on sight to judge texture, one might say, perhaps a bit misleadingly, that sight does not discern the real texture at all, and that the true or real texture is not seen, but rather, is felt, by touch. One would not mean that there is, in some literally separate world of touch, a true or real texture numerically nonidentical with the texture one sees. One would instead be making an essentially epistemic point in a way which runs on ontological danger—the danger of suggesting that there are two textures and two "realms."

Plato subjects his readers to a similar danger with his talk of an "intelligible realm," but we need not succumb to it or conclude that he himself did. In speaking of an intelligible realm he was contrasting the epistemic reliability of dialectical thought with that of sense perception.

What, then, of Plato's locating the form or paradigm of the best city ἐν οὐρανῷ, "in heaven" (*Republic* 592B)? It is important to note that in context Socrates is also made to describe this city as lying ἐν λόγοις, "in accounts." Given that this passage is the end and summation of their description of the best city, that it completes the task begun back in book 2 when they set out to establish a city in an account, it seems plain that their own description, or λόγος, and descriptions, or λόγοι, like it in the future will be the locus of this city. (See *Republic* 369A, 372E, 427D. Cp. *Laws* 702E.)

But why, then, does Socrates also say the city is a παράδειγμα ἐν οὐρανῷ, a "paradigm in heaven"? He has hardly finished saying that one can be a citizen of it here and now, after all. But if one looks at past uses and senses of οὐρανός remembering that Socrates has also said the city is ἐν λόγοις, "in accounts," one can discern a plausible interpretation. One of the chief conventional uses of οὐρανός was to designate the abode of the immortals. We have already investigated in earlier chapters the way in which Plato expected an account of a form to be "immortal" and "indestructible," and he did not hesitate to have his spokesmen indicate that any such account would be θεῖος, or divine (*Phaedo* 85D; *Phaedrus* 259D). Thus, in assigning this city both to a "location" ἐν λόγοις and to one ἐν οὐρανῷ, Plato is, I think, indicating that he deems this account irrefutable or divine, and that the form of city which it describes is the only genuine or true city, the form mongrelized in lesser organizations called cities (*Republic* 543E–544A). It is the just city, embodied in a true account.[60] It is a form which occurs in adulterated form in actual cities, but in pure form is apprehensible only by the activity of the best part of the psyche. Early Greek readers would have had every reason to react to such forms as

The "arguments for the existence of forms"

familiar. And this is precisely the untroubled reaction Plato attributes to almost all of his Socrates' interlocutors.

The "arguments for the existence of forms"

Still, it may be objected that if the early and middle Platonic forms were familiar, Plato would scarcely have found it necessary to argue that such entities exist. Such a remark would be wholly correct, but no objection; for Plato never argues for the *existence* of forms. In the passages in which he is alleged to do so, he has invariably presumed that they exist well before he gives his alleged arguments, and the interlocutors in the dialogues in question have not raised the slightest objection to this. He argues, not that forms exist (unless one begs all the interesting questions by using the interpreter's word "form" other than as Plato uses his terms εἶδος and ἰδέα), but rather that these forms which have been agreed to exist must have certain characteristics. He is arguing for their having these slightly controversial characteristics, not for their wholly uncontroversial existence. We shall consider each of these alleged arguments in turn.

It is sometimes thought that Plato has Socrates offer an argument for the existence of forms at *Phaedo* 74A–B, for example. If he does, the *Phaedo* is badly put together, for the participants have freely conceded the existence of such forms at 65D–E; hence, no occasion for such an argument would have been established. But in fact an occasion is established for his discussion of forms at 74A–B, and it shows that this discussion is no argument for their existence. At 74A12–13 Simmias again agrees most emphatically that such a form—αὐτὸ τὸ ἴσον, or "the equal itself"—is real. At 74B2–3 he is equally emphatic that they understand what it is. Socrates then asks the question that motivates the ensuing discussion, which interpreters allege offers an argument for the existence of forms: Πόθεν λαβόντες αὐτοῦ τὴν ἐπιστήμην; that is, "Where do we get the understanding of it?" Plainly, this commits the fallacy of many questions if the existence of such forms is at all in question. It would be like asking a robbery suspect who proclaims his innocence, "When did you first case the job?" But the existence of such forms is not in question at all, having just been conceded enthusiastically at 74A12–13, as it had been earlier at 65D–E.[61]

What *is* in question here is merely the way in which we come to understand a form which is, like all forms, καθ'αὑτόν or εἰλικρινής, by which Plato means to indicate that it is apprehended as pure, unmixed, and "true" or "real," ἀληθής. Hence, when he points out at 74B7–C1 that the equal pieces of wood and stone which we sense sometimes appear unequal, he is merely applying the general principle conceded at 65D–E—that τὸ ἀληθέστατον, or what is most genuine or real, is not apprehended by any sort of αἴσθησις, or sense perception. The particular things we perceive are apprehended as inconstant mixtures of opposites, and indeed, as 70D–71A claims, they change into their opposites freely. The entities grasped by the mind, being ἀληθέστατα, "truest," and most constant or genuine with respect to themselves (αὐτὰ καθ' αὐτά), do not present contradictory εἴδη, or appearances, to the mind which apprehends them. Hence they are not the same as the shifting things apprehended by the senses in that they have a simplicity, purity, and constancy lacked by sensible things. We could not have come to an awareness of the sort of purity possessed by the equal itself on the basis of sensing things which lack this purity. Thus, Plato argues, we must apprehend the equal itself not by sense perception but by what he calls recollection. That is all this argument is designed to show.

The erroneous view that Plato argued for the existence of forms is quite old, but also quite current. Alexander of Aphrodisias reports that Aristotle, in his lost work on forms, criticized Plato's having argued for the existence of forms in ways which contravene his putatively exhaustive distinction between entities which are πρός τι, "relative to something," and entities which are αὐτὰ καθ' αὐτά, "absolute" or, more accurately, "the same in comparison with themselves."[62] G.E.L. Owen suggests that Alexander's version of Plato's alleged argument is "substantially faithful to his sources in Plato," though he concedes that Alexander "takes pains to sharpen the logical issues they involve."[63]

These sources Owen finds at *Phaedo* 73C–75D and *Republic* 523A ff.[64] The *Phaedo* passage has been interpreted above, and we have maintained that it is no argument for the existence of the forms. Thus, if being substantially faithful to one's sources requires analyzing them to discern the point actually being argued for as conclusion, rather than devising a conclusion of one's own for which premises in the argument would have been poor reasons, Alexander's Aristotle is less than faithful to his sources in the text of the *Phaedo*. This lapse of faithfulness to sources is repeated if one takes one of those sources to have been *Republic* 523A ff.: not only has the existence of forms been assumed without question in preceding passages in *Republic*, book 7 (most notably in the Cave passage at 519C–D), but it has been assumed also in preceding books (e.g., in book 6 at 511C). Moreover, the context indicates that the existence of forms is not the point at issue in 523A ff. The point is how to educate potential guardians to use sense perception to provoke the exercise of λογισμόν τε καὶ νόησιν, or "calculation and reasoning." Plato suggests that many sense perceptions are sufficient in that they are epistemically dependable reports on the current state of what one is perceiving. As a clear example he cites looking at one's finger. Sense perception never represents it as anything but a finger, nor does it provide one with occasion to ask the dialectical question "What is a finger?" We ask such dialectical questions when sense perception presents us with something problematic, and a finger is not problematic. To be problematic in the way required to provoke a dialectical question is to present one with what, at first sight, one can only describe in an incoherent way. It is to present one with a mixture of opposites in what seems to be, but cannot be, one thing. Plato recommends directing students' attention to the perception of problematic things in order to awaken reflective thought in them, and thus to induce them to ask and begin to answer dialectical questions. This, and not a wholly unnecessary proof that some things have paradigms beyond our confused perceptions of them, is the point of this passage. Plato did not argue the existence of forms here, for he did not need to.

In the *Cratylus* at 439C8 ff., Socrates begins what might also be taken as an argument for the existence of forms, since at 440B–C he gives what appears to be a *reductio ad absurdum* on the view that they do not exist. Yet on closer examination, it is plain that such an interpretation misconstrues the line of argument. The very first thing the Heraclitean, Cratylus, concedes at 439C8–D1 and D5–6 is that beauty itself, good itself, and the like, are real, and that such a form is necessarily "always such as it is" (τοιοῦτον ἀεί ἐστιν οἷόν ἐστιν). Thus again, *before* what might be taken to be the argument for the existence of such forms, their existence is in effect conceded. All Socrates does in the ensuing lines is to drive home to Cratylus the impossibility of reconciling this concession with his general view that "all things are changing and nothing remains fixed" (440A8–9), noting in so doing the role of forms as the stable ground presupposed by any talk of γνῶσις, or understanding, at 440A10–C1, an understanding Cratylus had evidently claimed to have at 384A2–3.

It is typical of Plato's dialectical method to offer arguments only when, in context, there is doubt about the conclusion for which he argues. We have seen that in the *Phaedo* and *Cratylus* there is no such doubt, the existence of forms being in effect conceded. Similarly in *Republic* 5, the existence of forms is readily admitted by Glaucon at 476A, and the question at issue is merely "Who are the real philosophers?" The distinction between forms apprehended by intelligence as unmixed, intelligible, and stable entities, and sensible things apprehended by sense perception as unstable mixtures of opposite forms, is intended not to establish the existence of pure forms but to differentiate the mode of life of the true philosopher from that of the lover of appearances, as emerges clearly at 479A–480A. The true philosopher loves to apprehend forms, while the lover of appearances loves to apprehend shifting sensible spectacles.

In the *Parmenides*, too, having asked if Parmenides and Zeno do not concede that there are forms, Socrates finds at 130B that they never say that forms do not exist; indeed, at 135A–E Parmenides explicitly agrees that there must be forms.

In the *Timaeus* at 51B ff. Plato offers the most nearly convincing candidate for an argument that forms exist. He has talked about forms on practically every other page of the *Timaeus* up to this point, but suddenly proposes to investigate more precisely. He poses two alternatives: either

1. There is a certain "fire itself by itself" (ἔστι τι πῦρ αὐτὸ ἐφ' ἑαυτοῦ) and all the other things they term "realities in accordance with themselves" (αὐτὰ καθ' αὐτὰ ὄντα), an intelligible form for each thing, or
2. There are only the things which we see or otherwise sense, and these alone have ἀλήθεια, "reality" or "genuineness."

The language of the first alternative, at 51C8, may suggest the identity of a doubter, for he uses the decidedly uncharacteristic phrase πῦρ αὐτὸ ἐφ' ἑαυτοῦ, where, as he immediately shows, he prefers αὐτὸ καθ' αὐτό to αὐτὸ ἐφ' ἑαυτοῦ. This is quite suggestive of the phrase αὐτό τι ἐφ' ἑωυτοῦ θερμόν at *Ancient Medicine* 15, where, as we saw, the author attacks Empedoclean medicine for its hypothesis that there exists a distinct thing called "the hot" which participates in no other form, and emphasizes that we all have at our disposal the same quite mixed foods and drinks.

But what would such a doubter question? Not, surely, that there are εἴδη. Up to this point in the *Timaeus* Plato has talked freely as if there were εἴδη, and as we saw, the author of *Ancient Medicine* likewise assumes that there are εἴδη. The point at issue is not whether or not there are εἴδη, but rather what sorts of εἴδη there are. That a thinker or perceiver apprehends an εἶδος was as uncontroversial as anything of a philosophical sort one could say to a Greek. That the εἶδος thus apprehended existed was likewise uncontroversial. The controversy, mild as it was, evidently, was over the purity or distinctness of εἴδη as we apprehend them. The Hippocratic writer notes that when perceived in food and drink, εἴδη are invariably mixed. Plato concedes this, but adds that when apprehended by νοῦς they are not apprehended as mixed, but rather as distinct and pure; and in contrasting what we apprehend by νοῦς with what we apprehend by the senses, Plato had other Hippocratic writers—Heraclitus, Empedocles, and Anaxagoras—on his side, as we have seen. Thus it is not surprising that this passage seems almost an afterthought in the *Timaeus*, a footnote, as it were, for the few who might be inclined to confuse εἴδη as sensed with εἴδη as apprehended by the mind.

Mixtures, ingredients, copies, and paradigms

We have seen that Plato inherited from predecessors the rudiments of the view that sensible things are mixtures of pure and intelligible ingredients. But he also views sensible things as copies or reflections or images of intelligible paradigms. These rather different views are found side by side in the same dialogues (as, e.g., in *Republic*, book 6, at 509E ff., and in book 5 at 476A), but do they cohere? This question will put the old controversy over whether or not Platonic forms are "immanent" or "transcendent" in a new light.

At *Republic* 476A Socrates is made to say: "Regarding the just and unjust, the good, the evil, and all the other forms the same account holds: each is itself unique [ἕν], but owing to their presenting themselves in community with actions, with bodies, and with one another everywhere, each appears to be many." There can be no doubt here that the unique form is the form apprehended by mind; nor can there be any doubt that it is this same unique form which presents itself in community with many actions, mixed with many other such forms. This is but an adaptation of the old notion that there are δυνάμεις, or powers, which appear in many places at once, mixed with other powers and obscured or "moderated" for this reason. It is not to the point to raise the objection of Parmenides at *Parmenides* 131B about making one and the same thing located at many places at once, like a sail covering many sailors, for it is obvious that a power or form is not a thing in this sense. It can be *in* a location but not *confined* to that location, as an army can have a detachment at one spot and also another detachment elsewhere and still be the same army.

Socrates is depicted as being wary of Parmenides' suggestion that such a line of reasoning would make the form itself distinct or separate from itself (αὐτὸ αὑτοῦ χωρίς), but this is of a piece with Socrates' youth and clumsiness as depicted in this dialogue; for elsewhere (*Phaedo* 65D, 67C, and 83A) Plato does not balk at talking as if the psyche, which we know to be immaterial on his view, were spread or distributed through the body, but capable of collecting or gathering itself up from all parts of the body into one mass. It would be still less problematic to view a nonpsychic form as mixing, mingling, or having community with many different things in different locations than to view a psyche as doing so, for he does not assume that there can be communications among the diverse portions of nonpsychic form.

The κρᾶσις, or mixture, model appears at many places in the *Republic* itself, as at 406A, with its reference to blending or mixing gymnastics with medicine. Parts of the city, at 548C, are described as mixed or blended with one another, and the timocratic city is said to be a mixture of good and evil. At 618B a given form of life is said to be a mixture of health, disease, wealth, and poverty, and at 586B Plato speaks of a mixture of pain and pleasure.

Those who impose a preconception of what a "transcendent form" is supposed to be on Plato's text rather than attending to his use of εἶδος and his mixture model may protest that what is blended in the above examples cannot be a form, since forms are "transcendent." But there is no escaping the force of passages such as 590B, where Plato speaks of the psyche's mixing with true reality and begetting understanding and genuineness as a result. The phrase τῷ ὄντι ὄντως, "what is really genuine," can stand only for Platonic forms, and the sexual language is no mere metaphor, standing as it does in a tradition which took such "mixing" talk as explanatory. He continues to describe even such entities as the psyche as being put together by mixture of forms when at *Timaeus* 35A he speculates that the Demiurge blended the same, the other, and being to produce it. He employs the same model, complete with mixing bowl, at 41D when he describes the mixing of the human psyche, and at 73C when describing the composition of marrow by mixing triangles with one another in due proportion. At 63E he describes the cause of roughness as being hardness mixed with irregularity, while at 48A he had described the origin of the universe itself as lying in a mixture of νοῦς, or mind, and ἀνάγκη, or necessity, each of which is termed an εἶδος elsewhere in the *Timaeus*.

W. D. Ross in his book *Plato's Theory of Ideas* compiled a list of the terms in the dialogues which suggest the "immanence" of forms in particular things, and a separate list which suggested their "transcendence," noting how in a given dialogue words from both lists will occur.[65] By regarding "immanence" and "transcendence" in the usual way as terms for the *location* of forms, Ross gives the distinct impression that Plato was caught in a vast muddle of his own making.

We are now in a position to diagnose and avoid that way of regarding "immanence" and "transcendence," however, and to discern that Plato was by no means so muddled as Ross suggests. It is striking that most of the words from the "immanence" list are closely associated with the mixing model which Plato inherited and used, while most of the words from the "transcendence" list are associated with the model of copy and paradigm.[66] Since these two models occur side by side in the middle dialogues, it seems most unlikely that Plato even unconsciously wished one to replace the other. It seems far more plausible that he had in mind distinct uses to which he put each. What might these distinct uses have been?

It is possible to appreciate the sense of Plato's model of copy and paradigm without going deeply into his theory of forms. It is possible, that is, to understand that model as having principally dialectical, epistemological, psychological, and political uses. That model conveys to us the way in which a person who has ἐπιστήμη and thus apprehends a form compares and contrasts sensible things with that form. He or she does so by regarding the sensible thing as "like" the paradigm, but a poor copy of it—and in some ways and from some points of view a copy of its opposite as well (*Phaedo* 74B7–C1; *Republic* 479A). It is an image, a confused image, of several perhaps antithetical originals, much as a mongrel dog might seem like a hound in some respects and like a pointer in others, yet be neither hound nor pointer. To be acquainted solely with such animals of colorful heritage is to fail to understand what a real hound or a real pointer is or does.

Is the mixture model put to different uses than the copy and paradigm model? Clearly it is. Its uses are ontological and causal. These are obviously connected with Plato's epistemology, since to understand is to understand something which is *real* or *genuine* on his view; yet these uses are distinct for all that. On the mixture model the form is like a pure chemical substance a portion, or μοῖρα, of which may be mixed in a confusing way with other such substances; it is then present in the compound, influencing the compound's behavior, but not obliterating all traces of its fellows. Plato uses the mixture model to explain how things *look* in contrast to what is *real*.

If one insists on relating the two models, one might liken a form to the first standard pointer, which sired many pups by dogs of other breeds or of no particular breed, and one might then liken sensible particulars to the offspring, adding that the original pointer is apprehensible solely by the mind, not by the senses. The two models are complementary, not contradictory.

Though the paradigm vs. copy and power vs. mixture distinctions are complementary in the above ways, they may also appear to stand in a certain tension. On the paradigm/copy distinction, a sensible F is deficiently F, and from things which are deficiently F one could never come to understand what it is to be perfectly F. To understand that, one would have to apprehend F itself, the perfect paradigm. It might seem that on the power/mixture distinction, there is no parallel deficiency in sensible F's, and hence no need for apprehending (or positing) a paradigm. This might seem so if one held that in order to apprehend F itself, all we need to do is to perform some intellectual operation (of abstraction, perhaps) on sensible objects which are F, separating the bits of F in them from other components in them.

The above tension is only apparent, however. Sensible F's are no more unqualifiedly F on the power/mixture distinction than they are on the paradigm/copy distinction. A sensible mixture is deficiently F, since it contains only a portion of F mixed in with portions of non-F, which obscure the portion of *F* and render it difficult, if not impossible, to identify *F* accurately unless one has just apprehended the paradigm or pure power *F* in isolation and is thus able to use it as a paradigm in judging sensibles. One could no more remove, single out, or abstract away Alfred's portion of the power of justice from his portion of the power of temperance if one did not first understand justice and temperance themselves than one could abstract away Alfred's resemblance to his paternal Uncle Herman from his resemblance to his maternal Aunt Jane if one were not first acquainted with Herman and Jane. Portions of powers are not, epistemically, any more helpful than resemblances to paradigms. Indeed, they are the same thing described in two different ways.

Forms, universals, and self-predication

On both models for conceiving of forms, however, interpreters often object that Plato was caught in quite a different muddle. Forms conceived as paradigm objects have the properties mirrored only imperfectly in their many copies, and forms conceived as powers working in various individual mixtures which they thereby empower must of necessity have or carry with them the power they provide. In that sense it will sound as if forms or powers are self-predicable.

This is often thought to be a logical scandal. The chief reason for this is that many readers have taken forms to be universals. They do so because they think Plato proceeded on the assumption that in cases where one name is applied to a number of entities, these entities have a single form. *Republic* 596A is readily cited in this connection. Since a universal is thought to be what a number of like things have in common, it is easy then to think that Plato is at work trying to develop a theory of universals, especially when he calls a form a ἓν ἐπὶ πολλά, or "one over many," and has Socrates explain patiently in early and early middle dialogues that he is not asking for a recital of particulars but for an account of "the one that runs through them all." (See, e.g., *Meno* 72C, 72E, 75A, and 74A.) Aristotle helps make this easier by claiming at *Metaphysics* 987b1–6 that Socrates tried to define universals, while Plato followed him in this, attempting to differentiate the objects of such definitions from sensible things.

It is less easy to think this, however, when one reminds oneself that whatever else Plato's forms may have been, in his ontology they were causes or powers. Some commentators go so far as to claim that for this reason Plato never got quite straight the difference between forms as natural entities capable of having a causal role and forms as logical entities capable of serving as universals or objects of definition.[67]

If he did not get this straight, however, then we are led to the brink of sheer paradox by Plato's talk of forms (now both universals and powers) as *having* the qualities they impart to individuals sharing in them. R. E. Allen has put the alleged difficulty here succinctly: "Proper universals are not instantiations of themselves, perfect or otherwise. Oddness is not odd; justice is not just; equality is equal to nothing at all. No one can curl up for a nap in the Divine Bedsteadity; not even God can scratch Doghood behind the ears."[68]

Allen details the familiar embarrassments for Plato's alleged view if forms are taken to be what he calls "proper universals."[69] A vast literature on the worst of these alleged embarrassments, the so-called third man, has sprung up in recent years.[70] The entire issue rests on a misunderstanding, however. It results from (1) attributing to Plato a view of forms as the designata of predicates in sentences rather than as powers operating in mixtures having no stable subject or substratum, and (2) a wholly misleading and anachronistic use of the term "universal." The first of these has been refuted by Gerold Prauss, who has shown that in Plato's early and middle period it never occurred to Plato to view a form as the designatum of a predicate, nor to conceive of λόγοι as subject-predicate sentences.[71]

The second of these must now be discussed. Historical controversies aside, the term "universal" is most likely to suggest to a contemporary reader something quite remote from a cause or power working in various particulars, albeit against the influence of other such powers. It is likely to suggest a mere abstraction, something arrived at by induction. Yet we know from *Phaedo* 74B7 ff. that such a form can be no mere abstraction, incorporating as it does a perfection never encountered in sense experience. Hence, we must hold resolutely apart the question, What, from our point of view, was Plato *actually* doing when he conceived of a form? (which is a philosophical question answerable perhaps in terms of induction and universals if we are still inclined to accept that sort of picture of thought processes) and the interpretative question, What did Plato evidently *think* he was doing in conceiving of a form? (which is not so answerable). We shall pursue the latter question, but the persistence of talk of universals must first be faced.

Allen remarks: "It is generally agreed that forms are universals, and in some sense that is surely true: 'One over Many' is the nub of the argument for their existence. In *some* sense, then; but in *what* sense?"[72] Here Allen concedes too much. Is it surely true that Plato's calling a form ἓν ἐπὶ πολλά, "one over many," warrants our saying that a form is in *any* readily understandable or helpful sense a universal? What does ἓν ἐπὶ πολλά mean?

It is usually taken to mean "one over many," where ἐπὶ is taken to be employed in a metaphorical extension of sense 5 in the Liddell-Scott-Jones lexicon, the sense suggesting literal extension over a space. The one form would then be "over" the many particulars presumably in that it would be an abstraction applying to and based upon each of them, a conception of them based upon an overview.[73] It is difficult, however, to believe that this is the right way to take ἐπί, given that Plato at *Parmenides* 132B–C showed that he plainly knew the difficulties involved.

There is an alternative reading of ἐπί which coheres better with Plato's use of forms as causes or powers and with the medical conceptions of forms upon which he was evidently depending for the ready intelligibility of his theory. One can take ἐπί in the phrase ἓν ἐπὶ πολλά in sense 4 of Liddell-Scott-Jones, the hostile sense in which a general is said to have proceeded against an objective.[74] To proceed successfully against an objective is to have conquered it, to have come to rule over it. The ἐπί of ἓν ἐπὶ πολλά can be likened to the ἐπί of ἐπικρατέω, "rule over," or ἐπιφερέω, "bring up," where a causal role is clearly indicated. In the Hippocratic treatise *On Regimen* (1.6) one finds forms treated as powers ruling over individuals and warring against their opposites, a conception derived from Alcmaeon's view that disturbances in health are owing to a power's having attained μοναρχία, or monarchy. Plato continues to talk in such ways in the middle dialogues, as we have seen, and evidently does so in order to give forms an explanatory role with regard to sensible things and their behavior.

One can illustrate this role aptly in terms of the paradigm and copy model. Suppose one is given a dog that is half pointer and half hound. If the dog occasionally points a pheasant, one may be inclined to say, "That is the pointer in him showing itself." If instead he follows an animal trail baying loudly, we may be moved to say, "That is surely the hound in him coming out." If he points, runs a few steps baying, stumbles and points again, we might say that the hound and the pointer in him are in contention. In so doing we would be talking much as Plato does in *Republic* 4 and 9 when he describes psychic conflict between the three distinct forms of which we are composed as a conflict of three animals sewn, as it were, into one skin, and as medical writers talked in describing a patient's crisis.[75] And we would be employing a simile of dog-breeding which Plato himself uses in book 2 to describe the problem of developing a guardian with exactly the right psychic constitution to act as a watchdog, not to be a neighborhood hazard or a totally tranquil pet. On his view the qualities things have are simply forms blended into them.

Forms can scarcely be universals if this is taken to suggest any connection with names. Plato regarded names as a very misleading guide to forms. Consider, for instance, his characterization of ἀντιλογική, or antilogic, at *Republic* 454A–455A. Evidently, its chief characteristic is its penchant for dividing things up on the lines suggested by conventional nomenclature. Plato thought this stood in the sharpest possible contrast with the procedure of διαλεκτική, or dialectic, which sought to divide things κατ' εἴδη, or along the lines dividing forms or powers. In the *Cratylus* at 436A–438E he describes the confusions and contradictions imparted to Greek by the legendary name-giver, thus showing that he thought the language far from ideal from a dialectical point of view concerned with forms or powers. Like the author of the Hippocratic treatise *On the Art* 2 before him, Plato is keenly aware at *Cratylus* 434E–435D and 439C–440B that forms are natural, while even simple names are conventional and epistemically unreliable in their conventional application. Even the famous assumption that if both a city and a person are called just, this will be owing to the same form, justice, is quite simply that in *Republic* 4—an *assumption*—which Plato at 434D–E treats cautiously as perhaps mistaken. If, therefore, a universal is construed as what all like-*named* things have in common, Plato knew very well that his forms could not be universals, and that names could at best be an imperfect and misleading guide to formal affinities.

As *Republic* 477 ff. makes clear, Plato evidently regarded the behavior of a thing as a far better guide to its form than its name could be. This is natural, given that his forms were primarily the old medical and Empedoclean quality-things or character-powers in a guise readily apparent to his early Greek readers.

Individuals, forms, subjects, and predicates

The way of conceiving of particulars and forms presented in this chapter provokes questions concerning Plato's view of predication, for it has been commonplace to treat Platonic forms as properties or qualities denoted by predicates.[76] But it is misleading to represent a Platonic form as a property or quality, for this suggests that on Plato's view there is some subject or substance of a logically distinct type which it is a property or quality *of*. There is no such subject or substance on Plato's view. What we take to be a subject or substance having certain properties Plato, very much in the Greek medical tradition, takes to be a mere mixture of things having the same ontological or logical status. A particular, on his view, is nothing but a mixture of portions of δυνάμεις and εἴδη, portions of which occur elsewhere as well, in mixtures of greater or lesser purity or strength. But wherever it occurs in sufficient strength, such a δύναμις or εἶδος, F, makes whatever it is present in appear F, much as water wets its container.[77]

This Platonic conception is difficult to express even if one has grasped it, as John Burnet evidently did. He remarked:

> The predicate of a proposition is always a form, and a particular sensible thing is nothing else but the common meeting-place of a number of predicates, each of which is an intelligible form, and in that sense there is no longer a separation between the world of thought and the world of sense. On the other hand, none of the forms we predicate of a thing is present in it completely, and this relation is expressed by saying that the thing "partakes in" the forms that are present in it. Apart from these, it has no independent reality; and, if we know all the forms in which anything participates, there is nothing more to know about it.[78]

In a number of ways this is an admirable remark about the relation of forms to particulars. But there is nothing to be gained by describing the portion or share of a form present in a particular as a property or a predicate of that particular. In fact, there is a good bit to be lost, for a property is necessarily a property *of* something, and a predicate is a predicate of some subject. But on Plato's view, forms were the only realities, and there is nothing suitable of which they could be predicated. To describe the form present in a particular as a predicate or property of it is to miss Plato's attempt to deconstruct particulars into forms or portions of forms without remainder. It is to give the unfortunate impression that Plato must have thought there are "bare particulars" or "empty containers" of which forms can be predicated, an impression close to the impression that forms are predicated of nothing at all.[79] But Plato conceives of particulars as being possessed by forms, and as being constituted by them wholly. This is indicated with special clarity at *Republic* 476A. Particulars are mere mixtures or communities of portions of forms, bundles of form-shares occurring together at a given time and place; and any structure the bundle has is not that of subject and predicate. The language of subject and predicate, possessor and property, belongs to another tradition of thought altogether, one not anticipated by Plato in the middle dialogues.[80]

The model of portions or shares differs in crucial ways from the model of predicates or properties. It does not foist upon the extralinguistic world of Plato the grammatical structure of Indo-European languages. Predicates are such that we can either predicate them truly of a subject or we cannot. But Plato conceived of participation as sharing in, and sharing in as being a matter of degree varying with the "size" of the share. On his view, then, participation was a matter of degree. This has been denied by Alexander Nehamas, who remarked, "There is not one shred of evidence that Plato thought of participation as an ordinal relation; particulars participate in the Forms in different respects or in different contexts, but never, so far as I can tell, in different degrees."[81]

But consider the following pile of "shreds": At *Timaeus* 58E, Plato remarks, Ἀπολέσαν μετίσχει μᾶλλον κινήσεως, or, "This being lost, it [fire] participates more largely in motion."[82] At *Philebus* 56C, Plato speaks of those arts which resemble music as participating less in accuracy (ἐν τοῖς ἔργοις ἐλάττονος ἀκριβείας μετισχούσας) than do those arts which resemble the art of the builder. In the *Laws*, at 889D, Plato speaks of certain productions as ἀληθείας οὐ σφόδρα μετίσχει, "sharing but little in truth." At *Phaedo* 93D he speaks of participating more or less in harmony (πλέον ἢ ἔλαττον ἁρμονίας μετέχει). A particular's having a property at all was to be accounted for, on Plato's view, by its having a share in a form, that is, by its participating in that form. Thus, it was only natural for him to explain a particular's having more or less of that property in terms of the "size" of its share of that form—in other words, in terms of the degree to which it participated in the form. There is nothing irretrievably counterintuitive about this. If a senator is held to be powerful by virtue of participating in the power of the Senate, then the degree to which the senator participates in that power and the size of the share the senator has in that power are simply two ways of speaking of the same thing.

Conclusion

In summary, then, we have found that in his early and middle period Plato employed and treated as familiar what in fact was a familiar conception of εἶδος or form derived in large part from ancient medicine and the speculations of Empedocles and Anaxagoras. According to this conception, forms were causes or powers showing themselves in their qualitative prominence over particular mixtures. Some εἴδη, those Plato termed νοῦς, "mind," or ψυχή, "psyche," were treated as causing motion in whatever mixtures they happened to be found in. Psyche, or ψυχή, was a form for the same reason that anything else one could apprehend was a form—it presented a certain "look" or appearance to the one apprehending it, either to the sense organs or to the mind itself.

The language of χωρισμός, or "separation," was intended to suggest that forms are distinct from the mixtures with which they share their qualities and that no form is confined to any such mixture. There is no good reason to attribute to Plato the view that there is another "world" in which these forms are located, nor to believe that this is what his χωρισμός language is intended to convey. The forms had a role in the only world Plato conceived of, a world which we can both sense and think about. When apprehended by thought, forms appear the way they are—simple and unadulterated by their opposites. It is for this reason that such forms are regarded as "absolutes," models, or paradigms. Thus the mixture model is put to ontological and explanatory use, while the paradigm/copy model is put to epistemological and moral use. Once we have seen this, we are in a position to address ἐπιστήμη as an understanding of truth and reality conceived on the paradigm/copy model. This will be our task in the following chapter.

5
Ἐπιστήμη, Reality, and Truth

Ἐπιστήμη on Plato's view was an understanding of real objects. In his early and middle dialogues, at least, Plato contrasted these objects with particular sensible objects in two ways which differ so vividly that one might easily think of them as rivals. In the preceding chapter, however, it was argued that these two ways of characterizing the objects of ἐπιστήμη are actually complementary. Plato's characterizing the objects of ἐπιστήμη as paradigm forms and particulars as more or less accurate copies served an epistemic function. It put his readers on guard against the epistemic unreliability of sensible particulars, which, on his view, are never perfectly, adequately, or perspicuously representative of what one wishes to understand. It set in sharp contrast the use of the senses in perceiving an object and the use of the mind in apprehending an object dialectically.[1] Sensible objects were held to be epistemically unreliable owing to their reminding one who sees them of too many paradigms, perhaps even of the opposite of the paradigm whose name the particular bears.[2] Thus, in using his paradigm/copy distinction Plato emphasizes that the objects of ἐπιστήμη must always be distinguished and conceived of in isolation from the confusing melange in which the senses detect them. Their "separation" from sensible particulars is epistemic separation.

Plato's characterizing the objects of ἐπιστήμη as δυνάμεις, or powers, and particulars as mixtures containing only a μοῖρα, or share, of the δύναμις one wishes to understand can also put his readers on guard against the epistemic unreliability of sensible particulars. If a particular is a mixture and contains only a μοῖρα, or share, of the power one wants to understand, this μοῖρα may be obscured by a share of another power, even an opposite one found in the particular. One can have ἐπιστήμη of the power, or δύναμις, only by distinguishing it and conceiving it in isolation.

The pure δύναμις, or power, is a "quality-thing," and numerically one and the same entity as the paradigmatic εἶδος, or form. Thus, Plato's two ways of characterizing the relationship between the objects of ἐπιστήμη and sensible particulars are complementary in a number of ways. First, the power/mixture distinction suggests an account of *why* sensible particulars can remind one of too much, and thus an account of their epistemic unreliability. These particulars can remind one of too much precisely because they *contain* too much; they are "impure," incorporating portions or "shares" of many powers as parts, even portions or shares of opposites. If such opposites are described in the account of what one takes to be one entity, the account will contain a contradiction. Plato, in fact, uses the principle of contrariety in *Republic* 4 to distinguish opposing ingredients in a sensible particular, a human being. Opposing tendencies in a particular are attributed to opposing powers in which the particular shares, as when Leontius both wants to view a pile of corpses and refrain from viewing it.

The power/mixture distinction complements the paradigm/copy distinction in a second way. It, too, suggests that in apprehending a power or form by the activity of the mind, one is apprehending something perfect. And it suggests a way of construing that perfection. The perfection consists in purity or lack of mixture with opposites. This is the perfection which can be missing in sensible particulars, as in an object which is both beautiful and ugly, though in different respects. A power or form, when apprehended dialectically by the mind alone (as contrasted with being sensed as a component in a particular), will transcend the confusion of the particular and appear "pure" and "unmixed" with its opposite. Only when apprehended in this way can a power or form be an object of ἐπιστήμη, for only in this way, when apprehended "alone" or "by itself," can it be reliably distinguished from other forms even in its influence.

The power/mixture distinction complements the paradigm/copy distinction in a third way. It offers an account of what powers or forms are doing in the particulars which participate or have a share in them. A sensible particular was said to be a mixture of portions of powers or forms which cause it to behave in various ways, perhaps opposing ones, or to have various qualities, perhaps also opposing ones. Epistemically, then, powers or forms are conceived statically as pure paradigms, substances not sullied by any admixture with their opposites. But ontologically, powers or forms are conceived dynamically as components, shares of which appear in the particular sensible mixtures in which their causal influence is sensed.

That the power/mixture and paradigm/copy distinctions were involved in Plato's conception of forms and particulars profoundly affected his views about what truth and reality consist in. Having now interpreted these distinctions, we are in a position to inquire into his conception of reality or truth, a conception central to his view of ἐπιστήμη as an understanding of reality expressible and testable in an ἀληθὴς λόγος, or true account. In this chapter we shall see that Plato's surprisingly widespread use of his paradigm/copy distinction generated serious difficulties for him in his account of why there can be both true and false accounts, and that he faced these difficulties with familiar weapons. In the following chapter we shall explore additional difficulties generated by Plato's use of these two ways of conceiving of the object of ἐπιστήμη, difficulties having sweeping dialectical, epistemic, and political consequences for his views in the late dialogues.

Paradigms, copies, and approximations

In applying his paradigm/copy distinction Plato held that the "truest" or "most real" x is the paradigm x itself. Anything else which is x is so by virtue of being and remaining qualitatively *like* the truest one, x itself.

The evidence of Plato's having been inclined to employ his paradigm/copy model when judging the relative "truth" or "reality" of particulars is plentiful in the dialogues.[3] That such judgments take as their point of departure comparison with ideal paradigms not apprehended by the senses, and that these paradigms are ἀληθέστατα, "truest" or "most real," is clear from *Republic* 485C–D, *Phaedo* 66E, and many other passages.

The character of this truth or reality as a qualitative perfection may be seen in Plato's characterization of his forms as paradigms which, if apprehended at all, would never seem defective to anyone anywhere. At *Hippias Major* 291D, Hippias finally understands what sort of thing Socrates is after in asking him to give a λόγος, or account, of beauty. Hippias remarks, "You seem to me to be seeking to reply that the beautiful is something of such sort that it will never appear ugly anywhere to anybody." Socrates responds, "Certainly, Hippias; now you understand beautifully." Similarly, at *Symposium* 211A the paradigm of beauty is put in sharp contrast with that which is in one respect beautiful but in another ugly, beautiful in some part but not in others, or beautiful in the opinion of some but not in that of others. Much as a Brittany spaniel fancier would term an animal "a *real* Brittany" or "a *true* Brittany" only if it was the clearest possible example of a Brittany at even the best shows judged by the most discriminating judges, so Plato will regard an entity as a paradigm only if under dialectical scrutiny it proves to be an absolutely clear, unambiguous exemplar not incorporating any of the defects of its mongrelized "offspring," "copies," or "images."[4] Defects consist in mixture with opposites.

This suggests that what Plato has in mind when he calls his paradigms or forms "pure" (καθαρός, εἰλικθινές) is a curious homogenity of "breed," a strong disposition to look and continue to look of a single type to one who apprehends them in the relevant way, no matter what point of comparison one may employ.[5] The same point is conveyed by Plato's otherwise opaque claim that such paradigms are "one" or "simple," not complex entities or mixtures. They are constant and homogeneous, and plainly much the better for that on Plato's view. At *Republic* 380D–381B, this emerges in Plato's description of God as "simple and less likely than anything else to depart from his own form," and of things which are divine as being like him in this respect. He remarks:

If a thing departs from its own proper form, must the change not be owing either to itself or to something else? (Necessarily.) Is it not true then that things in the best condition are least changed or moved by other things? Consider the effect of food, drink, or exercise on the body, or that of sun, wind, and similar influences on a plant; are not the healthiest and strongest least changed? (Certainly.) And is not the bravest and wisest psyche least influenced or changed by external influence? (Yes.) And by the same account even all composite things such as implements, buildings, and clothing, suffer least from time and other influences if they are well made and in good condition. (That is so.) Then everything which is in the best state either naturally or owing to technical treatment or both admits the least change by something else. (Evidently.) But surely God and divine things are in every way in the best condition. (Certainly.) By this then God would be least likely to have many forms.

Plato clearly thought the forms or paradigms to which he appealed divine, and thus changeless, simple, and, accordingly, good. And anything which was to be *like* one of these paradigms had to bear up under scrutiny in the same stable, homogeneous way. He adds at 381C, "The most beautiful and best possible remain always simply in their own form." This coheres with the contrast drawn between sensible things and forms or paradigms at *Republic* 478E ff., where sensible things are characterized as mixtures of opposites in their appearance, and forms as "one" (479A)—that is, as remaining always the same and unchanged (479C).

Note, for example, the passages cited above from the *Hippias Major* and *Symposium*. Carefully scrutinized, most allegedly beautiful things will prove to have some ugly features, to look ugly in some circumstances or to some people. By hypothesis, beauty itself, the really beautiful paradigm, is not subject to such disabilities, but can withstand the most exacting scrutiny of its features for signs of its opposite.

The meaning of Plato's phrase καθ' αὑτόν, usually rendered "absolute," can be clarified in many of its more perplexing applications by appeal to this paradigm/copy distinction as its basis.[6] It is a commonplace that Plato regarded his forms or paradigms as "absolute" and not relative to anything else (πρὸς ἄλλον), but the basis for this is often left unclear. The phrase καθ' αὑτόν often means "over against itself" or "compared with itself" when Plato applies it to forms.[7] For example, only beauty itself, the paradigm, is free of admixture with ugliness so that it can withstand a comparison of each of its features with every other. Other beautiful things, such as those we see, cannot withstand such scrutiny, but are beautiful only in a relative way owing to their resemblance to the paradigm. They will have parts which, when compared with one another, will appear to have opposite characteristics. As Plato suggests at *Phaedo* 78D–79A and 80B, *Symposium* 211A, and *Republic* 590A, such particulars are not μονοειδής, or single in form, as the paradigm of beauty is, but are πολυειδής, or multiple in form, and hence present a confused appearance. It is this confused appearance which "hides" each of the forms contributing to the appearance of a particular, and thus prevents its being ἀληθής in the sense of "unhidden."[8] Only what is apprehended as standing by itself, distinct from other entities, can be regarded as "unhidden."

The paradigm/copy distinction as applied to accounts

Today we speak freely of true love, true friendship, and the like, where "true" is replaceable by "real" and "real" by "genuine," "unfeigned," or "not simulated." But such uses of "true" in English involve nondiscursive entities. This use of "true" with nondiscursive entities stands in sharp contrast with our use of it with discursive ones such as statements or accounts, for when we call something a true statement, we do not mean simply that it is a *real* statement or an unfeigned one; for it could be false and yet be a real statement. It could not be false *unless* it were a real statement. In calling a statement "true" we mean not merely that it is a real statement but that it corresponds with the facts, that the world is as the statement says it is. Indeed, it would be plausible to claim that for us, the nondiscursive use of "true" is parasitic upon the discursive one. Alan R. White has remarked:

When an X, e.g., a statement or a story, is characterized as true in virtue of what is said in it rather than for itself, such an X is a true X if and only if what is said in it is true. When on the other hand an X, e.g., a Corgi or courage, is characterized as true other than because of what is said in it, an X is a true X if and only if it is true to say that it is an X. The former use of "true" is primary. "This is a true Corgi" implies, but is not implied by, "it is true to say that this is a Corgi."[9]

Gregory Vlastos finds the same order of priority in Greek uses of terms for "true." He remarks, "In Greek, as in English, the predicate, 'true,' applying primarily to propositions, may also apply, derivatively, to things described by propositions—to objects, persons, stuffs, states, processes, dispositions, and the like."[10]

Whatever may be said of other Greeks, Plato's order of priority or derivation was quite the reverse of the familiar one described by White and Vlastos. Plato applied his paradigm/copy distinction to λόγοι, or accounts, holding them "true" or "false" by standards parallel to those he invoked in judging a polis a real polis or not. He had no distinctive discursive use or sense of his terms for "true" and "false," no notion of a proposition, and no easy way to interpret the relation between meaning and truth. These are the principal claims to be argued in this chapter.

If Plato employed his paradigm/copy distinction in judging whether or not an account is true, this judgment amounts to assessing whether an alleged account is a *real* account—that is, a close approximation of its paradigm—or merely an imitation or counterfeit account. It is difficult for us to understand how anyone could employ the distinction in this way. It seems plausible to us today to construe the giving of an account as the uttering of certain propositions, and the account itself as these propositions. If we were to apply Plato's paradigm/copy model here, it would seem to follow that a false account would be an imitation proposition, in other words, a piece of nonsense which resembles a proposition but isn't. This would fail to account for the fact that in order to say anything false one must utter, not nonsense, but a real proposition. It would seem that on Plato's view it would follow that every proposition one could utter, including all the ones we would judge false, are equally real propositions. Thus, if all there is to being a true X is being a real X on Plato's view, it would then seem to follow that all accounts, being equally real, are equally true, and that falsity, as we conceive of it, is impossible. Yet we know that Plato did not accept every account offered as a true account. How then could he evade the sophism that every meaningful account is a real—that is, true—account?

It would be foolish to slight the difficulties Plato had in combatting this sophism, or to insist that Plato evaded these difficulties more successfully

The paradigm/copy distinction

than Moore and Meinong, who experienced similar ones. Nevertheless, we are not more obliged to expect Plato to combat the sophism by our familiar means of giving priority to the discursive use of "true" than we are obliged to expect him to combat Spartans with jet planes rather than javelins. He did not discriminate the true from the false as we do. He did so, rather, as a natural extension of his paradigm/copy model, with ingenious additions.

There are many signs of this. In Chapter 2 it was pointed out that he plainly used his term for "account," λόγος, in several senses, the third of which we might now call the "fancier's sense"; λόγος in this sense suggested the closest possible approximation to a paradigm, the form of λόγος. The term is employed in this sense at *Republic* 533C, *Symposium* 202A, *Phaedrus* 276A, *Statesman* 286A, and *Laws* 967E. It also bears this sense in the otherwise perplexing locution οὐκ ἔχει λόγον, which is often rendered "that does not make sense." The locution actually has a meaning closer to that involved today when one person offers a second an explanation of sorts, and the second responds, "That is no explanation," meaning, presumably, "That is not *the* explanation." Much colloquial talk today, especially in sports, reflects a similar line of thinking: "I wouldn't call Starr a coach. His win-loss record doesn't compare with Lombardi's." Or consider an appreciative student's remark as he walked out of a colleague's class: "Now that's what I call philosophy."

At *Gorgias* 465A–B Socrates is berating various forms of what he calls κολακεία, "flattery," namely, cookery, cosmetics, the art of attractive dress, sophistry, and ordinary rhetoric.[11] His complaint against all these is that their practitioners have no account to give of what they offer. He plainly does not mean they are at a loss for sales pitches. He had got one shortly before from Gorgias. He means that such flatterers' remarks will not withstand serious scrutiny, that their attractiveness is meretricious compared with that of a real account. The flatterer's alleged account will parse, and is hence an account in one sense, in that it is a grammatical statement. It is defended after a fashion, and is thus an account in a second sense. But it is not an account in the paradigm-fancier's sense, any more than a cockapoo is a poodle or a counterfeit drachma a drachma.[12] Flatterers construct imitations but not scrupulous likenesses of the real thing, and do so whether they work in the medium of words, wax, plaster, or peace negotiations.[13] They cannot replicate or even approximate closely what they do not understand, though they may very well ape those who do attempt to approximate it. Plato's definitive characterization of the sophist at the end of the dialogue *Sophist* is as an ignorant imitator.[14]

On Plato's view a particular is an "imitation," the original of which—

perhaps at several removes—is a form. This form provides its identity. Insofar as the particular can be said to *be*, it is what its form makes it. If it had no form, it would not be anything at all.

This is perhaps why Parmenides is made to concede at *Parmenides* 135B–C that if one denies there are forms one utterly destroys the power of carrying on dialectical discussion. He is not suggesting merely that without forms there would be nothing for such a discussion, or λόγος, to be *about*. He is suggesting also that there would be nothing for such a λόγος to *be*. There would be no form of λόγος, or accounthood, for it to share in. The character of every particular is derived from the δύναμις (or power), the εἶδος (or form), which dominates it, on Plato's view, and this power or form is precisely what this passage indicates would be lost for discussions or accounts if there were no forms whatever.[15]

A particular account is thus on a par with a particular bed. Each is true or real to the extent that it resembles and continues to resemble under close scrutiny the paradigm from which it gets its name. The relevant characteristics of the paradigm are, of course, different. Accounts do not have to permit comfortable reclining, and beds do not have to contain defenses against objections. But each has an original and must measure up to it if it is to be judged true to its type. The major respects in which a λόγος must measure up were sketched in Chapter 2.

The real *account* is perhaps the divine account which Simmias, who accepts the theory of forms, contrasts with human accounts at *Phaedo* 85C–D. That would be the form of account, just as the divine bed in *Republic* 10 is the form of bed. This form of accounthood is, I think, what Socrates is referring to at *Phaedrus* 270C–D when he says that he and Phaedrus must look at what Hippocrates says about nature *and* at the true account. He is not prejudicing the discussion of whether or not Hippocrates' account *is* true; the "and" is not meant to indicate that sort of distinctness. He is indicating, rather, how such a discussion proceeds on his view, by comparing *an* account, in this case Hippocrates', with the *true* account, by which he means not "the facts" about the subject under discussion but the form of accounthood itself, the type-form to which a true account is true.

Since "truth" for discursive as well as nondiscursive entities is a matter of being true to type, and since its being true to type is what we are imputing to an entity in calling it a "real *X*," it is understandable and important that Plato uses the Greek verb for "is" in absolute constructions indifferently of accounts and beds. The embarrassed translator has him saying "is so" of accounts and "is real" of beds, and thus suggests, misleadingly, that Plato is describing or conceiving of these differently. But he is not. He also employs the nouns for reality and truth as if he thought them synonymous when applied to entities the mere existence of which was not in question.[16] Plainly, the reason they were employed as if he thought them synonymous is that he actually thought them synonymous when so applied. Both reality and truth amounted to a dependable genuineness of quality, an approximation to a stable type or paradigm.

Even at *Sophist* 257B, where we might be inclined to suspect most strongly that a correspondence theory of truth is at least being hinted at, Plato treats the truth of an X as its resemblance to the real X, the paradigm, and he treats what translators render sometimes as "nonbeing" and sometimes as "falsity," τὸ μὴ ὄν, as "otherness" or "difference" with respect to the real X, whether X is discursive or not. Falsity and nonbeing have nothing to do with existence. They are both paradigm deviance.

This explains why Plato's remarks about falsity in the *Sophist* are hedged about fore and aft (235A ff. and 264C ff.) with remarks about nondiscursive fakes and phonies.[17] As in the *Gorgias* at 465B–C, the sophist's remarks are treated at *Sophist* 236C as being comparable to a cosmetician's performance. Λόγος is explicitly treated as a γένος at *Sophist* 260A, a form or natural kind on a par evidently with bedhood, beauty, and health. Particular λόγοι, or accounts, are treated as vehicles for phoniness and fakery on a par with the vehicles provided by shell games at *Sophist* 235C.

The sophist whose account of justice is false imitates, not justice or accounthood, but a wise and just person's account of justice. A sophist's account is judged false, not because it fails to correspond with the reality it might be thought to be about, but because it is itself not very much like the real account.[18] As *Republic* 598E ff. indicates, copies of copies are less true than copies of the true paradigm, the real thing. An account is essentially *about* something, but it is *itself* something—a good or bad image of λόγος, the power or form in which all λόγοι or accounts share.

The entities which we call accounts are, on Plato's view, a multiplicity of like-named things. For any such multiplicity he posits a form, as he indicates at *Republic* 596A7–B8. The burden of proof, given Plato's general view about there being a form for each such multiplicity, is upon anyone who wishes to *deny* that there is a form for the multiplicity of λόγοι, or accounts. An account was a particular which he conceived of as coming out of the mouth on one's voice (*Sophist* 263E). In his claiming repeatedly that one who understands something can give an account of it, there is no suggestion that he meant to say *the* account. An account is a good image, not of X, which it is *about*, but of λόγος, or accounthood itself, in which it shares.[19] An account of triangularity does not have three corners, but it has an original nevertheless, and this is the very original which serves for all other accounts which are real or true accounts.

That Plato employed his paradigm/copy distinction in judging accounts just as he did in judging non-discursive particulars is borne out by the terms he employed as opposites for ἀληθής, his principal term for "true." There are few considerations which mark off one sense of a term from another as decisively as the use of distinct opposites for the term in its different senses. Aristotle clearly noted this.[20] "Sharp" does not mean the same when applied to cutlery as when applied to musical notes, since "dull," the opposite in the cutlery case, does not mean the same as "flat," the opposite in the musical one. If we went about speaking both of knives needing sharpening and of notes needing their pitch raised as "flat" or "dull," this would be a sign that we had overlooked a powerful and obvious means of differentiating two senses of "sharp" and that perhaps we had failed or declined for some reason to differentiate them at all.

Plato had available a term—κίβδηλος, "base," "adulterated," and hence "counterfeit"—which would have made a serviceable opposite for ἀληθής in a nondiscursive sense had he wished to reserve it for use in nondiscursive cases and the other opposite—ψευδός, "false"—for use in discursive cases. In fact, however, he used both opposites indifferently in discursive and nondiscursive applications.[21] At *Republic* 507A, for example, Socrates is not confident that he can give an account of what he calls the offspring of the good, far less of the good itself, and he warns Glaucon lest he deceive him with a κίβδηλος λόγος, a bogus account.

If this example were isolated and seemed stylistically calculated, one might regard it as metaphorical—as a Goodmanesque extension of counterfeiting terminology across category lines.[22] But the example is not isolated. Nor does it appear stylistically calculated. Plato was so wary of poetic and figurative language (witness his famous strictures on it in *Republic* 3 and 10) that he generally seems to have posted some sort of warning when he thought he was indulging in it. See, for example, *Meno* 86B–C, *Phaedo* 114D, *Phaedrus* 246A, and *Timaeus* 29C–D. In the context of the very passage in which he warns against his possibly offering a counterfeit account, he is acutely self-aware and calculating about figurative language. He explicitly warns the reader in advance about the Sun, Line, and Cave similes at *Republic* 506D–507A, 517B, and 533A. Elsewhere, at *Phaedrus* 261D ff., he comments on the slipperiness of such figures and the difficulty of ascertaining whether or not the comparison they suggest is accurate. But neither in the *Republic* passage nor elsewhere does he let drop a word of warning about the propriety of lumping together being a false claim and being an adulterated or *ersatz* product.

On the contrary, this "lumping" comes naturally to Plato. In the *Laws*, which is guarded and unmetaphorical almost to a fault, the Athenian lawgiver who serves as Plato's spokesperson delivers himself of the following at 916D: "Adulteration [κιβδηλεία] must be regarded by every man as being the same natural kind [ὡς ἕν τι γένος ὄν] as falsehood [ψεῦδος] and fraud [ἀπάτην]." And Plato was shortly as good as his word in associating these notions much as he always had. At 916E his lawgiver declares, "No man, calling the gods to witness, shall commit either by word or deed any falsehood, fraud, or adulteration." Plato evidently saw no relevant difference between the adulteration committed in passing off an alloy of gold as pure gold and the adulteration committed in passing off a likely sounding story as an account.[23] Speech acts and their qualities were on a par with other acts and their qualities.

Plato's standard for judging truth and falsity in accounts no doubt achieves a sorting of accounts into roughly the same two groups we would generate were we asked to sort by our own standards. But this should scarcely surprise us. What a λόγος is supposed to do is to tell about things that are as they are (*Sophist* 263B), much as what a shuttle is supposed to do is to weave. It measures up to its standard or falls short of it in what it does. It is judged by reference to a paradigm precisely as any other particular is. And the paradigm is a δύναμις, or power, having a distinctive activity. Fire imparts heat (*Phaedo* 105C), and justice, a specialization and restriction of function. Λόγος imparts a correct and psychologically convincing sorting, a distinguishing, articulation, and clarification of boundaries, "gathering" like to like, and distinguishing or "separating" the unlike.[24]

Destructive testing and the survival of the true or real

Plato's tests for truth and falsity in accounts and elsewhere bear out the thesis that he employed his paradigm/copy distinction as his primary device for conceiving of and assessing particulars in epistemic contexts. Whatever was false, on his view, could be so judged because it would not maintain its putative identity under scrutiny or test. And a sensible thing's identity, as noted earlier, was simply its predominant or seeming likeness to a given paradigm. In the dialectical testing of a particular account, the questioner looked to the paradigm of λόγος and judged the answerer's λόγος by comparison with that. Whatever else one may say about this paradigm, it contained no admixture or confusion of opposites, and hence no excuse for incoherent descriptions.

Given that Plato employs an ideal or paradigm of λόγος, or accounthood, and that there would seem to be no obstacle to a person's grasping just this paradigm or ideal without grasping others, it becomes clearer why Plato could have thought it possible for Socrates to proceed in all honesty as he portrayed him. He portrays him as being able to test an alleged λόγος for its truth or falsity without ever understanding or discovering anything about what it purports to be an account of save that it is or is not a stable paradigm of the fancier's sort.[25] Socrates may not understand much about virtue, but he has an extraordinary grasp of accounthood, and that is enough to equip him to test the accounts offered him by putative experts. This understanding of accounthood is the midwife's expertise which he claims in the *Theaetetus* at 149A ff. and 161A–B.

The need for this midwife's expertise on the part of the dialectical questioner explains something which is otherwise a mystery, namely, Plato's characterization of ἐπιστήμη, or understanding, in terms of the ability to give *and receive* an account (as at *Republic* 534B and *Theaetetus* 202B–C). In Chapter 2, using *Theaetetus* 151C–D as the principal text, we dealt at length with the ability to give accounts, on the understanding that someone was, of course, eliciting and receiving such accounts in Plato's dialectical practice. It is now clear that Plato thought there were two distinct sorts of understanding or wisdom, one consisting in the ability to give accounts, and a second, more basic sort consisting in the ability to elicit and assess accounts. It is this latter ability which Socrates claimed, as at *Theaetetus* 161B. It remained basic to Plato's epistemic, psychiatric, political, and moral enterprise. The psychic midwife had the ability to distinguish the bogus from the genuine among accounts, to sift or sort one's mental contents and help one remove anything mixed or impure.

Plato hit upon a useful simile for this dialectical sifting in Greek metallurgical lore. Having grown up in metallurgically sophisticated Athens, he was evidently familiar with various potentially destructive ways of testing alleged samples of a precious metal, and he extended to nonmetallurgical areas the view that a "true" X is an X which will survive analogous testing.[26] The full βάσανος, or torture, for gold, coupelation and cementation, would yield a worthless plaque of salts if one tried to pass off base metals as gold and they were submitted to this test. Alloys of gold would emerge at appropriately reduced weight and volume with the impurities removed. What was left in the pot at the bottom of the furnace was gold, pure or real gold. No matter how many times one "tried it in the fire" thereafter, it would emerge intact.

So, at *Statesman* 303D–E, Plato has been trying to get an account which would separate off other arts from that of statesmanship, and has already eliminated some. He remarks: "Another group remains, which is still more difficult to separate, because it is more closely akin to the kingly kind and also harder to recognize. It seems to me that our situation is like that of those who refine gold." He continues: "The craftsmen first remove earth and stones and many things of that sort; and after that there remain the

Destructive testing

valuable substances which are mixed together with the gold and akin to it—copper, silver, and sometimes adamant—and these can be removed only by fire. They are removed with difficult tests by smelting, leaving before our eyes what is called unalloyed gold all by itself." If Plato's dialectical smelting is successful, he will secure an account of the statesman alone, one which does not apply even to similar kinds of people, far less to disparate ones. If the truth is *in* one, he is confident that sufficient dialectical testing would remove *all but* the truth, as smelting or refining removes all but the gold from ore.

Given the special sensitivity to incoherence even in this late dialectical testing employing division schemata, Plato's view is likely to strike the modern reader as involving a confusion, a confusion between surviving tests for incoherence and being true. Whether we take this as a confusion or not, Plato had long depicted Socrates as if he saw no distinction between these. At *Gorgias* 508B–C, for example, Socrates had told Callicles, "Very well; either we must refute this account, that it is by the possession of justice and temperance that the happy are happy and by that of vice that the wretched are wretched, or, if this is true, we must look at what stands. Those former things, Callicles, all stand, . . . and what you supposed Polus to be conceding from shame is then true."[27] This is quite like what he had told Polus shortly before at 482B–C: that he would have to refute Socrates' account or else be in disagreement and discord with himself. And shortly before, at 480E, Socrates had said, "Well, either it [what went before] must be upset, or this necessarily stands."[28] Still earlier, at 466D–467A, Socrates had challenged Polus to refute him, and had added, "Otherwise, if you leave me unrefuted, the orators who do what they think fit in the cities, and the despots, will find that they get no good in doing that . . ."

This is not just Socratic *chutzpah* appropriate for confrontations with sophists. In talking with the congenial Glaucon at *Republic* 610A–B, Socrates remarked, "Either, then, we must refute this and show that we are mistaken, or, so long as it remains unrefuted, we must never say that . . ." Similarly at *Sophist* 259A, the Eleatic stranger, in speaking with the tractable Theaetetus, remarks, "But as for our present definition of not-being, one must either refute us and show that we are wrong, or, so long as he cannot do that, he too must say, as we do, that . . ."[29] As late as *Laws* 899C we find Plato's Athenian stranger saying of the atheist, "Either he must teach us that we are wrong, . . . or, if he is unable to give a better account, he must be persuaded by us, and for the rest of his life live in veneration of the gods." This agrees with Plato's explicit criterion of truth and reality at *Republic* 582B, where it is urged that we are to judge what is true or real by experience, understanding, and an account. If a well-tested account stands as coherent, then we have sufficient reason to believe it is true, for it stands as its paradigm does.

Given that Plato and evidently Socrates before him proceeded as if surviving extensive tests for the incoherence of one's account was not only necessary but sufficient for ἐπιστήμη, or understanding, up until the *Laws*, and given that they thought one can understand only what is true or real, as claimed at *Republic* 477A, it is scarcely surprising that the same or similar tests for coherence, on their view, suffice for the mere truth of an account. In looking for the truth about understanding at *Theaetetus* 146A, for example, Socrates speaks of "getting through without making a mistake," as if that were enough, and the sort of mistake he was looking for was plainly the answerer's falling into incoherence.[30] Incoherence, on his view, is a sign of having hit not on what is fully stable or real, which is perfectly harmonious and coherent, but on confused and shifting things which are not very real or genuine at all owing to their having warring powers at work in them.[31] If one's account has been thoroughly tested by one who understands what accounthood is and it has measured up, then this is enough. The truth is, after all, *in* each of us on the theory of recollection, though Plato speculates at *Phaedrus* 248E–249A that it might take 3,000–10,000 years to extract it from us, even allowing time off for good behavior.

At *Gorgias* 527A, for example, Socrates says that no account is better or truer than the one he has given, since the alternatives have been refuted, and his account alone remains unshaken. That this sort of sturdiness in the face of attempts to find confusion or incoherence was the relevant dimension in which a λόγος was to measure up to its paradigm is indicated by the terms Plato employed as synonyms or near-synonyms for ἀληθής: ὑγιής, "healthy," σαφής, "certain," βέβαιον, "enduring" or "stable," and in the superlative, ἐρρωμενέστατον, "strongest."[32] Likeness to the paradigm of λόγος was not correspondence to it; it was dialectically ascertained similarity in ability to endure coherently.

Given that this similarity is a matter of degree, this renders understandable Plato's otherwise loose-sounding practice of employing degree constructions with ἀληθής, his principal term for "true."[33] When *we* speak of one claim as truer than another or characterize a remark as the truest we have heard on the subject, we are apt to treat the degree construction as appearing only at the level of surface grammar.[34] We will read "truest" as "closest to the truth," perhaps, and "truer" as "closer to the truth," preserving the conviction that, strictly speaking, either a claim is true or it isn't. For us, "true" is no more qualifiable than "unique."[35]

But similarity to a paradigm is qualifiable and literally a matter of degree. If the interpretation advanced thus far is correct, one would be sur-

Destructive testing 133

prised if Plato did not treat truth and falsity as literally a matter of degree. That he does so treat them when he speaks of nondiscursive entities has been pointed out by Gregory Vlastos.[36] That Plato also does so when he speaks of discursive entities has not received sufficient notice, perhaps owing to the natural but mistaken belief that he must be using his terms for "true" and "false" in our discursive sense, and that his degree constructions with his terms for "true" accordingly must occur only at the level of surface grammar, as our own are thought to.[37] But as we have seen, Plato did not use his terms for "true" and "false" in a discursive sense. Hence it was open to him perhaps to use his terms for "true" as if they were quite literally subject to degree, and he did so use them.

The recognition of this use helps explain a number of otherwise intractable puzzles in the dialogues, especially when one also recognizes the range of uses to which such degree constructions may legitimately be put. Thus, despite his employing exacting paradigm fanciers' standards for truth, he was able nevertheless to speak occasionally of putatively inferior physical objects *and* claims about them as "true."[38] As he was evidently aware, the positive degree of adjectives subject to degree is indefinite and quite unpositive in its force.[39] To call a person "tall" is compatible with the person's being seven feet in height or only three feet. One may mean that the person is tall for a basketball forward or tall for an eighteen-month-old. Similarly with Plato's term for "true," ἀληθής. It may express anything from a fairly low degree of dialectically ascertained or projected stability to the highest conceivable degree of it.

This in turn allows one to explain why Plato appeared to sense no awkwardness at *Gorgias* 508B–509A when he had Socrates claim emphatically that his account was true and *also* that he did not understand such matters, but was laying down an hypothesis. From our point of view, if S is very emphatic about *p*'s being *true*, then S had better be equally emphatic about *understanding* that *p* on pain of being charged with confusion. Not so for Plato. Understanding, on his view, required the very highest degree of truth or stability for what was understood, yet one could be sure that a claim was *true* in that it had demonstrated *some* dialectical staying power and had not yet been refuted even though one was not sure it could withstand really strenuous tests. Callicles, whose tests Socrates' views had passed, he explicitly likened to a touchstone, and touchstones could test gold only at a superficial level.[40] But a superficial test was still one sort of *test*, which many accounts would quickly fail.

It is understandable, then, that in looking for the truth Socrates, without necessarily having to understand piety, could be made to criticize Euthyphro at *Euthyphro* 11C for having views on piety which "wander," and Callicles at *Gorgias* 491B–C for "never saying the same thing twice on the same subject." In the *Euthyphro*, again in aspiring to the truth, Socrates expressed an ambition to have views which would sit still under relevant scrutiny, and when one of his views appeared to have done so in even a rudimentary way at *Gorgias* 507C, he did not hesitate to call it true. The true or real was βέβαιον, "enduring."

When Socrates examines accounts in the early and middle dialogues, the chief thing he seems to be looking for and hoping he will not find is the sort of shiftiness under examination which promises incoherence and hence refutability. At *Theaetetus* 202E Socrates says he will hold earlier claims hostage against the intrusion of alien ones later. At *Protagoras* 336C–D Alcibiades indicates that despite Socrates' claim that he has a poor memory, he will not forget the point at issue, which is the truth of the initial account proposed. Socrates is looking for an account which is certain and coherent, and unless he finds it, he will conclude that he has not found the truth. If he does find it, he will conclude that he has found the truth.[41] At *Phaedo* 90C, for example, he is expressly seeking an account which is true, that is, enduring.

This is likely to strike the modern reader as embodying a nest of related confusions. It seems to conflate its being true that *p* with S's having good reason to judge that *p*, just as Plato's way of treating certainty seems to conflate its being certain that *p* with S's being certain that *p*. It is irrelevant to the truth of the proposition that justice is the interest of the stronger that Thrasymachus does or does not have good reason to judge it to be true. It is still less relevant that he is or is not certain about the truth of this proposition.

But there lies the problem, or rather two problems: it is not a proposition that is in question, nor is it truth in our discursive sense. Today we are perhaps inclined to think that the meaning of an account or statement lies in the proposition or propositions it expresses, but no such account of meaning was dreamt of by Plato. We turn, then, to Plato's actual theory of meaning as it bears on the truth of the sorts of accounts which those who possessed ἐπιστήμη were allegedly able to give.

Meaning, thinking, and reality

As Jaako Hintikka has argued, neither Plato nor Aristotle had a notion of a proposition.[42] This is not to say that they had no inkling that one could say the same thing in different ways but, rather, that they had no conception of a temporally definite meaning correlate for sentences. It is worth recalling again that λόγος, Plato says at *Sophist* 263E, comes out of the mouth. But he did not conceive of it as coming out of the mouth on some occasion which could be indexed for all time as t_1. Greek timekeeping and calendar-keeping were scandalous.[43] It would not have occurred to a Greek philosopher that what you said when you said *p* on one occasion was not precisely the same as what you said when you said *p* on another occasion, even if it was true on the first occasion and false on the second. Aristotle is quite explicit about this in two works Hintikka cites, *Categories* 4a34–b2, 4a24–29, and *Metaphysics* 1051b13 ff. He is also quite plain about it at *De Anima* 428b8–9.

It should not surprise us, then, that since Plato thought ἐπιστήμη both infallible and of the truth, he thought that, strictly speaking (which is how paradigm fanciers speak), one could have ἐπιστήμη only of changeless things. Nor should it surprise us that Plato evidently thought at *Philebus* 58A ff. that the highest degree of truth was possessed only by accounts which hit upon such objects. This is why he characterized ἐπιστήμη as truer than opinion in *Republic* 6: its *objects* are truer, on his view, than the objects of opinion. This indicates also how the difficult passage at *Republic* 476C ff. develops a treatment of the objects of opinion and ἐπιστήμη which actually coheres nicely with the seemingly incompatible treatment of ἐπιστήμη and opinion at *Meno* 98A ff. The *Meno* passage characterizes the difference between ἐπιστήμη and opinion in terms of the difference between an animal one has securely tied so that it will not wander off and an animal one lets run loose, trusting it to stay about without being tied. The *Republic* passage, in effect, characterizes *tying down* an opinion and hence converting it into ἐπιστήμη in terms of tying it *to* something secure, the forms. That this was the thrust of the *Meno* passage itself should perhaps have been guessed from Plato's identifying the tying-down process with dialectical questioning and answering designed to promote clear recollection at *Meno* 85C–86B and 98A. (See also *Phaedrus* 249B.)

It is principally *people* who mean on Plato's model, just as it is people who hear and see.[44] Words by themselves have no meaning or reference.[45] As we see from *Epistle 7*, 343B, Plato evidently thought the conventions for the use of nouns and verbs, and hence for the meaning of accounts, were not fixed with sufficient firmness.[46] Thus, one would expect his Socrates to try to get at what the speaker had in mind rather than what the words by themselves might be taken to mean. One was to investigate, not according to names (κατ' ὀνόματα), but rather according to forms (κατ' εἴδη), he notes in several places, as at *Republic* 454A–E. This is why, I think, Plato depicts Socrates as asking, not for *the* account of X, but for *an* account of it. An account was a series of occasion sentences tailored to the questions of a possibly idiosyncratic questioner and the conventions obtaining at the moment. It was to satisfy *that* hopefully maieutic questioner. It was to be an image of accounthood having as its meaning the forms which it was intended to be about and to arouse thoughts of in the intended hearer.

It is not surprising, then, that *written* accounts fared so badly on Plato's view. He treated written remarks by authors who were dead or otherwise unavailable for questioning as a dog fancier would treat a stray animal having no one to vouch for its pedigree. He remarks that a written account is like an orphan who does not know which strangers to talk to and which to avoid, and so is mute and defenseless.[47]

Plato's point is not just the congenial one that philosophy is best done *viva voce*. The point is, rather, that an account in the third sense is an occasion piece—by S, to Z and about *X*. Plato cannot, question Protagoras on what he *meant*, so Plato cannot tell what Protagoras was getting at. If Plato cannot tell what Protagoras was getting at, he cannot tell whether or not Protagoras' account was true.

So he was not examining a proposition: he was examining a person, who possibly had got at something *real*. But if the person had got at something real, then his or her account of it would be a real (i.e., true) account, partaking of the stability and uniformity of the real, and thus measuring up to the paradigm of accounthood. As *Timaeus* 29B emphasizes, the truth of an account varies directly with the "truth" or genuineness of its objects. Since these objects are its meaning, the truth of an account for Plato was dependent on its meaning.

Plato's sole semantic notion was that of referring, and meaning, on his view, was reference. Referring, moreover, was not solely a semantic notion but a psychological one as well. Thought, on his view, always had a referent; it was always *about* something (περί τινος), and that something could be more or less real or stable.[48] As he indicates at *Timaeus* 29B–C, *Philebus* 59A–B, and *Republic* 519A–B, the truth of what one thought depended upon the reality or stability of what one thought *about*. Since statements or accounts were thought to be mere images of what one thought, the truth of what one said was a matter of the flightiness or the stability of what one thought *about* and thus referred to.

Both the quality of an account and the quality of the thought of which it is an image will be directly proportional to the quality—that is, the stability or reality—of the object thought about. Thinking about sensible things, Plato indicates at *Republic* 479B–C, is like entertaining the sorts of remarks bearing a double sense which jesters make at banquets: "For these things, too, equivocate, and it is impossible to conceive firmly any of them to be or not to be or both or neither." But conceiving firmly is at the very least necessary for conceiving truly on Plato's view. It is not merely necessary, however; it is sufficient, provided the conceiving or thinking in question will withstand thorough dialectical testing. The truth, he says, is never refuted, and when he comes across an account which has been well tested but not refuted, he does not hesitate to call it true.[49]

This model for thinking, peculiar as it may seem to us today, was a natural one for Plato to adopt, since something quite like it was evidently the received view from Homer's day at least to that of Empedocles. Aristotle at *De Anima* 427a19 ff. describes the earlier version of it as follows:

Thinking, both speculative and practical, is regarded as a form of perceiving; for in both cases the psyche judges and is aware of something which is [κρίνει τι ἡ ψυχὴ καὶ γνωρίζει τῶν ὄντων], and indeed the older philosophers assert that thinking and perceiving are identical [τό φρονεῖν καὶ τὸ αἰσθάνεσθαι ταυτὸν εἶναι], as, for example, Empedocles, who has said, "Wisdom grows with a man according to what is available to him," and in another passage, ". . . whence it befalls them always to think different things." Homer's phrase, again, "Such is understanding," suggests the same thing. For all these suppose that thinking is a bodily function like perceiving, and that men both perceive and recognize like by means of like, as we have explained at the beginning of this treatise [bk. I, ch. 2]. And yet they ought to have made some mention of error at the same time; for it seems to be more natural [οἰκειότερον] to living things, and the psyche spends more time in it. From their belief it must follow either that, as some say, all the things which appear to us are real [πάντα τὰ φαινόμενα εἶναι ἀληθῆ] or that error is contact with the unlike; for this is the opposite of recognizing like by like.

Plato did not, of course, hold that thinking was a bodily process, but in other respects his treatment of thinking coheres with this earlier one, and he attempts to meet precisely the problems Aristotle mentions here at 427b1–6, 15 ff.—the nature and origin of error, and the status of the objects of imagination. Plato did hold that error was, in a sense, contact with the "unlike"; he attributed it to the contact of the psyche with the body or the reasonable part of the psyche with the unstable, less reasonable parts. He explained the quality of thought as being correlated in ἀλήθεια with that of its object; hence error had its origin in the ontological slum of confused sensible objects about us.[50] Given his conception of reality as genuineness he could not agree that all the things which appear to us are real in that sense, for he held that the sensible ones are qualitatively unstable and hence epistemically undependable—not genuine or true. But he did think even ephemeral and unstable things real in the trivial sense that they exist. Thinking truly, however, was on his view thinking about what is genuine, enduring, and true. To think less than truly is to think about what is less than true. Thought takes on the quality of its object, and all thought has an object. Only the truest has an eternally enduring object.

Negation, falsity, and meaning

That Plato employed over a wide range his paradigm/copy distinction and his model of thinking as referring to an object allows one to explain (and hence is supported by) a number of otherwise stubborn puzzles about his treatment of an argument in the *Theaetetus* and *Sophist* that falsity is impossible. Interpreters have long been amazed that Plato would treat with such serious attention what strikes them as a straightforward sophism calling for no special attention whatever. This alleged sophism was best stated in the *Theaetetus*, the dramatic predecessor to the *Sophist*, where it finally evokes Plato's attempt to cope with it definitively.[51] The alleged sophism went about like this at *Theaetetus* 188E ff.:

1. If one touches, hears, or sees anything, one touches, hears, or sees something, and if something, then a thing that is.
2. So if one thinks, one thinks something, and if something, then a thing that is.
3. If one thinks what is not, one thinks nothing, since what is not is nothing.
4. If one thinks nothing, one does not think at all.
5. Hence it is impossible to think what is not.
6. But it was agreed that to think what is not is the same as to think what is false.
7. Hence it is impossible to think what is false.

Had Plato been concerned to develop a theory of truth and falsity congenial to modern readers rather than a theory of thought and meaning in the tradition discussed in the previous section, points 1–7 would have furnished two lines of attack. He could have argued, as Gregory Vlastos and Charles Kahn have, that the Greek verb for "is" is quite ambiguous—since it can mean "is true," "is genuine," or "exists"—and no less so when coupled with negation.[52] Or he could perhaps have been led into a more congenial theory had he attacked the misleading analogy in surface grammar between verbs of touching, seeing, and hearing on the one hand, and verbs of thinking, knowing, and saying on the other. To the dismay of many modern readers, he seizes neither of these handles on the problem, nor does he eschew what Dennis Stampe has called "mental ophthalmology."[53]

That he did not seize the second is understandable. He did not see the analogy between sensing X and thinking about Y as being at all misleading; in fact, he frequently employed and asserted it himself, as at *Theaetetus* 160A and *Republic* 508C ff. That he did not seize the first is equally

Negation, falsity, and meaning 139

understandable given the evidence of his deep commitment to the use of a paradigm/copy distinction in characterizing the form-particular relationship in both discursive and nondiscursive contexts. It is a tribute to Plato's enormous philosophical resourcefulness that having closed off these options he found any way of seizing on the problem at all.

Instead of taking one of these now more obvious ways of dealing with the alleged sophism, Plato offers us a new treatment of negation, seemingly the most innocent element in the problem. Formerly, he tells us at *Sophist* 258E ff., he was inclined to think that "not-*X*" signified the opposite of *X*. And indeed, there is evidence of this. At *Protagoras* 332B he had argued that if one's behavior is not temperate, then it is intemperate or foolish.

In the *Sophist*, however, he abandons this view, though not for the reasons we perhaps would. He still treats meaning as an intentional, psychic reaching out to something. He still talks as if meaningful speech could not fail to *refer* to something, so he is faced with the problem of making "what is not," which sounds like nothing, into something, a nameable thing among other nameable things, *or* acquiescing in the sophism that putatively false statements mean nothing at all, while meaningful statements are all true.[54]

To avoid this, he construes negation as signifying otherness or difference, not oppositeness.[55] "What is not" is understood as an incomplete expression, with "not" signifying difference from some understood but nevertheless genuine and real *X*. On this construal, to give an account which *is not* (i.e., to say what is false) is to give something which is *other than* or *different from* the paradigm of λόγος, or accounthood, that is, something which, in large part at least, is *not* sufficiently *like* the paradigm.

An account in the first or second sense of Chapter 2 on this view is correlated with a perceived, imagined, or remembered network of interwoven things to which it refers, just as the thought of which it is an image is a thought of such a network. As Plato claims at *Republic* 479C, it is impossible to conceive firmly of such things. In an epistemically ideal world, sentences and the thought behind them would hit on clearly recollected networks of intertwined forms as their meanings, and since this network would be fully real or true, such sentences would measure up fully to the ideal of λόγος and thus be fully real or true accounts. Many actual sentences miss the mark and evince the speaker's having hit instead on targets other than these. They refer to confused and ephemeral networks of perceived or imagined things.[56] These sentences are less than true because what they refer to is less than real and thus other than genuine. It is by hitting on what is real as its intended meaning or referent that an account acquires its own power to endure and thus measures up to the paradigm of λόγος.

Such platonic paradigms were not ontological mongrels which struck one now as this, now as that, but had on Plato's view a purity of type, a coherence and simplicity of apparent quality, which he hoped to see imparted insofar as possible not just to human accounts but to all of human life. This single quality, whether exemplified discursively or otherwise, he called ἀλήθεια—truth, genuineness, or reality.

The models to be imitated were his forms. As he indicates at *Republic* 534A and 476E–477B, they were the objects of the truest accounts and the things to which the attention of one who had ἐπιστήμη had to turn. They remained so in the late dialogues despite important developments in Plato's ontology. We turn now to these portentous developments.

6
Eleaticism, Division, and Ἐπιστήμη in the Late Dialogues

In the preceding chapter it was argued that Plato held an extraordinary view of truth and reality, one which embraced under a single conception both discursive and nondiscursive particulars. It was argued that he

1. applied the Greek terms corresponding to our "true" and "real" in ways which indicate that he meant the same by both—being genuine or true to type, the type being the form or paradigm discussed as the object of ἐπιστήμη in Chapter 4.
2. recognized that being true to or resembling such a type was a matter of degree, and hence spoke freely of degrees of truth or reality;
3. posited such a type or form of λόγος for discursive particulars or accounts to be true to, just as he had posited similar forms for nondiscursive particulars to be true to;
4. conceived of accounts as true only to the degree that they resembled their paradigm type;
5. conceived of the respect in which particular accounts were to resemble their paradigm type as being assessable in the same general way in which the resemblance of particular nondiscursive artifacts to their paradigm types was assessable, namely, by discerning whether or not they endured or survived as genuine, real, or true to type under type-relevant tests, tests keyed to what the paradigm, conceived also as a power or δύναμις, *did* or *caused*;

6. conceived of the type-relevant tests for a λόγος, or account, in such a way that the accounts which would emerge as true are at least a proper subset of the ones we would count as true, since the power of λόγος was thought to be the power to discriminate, sort, select, and order accurately, without clarity or confusion;
7. conceived of falsity or phoniness as a failure to be true to a claimed or apparent type;
8. conceived of this falsity or phoniness as being certifiable by type-relevant tests;
9. attributed both the falsity or phoniness of accounts which do not survive such tests and the truth or genuineness of accounts which do survive them to the causal influence of the objects attended to by the one giving the account; hence,
10. conceived of the objects of false accounts as existing but not "real," that is, not genuine objects of their claimed type; these "false" objects are either sensed or imagined but not apprehended by the dialectical activity of the mind;
11. further conceived of the object of an account as being its referent, and hence its meaning in the only sense of "meaning" he recognized;
12. characterized the referent of a false account as *other than* the real form claimed as its referent; and
13. conceived of a false account as meaningful in virtue of its having a referent, but false in virtue of its not isolating a pure form as genuine and hence "true" referent.

We have seen, then, that both of Plato's ways of describing the form vs. particular relationship—as a paradigm vs. copy relationship, and as a power vs. mixture relationship—figured in his account of truth and falsity, and that his ingenious account of falsity or nonbeing as "otherness" in the *Sophist* allowed him to evade the charge that all meaningful accounts are true, and thus to meet the chief difficulty involved in his embracing both discursive and nondiscursive particulars under his paradigm/copy distinction.

Of Plato's two ways of distinguishing forms from particulars, the power/mixture distinction is the more suggestive. Being the more suggestive of the two models for the relationship between forms and particulars, it was accordingly the more difficult to employ without generating confusion. It was important for Plato to employ it well, since he had much riding on the epistemic, ontological, and causal views it expressed. A person who, on the *Republic*'s account, had understood and distinguished these powers or quality-things in dialectical isolation would with some additional effort be enabled to recognize them at work even in confused particulars, and to guard against their having undue influence. *Republic* 520C shows clearly the political importance of Plato's epistemic and ontological view. A person who had apprehended the forms would stand to an ordinary statesman as one who is awake stands to one who is dreaming, and would be able to demonstrate this by giving a clear, coherent, and defensible account of such forms, as Plato indicates at *Republic* 533C–D. No ordinary statesman could give such an account. Giving such an account would be a test, and a very powerful one, for it would provide necessary and sufficient conditions for certifying the presence of understanding. One who failed would, of course, be politically defective in understanding, and hence in ἀρετή, "excellence" or "virtue." But one who passed would be politically perfect, and rightly certifiable as such.

It is plain, then, that Plato had much invested in an epistemic, dialectical, and ontological system which permitted such tests and the political risks they licensed one to take. In the remainder of this chapter it will be argued that Plato found himself unable to maintain the entire epistemic, dialectical, and ontological system involved here, and that he accordingly had to revise drastically downward the political risks he thought we could rightly take on the basis of dialectical testing. The root of his difficulty was ontological. He found a crucial difficulty in his power/mixture model as he had earlier presented it and built upon it.

Some scholars have previously argued that Plato found this power/mixture model difficult to maintain. The interpretation to be offered in this chapter differs from such arguments in its diagnosis of *when* Plato recognized this difficulty and in its diagnosis of *what* the difficulty was. We turn now to previous accounts of the difficulty and Plato's recognition of it.

Did Plato abandon the power/mixture model?

John Brentlinger has described the similarity between Plato's view of forms as mixed into sensible things as perceived ingredients and his predecessor Anaxagoras' view that "a perceptible mixture, a particular physical thing, *has a quality* through one of its portions (μοῖρα) only if the latter bears a certain relation, call it 'Q', to all other parts to which it is contrary or opposed. This relation is simply quantitative preponderance. The qualities of a particular correspond to a subset of its parts."[1]

Brentlinger rightly notes similar views in Plato's *Laches* 191E7–8, 192A1–4, *Euthyphro* 5D1–6, and *Lysis* 217D–E. But he refers to these Platonic shares or portions of a form as "immanent properties." This phrase may suggest that a μοῖρα plays a logical or conceptual role, not a causal one. Still, he comes very close to recognizing their status as traditional Greek δυνάμεις, "quality-things" or "powers," when he remarks (p. 67) that Plato "describes these properties as themselves having the property they confer upon things they are present in: that is, the presence of the immanent property, in a particular, gives the particular the quality in the way in which salt gives its quality to soup or coloring to cake." He continues: "In two basic respects, then, Plato's earlier view seems in agreement with the Anaxagorean concept of property. A color quality such as white is related to perceptible things as part to whole. And the quality is a kind of stuff constituting a source by the presence of which perceptible things take on the quality, as a pigment, or ingredient in cooking, gives its quality to a mixture."

Brentlinger takes the *Phaedo* to reject the view that quantitative preponderance of an immanent part over others accounts for the perceived quality of a particular, and he interprets the *Phaedo*'s talk of forms as "separate" from particulars to indicate that Plato no longer claims the old relation, "Q," to hold, that a new relation of imitation holds instead. The *Phaedo* is a middle dialogue, and not one of the late ones with which we are primarily concerned in this chapter, but since the change of view Brentlinger claims Plato is making in the *Phaedo* resembles closely the change other scholars claim Plato makes in later dialogues, it will be useful to examine Brentlinger's arguments in more detail here. He remarks (p. 69):

Plato's conception of immanent properties is completely divorced from the Parmenidean influence which led Anaxagoras to hold them to be eternal, since his view is that they may come-to-be and pass-away (102d–e). Thus the need for the relation Q is dispensed with in Plato's theory: a one-one correspondence can obtain between qualities which are "true" of a particular and its immanent properties. Further, the immanent properties need not be considered parts of the particular they are present in. For change of quality is not to be explained by Plato as exchange of separable parts.

Is it true that *Phaedo* 102D–E suggests that Plato's view is now that "immanent properties" come to be and pass away? Consider Tredennick's admirably clear translation:

I am saying all this because I want you to share my point of view. It seems to me not only that the form of tallness itself absolutely declines to be short as well as tall, but also that the tallness which is in us never admits smallness and declines to be surpassed. It does one of two things. Either it gives way and withdraws as its opposite shortness approaches, or it has already ceased to exist by the time that the other arrives. It cannot stand its ground and receive the quality of shortness in the same way as I myself have done. If it did, it would become different from what it was before, whereas I have not lost my identity by acquiring the quality of shortness—I am the same man, only short—but my tallness could not endure to be short instead of tall. In the same way the shortness that is in us declines ever to become or be tall, nor will any other quality, while still remaining what it was, at the same time become or be the opposite quality; in such a situation it either withdraws or ceases to exist.[2]

The final sentence here is crucial: 'Ἀλλ' ἤτοι ἀπέρχεται ἢ ἀπόλλυται ἐν τούτῳ τῷ παθήματι. This line (102E10–103A1), like a preceding one (102D10–E1) and a following one (104C1–2) affirms that one of two things happens to an opposite in us when its opposite approaches, and the occurrence of either of these two would prevent the opposite in us from having to accept that approaching opposite as true of it. Brentlinger overlooks Plato's having included as one of these two alternatives the very one required by *continued* adherence to the Anaxagorean view which he claims Plato is here rejecting. And not having noted that Plato describes this alternative, he also overlooks Plato's not having said which of the two alternatives he describes actually obtains. Hence, for all that *Phaedo* 102–103 shows us, Plato may well continue his adherence to the Anaxagorean model. Indeed, since the very point of the larger passage, 102–107, is to set the stage for the view that since the psyche carries with it life, which is the opposite of death, the psyche upon the approach of death *must* "go away," it is quite implausible to construe this introductory part of the passage as undermining the point by positing the destruction of what Plato concludes at 107A is immortal and indestructible.

Perhaps Brentlinger sees Plato as having abandoned the Anaxagorean mixture model for a paradigm/copy model because there was what strikes us perhaps as *reason* to abandon it, reason provided by what some scholars have come to call "incomplete predicates."[3] Plato is sometimes thought to have called attention to such predicates at *Republic* 524C.[4] Brentlinger remarks (pp. 70–71):

Plato is focussing attention upon "incomplete" predicates. Though often used in ordinary discourse by themselves, other information must be supplied from the context or background assumptions of the discourse. Hearing "O'Brien is huge" we understand the assertion to be that O'Brien is a huge man. Similarly for sentences using the other predicates Plato mentions: "the cat is heavy," "the bed is hard," "the milk is thick." Similarly for "one": "Mary is one" is scarcely meaningful unless context supplies an addition such as "thing" or "girl who can do the job." And similarly for all of the predicates that are mentioned in the *Phaedo* as connoting forms: "just," "good," "pious," "beautiful," the cardinal numbers, and "large." Each requires a completing substantive or general term, expressed or understood, or statements in which they occur will be ambiguous. An apparent, though only apparent, exception is "equal."

Plainly, a problem of ambiguity is not the same as a problem of being "scarcely meaningful"; it is more nearly a problem of having entirely too many possible meanings. But we shall pass over this difficulty in understanding Brentlinger's charge. The actual focus of his objection is that he sees "incomplete" predicates as unaccountable on what he takes to be Plato's theory of predication as presented in the *Meno*. He remarks (p. 71): "According to the theory of predication in the *Meno*, predicates which stand for πρός τι ["in relation to something"] properties must be interpreted as logically simple, 'complete' predicates. 'Good' has the same meaning in 'good man,' 'good action,' 'good pruning hook'; 'large' means the same in 'large man' and 'large cat.'"

Having construed as a theory of predication Plato's claim at *Meno* 74A9 and 75A4–8 that if a group of things is called by the same name, there is an entity present in every member of the group (p. 68), Brentlinger remarks that this theory of predication is totally and obviously inadequate to handle incomplete predicates.[5] He charges (p. 72) that Plato "cannot construe properties as immanent parts of the wholes which have them, as the properties corresponding to incomplete predicates are logically related to the other properties. The largeness in a cat is logically connected with its being a cat, and this connection is unrecognized by the theory that the two properties are merely conjoined in the same animal." Brentlinger further claims (p. 73) that Plato saw the inappropriateness of his earlier conception of predicates, and that his having done so motivates him to separate forms from particulars in the *Phaedo*:

The largeness of a thing cannot be a part of it, nor can its Beauty or Goodness, Equality or Oneness. These qualities are present or absent relative either to the thing as a whole or another thing. They are logically dependent upon the sort of thing they are in or its relations. Incomplete predicates, therefore, are related to the separation of the forms in this way: they require a different conception of the relation between a thing and its qualities than whole to part.

It has been argued before that in his mature dialogues Plato found it difficult to maintain intact all that he had said earlier in distinguishing forms from particulars, though scholars have differed in where they saw this alleged maturity emerging and in the particular views they regarded Plato as having difficulty in maintaining. G.E.L. Owen argued that in the late dialogues Plato abandoned paradigm/copy talk. And Gerold Prauss has argued that Plato overthrew his earlier power/mixture talk in favor of a subject/predicate model dependent not, as in Aristotle, upon an antecedently apprehended substance-attribute structure in particulars, but dependent, more nearly as in Kant, upon the coupling of subject and predicate in a judgment about what is still apprehended as a mixture.[6]

Owen's view, however, has been convincingly rebutted by H. F. Cherniss, most especially in its use of stylometric evidence.[7] And against

Prauss's view, it will be shown in the next section that in late dialogues Plato continued to hold the view that sensible particulars are compounds or mixtures of δυνάμεις, not overthrowing this view even at the level of the judgments we present in λόγοι, or accounts. This section will thus serve also as an argument against Brentlinger's claim that Plato abandoned the mixture model in favor of a paradigm/copy model in the *Phaedo*, for it will show that Plato continued to employ the mixture model in much later dialogues, such as the *Philebus*.

There are, however, more specific and direct points which need to be made in regard to Brentlinger's argument, for his argument evinces difficulties we typically encounter if we take Plato to be pursuing a confused combination of philosophical logic on the Anglo-American model and causally interesting metaphysics on the pre-Socratic model. Against the sort of view Brentlinger presents, it must be noted that

(A) Neither the *Meno*, the *Phaedo*, nor the *Republic* suggests that Plato is interested in presenting a theory of predication, if by that one means either a grammatical theory of sentence parts or an epistemological theory of the difference between identifying a subject and characterizing what one has identified. His acceptance of the pre-Socratic mixture model prevented his developing a notion of a stable subject, for what we take to be a subject on that view is a melange of portions of δυνάμεις, or powers. This melange might be thought to be simply a collection of subjectless predicates. But as was argued in Chapter 4, without the notion of a subject having ontological status coordinate with its predicates—a notion first exploited philosophically by Aristotle—there is no use in speaking of predicates or in characterizing a discussion of δύναμις as a theory of predication.[8] Hence any difficulties one poses for Plato's views by construing them as if they were intended as a theory of predication are gratuitous.

Moreover,

(B) On Plato's view of meaning as characterized in previous chapters, words such as "just" and "good" do not *connote* forms as Brentlinger suggests (p. 70). Rather, they *denote* forms. Denotation is the only notion of meaning Plato has.

Brentlinger himself appears to have been aware of but undeterred by A, for he concedes (p. 71): "Indeed it should be understood that Plato does not himself speak of predicates at all in this connection; he speaks of *things* which have their character πρός τι ("in relation to something": see

Republic 437b ff.). Things which are good, heavy, hard and things which are double, half, or equal, alike have their character πρός τι."

Since Plato is describing not predicates but things, to raise against his view any objection which construes him as having described predicates or conditions for their use is beside the point. Brentlinger takes Plato to be discussing the "logically necessary conditions" for being this or that, not the causal powers at work in a thing which make it this or that, and in so doing he uses "logically necessary condition" much as Norman Malcolm uses "criterion" in his discussion of dreaming.[9] Such logically necessary conditions may well have to do with what a term such as "equal" or "just" connotes. But they may also be irrelevant to the interpretation and to the critical assessment of Plato's account of what the term denotes. Plato was interested in denotation, in actual characterization of the referent of a term, as he shows in many places—for example, at *Republic* 505C–506A. In his account of the psyche, for example, as we argued in Chapter 3, he is describing relations among what he takes to be actual psychological agents at work in us, not logically necessary conditions which illuminate an ordinary concept we already have and can use in philosophically impeccable ways. It is true that Plato's characterization of the referent of a term such as "just" makes sense only against a background or in a context, but this is no objection to his view, since it is equally true of anyone's characterization of anything whatever, and holds no more of Plato's account of equality than it does of his account of clay at *Theaetetus* 147C.

Yet Plato did see a difficulty in his previous way of contrasting forms with particulars. He apparently did not see it in the *Phaedo*, nor does it surface for many years after he had written that dialogue. But this difficulty is in part responsible for the ease with which critics of Plato, from Aristotle to our own contemporaries, have been able to see Plato as having mixed philosophical logic with metaphysics in ways which generated quite impossible conclusions. Our problem now is to describe that difficulty and to test our description of it against the consequences one would predict that its recognition would have for Plato. It will be argued below that the difficulty was, in fact, an ambiguity in Plato's previous talk of the purity, simplicity, or "absoluteness" of the forms.[10] It will be argued further that Plato recognized this difficulty, and that once having corrected it, he made precisely the dialectical and political changes in his views which were required as consequences of the correction.

This ambiguity was between (*a*) the purity of forms narrowly conceived as their not being mixed with their opposite forms in such a way that opposite modifies opposite rather than each modifying or contributing to the "look" of the particular mixture in which they are both found, and (*b*) the purity of forms conceived in an extreme Eleatic way as their not being

Sensible things as compounds 149

mixed with any other forms whatever, not even in the ways required for a form to have any quality other than that suggested by its name. Plato's correcting this difficulty proved to be portentous for his political system, for that system was founded upon what he thought dialectical testing could certify epistemically, and that, in turn, was founded upon his view of the ontological structure of what he thought accounts described, the forms. It will be argued, then, that Plato recommended the political system of the *Laws* as a way of cutting his political coat to fit his shrunken epistemic cloth, a cloth which shrank, as it were, to fit what dialectic could certify on the basis of an ontology rid of confusions over what the purity of forms consisted in.

Our first step in this argument will be to examine Plato's talk of compounding and of purity in the later dialogues.

Sensible things as compounds of εἴδη or δυνάμεις in the late dialogues

In the *Philebus* at 23C Plato sets out to characterize πάντα τὰ νῦν ὄντα ἐν τῷ παντί, or "all that now is in the universe." He offers a sweeping characterization of his late ontology under four headings, each termed an εἶδος, or form: πέρας, or limit; ἄπειρον, or lack of limit; τὰ μεικτά, or the mixtures of limit and lack of limit; and the cause of such mixtures, νοῦς.

On some interpretations of the middle Platonic εἴδη, as literally separate from physical things and located in another world, this late ontology seems to have little to do with the εἴδη.[11] But in Chapter 4 it was argued that such interpretations of middle-period εἴδη are mistaken, and that the early and middle εἴδη are the familiar Greek δυνάμεις, which may be sensed as constituents compounded into particular things and yet grasped better in isolation by the mind. This conception of εἶδος is maintained in late dialogues, as the *Philebus* will show.

Each of the four εἴδη in Plato's four-part ontology is a δύναμις; each is described either in terms of what it is able to do (δύνασθαι) or in terms of what it does or accomplishes (ὃ ἀπεργάζεται).[12] Mind, or νοῦς, is the cause of mixtures, Plato suggests at *Philebus* 26E–27B, 28C, and 29D8–10. These mixtures or compounds are formed from the πέρατα, or limiting forms, and the ἄπειρα, or unlimited ones (27B9–12). The πέρατα at 25D–26C are assigned the role of conveying symmetry, harmony, and order to a mixture. The ἄπειρα—such as more or less, emphatic or gentle, etc.—lack precision and definiteness until bound by the πέρατα. By themselves they convey disorder and imprecision, Plato suggests at 24B–D.

Scholars have disagreed about what Plato intended by the μεικτά, some thinking that they are perhaps forms, others thinking they are particulars. It is evident that Plato now regards both forms and particulars as having a complex nature, and hence, that he may intend us to think of both as μεικτά. A particular may gain in complexity owing to the complexity of a form in which it participates. Even as early as *Phaedo* 103–105, it was obvious that a particular campfire must be hot because it participates in fire, which is always hot. If a form such as fire is thought to have a complex nature in that it always carries with it (has mixed in it) another form, then it would be natural for Plato to describe fire itself as one of the μεικτά. Later in the chapter we shall consider the complexity of forms.

Here, however, our concern is with sensible particulars as compounds in the *Philebus*. Plato wished to characterize such particulars as μεικτά, or mixtures, even here. He argues that νοῦς, or mind, in which we participate, causes mixing; and at 26E, he further specifies at least some such mixtures as γιγνόμενα, "things which become" or "things which happen." As 59C indicates, intelligible forms do not "happen" or "become" on his view; hence, it is evident that some of the μεικτά he is describing are sensible things and happenings, and that he has not abandoned his former view of such things as compounded of forms.

This is evident also from 25A–E, where Plato reminds us of the medical origins of this theory by remarking that combining opposites properly *produces* health. If the form of health is stable and enduring, it is not produced. And *Philebus* 59A–C indicates that forms are thus stable and enduring. Hence, it is evident that Plato is speaking of health as it is produced in people. Plainly, he is still employing the old medical κρᾶσις model for particulars. He has made that model overtly more sophisticated by specifying some constituents in a compound as tending towards precision or limit and others as tending towards the lack of these, but the basic model is unaltered. It involves conceiving of an εἶδος or δύναμις as parcelled out into particular sensible things, each of which has a μοῖρα or portion of it and is modified by that form or power without having the power to modify it in turn. This is illustrated at 29B–C, where he contrasts the elements in us (fire, e.g.) with the elements ἐν τῷ παντί, "in the universe," calling our portions relatively small and weak, and noting that they can draw nourishment from greater and stronger portions elsewhere. The resemblance to Anaxagoras' version of the old medical model is especially evident in the talk of cosmic elements' "nourishing" ours at 29E and in the relation between cosmic νοῦς and the νοῦς in us at 30D.[13]

The above interpretation of the *Philebus* differs sharply from one developed by Gisela Striker.[14] Striker, deeply influenced by interpreters in the English tradition, takes Plato's talk of forms in the *Philebus* to be talk of both concepts (*Begriffe*), and classes, though she admits (pp. 37, 40, and 51) that Plato has no expression for *Begriff*. She interprets Plato's use of language suggestive of the power/mixture model (at *Philebus* 24A9 and 24D1, e.g.) as metaphorical, and appears to construe his talk of putting one form in the class of another or collecting forms or impressing upon several a single φύσις, or nature (25A, D) as a literal description of conceptual operations.

Striker's interpretation raises large questions of interpretative methodology. How are we to decide which of two seemingly incompatible Platonic descriptions of the same sort of phenomenon is "metaphorical"? The issue at stake here is what Plato's view of meaning was—whether he was concerned with the analysis of concepts or with an account of what he conceived to be real, extralinguistic entities. We have already argued that his concern was with the latter, and Striker's own admission that Plato does not have an expression for *Begriff* only strengthens the argument: Philosophers develop or invent words to express what they intend to get across, and Plato is no stranger to this process, having evidently coined συνοπτικός as well as other terms. It seems much more likely that if we have to take either his talk of forms' mixing and dwelling with one another or his talk of collecting them or impressing them with a single nature as metaphorical, we had best choose the latter. His talk of mental operations with forms, as if they were so many intellectual counters, is a figurative way of expressing the recognition of antecedently existing, extraconceptual relations among forms. And on this interpretation, by contrast with Striker's, the *Philebus* may be viewed as an orderly but quite significant development of the power/mixture model we have seen Plato adopt from his predecessors and improve in its power, range, and plausibility, a model essential to his philosophy's having the practical, causal importance he had always claimed for it and continued to claim for it in the *Philebus*.[15]

The *Philebus*, however, is not the only dialogue interpreted by some scholars as indicating that Plato abandoned his earlier power/mixture model. If, as most scholars believe, the *Philebus* is a later dialogue than the *Sophist*, then nothing Plato said in the *Sophist* undermined his adherence to the view that sensible particulars are compounds or mixtures of δυνάμεις or εἴδη. Yet it is sometimes alleged that in the *Sophist* Plato gave up his mixture model of particular things as compounds of δυνάμεις or εἴδη. What basis is there for this allegation?

Plato does in fact complain at *Sophist* 242C ff. about all those who had ever undertaken a critical account of the number and nature of realities, and his complaint is phrased in terms which might suggest that the ancient mixture model itself is under attack. but on closer inspection one finds that his complaint is rather that (*a*) these writers treat us like children when they speak of realities as warring or friendly, becoming friends and having children, and the like (242C–E), and (*b*) they do not take sufficient care to render their views understandable (243A–B). *He explicitly draws short of saying that their views are false* (243A). He complains, rather, that they are badly expressed. Indeed, it will be seen that he maintains the old mixture-model in the *Sophist*.

Plato does not, however, leave the mixture model unimproved, for he claims that in such a mixture certain forms have rather different roles. The claim is reinforced at *Statesman* 309A–B, where these roles are likened to those of warp and woof in a fabric designed and woven to be both soft and strong. Portions of opposing forms mixed into a particular can be got to work together, on this view. This talk of mixture need not seem ad hoc even when expressed in English, since one of the meanings of "mixture" is "a fabric woven of variously colored threads."

It has been thought that the recognition of the different roles played by different forms in a mixture constituted a major revision in Plato's views, and that it is *dependent* upon his having recognized explicitly for the first time in the *Sophist* that a sentence has a subject-predicate structure. It has been thought to be dependent upon this insight on the ground that Plato describes a sentence as being formed of nouns and verbs *interwoven*, and also describes εἴδη, or forms, as being interwoven. This has suggested to some that Plato here abandoned his earlier view of the structure of sensible things as we judge them in favor of a view modeling their structure as we judge it on the structure of a sentence. It has even been suggested by Prauss that just as a sentence is a human production having no reality in the nonhuman productions we apprehend, so is the interweaving of εἴδη, or forms, underlying that sentence.[16]

On closer inspection, however, it is evident that Plato's insight into the subject-predicate structure of sentences has no such ontological importance. Far from modeling the sensible world or even the sensible world as we judge it on the structure of the subject-predicate sentence, Plato seems to regard this newly recognized subject-predicate structure itself as needing a model in terms of something more familiar and more easily grasped. This is natural, for successful models must always be more familiar and more readily grasped than that which they are employed to illuminate.

Plato finds such a familiar model for the subject-predicate structure of sentences in the interweaving of warp and woof in a fabric. He employs this same model to explicate the relationship between forms in sensible particulars. On his view then, the sensible world is more nearly cloak-textured than *logos*-textured.[17] Indeed, λόγοι *themselves* are cloak-textured.

Sensible things as compounds 153

Plato's use of the seemingly novel language of συμπλοκή, or interweaving, to suggest both that nouns have different roles than verbs, and that some forms bind together or "limit" things while others need binding and unifying, should not be taken to suggest that as he conceives of it this insight is incompatible with or even different from what he had intended to convey by his earlier language of compounding, mixing, or harmonizing disparate εἴδη in particulars. He employs the language of interweaving not as a *replacement* for compounding-language but, rather, as a structurally more precise *variant* of it. In the *Sophist* itself the older language of compounding or mixing is used far more frequently than the new language of weaving, and it is used, moreover, in passages both preceding and following passages employing weaving language.

At *Sophist* 252E, for instance, he accepts the premise that necessarily either (*a*) all things mix with one another (συμμίγνυσθαι), (*b*) none do, or (*c*) some do and some do not. He explicitly accepts *c* as the correct alternative at 252E7–8, and at 253B10–C4 he speaks of a mixture of forms and of a harmonizing or fitting of some of these with one another. As we have seen in previous chapters, the language of harmonizing or fitting is often employed by Plato in early and middle dialogues, and we now see it maintained in a late one to describe precisely what it has been used to describe earlier at *Republic* 443C–444A—the relation between forms in an individual compounded of those forms. At *Sophist* 253B–D he characterized the philosopher's ἐπιστήμη as an understanding of which forms mix, fit, or harmonize with one another and which do not, of which bind things together into wholes and of which cannot be so bound. He pursues the old compounding or mixing model at 254B–D. He speaks variously in the *Sophist* of such mixtures as one form's permeating another (255E), as one form's sharing in another (256A) and as a small portion of a form being distributed into each thing (258D–E). This last expression should not perplex us: being νοητά, or intelligible, forms are not *confined* to places as αἰσθητά, or sensibles, are, though they are *present in* sensibles. And they are present in them as strands woven into a fabric are present in that fabric.

Significantly, even the first comment on the interwovenness of εἴδη with one another at *Sophist* 259E is immediately rephrased in the old language of mixtures at 260A3.[18] And the old language of σύνθεσις, or putting together, occurs again at 263D.[19] The language of interwovenness is not an especially effective vehicle for suggesting a subject-predicate structure or even a structure like a subject-predicate structure. In fact, it was used in characterizing the establishment of any sort of strong and not disorderly bond between essentially disparate elements. This, and not a *logos*-texture, is what it is employed to express. It is so employed in the sequel to the *Sophist*, the *Statesman*, at 309B, where Plato speaks of diverse elements in human nature as being *woven together* by the statesman. At *Timaeus* 80C he uses the language of interweaving to characterize the bondedness and texture of a world without void. That the language of interweaving can be used of the existence or the establishment of such bonds by no means gives it a paramount role in Plato's thought, however, for in this same passage he speaks of these natures as capable of *mixture with* one another (σύμμιξιν πρὸς ἄλληλας). "Weaving" and "interwovenness," then, are not intended to convey any point which could not be intended or conveyed by one using the language of mixture or compounding, for Plato uses them as if they had the same meaning for him, and uses only mixture language in the still later dialogue *Philebus*.

Not only is mixture language maintained in the late dialogues, in which Plato allegedly switched to a new view of reality as "*logos*-textured," but language suggestive of the allegedly new interwovenness model occurs in Pindar's *Olympian Ode* 1. 28, well before even the putatively early or middle Platonic dialogue *Cratylus*, in which it also occurs. At *Cratylus* 388C Plato characterizes a name as an instrument for teaching and for separating reality, as a shuttle is an instrument for separating the web in a fabric. Even here, then, one sees reality conceived as a fabric comprised of warp and woof, of disparate strands having perhaps disparate functions, though not all the consequences of this conception are drawn out. Yet Plato was not ignorant of these consequences in dialogues of the middle period, for he recognized the disparate roles of different δυνάμεις or εἴδη in particulars in the *Republic*'s description of what is needed in a competent guardian of the state. At 410D–411E he speaks of the difficulty of combining the gentle and spirited natures into one person, and at times employs metallurgical language standardly used to describe the alloying of disparate metals. Plainly then, he had long been aware that in a compound thing, some forms contribute strength and coherence while others contribute different characteristics. This is merely reaffirmed, more vividly perhaps, in the *Statesman* at 305E ff., and expressed in a more general way in the *Philebus*' talk of πέρας and ἄπειρον in mixtures.

Neither the language of weaving nor the language of subjects and predicates which it is intended to illuminate are necessary, then, in understanding how Plato in the late dialogues conceives of the relationships between εἴδη or δυνάμεις in particulars. And when Plato sets out to describe the relationships between εἴδη and δυνάμεις as they are apprehended dialectically and epistemically by the philosopher, not as they are apprehended by the senses, he usually employs neither sort of language, but speaks rather in terms of a whole cut or divided at its joints. (See, e.g., *Sophist*

253B–D; *Phaedrus* 265E; *Statesman* 287C). If we are to understand Plato's conception of the structure of what he says a philosopher must understand, we must consider his method of division in detail. But in order to understand this, we must first consider the extreme Eleatic challenge which seems to have elicited it by suggesting that forms are not complex at all, but are entirely simple and indivisible. We turn, then, to that challenge.

The challenge of extreme Eleaticism

In order to emphasize the distinctness of intelligible forms and particulars compounded of forms, Plato had long insisted that the *intelligible* form, the form apprehended dialectically, is μονοειδές, "singular in form," while a sensible particular is πολυειδές, "multiple in form." The exact force of this contrast had not been made unambiguous, however, and seems to have varied in potentially incoherent ways.

At *Phaedo* 78D, for example, the singularity in form which Plato seems to be attributing to forms and denying of sensible things is *constancy* of quality over time. A form such as beauty is not at one time beautiful and at another not beautiful. It is always "such as it is"; it always has the quality its name suggests, while beautiful bodies and the like may well lose that quality. The same point seems to be intended at *Phaedo* 80B, *Symposium* 211A, and *Hippias Major* 291D.

A related but distinct point is suggested by *Parmenides* 129C, where Socrates views it as not at all marvelous if a particular such as himself participates in opposites such as one and many, but views it as beyond belief that the forms considered by themselves do so. Socrates may be "many" because he has many parts, but unity is not many, and the forms of rest and motion considered by themselves cannot be mixed together and separated. Here, he seems to be suggesting that sensible particulars are compounded of opposites, while forms are not so compounded. If they had been compounded of opposites, they could not be abiding and constant in quality, for what has been put together by compounding out of opposites can be taken apart.

He may have been attempting to make the same point at *Symposium* 211E, but does so in a potentially misleading way. In speaking of the form of the beautiful he calls it μονοειδές in a context in which his illustration perhaps suggests too much. He suggests not merely that this form is pure or simple in that it is not blended with its opposite, but also that it is "not infected with the flesh and colour of humanity, and ever so much more of mortal trash."[20] Plato may have regarded "the flesh and colour of humanity" and the like as itself suggesting the opposite of beauty, but he does not say that he does so here, and hence might be taken to mean not merely that beauty itself is free from its opposite but that beauty itself is free from communion with all other forms as well, even forms which neither are nor carry the opposite of beauty.

To take Plato to have meant this would be to take him as an adherent of extreme Eleaticism, which involved preoccupation with the one-many contrast—with the view that simplicity amounts to singularity of quality, a singularity incompatible with the complexity of permanent and invariant qualities which even a form must have. Fire, for example, must not only be fiery, but hot, and it must have being as well. Justice must be just, virtuous, and enduring. Extreme Eleaticism would make this impossible. No form could have as a permanent feature more than the one quality suggested by its name. Thus, no form save Being itself could *be*. Could Plato have worked himself into such a position?

In the *Symposium* passage mentioned above, 211E, Plato does not go so far as to say that a form is not associated with *any* other forms, but the features with which he says beauty itself is *not* associated seem miscellaneous enough and perhaps remote enough from being individually or collectively the opposite of beauty that an extreme Eleatic interpretation of his meaning is not ruled out. Indeed, the extreme Eleatic position has been attributed to the early and middle Plato by Gerold Prauss.[21] On this view, if a form is a unity (and every form is), it can have no complexity whatever, and its character is exhausted by its name. Heat is hot, period. The form can be named and recollected, but it can never be described. Can Plato ever have held such a view?

It is difficult to see how he could. His holding such a view would render utterly baffling his entire early and middle dialectical enterprise of trying to elicit λόγοι, or accounts, of forms. Worse, it would blatantly contradict one explicit presupposition of that dialectical enterprise: that forms do have association, communion, or relation with one another. As Hamlyn rightly emphasized, Plato flatly tells us at *Republic* 476A that forms have κοινωνία, or community, with actions, with bodies, *and with one another*.[22] Since forms do not change, any community they have with one another must be permanent. As Ross saw, this community of forms is also presupposed by *Phaedo* 103–105, where Plato recognizes that one form may *always* carry with it another, as threeness carries with it oddness or fire, heat.[23] Moreover, Plato could scarcely have held, as he did at *Protagoras* 331B, that justice is holy and holiness is just if forms have no community with one another. Still worse, at *Phaedo* 105B–C Plato had explicitly rejected as "safe but stupid" the line of thinking demanded by a causal projection of extreme Eleaticism—that a thing is hot by reason of heat only. He holds, rather, that it can be hot by reason of sharing in fire, which

The significance of Theaetetus *200 ff.* 157

in turn has permanent community with heat, much as a person can be just by participating in holiness, which in turn has permanent community with justice. If a form F1 has permanent community with a second form F2, then F1 will carry with it F2 in all particulars participating in F1.

It is clear, then, that Plato could never have consistently embraced such an extreme Eleaticism, though his exaggerated language of singularity, purity, simplicity, and the like strongly suggest that he did embrace it inconsistently for a time. But if he could not consistently embrace it, who could? It cannot be said with certainty who the proponents of such extreme Eleaticism were in Plato's day, but it is believed that Antisthenes was prominent among them. Aristotle at *Metaphysics* 1024b33 attributes to Antisthenes the view that it is impossible to describe anything save by its own proper λόγος, one term for one thing (ἕν ἐφ ἑνός). Thus, about the one it would be possible to say merely that it was one. At *Parmenides* 141E, Plato caricatures such a view by showing that on its premises it would not even be possible to say that the one *is* or even that the one is one. And he again refers to it scornfully in the *Sophist* at 251B as the view of "youths and oldsters whose learning has come to them late"; they are said to hold that one must not call man good, but must call the good good and man man.[24]

As is evident from the *Parmenides* at 142A, Plato is aware that extreme Eleaticism in its emptying a form of all not suggested directly by its name was quite incompatible with his view of forms as the most appropriate objects for understanding, for he depicts Parmenides as admitting that on the Eleatic argument the one would have neither a name nor an account, and that no one could have understanding, perception, or even opinion of it. But it was one thing for Plato to be *aware* of the dire epistemic consequences of extreme Eleaticism and quite another to show precisely how these consequences might be avoided by a theory which nevertheless managed to characterize forms as differing from sensible compounds in "purity." He turns to the challenge such an extreme Eleaticism presents to his own view in the *Theaetetus* and *Sophist*.

The ontological, dialectical, and epistemic significance of *Theaetetus* 200 ff.

The issue of avoiding an extreme Eleatic interpretation of the claim that forms are in some sense "simple" or "pure" comes to a head in the *Theaetetus* when Plato reflects on his former use of the ability to spell words and to recognize the same letters in many different words as a model for ἐπιστήμη and on his suggestion that forms are like those letters appearing in many such words. The passage in which he had done this most clearly was at *Republic* 401E–402C, where he argues that the guardians must be able to recognize such forms as moderation, courage, liberality, and their opposites in all their combinations wherever they appear.[25] He had argued that when λόγος comes to a person who has been properly nurtured, the person is like one who has learned his letters and can recognize and distinguish them in words both small and large. He even suggests that we have not really learned our letters until we can do this, which by analogy suggests that we have not come to understand forms until we can spell them out in combinations wherever they appear.

As Plato came to recognize in the *Theaetetus*, this is potentially a very misleading and counterproductive analogy. It suggests that Plato holds a quasi-Eleatic ontology of logically simple forms to which he could not consistently have committed himself, and it has consequences disastrous for his epistemological views as well. Nowhere in the middle dialogues does he give evidence that he had then thought through the unfortunate implications of this spelling analogy. We turn, then, to the arguments at the end of the *Theaetetus*, in which he finally recognized and diagnosed both the damaging ontological connotations of this spelling analogy and its even more damaging epistemic implications.

At *Theaetetus* 200 ff. Socrates and Theaetetus are doggedly pursuing that account of ἐπιστήμη which will make them contradict themselves least. They want the truest account (τὸν ἀληθέστατον λόγον, 200D, 208B). Presumably, this would be that account which would permit them to contradict themselves not at all. And their previous attempts had fallen lamentably short of this goal, so in context they are making a final effort to achieve it.

Theaetetus remembers someone's having given an account according to which ἐπιστήμη, or understanding, is μετὰ λόγου ἀληθὴς δόξα, "true opinion with an account." The one giving it also held that τὴν δὲ ἄλογον ἐκτὸς ἐπιστήμης, or "whatever is unaccountable is beyond understanding" (201C–D). The second point is immediately reiterated: καὶ ὧν μὲν μή ἐστι λόγος, οὐκ ἐπιστητὰ εἶναι, "and things of which there is no account are not understandable" (201D). The first is also repeated: ἃ δ' ἔχει [λόγον understood] ἐπιστητά, that is, "and those having an account are understandable."

This account as Theaetetus gives it purports to do three things: (1) it purports to tell us what ἐπιστήμη *is*; (2) it purports to tell us what sorts of things are ἐπιστητά, or understandable; and (3) it purports to tell us what sort of things are *not* ἐπιστητά, or understandable. Moreover, the account seems to articulate precisely what, from a dialectical point of view at least, one might take Plato's own account of ἐπιστήμη to be on the basis of the *Meno* and *Republic*. Hence Theaetetus' three tasks are of great interest for understanding Plato's own assessment of his early and middle epistemological views.

The operant notion in all three tasks undertaken by Theaetetus' account is that of a λόγος, or account. It is in terms of the ability to give an account that ἐπιστήμη itself is conceived, and in terms of admitting or not admitting an account that things are conceived to be objects of ἐπιστήμη or not. Hence, it is natural for Socrates to press for an explanation of the alleged way of distinguishing what *admits of* an account from what does not, as he proceeds to do.

Theaetetus is unable to remember any more, however, when Socrates asks him to tell how his source distinguished between the things which are ἐπιστητά and those which are not. He has just dimly remembered the account itself, although he says he is sure that he could follow it if someone else were to develop it.

This rather coy invitation to Socrates and the tone of the entire passage here, together with the failure to specify the name or school of the source, should itself suggest that the Platonic Socrates is the source of the view Theaetetus has remembered; and this is borne out by Socrates' response. He says, Ἄκουε δὴ ὄναρ ἀντὶ ὀνείρατος. That is, he tells Theaetetus to listen then to a dream which bears *some* relation to another dream. The precise relation intended by ἀντί has been controversial. Hicken has suggested that ἀντί here means "in place of," while Prauss, who takes it to mean something like "against," interprets it as having connotations which contradict those of the dream at *Cratylus* 439C–D.[26] Hicken is, I believe, right about the meaning of ἀντί here, while Prauss is right in looking to the *Cratylus*' dream as Plato's intended referent. That dream was the Platonic Socrates' own.

But the epistemic status of dreams in Plato is no easy matter to determine.[27] As early as *Apology* 21B–C Socrates is depicted as thinking that their meaning (if not exactly their truth) needed careful investigation, and this is borne out at *Phaedo* 60E. At *Republic* 572A–B Plato makes the truth or falsity of what is conveyed in dreams dependent upon the quality of a person's waking life. Since we all dream but few of us live high-quality lives on Plato's view, this suggests that dreams are to be regarded with great caution because they may well convey falsehoods. At *Republic* 383A he objects to the Homeric passage at *Iliad* 1. 34 in which Zeus is said to have deliberately misled Agamemnon by sending him a certain dream. But he does so, not on the ground that the content of dreams is true, but rather on the ground that poets should not be allowed to portray the gods as misleading people. That people are misled, and misled by what they dream, is never denied.

Plato's theory of the psyche offered him good reason for this reserve about dreams. In a striking paleo-Freudian passage at the *Republic* 571C–574E, it is claimed that in some dreams only the body-loving or possession-loving part of the psyche is awake. This is the part which thinks in the grossest physical terms, on his view. This scarcely enhances the epistemic status of dreams as Plato conceives of them, for the body-loving part is the one which can have no share in λόγος of the finest sort and hence no share in ἐπιστήμη. *Republic* 572A–B indicates that if this part of the psyche is well trained by the others, it *may* dream with some degree of truth, but Plato does not seem to have viewed even this as likely. At *Statesman* 290B the stranger, in reaffirming something said before, must insist that it was surely no dream which made him say it, as if it would be even more questionable if it had been.

Plato not uncommonly declares less-than-admirable mental states to be dreamlike, as at *Meno* 85C and *Republic* 476C. Even in the *Theaetetus* itself, at 157E ff., Socrates has scarcely complimented the epistemic status of dreams by suggesting that dreamers and those who are insane are alike in having false views. He does admit at 190B that there are some errors so obvious that we do not make them even in sleep, but the use of this qualifying term meaning "even" suggests that he thinks dreams are shot through with falsehood and blunders even if not constituted solely of these. This invites our mistrust of any account having its origin in a dream, as the one Socrates is about to give is claimed to.

It equally invites our mistrust of any *question* one may be inclined to ask in a dream. Note that what Socrates says he often dreams of at *Cratylus* 439C–D is not an assertion that there are certain forms, but rather a *question* about whether one should say there are such forms. In his clear waking moments neither Socrates nor anyone else in the middle dialogues is ever portrayed as seriously questioning whether or not one should say there are such forms, for it is taken for granted that forms are the most real of all entities. Forms provide the conditions which render questions and the assertions that answer them intelligible, the *Parmenides* 136B suggests.

It is no accident that (*a*) on Plato's view the psyche is dominated in dreams by the body-loving part, (*b*) Plato finds it necessary at *Sophist* 264 ff. to contrast sharply with the "friends of the forms" those "giants" who "drag everything down into body," and (*c*) the way Plato's middle views about forms had been expressed is shown to be inadequate by a "dream" which construes forms as indivisible things on the model of rather bodylike "letters" in the *Theaetetus*. The conceptual apparatus of dreams is that of part C of the psyche—the "giant," body-loving, acquisitive part—and such an apparatus, whether it figures in answers or in questions, will distort and misrepresent reality, on Plato's view.

The significance of Theaetetus *200 ff.*

The dream Socrates relates as an elaboration upon Theaetetus' middle-Platonic account of ἐπιστήμη and its objects is a fitting one to put in place of the *Cratylus*' dream-question about forms, for it would require a negative answer to that question. It would require one to say, "No, we should not say there are such forms, for there can be no λόγος of them." Forms in early and middle dialogues were always posited as the objects of a λόγος in the paradigm sense and as the entities of which we have ἐπιστήμη. But if they are dreamt of or otherwise described in such confining terms that they are beyond λόγος and hence beyond ἐπιστήμη, there would be no reason to say there are such forms. And thinking of forms in terms of letters *is* confining in this way. If understanding something is being able to "spell" it, if one cannot spell a letter, and if a form is like a letter, then one cannot understand a form. If forms were like letters, they would be pure in the sweeping, Eleatic sense. And such forms would not be understandable. Yet Plato had claimed in middle and late dialogues that if there were no forms, there could be no ἐπιστήμη, no λόγος, and no δόξα or opinion either. (See, e.g., *Parmenides* 135B.) And he takes it as obvious that there are these things, and sets out to understand them. Truly, [only] a "dream" would render understanding forms impossible. Plato in the *Theaetetus* awakens, as it were, from such a dream.

A number of able scholars have denied that important passages in the *Theaetetus* refer to the forms.[28] They have said that the dialogue minimizes reference to forms in its attempt to develop an account of ἐπιστήμη. It does so in order to show how futile such an attempt is, and hence indirectly how necessary the forms are for any adequate conception of ἐπιστήμη. This interpretation is, I think, mistaken for the following reasons:

1. The *Theaetetus*' silence about forms is not complete: Theaetetus' account of ἐπιστήμη is verbally identical with what one would take to be Plato's own in middle dialogues, and it mentions the entities that are ἐπιστητά, which we know to be the forms on Plato's middle account.[29]
2. While it is true that much of the argument following the dream passage in the *Theaetetus* is phrased in terms of sensible or bodily things, any argument applicable to these as indivisible components of things which are allegedly ἐπιστητά is equally applicable to intelligible ones so long as one mistakenly conceives of those intelligible ones in excessively bodylike terms, as in a dream one would, on Plato's theory.[30]
3. Even Theaetetus' Platonic-sounding conception of ἐπιστήμη as true opinion together with an account, or λόγος, is refuted and aban-

doned in the *Theaetetus*, and that conception itself made reference to the entities which are ἐπιστητά, or understandable—that is, to the forms as conceived of in the middle dialogues.

This third point has sometimes been denied on the ground that Theaetetus' Platonic-sounding account of ἐπιστήμη does not itself give an interpretation of what it is to give a λόγος, or account, and while three such interpretations are examined and rejected in the *Theaetetus*, not every plausible one is. This is taken to indicate that we are meant to think of another.[31]

This denial is by no means groundless. At 202C–D Socrates asks Theaetetus if he is satisfied to state that δόξαν ἀληθῆ μετὰ λόγου ἐπιστήμη εἶναι, in other words, that "true opinion with an account is understanding." Theaetetus says that he is, and Socrates might appear to be agreeing with that part of Theaetetus' account when he responds at 202D, Καὶ εἰκός γε αὐτὸ τοῦτο οὕτως ἔχειν, "And probably this statement itself is so." Hence, it is tempting to agree with Sayre's claim that in the *Theaetetus* Plato has not abandoned his earlier view of what ἐπιστήμη consists in, but has perhaps just noted a number of things an account, or λόγος, cannot be, leaving it to the reader to remember or work out what it must be.[32]

This temptation ought to be resisted, however, for two reasons. First, Socrates does not say that the claim Theaetetus has now made as to what understanding consists in *is so*, but only that it is εἰκός, "probable." Socrates' "probable's" are almost worthless as signs of lasting assent when one surveys them as a body. He uses εἰκός of all sorts of sophistries that he subsequently exposes. Hence, his using εἰκός here is merely a good reason to be wary.[33]

This wariness is vindicated at the end of the *Theaetetus*, as has traditionally been maintained, when Socrates asks, rhetorically, Οὐκοῦν ταῦτα μὲν πάντα ἡ μαιευτικὴ ἡμῖν τέχνη ἀνεμιαῖά φησι γεγενῆσθαι καὶ οὐκ ἄξια τροφῆς; "Then does our midwifery declare to us that all the offspring that have been born are mere wind-eggs and not worth rearing?"[34] The offspring, one will recall from 149A–151D, were to be the various *accounts* of ἐπιστήμη submitted for examination. If all of them are likened to intellectual flatulations, then of course so is the final one articulating what appears to be the view of the *Meno* and *Republic*. There are two chief epistemic reasons for rejecting the final one. The first is that even if one can analyze a whole into its components, this provides no assurance that one can recognize those same components in other wholes, and hence no assurance that one has ἐπιστήμη of them, much as the ability to spell Theodorus' name would give no assurance that one had understood the spelling of it and become a good speller, for one might not be

The significance of Theaetetus 200 ff.

able to spell "Theaetetus," which contains the same first syllable. This reason for rejecting that final account has force quite apart from the second reason—the unfortunate suggestion that forms are simple, as letters are—for whether they are simple or not, Plato will not concede that one understands them either in *Republic* 401E or 402C or in the *Theaetetus* at 207D–208B unless one can recognize them in all their combinations and mixtures.

A second reason for resisting the temptation to think that Plato has not seen difficulties in the basis for his old account of ἐπιστήμη lies in the fact that Socrates' reason for saying that account is probable is consistent with his rejecting the account itself. That reason lies in a rhetorical question which he asks at 202D: Τίς γὰρ ἂν καὶ ἔτι ἐπιστήμη εἴη χωρὶς τοῦ λόγου καὶ ὀρθῆς δόξης; that is, "For what understanding could there be *apart from* an account and true opinion?" If we take this reason as indicating what makes the account seem probable to him and hence what he is inclined to agree with, it is not the account itself taken as a statement of necessary and sufficient conditions for understanding, but rather the account taken as a statement of a necessary condition only. As has already been noted in Chapter 2, Plato continues to treat the ability to give an account as a necessary condition for understanding right up to the end of book 12 of the *Laws*; hence, it is perhaps not surprising that he wishes to salvage at least this much from Theaetetus' ambitious account. But taken as a whole he viewed this account as a "mere wind-egg," a "dream."

His ontological reasons for viewing it in this way may be understood in terms of the spelling analogy which he examines here as a way of interpreting this account and its ontological connotations. This spelling analogy was to be a "hostage" for the theory which had been expressed in terms of it (202E). Presumably, risk to a hostage is to be regarded as threatening to the one against whom the hostage is being held. But what is the theoretic counterpart here to the one against whom the spelling analogy is being held hostage? Clearly it is the conception of the allegedly simple and hence unanalyzable elements into which one analyzes an understood thing. But who had expressed such a conception? Gillespie and Ross have argued plausibly that Antisthenes was a likely candidate.[35] I think it most probable that Plato has not just Antisthenes in mind, however, given his own earlier emphasis upon the forms' simplicity, purity, and lack of parts. This spelling analogy is being held "hostage" not merely against Antisthenes' theory (to which it proves fatally embarrassing) but against Plato's as he had sometimes misleadingly expressed it earlier in speaking of forms as μονοειδές, "singular in form" or "simple."

In the period of the middle dialogues such as the *Republic*, when Plato was concerned to emphasize that forms as grasped noetically have a stability or chronological simplicity not possessed by compound sensible things, it evidently did not occur to him that the spelling model suggested an epistemically disastrous sort of simplicity—one incompatible with his further view that one can give an account of forms and can hence have understanding of them. Nothing can be *said about* a completely simple thing if saying anything about it requires that it have parts and that the account analyze it into these parts. At *Republic* 380D–381B, for example, Plato's argument is an epistemically disastrous non sequitur which sacrifices the intelligibility of the "divine things," or forms, for the sake of their immunity to change.

By the time he wrote the *Theaetetus*, however, Plato set out to salvage what he could from this epistemic disaster by renouncing the traces of Eleaticism which had infected his previous accounts of forms. He recognizes at 202B that if giving an account of something involves breaking it down into simple parts one can enumerate, then there can be no understanding of such parts, but more importantly, no understanding of such wholes either. As Socrates pointedly inquires at 203D, "He is ignorant of each, and understanding neither he understands both?" One can scarcely analyze understanding as a complex lack of understanding, but this is what the conception of λόγος in question requires, for the elements in the complex are ἄλογα καὶ ἄγνωστα, "unaccountable and beyond understanding," if conceived on the spelling analogy.

Not just the spelling analogy itself but any language suggestive of the wrong sort of simplicity or "purity" for forms as understandable is in question here, and there was much language in the middle period which might have been taken as suggestive of this. Talk of purity, lack of parts, indivisibility, lack of mixture, and the like all might be taken to suggest a simplicity incompatible with being an object of an account and hence of understanding. They might suggest that a form may be given a name but not an account, that it can be *referred to* but not described. But Plato can scarcely have held this, given his resolute call for accounts or *descriptions* of forms such as justice and moderation.

If Plato is going to hold for any epistemic purposes at all that it is possible to give an account of a form, then he owes us an ontology which renders this possible. This is the ontological debt incurred by the *Theaetetus*. If Plato wishes to test people's understanding by asking them to give an account, then he must explain how the entities of which he wishes accounts are sufficiently complex to *allow of* an account. Otherwise, he would be forced to allow the *Phaedo*'s "safe but stupid" claim that heat is hot to serve as an adequate account of heat, and the *Sophist*'s late learners's claim (251B) that "good is good" to serve as an adequate account of the good. He was no more satisfied with such "accounts" in his late period than he had been in his middle one.³⁶ Hence, he incurred the obligation to explain to himself and to others how some alternative sort of account might be possible without compromising the distinction between (*a*) particulars as compounds of δυνάμεις or εἴδη, and (*b*) νοητὰ εἴδη, "intelligible forms," which are in some sense pure or unmixed.³⁷ He attempted to meet this obligation in the *Sophist*.

The ontological basis for dialectical account-giving in later dialogues

The *Sophist* reads from the beginning like a philosophical apology for earlier mistakes. To detect this, of course, one has to read it from the beginning, something contemporary interpreters have not always encouraged.³⁸ But as Plato himself reminds us in quoting a Greek proverb at *Laws* 753E, "The beginning is half of everything." I take the opening passages in the *Sophist* to be not mere repartee but an essential aid to the understanding of what Plato is up to in the *Sophist* and of the way in which the views developed in this dialogue relate to his earlier ones.

Socrates begins by speculating at 216B that the Eleatic stranger whom Theodorus has brought along may be some sort of refutative divinity who has come to watch over them and refute them because they are so vulgar in their accounts. Readers have often missed the significance of this comment owing to their accepting Theodorus' construal of it.³⁹ Theodorus takes Socrates to be worried about the stranger's possibly being some sort of sophistic quibbler, since his response to Socrates at 216B–C is to reassure him that the man is not given to quibbles but is a philosopher.

Taking Theodorus' implied reading of Socrates' reference to a refuter at face value is mistaken for three reasons. First, Theodorus as he has been made known to us in the dramatic predecessor, the *Theaetetus*, is singularly unqualified to understand a Socratic remark about a refuter. He has shown himself to be a dialectical duffer in a number of ways, but most importantly in the relevant one—he plainly does not know the difference between the quibbler's rhetorical refutation and genuine dialectical refutation, as he shows at 162A: "So I should hate to bring about the refutation of Protagoras by agreeing with you." Contrast *Gorgias* 472B–C on the refutative irrelevance of claims or concessions by anyone other than the author of the alleged account, and 474A–B to the same effect. *Protagoras* 347C likewise expressed a dim view of taking into account claims by anyone other than the person whose account was being examined. Plato has evidently not given up this line of thought, for in the *Theaetetus* itself at 166A–B, Socrates imagines how vehemently Protagoras would protest if they thought him refuted by the allegedly quite un-Protagorean remarks of some self-styled defender. The force of this protest is tacitly conceded by Socrates' subsequent practice, which is to attempt to refute Protagoras out of his own mouth, as at 171A–C.

Secondly, when had Socrates as Plato portrayed him ever been known to shrink from an encounter with a sophistic quibbler? Plato consistently portrays him as regarding such encounters with a certain relish. (See, e.g., *Hippias Major* 287B and *Protagoras* 328D.) And Plato has not changed his mind about the delights of refuting such pretentious people, since he has his spokesman in the *Sophist* itself, the Eleatic stranger, reiterate them at 230C. Thirdly, how could a quibbler possibly be called a divinity by the ultrapious Socrates? Despite his penchant for irony, he is not given to using the term θεός, "god," in vain. A divine refuter would likely be a dialectical one. Why then does Socrates expect to meet a dialectical refuter? Which of his accounts is φαῦλος, "worthless" or "vulgar"?

One is immediately reminded that the *Sophist* is the dialectical successor to the *Theaetetus*, and that the *Theaetetus* ends not just in the failure to say what ἐπιστήμη is, but in the refutation of the external, dialectical account of it which is suggested in the early and middle dialogues. Socrates, then, would have sufficient reason to deplore certain of his accounts as φαῦλος given this alone. But Plato is evidently after even bigger game here than what might earlier have seemed to be his account of ἐπιστήμη.

We are immediately given an inkling of what the rest of the *Sophist* contains when at 217C Plato reminds us of Socrates' last encounter with an Eleatic. That was in the *Parmenides*, where

(*a*) Socrates had suffered considerable embarrassment at the hands of Parmenides himself when he had stated rather crudely the early and middle theory of forms;[40]
(*b*) Socrates had been quite unable to defend himself against or even to diagnose clearly the mistakes he allowed Parmenides to get away with in thus criticizing his statement of the theory; yet
(*c*) Parmenides had been depicted as indulging in what amounted to a *reductio ad absurdam* on extreme Eleatic methods and assumptions.

Subsequently, Plato in the *Theaetetus* finds in his own expression of the theory of what is capable of being understood (which is, for him, the theory of forms) an analogy which shows an almost Eleatic weakness— the analogy between the ability to spell a word and the ability to give an account. And it is indeed his statement of this very theory of the forms as the objects of understanding which is in for modification in the *Sophist* itself.[41]

The theory is introduced as that of the "friends of the forms." As we

The ontological basis for dialectical account-giving

have already seen, it was perfectly appropriate for Plato to write as if the forms had many friends, given Hippocratic and other Greek contributions. Such friends are credited with the view that there are entities which are intelligible, bodyless, perfectly real, and powerful, though unchanging in identity and power (246A–247C).

It is significant that the theory is contrasted with that of the "giants" who conceive of everything in bodily terms and deny that anything exists but body. It is even more significant perhaps that Socrates himself had been portrayed in the *Theaetetus* as all but playing into the hands of the "giants." When at 147A–C he gives a model for Theaetetus to follow in attempting to give an account of ἐπιστήμη, he invites Theaetetus to give him something on the order of "Clay is earth mixed with moisture." Theaetetus' own model, an account of square roots (147D–148A), seems more appropriate if one is to conceive of forms as intelligible rather than as bodily, and Plato's choice of his own associate, Theaetetus, as having come closer to an adequate example than did his previous spokesman, Socrates, is perhaps no accident. Moreover, in the *Sophist*, Socrates merely listens after 217D.

In the *Sophist*, however, Plato finds that he can make no headway against the giants on behalf of the friends of the forms unless he can manage to say what being or reality is if not bodily. Yet he cannot say what it *is* without implicitly or explicitly saying also what it is *not*. (This appears to be part of the force of 241D and 243B–C.) And he cannot say what it *is not* without overcoming the ancient Parmenidean superstition articulated in Fr. B8 on saying that what is not *is*. If Plato is to be able to say sensibly that reality *is not* corporeal or *not the same* as motion, he must explain the sense of the "not" so as to meet the quibble that one cannot sensibly say this sort of thing because it suggests that nonbeing is real, which would be akin to a speaker of English treating "Nothing" as a name having reference.

As we saw in Chapter 5, Plato's solution to this problem was to distinguish being opposite and being other than. This is the key to the articulation of forms proposed in the *Sophist*. It allows him to distinguish and divide forms, to say that *X* is not *Y* without thereby placing *X* and *Y* on the same ontological footing as opposites. (See, e.g., 257B–C.) Some forms, on his view, had no opposite against which they were in contention; they had only an "other" or complement form, as it were. Such complement forms were not themselves definite, unified powers having distinct qualities, but were merely the heterogeneous complements to the forms which were.[42] This allows Plato to distinguish Greeks from barbarians, for example, without thereby suggesting that there is some positive feature possessed by all and only barbarians comparable to the feature which tied

Greeks together as speakers of the same language. Barbarians were simply people who did not speak Greek. Plato is now willing to speak, as in the *Philebus* (at 53D–54D, 23C–27C) and *Timaeus* (52B, 50C–51B), of forms which are obscure, indefinite, difficult to understand, and definable only in terms of what they are other than. To be a barbarian was to lack Greek (*Statesman* 262D–E), and to be unlimited was to lack limit.

The ontological debt Plato owed us at the end of the *Theaetetus* was the corollary of a dialectical debt: there is some sense in which one can give a λόγος of a form if and only if a form must partake of complexity. That is, to put it at its Antisthenean worst, the form must partake of what it is not. So long as negation is thought to signify oppositeness, this suggests that a form partakes of its opposite, and the form is thus as "impure" or "mixed" as the sensible things partaking of it. A description or account of a form might then be incoherent. But with Plato's conception of negation as signifying merely otherness and not oppositeness, this embarrassing conclusion about forms is avoided. Forms *are* mixtures in the sense that they combine with or share with other forms which give them the sort of complexity required if we are to be able to say anything informative about them; but they are not mixtures in the sense in which sensible particulars are—they are not mixtures of opposites, but merely of "others." Each form which has an opposite is not only *other than* that opposite; it "does not submit to it," does not "mingle with" it (253B–E).

This much having been clarified in the *Sophist*, Plato subsequently feels free to call the forms εἰλικρινές, "pure," and ἀμεικτότατα, "the most unmixed of entities," as *Philebus* 59C, where what he has in mind is ἀλήθεια, "reality," in the sense of genuineness or freedom from opposites or susceptibility to an opposite. But at 63B–C he declares that it is neither altogether possible nor useful for any form to be μόνον, "alone," ἔρημον, "stripped bare," or εἰλικρινές, "pure." What he has in mind here is evidently not association with opposites, but association with *others* which are not opposites. The good life, for example, is a mixture or compound of genuine or true pleasures and νοῦς. This is plain from as early as 21B ff., where Socrates in effect *divides* lives of pleasure into those lived with νοῦς and those not so lived, finding that only the former are good. Similarly at 21D–E, he in effect divides lives lived with φρόνησις, νοῦς, ἐπιστήμη, and the like into ones lived with pleasure and ones lived without it, noting again that only the "mixed" ones are good. This division applies, of course, to actual lives and may be considered a taxonomy of lives, but it is a division of forms considered noetically in terms of their relationships with other forms.

These relationships are as permanent as one's relations to others in one's family tree, and to give an account is to trace one's way through a branch-

The ontological basis for dialectical account-giving 169

ing structure reminiscent more of Odysseus' account of his lineage (*Odyssey* 8. 83 ff.) than of an analysis into parts. An account now says what the accounted-for entity is a *part of*; it need not analyze what parts it *has*. It says which more generic *others* the form in question is a division *of*, and it plots the place of this division within a much larger whole.

The structure of dialectic as explicated above is as one would expect on the basis of the way Plato treats dialectical practice and ἐπιστήμη from the *Sophist* on. Dialectic, he claims at *Sophist* 253D, involves division by forms. He is describing what it is to give an account of a form. It is to map it in terms of its relations to other forms, to show which forms combine with which and which do not so combine. And though such a map may be treated as informative about what is possible for sensible particular things, he has nevertheless made a radical distinction between talking about sensible particulars, which incorporate not merely complexity but confusion of opposites, and talking about forms in their opposite-free complexity.

The account of dialectic developed in later dialogues is perhaps not incompatible with the conception of ἐπιστήμη suggested at *Republic* 401E–402C, where ἐπιστήμη is likened to the ability to spell any word and to recognize which letters combine and which do not. It is, however, incompatible with pushing the spelling model further than intended by asking how one can spell letters. The new account of dialectic suggests a structure and an order to the process of charting the relations among forms. Since these relations are now construed as inclusion and exclusion, and no letter is included in another, the old model of giving an account is now seen to be misleading in at least this one respect, and a new conception of what it is to give an account is developed.

To give an account dialectically is now to venture an hypothesis about which district of the forms a given form may be found in and how it differs from others in this district. It is to divide up the *district* patiently until one locates the quarry. It is to break down into parts, not the object of the account itself (which is the line taken in *Theaetetus*' spelling analogy and even in the account of particular psyches in the *Republic*), but rather, the neighborhood of forms in which the object of the account resides. It is to eschew that resolutely thing-oriented mode of thought evident at *Theaetetus* 207A–C in the line that giving an account of what a wagon is will be like analyzing it into *its* parts. Instead of looking inward to the internal constitution of the object of an account, it looks outward to its external relations. Thus, sophistry is to be located precisely within hunting, not disassembled like a wagon. Dialectic in its constructive phases is now structurally more akin to cartography or to genealogy than to analysis.

In the *Philebus* Plato notes a number of likely errors in the pursuit of precise intellectual cartography. He combats, in effect, the frivolous and impatient tendency to say of hunting, for example, that it has infinitely many divisions, and one of these no doubt is sophistry, offering that as an account. This seems to be the object of his scorn at *Philebus* 16D–17B, where he speaks of the uselessness of saying of sound either that it is one or that it is infinite in its divisions, saying at 18C–E that if one is to have musical ἐπιστήμη, one must understand how many divisions sound has and precisely what these are, for as he reminds us at 17D, these have different effects.[43] To break up a larger form immediately into an indefinite or infinite number of subforms is to renounce the task of dialectic, which demands an exact accounting of divisions in their important differences one from another and an exact "locating" of whichever one of these was the object of our account.

The old dialectical procedure of looking for contradictions in the answerer's replies remains important in two ways. It serves, as *Sophist* 230B ff. shows, as a way of preparing the ground for such a cartographic procedure by clearing away pretensions to understanding which might suggest that no such procedure was needed. But it also serves as a check upon the cartographic procedure itself once it is underway, as *Statesman* 268B–C indicates. It provides no guidance as to which cut to make next, but it can discredit some cuts as illegitimate, for it can lead the one who has made them to admit that "the same form is other" or "another the same," as when the stranger finds at *Statesman* 275A that he has divided in such a way as to allow the confusion of disparate manners of ruling, or at 266C, when he has failed to distinguish people from pigs.

As his pilot project with fishing indicated at *Sophist* 218D ff., Plato had no reason to suppose that one could not successfully map a given form within a larger network of related forms. Later (253D), various sorts of sophists are tracked down, and an account is thereby given of who or what they are, an account which allows one to avoid "confusing the same form with another or another with the same." In reinterpreting dialectic as division Plato seems, then, to have preserved the ability to give accounts of forms as at least a necessary condition for understanding, a condition which it is possible perhaps to meet. The dialectician, who can "see" the forms themselves in their relations with one another, is able to track a given form in an account which places it within another, larger form and differentiates it from related forms. He is able, presumably, to recognize such forms and differentiate them in sensible particulars as well. Plato, then, has overcome the misleading connotations of the spelling analogy. He has not, however, overcome a fatal difficulty which that analogy first betrayed to him in the epistemological view he had held in his middle period. We turn now to that difficulty.

The epistemological insufficiency of dialectical testing in the late dialogues

Theaetetus' suggested view that understanding is true opinion with an account is rejected in part for the following reason: Suppose one takes it as a sufficient indication that I understand how to spell Theodorus' name that when asked to do so I correctly break it down into the series of letters t, h, e, o, d, o, r, u, and s. But suppose that when asked to spell Theaetetus' name I break it down as follows: t, e, a, e, t, u, and s. The first syllable of each name ought to be the same, but I have not made it so. Plato would conclude that I do not understand how to spell either name. He would judge that I have the right *opinion* concerning the spelling of Theodorus' name, but I lack understanding, as he indicates at *Theaetetus* 208A–B.

In Chapter 2 it was argued that the vast power which Plato confers upon his guardians in the *Republic* attests to his belief not merely in the necessity of dialectical testing as a way of certifying understanding or wisdom but in its sufficiency as well. At *Republic* 520C successfully passing dialectical tests was treated as tantamount to guaranteeing one's infallibility in recognizing the "shadows on the wall of the cave" in terms of their originals, of spotting in confused sensible particulars their component forms. So long as an account of a form was carelessly conceived of on the analytical model of breaking *it* down into its component forms, as when one breaks a word into component letters or analyzes clay as earth plus moisture, particular things and forms might seem to have similar structures, and accounts of these structures might seem parallel.

We have seen how Plato detects the inadequacies of the view that a form is sufficiently like a sensible thing to render talking about a form and talking about a sensible thing similar. On the view that they are similar, one who was being asked about a form would run out of answers in an epistemically embarrassing way. In the late dialogues Plato restructures dialectical accounts of forms in a way that avoids this sort of embarrassment, as argued above. Thus, in restructuring dialectic as he did in the *Sophist*, Plato ensures that the answerer to a question such as "What is a sophist?" need not run out of answers in any embarrassing way, since his task is to map or track his quarry within a larger whole, not break the quarry down into simple parts. But in saving dialectic in this way, Plato has ensured that the series of answers can have no starting point other than a potentially problematic one, for this whole within which it starts is indefinitely large, and to press Plato's tracking figure a bit further, it can be crossed from many different directions, each demanding a new map.

The resemblance to the problem of being able to spell "Theodorus" but not "Theaetetus" is plain. In dialectical division, one is required to draw no more than the analog to a trip itinerary, not the analog to a road map of an entire state. One is asked in effect, "*Assuming* the sophist is some sort of hunter, can you track him down?" One is allowed to start with hunting and track the sophist to his final lair through various subdivisions of his genus. But it is obvious that these various subdivisions ("image-making," e.g.) could have been crossed from indefinitely many other directions (assumptions) on tracks leading to quarries other than the sophist.[44] The ability to track the sophist through image-making gives no assurance that one understands image-making or, for that matter, the sophist, any more than the ability to say in correct order the letters in Theodorus' name gives assurance that one understands the spelling of it.

That we are not pressing the mapping figure too far is indicated in the sequel to the *Sophist*, the *Statesman*, where at 252B–C the stranger concedes that the division of areas of understanding which they had employed in mapping the sophist will not be appropriate for mapping the statesman, though statesmanship too is held to be an area of understanding. The analogy between a division schema and a trip itinerary is accurate, given that the stranger himself says that the reason they require a new division is that the statesman's ἀτραπός, "path," through this maze is not the same as that of the sophist. How then can dialectical division certify that the answerer understands *every* path, every nook and cranny, in the territory over a confused copy of which a guardian must preside? Pretty clearly, it cannot do so in any finite series of questions and answers, however useful it may be in disposing of some pretenders and other unworthies. It cannot establish that the answerer *understands* the subject in question. It can only establish that *so far* the answerer does not seem to have *misunderstood* it.

Yet the epistemic demand for this wide and detailed a dialectical range—for the dialectical counterpart to a world map, not a filling-station attendant's directions—is emphatically not abandoned in dialogues after the *Sophist*. At *Statesman* 280A–B, the stranger says that in order to be *sufficient*, an account must distinguish its object not merely from *some* others but from *all* others. The same point is emphasized at 281C–D. But distinguishing the object of an account from all others would require an understanding not simply of that object but of all others as well. It would require an understanding of everything taken *distributively* in order to allow one to combat the danger of confusing some of the myriad forms referred to at *Sophist* 254C, and to combat also the danger of being led to confuse them by contentious reasoning playing on a series of small but misleading resemblances, a danger recognized at *Sophist* 231A and *Phaedrus* 261E ff. Moreover, it would require an understanding of everything taken *collectively*, for otherwise one could not be confident that no division of importance had been left out of account.

An understanding of everything taken collectively is inconceivable on Plato's new model of dialectical division. To understand is to be able to "map" accurately within a larger genus. The largest genus, taken collectively, cannot conceivably be an object of understanding. It can be divided, as Plato does in his daring division of "all that now is in the universe" at *Philebus* 23C, but taken as a whole, it remains an hypothetical starting point inherently beyond our dialectical grasp. The problem in understanding it parallels Aristotle's problem of saying where the universe is. If "whatever fixed, environing surface we take our reckoning from will be the place," then the largest such surface, the universe, must be nowhere (*Physics* 212a–b).

An understanding of everything taken distributively may be conceivable, but Plato is not optimistic about its occurring. In the *Sophist* the Eleatic stranger asks the evidently rhetorical question, "Is it possible for a human being to understand all things?"[45] The answer suggested in context clearly seems to be negative. More importantly, even if such understanding were possible for a human being, it would not be possible to demonstrate it dialectically by the new division procedure, for the multiplicity of forms, the myriad "paths" through them, and the difficulty of finding some stable and commonly understood terminology for discussing them all plague Plato's new procedure. The best one could demonstrate dialectically would be a true opinion which has stood up to testing so far, *given* a certain starting point and a certain path from it towards one's presumed quarry. This would give little or no assurance that one could cross so vast a territory again from yet another starting point and not confuse that quarry with another. Yet such dialectical tests are still thought to be necessary, and Plato clearly would not concede that a person who failed them had any right to claim an understanding of the area in which he or she got "lost" or confused. But these tests are plainly *not completeable* in practice and hence not sufficient to certify the presence of ἐπιστήμη.[46]

The problem of finding a suitably stable terminology loomed ever larger for Plato in the late dialogues. With his increased linguistic sophistication came a recognition that the terms in questions put to a dialectician could be taken in a number of different ways calling for a number of different divisions, and that these ways evolve and multiply rapidly. (See, e.g., *Sophist* 231C–232A, *Epistle 7*, 343B–E.) In his own time the term for "sophist" had more (and worse) meanings than it had possessed two generations earlier. That an answerer is able to map the sophist in one sense of the term by no means assures one that he will not confuse new sorts of sophists with nonsophists or with the sort of sophist he has mapped. And Plato thinks the political consequences of such confusion potentially disastrous. But he evidently sees no cure for this. Successful dialectical performance up to a lifetime—and perhaps even beyond—can no longer be used in the confidence that it will differentiate infallibly between those whose opinion has held up a long time under test but will crumble eventually and those who have genuine understanding, which cannot crumble.

One of the most remarkable features of the *Laws* and *Philebus*, then, is precisely what one would predict on the basis of the above interpretation: Plato casually lumps together true opinion and understanding as if there were practically no difference between them.[47] He had been at pains to distinguish these sharply in dialogues from the *Meno* (98A ff.) through the *Republic* (534A ff., 506C, 476D ff.). And probably he still believed even in the *Timaeus*, *Philebus*, and *Laws* that true opinion and understanding are different psychic conditions.[48] But he now lumps them together because he no longer has a practical and sufficient dialectical way to distinguish true opinion, which lasts for a period of time, from understanding, which is indestructible. The person who has understanding makes no mistake. The person who has true opinion, as Plato notes as early as *Meno* 97B–D, makes no mistake so long as he has it. The person who has passed dialectical tests by dividing a given genus has merely made no mistake so far. Is that good enough?

As noted at *Meno* 98A, the chief defect of true opinion lies in its being prone to depart unexpectedly. Plato recommended tying it down so that this could not happen, but on his modified conception of dialectic, one never knows when one has *finished* tying it down. The genus one is given to map may not be large enough, given the responsibilities of one's office, and the terms in which one is asked to account for it may have multiple and shifting meanings that open many possibilities for confusion. Moreover, the largest area is inherently unmappable. The largest genus has no larger genus within which a dialectician can locate it as a division. Hence, no dialectician could conceivably have ἐπιστήμη of everything collectively.

In Chapter 2 we discussed in some detail Plato's startling mistrust of even the most thoroughly tested officials in the *Laws*. This mistrust indicates that he thought it quite conceivable that the apparent virtue these officials had displayed previously—the true opinion they had argued for and acted upon—might suddenly fail them. We are now in a position to understand why, after writing the later dialogues, he would have thought this. I submit that this is owing to his realization that the ability to survive dialectical testing as he now conceived of it is a necessary condition for understanding and excellence, but not a sufficient one. If one has understanding, one will pass such tests. But we commit the fallacy of affirming the consequent if we claim that one who has passed such tests has understanding. And Plato wisely draws back from this fallacy, and from any political arrangement which would rest upon it, as that of the *Republic* would. The utopian element in Plato's *Republic* was, at bottom, *epistemic*.

Plato's uneasiness about his previous political recommendations had already begun to show in the sequel to the *Sophist*, the *Statesman*. At *Republic* 472B–473A Plato had spoken confidently of approximating the pattern of the just person described in the dialogue, with no hint that such an approximation calls for political arrangements different *in kind*, not merely in degree, from those of the *Republic*. On Plato's view, a just person might well be a shepherd over others, as *Republic* 440D indicates, and divine, as 590D–591A suggests. But in the *Statesman*, at 275C, Plato notes that "the form of the divine shepherd is greater than that of the king, whereas the statesmen who now exist here are by nature much more like their subjects, with whom they share much more nearly the same breeding and education."[49]

The difference in σχῆμα, or form, between the shepherd having total discretion and the statesman now strikes Plato as very significant, for insofar as a person exercises unchecked power while lacking ἐπιστήμη, that person is not a statesman or king but a tyrant, as he indicates at *Statesman* 301B–C. The difference is so significant that Plato now regards it as calling for a different political structure. One who is not certifiable as a king or statesman of the divine sort cannot be allowed to rule in a way which even approximates the unfettered case-by-case approach of the divine shepherd. With mere approximations of the divine shepherd we must, he says at 301E, follow in the track of the perfect and true form of government by coming together and making written laws. Plato's refined solution in the *Laws* is to spread political power about in legally circumscribed quantities (945D–948B, 915D, 713C).

The *Statesman* is somewhat more pessimistic in its reason for subjecting rulers themselves to laws than the *Laws* itself is, and more pessimistic than Plato's revised conception of dialectical testing would really warrant. The *Statesman* perhaps exaggerates the implications of Plato's new conception at 275C and at 301E by suggesting that there are not at present any who are worthy of unchecked power; all he need have concluded on the basis of his new conception of dialectical division is that there are none who can safely be certified as being worthy of it.

In the *Laws* Plato appears to have got clearer about the exact implications of his views on dialectical testing, and he was more careful in avoiding this exaggeration. As 875C–D shows, Plato believed that some rulers could be trusted with no law over them. Thus, he would have rejected as unjust today's sweeping cynicism about all persons in political positions. But he believed that we have no way of telling who the trustworthy people are until they are dead. And the political stakes involved in unfettered power are too high to wager on the outcome of inconclusive tests. Hence, at *Laws* 802A, for example, he insists that it is not safe to honor with hymns and praises those who are still living. They must traverse the whole of life and reach a noble end before he will praise their virtue or understanding. Such honor or trust is not safe politically, but the *reason* it is not safe politically is that it is not safe epistemically. It is not safe epistemically because dialectical and other tests are not sufficient to certify complete understanding of a realm of forms having the complex genus-species articulation Plato's quasi-cartographic conception of dialectic as division suggests.

Thus, Plato in the *Laws* had come to mistrust, not human nature, but rather human efforts in applied epistemology, human efforts to certify a person as wise, virtuous, and irrevocably trustworthy in that person's own lifetime.[50] This is not complete skepticism, for he is confident that dialectical and other tests can certify that someone *lacks* understanding, and he remains confident that rare people can attain understanding. But no tests, not even the most probing dialectical ones, can certify that such persons have attained understanding.

Plato's caution about the efficacy of dialectical tests and the degree of confidence one ought to have in those who pass them is reminiscent of dialogues preceding the epistemically less cautious *Republic*. At *Meno* 86B–C, for example, Socrates is made to say in defense of inquiry: "Some things I have said of which I am not altogether confident. But that we shall be better and braver and less helpless if we think that we ought to inquire, than we should have been in the idle fancy that there is no understanding and no use seeking to understand what we do not understand—that is a theme upon which I am ready to fight, in word and in deed, to the utmost of my ability." On this line of thought, the results of inquiry will be well-tested hypotheses which are, in the words of the *Statesman* 284D, "beautiful and sufficient for now." They will be accounts given in the realization that "nothing in human life is ever at rest" (294B). Such accounts will not be certifications of understanding, verified and immune from further testing. But if they have survived appropriate dialectical examination, they will be the best we can obtain at any given time. Again, Plato's final view is reminiscent of one he had earlier attributed to the condemned Socrates in the *Crito*: "I am not only now but always a man who follows nothing but the reasoning which on consideration seems to me best. And I cannot, now that this has happened to us, discard the arguments I used to advance, but they seem to me much the same as ever, and I revere and honour the

The epistemological insufficiency of dialectical testing 177

same ones as before. And unless we can bring forward better ones in our present situation, be assured that I shall not give way to you."[51]

Not only are such hypotheses or arguments the best we can get at any given time, and the ones we had best act on; but those who have offered and defended them successfully are the best we can get for political purposes at any given time. Political experience both in Plato's time and in ours indicates the wisdom of this conclusion forced upon him by his revised ontology. In that day, as in this, it proved wise to trust the well-tested hypothesis and the well-tested, closely examined person, while realizing that such tests are not decisive, that such trust may have to be withdrawn, and that when and if it is withdrawn, we shall want to have reserved to ourselves the power to recover whatever political stakes we have wagered. Thus, a healthy, moderate caution about large claims to exceptional wisdom and excellence proved to be the soundest epistemic foundation for something resembling a democracy, a system which recognizes that all of us are, in Plato's words, "capable of distinguishing better people from worse" owing to "something divine and well-aimed" in us.[52]

Conclusion

We have examined from several points of view Plato's conception of what he regarded as the finest condition of the psyche to which humans can aspire, the condition of ἐπιστήμη. In Chapter 1 it was argued that "knowledge," our conventional word for this condition, can be seriously misleading in our attempt to comprehend and assess Plato's views. In Chapter 2 we asked how this condition of the psyche shows itself, on Plato's view, in the discussions engaged in by those who possess ἐπιστήμη, and how their discussions differ from the discussions engaged in by others. In Chapter 3 we considered what, on Plato's view, such discussions show psychologically about the internal condition of those who have ἐπιστήμη. In Chapter 4 we asked what the discussions of those who are in this condition are about, and we explicated Plato's theory of forms or powers. In Chapter 5 we considered what, on Plato's view, is distinctive about these forms or powers—their complete "truth" or "reality"—and we interpreted the extraordinary conception of truth or reality which Plato held. In Chapter 6 we examined Plato's later conception of the extrapsychic objects to which one who has ἐπιστήμη attends, his conception of a form or power as "located" within a fabric of forms that one can depict in a division schema. We considered the substantial dialectical, epistemic, and political implications of his having adopted this view of forms or powers, and noted that his adopting it accounts for much that is otherwise baffling in the later dialogues.

In the Introduction it was suggested that we know little of the positive views of Socrates, and cannot distinguish these from the views of Plato on the basis of the available evidence. Nevertheless, we know something of the activities of Socrates. We know, in particular, that he spent his time in discussion, discussion so remarkable that those who heard it could scarcely help wondering how it was possible. Philosophy, for Plato, appears to have begun in wonder engendered by Socratic discussion. Such wonder at discussion, especially probing, illuminating discussion, remains a powerful force even today.

Two human abilities are remarkable perhaps above all others. The first is our ability to carry on discussions with one another. The second is our ability to turn the first upon itself, to reflect upon and discuss critically our own discussion.

Conclusion

The exercise of the first ability is the bonding agent in human culture, the tie which links us in political, economic, educational, and other human communities. In this type of discussion we attempt to convey and arrange the satisfaction of whatever practical wants, needs, and preferences we have.

The exercise of the second ability is our only check upon the first. To adopt a Greek figure made more accessible today by cybernetics, this exercise is the κυβερνήτης, or "helmsman," capable of steering the first more intelligently by reflecting critically upon the dangers to which it is exposed and the alternative "destinations" to which it can proceed. It is of a logically higher order than the first, for it involves the use of predicates which range, not over concrete things, but over lower-order predicates. Just as "Brown is a color" is a statement of a higher logical type than "Jersey cattle are brown," so "Discussion is possible only because . . . " is of a higher logical type than "Defeat of the treaty being considered by the Senate would be a setback/boon to the cause of world peace."

The ability to make and assess such higher-order statements is a prerequisite of autonomy. A discussion ranging over discussions permits us to envisage and express a preference ranging over preferences.[1] It can help free us from bondage to our present preferences by allowing us to articulate, compare critically, and choose among alternatives. It permits us to discuss not simply talcum powder and treaties, but the like and dislike of various brands of each. It allows us to conceive of what might otherwise seem a bald given of discussion as itself open to rational discussion and assessment. And it equips us to explore the pathology of discussion gone awry.

Had humans not been capable of discussion at all, we would almost certainly not have been able to deviate very far upwards or downwards from the "cultural" level of the better-organized baboon troops. Had we been incapable not simply of discussing this-and-that but of discussing the prerequisites, canons, and limitations of discussion itself, we should not have known either the love of wisdom and understanding portrayed in the Platonic dialogues or the contempt for it displayed in the speeches of a Goebbels or an Idi Amin. We would have lacked the capacity to appreciate the beauties and the terrors of human civilization. A human species deprived of discussion of any sort would be arguably another species altogether. Though we are perhaps not, as Linnaeus generously put it, *homo sapiens*, we are emphatically *homo loquens*. Our loquacity has made us what we are.[2] In a profound sense our identity is that of users and abusers of words. Saint John said perhaps more than he knew when he wrote Ἐν ἀρχὴ ἦν ὁ λόγος, "In the beginning was the Word." Here, surely, was *our* common beginning at least.

Plato's philosophy was founded, first and last, on the requirements of discussion. He had seen discussion abused by political and educational opportunists of all stripes and knew well the price we pay for an uncritical attitude toward it. But he also knew the price we pay for a hypercritical attitude toward it, an attitude of misology which, if it were indulged fully, would silence every tongue and still every pen.[3] Plato had not simply observed the abuse of discussion, however; he had had the good fortune to see it used expertly by Socrates to get at quite elusive truths—such as the truth about an alleged expert's competence or lack of it. And he believed it capable of still more constructive use, for he had seen it raised to the level of a τέχνη, an art or discipline, holding forth the promise of wisdom or understanding.[4] He wished to explore fully what makes such disciplined discussion possible and how it differs from the undisciplined discussion in which we can grievously mislead one another and even ourselves.

In order to articulate the requirements of disciplined discussion—the discussion Plato termed "dialectical"—he adopted for his own purposes the notion of a form or power developed by his medical and philosophical predecessors, a notion we have seen to be in wide currency in his day. Despite its currency, Plato was aware that one might be tempted to disallow such forms or powers. But he evidently believed that disallowing them would render utterly incomprehensible our admitted power of carrying on a disciplined discussion, and as he showed at *Parmenides* 135B–C, he would countenance nothing which did this. This is one of Plato's nearest approaches to what we might now develop on his behalf as an argument that there must be the forms or powers which his discussants so readily assume exist. If developed, it would take the form of a simple *modus tollens*: if there are no forms or powers, discussion is impossible. But discussion is possible, so it is not true that there are no forms or powers.

The understanding of the first premise of this tacit proof amounts to the understanding of the rudiments of Plato's entire philosophy. Plato judged that he had to posit forms or powers, since

- A. He was concerned to explain how discussion could take place.
- B. He conceived of discussions as reflecting the mental state of the discussants.
- C. He conceived of such mental states as founded upon what we would term veridical experience of objects.
- D. He attributed the varying quality of these mental states to the varying quality of their objects.
- E. He conceived of ἐπιστήμη as the best mental state, the one having the best objects.

F. He conceived of the best discussions as reflecting the best mental state, the one involving attention to the best objects.
G. He posited intelligible forms or powers as these objects.
H. He accounted for the ability of those who perceive these objects to hold discussions with those who perceive inferior objects in terms of
   (i) These inferior objects' sharing in or resembling the intelligible forms or powers, and
   (ii) our common ability to "recollect," if only dimly at first, these intelligible forms which inferior objects resemble or share in and thus "remind" us of.

Perhaps the least acceptable components in Plato's system today are C and D. Ryle, perhaps rightly, pilloried such flashlight models of the mind, models which require objective ontological slums to support shabby thoughts.[5] But in the remainder of Plato's system, a system shorn of so wholesale a realism, there remains not simply a collection of historically important ideas but an *orientation* which continues to attract important philosophers. This orientation lies in Plato's point of philosophical departure, his overriding concern with how it is that we are able to hold any sort of disciplined, critical discussion with one another. If we take this as our philosophical point of departure, our views about *meaning* and about everything dependent upon this central element are likely to be quite different than if we take, instead, a concern with the truth conditions of what we say.

From this point of departure we need an idea of meaning precisely because we are members of a community engaged in political, educational, and economic discussion with one another, and because we realize that such discussion can go awry. As Hilary Putnam put it,

A language made up and used by a being who belonged to no community would have no need for such a concept as the *meaning* of a term. To state the reference of each (simple and defined) term and to describe what the language user believes in connection with each term is to tell the whole story. . . . But as soon as language becomes a communal instrument things change. How could *discussion* take place if we assume *nothing* about what all speakers believe?[6]

This final question is a modern expression of a concern which parallels Plato's at *Parmenides* 135B–C, a concern with the common basis for disciplined discussion, a basis Plato finds, rightly or wrongly, in forms or powers existing independently of discussion and serving as the referents for dialectical inquiry.

It was suggested in Chapter 5 that Plato's sole notion of meaning was reference. This now requires a certain elaboration if the above comparison with Putnam's view is not to be misunderstood. It will be helpful in expressing this required elaboration if we attend to another remark of Putnam's:

> Meaning is a several-component affair. . . . One component of meaning is *reference* (extension). . . . Another major component, in my view, is *stereotype*—and stereotypes are nothing but sets of beliefs or idealized beliefs associated with terms. (E.g., the belief that tigers are typically striped orange and black is part of our stereotype of a tiger.) The need for stereotypes is *not* primarily to fix extensions; that can be and often is done by experts using criteria that are not 'part of the meaning' in any sense. The stereotype associated with 'gold,' for example, is all but worthless for fixing the extension of the word. . . . *Language is used not only to verify and falsify and classify*; it is also used to *discuss*. The existence of standardized stereotypes, and hence of meaning, is a necessity for *discussion*, not for classification.[7]

Plato's theory of forms as *recollected*, and as having pre-recollected memory traces one can regard as opinion, is a theory of what Plato as well as Putnam regarded as a necessary component in our common basis for discussion. The theory differs from Putnam's, as Putnam's phrase "nothing but . . . " makes vividly clear. For Plato, unless we assume that there are forms, that we have all "seen" them, and that they are therefore accessible to us as stereotypes, we have no common basis for communication or for cooperative inquiry, as he suggests at *Meno* 80D–E and 86D. Plato would agree with Putnam that the requirements for common discussion are more exacting than those for simple classification. Even in their ignorance of stereotypical forms and their acquaintance with mere shadows of these, the wretched inhabitants of Plato's Cave in the *Republic* can classify the shadows on the wall. But their discussion and the common life that depends upon it are held in a certain inevitable bondage until they understand the stereotypes which are necessary to give firm and stable meaning to the claims they make to and upon one another.

How does Plato's interest in forms as stereotypes make it advisable to elaborate now on the claim that his only notion of meaning was reference? It does so in just this way: we have seen that he believed that the contents of all extra-imaginative experience are determined veridically by the objects of varying quality which one experiences. He indicates this in his repeated talk of turning the mind's "eye" upwards away from defective objects, as if what we would call the truth of its reports—the correspondence between these reports and what they describe—were a constant.[8] Since forms on Plato's theory of recollection serve as stereotypes, and on his theory of dialectic they serve also as the referents of the truest accounts, Plato apparently attempted to unite in one conception both the notion of stereotype and the notion of referent.

Conclusion

If today we adopt as our point of philosophical departure a concern with accounting for the possibility of *discussion*, as both Plato and Putnam do in their different ways, we shall probably wish to join Putnam in distinguishing stereotype from reference, and shall probably regard Plato's view as daringly simple but too sparing in its distinctions. Yet in pursuing our answer we shall find it necessary to wind our way systematically across the sometimes jealously guarded boundaries between disciplines conventionally regarded as distinct—linguistics, psychology, educational theory, epistemology, ontology, the philosophy of science, ethics, and political science. And we shall find it necessary, as Plato did, to regard as of secondary importance any distinction not conducing to this overriding concern.

It remains to be determined whether or not an overriding concern with what makes disciplined discussion possible is an adequate philosophical point of departure. But even if it were to prove inadequate, this concern could not be evaded responsibly. The peremptory demands of practical political, economic, and educational discussion and our propensity for talking past one another in such discussion even when it is vitally important not to do so will ensure that Plato's concern with the grounds for disciplined discussion will retain very nearly the centrality he gave it. If we do not start with his concern as overriding, we shall at least have to end with it if our philosophy is to have the synoptic power to which his so clearly aspired.

Notes
Glossary
Index

Notes

Chapter 1: Knowledge and Ἐπιστήμη

1 This has occurred to a number of other scholars as well. R. S. Bluck remarked: "Plato . . . was concerned with something different from what we ordinarily call knowledge" ("Logos and Forms in Plato," *Mind* 65 [1956]: 526). John Gould, in *The Development of Plato's Ethics* (Cambridge, 1955), ch. 1, correctly noted that ἐπιστήμη for Plato was not merely what we now call "knowing that. . . ." N. R. Murphy (*The Interpretation of Plato's Republic* [Oxford, 1951], p. 98) recognized some of the inadequacies in translating such epistemic terms as γνῶσις by "knowledge," and even suggested that "understanding" would serve better (p. 99). But he did not follow up on his suggestion. The linguist John Lyons (*Structural Semantics* [Oxford, 1963], p. 98) notes that "classical scholars are conscious of the inadequacy of translation as a method of stating the meaning of such terms as τέχνη, ἐπιστήμη, [and] σοφία." Lyons's own procedure, while of great linguistic interest, would be philosophically perverse for reasons which will be apparent from the following two claims he makes: "The principle I have adopted, with regard to the interpretation of the passages in which Plato explicitly defines or discusses the lexemes that fall within the scope of the inquiry, is the following: I attempt to elucidate them in terms of other passages in which the lexemes in question are used, as it were, unconsciously. This is in accord with a principle familiar in linguistics: to accept everything that the native speaker says *in* his language, but to treat with reserve anything he says *about* his language, until this has been checked" (p. 140). "It might almost be said that explicit definition of a term by an author is evidence that it does not generally mean what he says it does" (p. 140, n. 1). First, it must be noted that Plato is not saying things "about his language" or telling us what "terms" mean; rather he is characterizing a condition of the psyche, ἐπιστήμη, for which his own language may have had no suitable word. If philosophers were restricted by Lyons's methods, no one could say anything new, and both thought and language would stagnate. If the interpretation of philosophy were carried on today by Lyons's methods, we might prefer to ask Quine's pest control man how he uses the term "web" rather than rely on explicit remarks in *The Web of Belief*. The creative philosopher is entitled and even required to take liberties with words where necessary to convey a new thought, and the occasions on which this is done may well be a small but enormously significant subset of the occasions on which this philosopher uses these words. That the philosopher understands (*Philebus* 13E, 55C, 57B) and even lapses frequently into uses of such words which are governed by less demanding criteria in no

way lessens the philosophical importance of his comparatively rare and distinctive uses.
2 J. L. Austin, *How to Do Things with Words* (Oxford, 1962). See also J. R. Searle's much-discussed book, *Speech Acts* (London, 1969), and Dennis Stampe's excellent critique, "Meaning and Truth in the Theory of Speech Acts," in John P. Kimball, ed., *Syntax and Semantics*, vol. 3 (New York, 1975).
3 E. A. Nida, "Science of Translation," *Language* (1969), pp. 483–98, esp. p. 494; also E. A. Nida and C. Taber, *The Theory and Practice of Translation* (Leiden, 1969), p. 14. Functional equivalence is only one among several proposed conditions for the exactness of a translation. E. Keenan, "Some Logical Problems in Translation," in F. Guenthner and M. Guenthner-Reutter, eds., *Meaning and Translation* (London, 1978), pp. 167–73, proposes the following four criteria as among those which two sentences must meet if they are to be counted as full paraphrases: the two sentences (*a*) "should be naturally usable in the same range of speech acts," (*b*) "must be true under the same conditions," (*c*) must remain the same in meaning if each has its meaning changed in the same way, e.g., by negating each, and (*d*) must have precisely the same ambiguities.
4 See H. P. Grice, "Meaning," *Philosophical Review* 66 (1957): 377–88, and Dennis Stampe, "Toward a Grammar of Meaning," *Philosophical Review* 77 (1968): 137–74, esp. 166–74.
5 This is not to say that what a writer or speaker *intends* one to think exhausts the meaning of what he or she says or writes. Intention is only one component of meaning. Reference is also a component of meaning, and what a writer intended us to think about it may well be false or misleading. When the existence of the referent is in doubt, or when we believe that by independent means we know more about it today than the writer did, then the historically interesting meaning-component is the author's *conception* of the referent as shown in what he apparently intends one to think about it. This is the situation today for most readers as regards the meanings of some of Plato's key terms.
6 An excellent example of what can happen when translators or interpreters fail to take into account the beliefs of their intended clientele is provided by Nida and Taber, *Theory and Practice of Translation*, p. 97: "A typical well-indoctrinated Thai Buddhist, who has no previous acquaintance with the Christian religion, would be likely to interpret the traditional translation of John 3:16 as follows: 'God so lusted after this material world that he sent his only Son so that anyone who is gullible enough to believe in him would have the misfortune of keeping on living forever and not dying.'" Lakoff, "Language in Context," notes problems in translating oriental honorifics. Mario Pei, *The Story of Language* (Philadelphia, 1949), pp. 426–31, gives numerous examples of words in other modern European languages which require cumbrous, colorless, and misleading circumlocutions to convey in English even a portion of their original force.
7 To say this is decidedly *not* to commit oneself to what has been called the exact translation hypothesis, namely, that anything that can be said in one

natural language can be translated exactly into another. Powerful reasons for rejecting this hypothesis have been articulated by Keenan in "Some Logical Problems in Translation," in Guenthner and Guenthner-Reutter, *Meaning and Translation*, pp. 157–89, esp. pp. 174–77. That one can talk adequately in English *about* words and sentences in another language is no argument that this very talk translates these words and sentences, for these words and sentences were not about words and sentences, and so their explanation in English does not have the same semantic properties as the original.

8 See, e.g., A. D. Woozley, *Theory of Knowledge* (London, 1948), ch. 8; A. J. Ayer, *The Problem of Knowledge* (London, 1956), pp. vii, 74; R. Chisholm, *Perceiving* (Ithaca, 1957), ch. 1. Many philosophers have resisted this influence recently. For the immense problems which arise if it is not resisted see Edmund Gettier, "Is Justified True Belief Knowledge?" republished with discussion and replies in M. Roth and L. Galis, eds., *Knowing* (New York, 1970). For a plausible contemporary view of knowing see Fred Dretske, *Seeing and Knowing* (London, 1969), esp. pp. 135–39.

9 For definitions of "application," "consequences," and related terms see Lyons, *Structural Semantics*, pp. 41, 73.

10 Some interpreters have doubted that this condition applied across the board on Plato's view. R. C. Cross, "Logos and Forms in Plato," *Mind* 63 (1954): 443, says that "ordinarily knowledge and logos go hand in hand," but thinks that in Diotima's speech at *Symposium* 211A Plato has claimed there is no λόγος and no ἐπιστήμη of beauty itself. A somewhat different interpretation seems appropriate; what Diotima is saying in this passage is that beauty itself does not present itself (φαντασθήσεται) as a certain face or as anything else having to do with the body, and not even as a certain account or a certain instance of ἐπιστήμη, nor perhaps as being in any other thing, such as an animal, the earth, the heavens, etc., but is always alone by itself (αὐτὸ καθ' αὑτό) and unique in form (μονοειδές). This passage does not tell us that there is no λόγος and no ἐπιστήμη of beauty; rather, it tells us a number of things with which beauty is not identical.

There have also been doubts about whether or not Plato thought it possible to give an account of the good itself. These are based upon a misreading of *Republic* 505A ff. and of *Epistle 7*, 341C. In the *Republic* passage Socrates is not made to say that the question of what the good itself is cannot be answered. Rather, he is made to say that *he* cannot answer it as yet; he suggests that they dismiss the question *for now* (ἐάσωμεν τὸ νῦν), not forever. The guardians of the best state will plainly have to do better (506B). And in the *Epistle 7* passage, Plato is commenting on those subjects about which he seriously concerns himself, with no hint that one of these is answering the question of what the good itself is. Moreover, he does not even claim that these subjects are outside the range of λόγοι, or accounts. He does say that his subject is ῥητὸν γὰρ οὐδαμῶς, or not such as to be expressible. But ῥητόν is subject to an ambiguity of the sort G. E. Moore pointed out in *Principia Ethica* (Cambridge, 1903), ch. 3. It can suggest either capacity for description or advisability of description. In context the latter is clearly intended by Plato, since he says that the best λόγοι of such matters either in writing or in speech would be his own, but that it would be inadvisable to give it for reasons which he details. One may try to justify refraining from what one thinks inadvisable, but not from what one thinks impossible.

11 *Republic* 534B–C in its context of emphasis on the crucial role of dialectic makes this point most clearly.
12 Skeptics leave one with the impression that they conceive of knowledge in this way, as does their recent defender, Peter Unger, in "A Defense of Skepticism," *Philosophical Review* 80 (April 1971): 198–219, given his treatment of the knower's certainty and of its not being an accident that the knower is right.
13 Phillips Griffiths, *Knowledge and Belief* (Oxford, 1967), p. 12.
14 Here we might be inclined to say that we know because we can trace our view back to persons who do have excellent reasons for it, but (*a*) we would still not know that they had excellent reasons, (*b*) such cases are a small subset of cases of knowledge, and (*c*) such ability to trace lines of epistemic authority still do not suffice for ἐπιστήμη on Plato's view. In the *Meno*, e.g., at 81A–B Socrates traces his belief in recollection back to people who were, he says, able to give an account; yet he himself does not claim to have ἐπιστήμη merely because they seem to, on his view. The crucial thing is that *he* cannot give an account.
15 For the distinction see Bertrand Russell, *Problems of Philosophy* (New York, 1912), ch. 5.
16 R. C. Cross and A. D. Woozley, *Plato's "Republic"* (New York, 1966), pp. 170–78.
17. *Republic* 476E–479E, 534B–C. The latter passage demands an account of the good, though the sun and the line similes freely employ the language of "seeing" or "apprehension" of it, and though Plato clearly denies that one who is unable to give such an account has ἐπιστήμη. What such a person has "seen" or "apprehended" is at best some image of the good, he remarks at 534C. See also *Theaetetus* 147B, and remarks on it by Lyons, *Structural Semantics*, pp. 121–22.
18 See, e.g., *Republic* 533E–534D, 582C–E. A few scholars seem to think that Plato employed ἐπιστήμη and its related verbs for knowledge and knowing by description, but reserved γνῶσις and its related verbs for knowledge by acquaintance. D. W. Hamlyn, surprisingly, posits this view in his often perceptive article "The Communion of Forms," *Philosophical Quarterly* 5 (1955): 290, when he remarks that "in the *Republic* 477a, the word initially used for 'knowledge' is 'γνῶσις', which expresses an acquaintance, although later in the same sentence 'ἐπιστήμη' (scientific knowledge) is substituted; this is not generally brought out in translations." I would suggest that translations are right in not bringing it out. The word γνῶσις can scarcely express an acquaintance in Plato if he uses it indiscriminately as interchangeable with a word which allegedly does not. Actually, both words are employed by Plato to express what we would call "acquaintance" *and* to express what we might call

"scientific knowledge" or "knowledge by description." At *Republic* 533C, e.g., Plato lays it down as a requirement for ἐπιστήμη that one have had a "clear waking vision" of reality, which surely suggests acquaintance, while at 477B and 478A he twice defines ἐπιστήμη as ἐπὶ τῷ ὄντι, τὸ ὄν γνῶναι ὡς ἔχει, using the verb γιγνώσκω, allegedly suggestive of acquaintance, in defining the noun ἐπιστήμη, allegedly suggestive of knowledge by description. There are many such passages in which Plato shows that he makes no distinction between knowledge by acquaintance and knowledge by description, at least insofar as such a distinction is marked by distinct philosophical uses for ἐπίστασθαι and γιγνώσκω. This is not to deny that Lyons is correct in pointing out that personal nouns *tend* to be the objects of γιγνώσκειν, even in Plato's corpus (*Structural Semantics*, p. 203). But Lyons's purpose was not philosophical interpretation of Plato's expressed views, i.e., of what Plato meant; it is rather the linguistic analysis of meaning relations typically holding among Plato's epistemic terms, with no weight given to relatively infrequent but philosophically portentous applications of these terms.

19 Cross and Woozley, *Plato's "Republic,"* do not quite say that Platonic ἐπιστήμη was such a confused amalgam, and their preface, which deals briefly but usefully with the pitfalls of translation and the disparities between Greek concepts and ours (pp. v–vi), would lead one to doubt that they could believe this; but their treatment of knowledge by acquaintance and knowledge by description on pp. 170–78 leaves one with the impression that perhaps they do believe it and are inviting readers to do so.

20 Gregory Vlastos, "The Paradox of Socrates," in Gregory Vlastos, ed., *Socrates* (Garden City, 1971), p. 6.

21 *Protagoras* 360B–E, as translated by W.K.C. Guthrie, in *Plato: Collected Dialogues*, ed. Edith Hamilton and Huntington Cairns (New York, 1961), pp. 350–51.

22 The way in which these became equivalent is detailed in Bruno Snell's masterful study, *Die Ausdrücke für den Begriff des Wissens in der vorplatonischen Philosophie* (Berlin, 1924), esp. pp. 87 ff. Plato has little technical vocabulary, and often employs as equivalents ἐπιστήμη, σοφία, νόησις, γνῶσις, φρόνησις, and σύνεσις. Snell's philological arguments are not vitiated by Lyons's more recent linguistic study.

23 Gilbert Ryle, "On Forgetting the Difference between Right and Wrong," in A. I. Melden, ed., *Essays in Moral Philosophy* (Seattle, 1958), pp. 152, 154.

24 Harold Cherniss accurately described "the fascinating and perplexing history of Platonic interpretation, which has been so largely a series of insistently charitable attempts on the part of Western philosophers and their acolytes, each to baptize Plato in his particular faith—having shriven him first, of course, by interpreting the heresies out of his works" ("Relation of the *Timaeus* to Plato," *American Journal of Philology* 78 [1957]: 234).

25 I take no position in this study on the question of which, if any, of the treatises in the extant Hippocratic corpus were actually written by Hippocrates himself. The date of this treatise is indicated on internal evidence by its mentioning in

a topical way the views of Melissus the Eleatic, who was prominent in the mid–fifth century, views quickly rendered passé by those of Empedocles and Anaxagoras.

26 E.g., Thucydides 1. 21, 6. 86. D. L. Page, "Thucydides' Description of the Great Plague at Athens," *Classical Quarterly* 47 (1953): 97–119, has documented Thucydides' familiarity with Hippocratic medical terminology of even the rarest sort, and regards it as highly probable that he was familiar with a number of the extant treatises of the Hippocratic school.

27 Friedrich Solmsen, "The 'Gift' of Speech in Homer and Hesiod," in his *Kleine Schriften* (Hildesheim, 1968), 1:1–15, has emphasized how important λόγος was to Homeric personae. Those who lack the gift of speech and yet try nevertheless to speak, as the unfortunate Thersites does, are pretty clearly the least wise among their fellows in the poet's scheme of things.

28 Xenophon, *Memorabilia* 3. 3. 11. Although the gift of "speech" in the sense of persuasive and moving eloquence suitable for controlling a mass of people was not thought to be coextensive with every other virtue, as Solmsen has argued, it does seem to have been assumed by the poet that what one has seen one can describe in a speech of some sort. In his invocation to the Muses in *Iliad* 2. 484 the poet suggests that they can tell him what he wants to know because they were present and saw it happen. On this passage see Ernst Heitsch, "Das Wissen des Xenophanes," *Rheinische Museum für Philologie* N. F. 109, 194–98.

29 Eric Havelock, *A Preface to Plato* (New York 1967), pp. 36–96.

30 J. D. Denniston, *Greek Literary Criticism* (London, 1924), p. viii.

31 *Iliad* 14. 235; *Odyssey* 3. 277 and 24. 442; see also Hesiod, *Works and Days* 731.

32 Cp., e.g., the following translations of *Iliad* 14. 235: Andrew Lang, Walter Leaf and Ernest Meyers (New York, n.d.), p. 258; George Chapman (New York, 1956), p. 287; William Cowper (London, 1802), 2: 60; Richard Lattimore (Chicago, 1957), p. 301; Ennis Rees (New York, 1963), p. 284; Francis W. Newman (London, 1971), p. 206; William Cullen Bryant (Boston, 1870), p. 49; Theodore Alois Buckley (New York, n.d.), 1: 260; Edmund, Earl of Derby (New York, 1865), 2: 60; W.H.D. Rouse (New York, 1950), p. 169. Or cp. these renderings of 24. 41: Lang, p. 441; Chapman, p. 478; Lattimore, p. 476; Rees, p. 492; Newman, p. 348; Bryant, p. 332; Rouse, p. 283.

33 David Hume, *A Treatise of Human Nature*, bk. 2, part 3, sec. 3. Sigmund Freud, *An Outline of Psycho-Analysis*, trans. and ed. James Strachey (New York, 1949), p. 5: "The power of the id expresses the true purpose of the individual organism's life. This consists in the satisfaction of its innate needs. . . . The forces which we assume to exist behind the tensions caused by the needs of the id are called instincts. They represent the somatic demands upon the mind. . . . they are the ultimate cause of all activity."

Kant's view of practical reason is closer to Plato's view than most modern views of anything which sounds cognitive. But it cannot be equated with Plato's. In chapter III of the *Kritik der praktischen Vernunft*, Kant, speaking of respect for the moral law, remarks: "Dieses Gefühl (unter dem Namen des

moralischen) ist also lediglich durch Vernunft bewirkt" (*Werke* [Weisbaden, 1956], p. 197). If Reason *produces* or *causes* this feeling, then it is distinct from it. Plato would say not that "reason" produces such a feeling but that it *has* that feeling. Indeed, the reasonable part of the psyche is identified in terms of its loving learning, wisdom, harmony, law, order and the like. See below, Ch. 3.
34 *Iliad* 5. 222, trans. A. T. Murray (London, 1965), p. 211.
35 "Know" is rarely used in such conative fashion. An example: A roulette player says, "I just *know* I'll win this time."
36 That ἐπιστήμη, σοφία, φρόνησις, νόησις, and νοῦς are often given the same application by Plato is evident from the following representative passages: *Phaedo* 98C (cp. *Euthydemus* 281B and *Protagoras* 352B–D); *Republic* 511D–E (cp. 534A), 506C, 598C–D; *Philebus* 12A (cp. 52E and 65E).
37 Kurt von Fritz, "ΝΟΟΣ and NOEIN in the Homeric Poems," *Classical Philology* (1943), pp. 79–93. Subsequent page references to this article appear parenthetically in the text.
38 Herodotus 3. 21; Lysias 2. 23; Xenophon, *Cyropaedia* 1. 6. 11, *Anabasis* 7. 6. 32; Isocrates, *Panegyricus* 175; Plato, *Protagoras* 310A, *Euthydemus* 304A, *Theages* 328A, *Phaedrus* 233D, *Theaetetus* 155D–E, *Apology* 20A (χάριν προσειδέναι).
39 Pindar, *Pythian Ode* 8. 18: εὖ μένει νόῳ, a "kindly 'intellect'"; Aeschylus, *Prometheus Bound* 164: ἄγναμπτον νόον, an "unbending 'intellect'"; Herodotus 8. 97: ἐκ παντὸς νόου, "out of all of his 'intellect,'" i.e., "with all his heart"; Plato, *Gorgias* 510B–C: ἐξ ἅπαντος τοῦ νοῦ οὐκ ἄν ποτε δύναιτο φίλος γενέσθαι, "and could never become a friend with all his 'intellect,'" i.e., "with all his heart."
40 G. S. Kirk and J. E. Raven, *The Presocratic Philosophers* (Cambridge, 1957), pp. 374–77, and S. Sambursky, *The Physical World of the Greeks* (London, 1963), pp. 81 ff., 190–91.
41 J. de Romilly, *Histoire et Raison chez Thucydide* (Paris, 1956), pp. 105–6, 135–36, 176, 178–79, 238–39, 299–303, has commented on what she regards as Thucydides' own rationalism in the interpretation of human action.
42 Heraclitus, *On the Universe*, fr. 107 (Bywater), in W.H.S. Jones, trans., *Hippocrates* (London, 1931), 4:503.
43 *On the Art* is so sophistic in style that Theodor Gomperz, *Griechische Denker*, 3rd. ed., (Leipzig, 1911), 1:374–77, thought Protagoras wrote it, while Jones, *Hippocrates* 2:188, speculates that it may have been written by Hippias of Elis. But it is clear that whoever wrote it, it belongs to the heyday of the great sophists who flourished a generation or more earlier than Plato. This has particularly interesting implications for a number of the more technical features of Plato's views, implications explored in more detail in Chapters 4 and 6.
44 For additional evidence see Michael J. O'Brien, *The Socratic Paradoxes and the Greek Mind* (Chapel Hill, 1967), pp. 24–26. It is probably fruitless to dispute over whether or not this is evidence of "intellectualism" or "naive intellectualism," especially without defining these. But O'Brien (p. 50) neatly

turns the tables on those who find such Greek locutions excessively "intellectualist" by citing parallel examples from English. Yet, having argued persuasively that a peculiarly Greek "intellectualism" is a myth (pp. 52–53), O'Brien shows a perplexing tendency to keep invoking it (pp. 83–84, e.g.).

45 E. R. Dodds, *The Greeks and the Irrational* (Berkeley and Los Angeles, 1968), p. 17.
46 J. L. Austin, "A Plea for Excuses," in *Philosophical Papers* (Oxford, 1961), p. 30. Interpretors might well bear in mind the maxim Paul Ziff calls "Occam's eraser": "Differences of meaning are not to be postulated without necessity."
47 See R. B. Onians, *The Origins of European Thought* (Cambridge, 1954), pp. 25–39.
48 Bruno Snell, "Das früheste Zeugnis über Sokrates," *Philologus* 97 (1948): 128–34, esp. 128–29, 132–33. Snell reaffirms his view in *Scenes from Greek Drama* (Berkeley and Los Angeles, 1964), pp. 58–68, esp. pp. 59–60, 66–67, and in *Szenen aus griechischen Dramen* (Berlin, 1971), pp. 61–74, esp. pp. 63–64, 70–71.
49 Ulrich von Wilamowitz-Moellendorff, *Einleitung in die attische Tragödie* (Berlin, 1889), p. 25, n. 44; Dodds, *The Greeks and the Irrational*, pp. 186–87; R. P. Winnington-Ingram, "Hippolytus: A Study in Causation," in *Fondation Hardt Entretiens VI* (Geneva, 1958), pp. 171–97; A. Lesky, *Geschichte der griechischen Literatur* (Berne, 1957), 348–49; Richard Lattimore, "Phaedra and Hippolytus," *Arion* 1 (1962): 11–12.
50 Jon Moline, "Euripides, Socrates, and Virtue," *Hermes* 103, no. 1 (1975): 45–67.
51 Pausanias 2. 32. 1–4; Euripides, *Hippolytus* 1424–30.
52 Thucydides 2. 38. 1, trans. Charles Foster Smith (London, 1920), 2:61.
53 A. W. Gomme, *A Historical Commentary on Thucydides*, 2 (Oxford, 1956): 302.
54 For the influence of Cleon, see Thucydides passim and Aristophanes' *Knights*. For the view of ἐπιστήμη, see Plato's *Protagoras* 352B.
55 Plato, *Protagoras* 352B–357E. It is surprising how often this passage has been taken as a profession of hedonism by Socrates. Socrates and Protagoras are ranged together *against* hedonism, though they have to argue, as they always do, from premises opponents will admit if they are to show their opponents' views are incoherent. Note 356D: "Now *if* our welfare consisted in doing and choosing things of large dimensions. . . ." Socrates never grants the antecedent of this conditional.
56 See *Philebus* 61D ff., where, having accounted for popular usage, Plato is more tolerant of it.
57 By "Aristotle" I mean Aristotle as represented in the *Nicomachean Ethics*. The *Eudemian Ethics* omits the context and qualifications we find on this question in the *Nicomachean Ethics*, and is thus a partial and defective text.
58 *Nicomachean Ethics*, trans. H. Rackham (London, 1962), p. 379. This way of taking τοῖς φαινομένοις is common. See W. D. Ross's translation (Oxford, 1925, vol. 9), the translation of Martin Ostwald (Indianapolis, 1962), and the

commentaries of A. Grant (Oxford, 1885), J. A. Stewart (Oxford, 1892), and H. H. Joachim (Oxford, 1951). For a more plausible view see G.E.L. Owen, "Tithenai ta Phainomena," in J.M.E. Moravscik, ed., *Aristotle* (New York, 1967), pp. 167–90.
59 Aristotle, *On the Soul* 427b3, 404a29; *Nicomachean Ethics* 1145b2–6; *Metaphysics* 1010b1, 1011a19 ff., 1004b18; *Rhetoric* 1369b26, 135620, 1402a26, 1402b23; *On the Heavens* 293a26. See Alexander of Aphrodisias, *in Aristotelis meteorologicorum commentarium*, 33.6–9 (Stueve).
60 Here I disagree also with W.K.C. Guthrie, *Socrates* (Cambridge, 1971), pp. 133–39, and *The Sophists* (Cambridge, 1971), pp. 257–60.
61 John Gould's suggestion that ἐπιστήμη can be construed as Rylean know-how (*Development of Plato's Ethics*, ch. 1) is inadequate for reasons cited earlier. Vlastos, "The Paradox of Socrates," p. 21, accuses Socrates of confusing a supreme degree of faith with knowledge.
62 Michael J. O'Brien, in construing ἐπιστήμη and σοφία as wisdom (p. 36, e.g., in *The Socratic Paradoxes and the Greek Mind*) overlooks the ability to give an account which Plato thinks necessary for the person having ἐπιστήμη.
63 Bluck, "Logos and Forms in Plato," pp. 527–28.
64 It is apparent that Attic Greek and current English are semantically anisomorphic in their epistemic terminology, much as they seem to have been in their color terminology. See Lyons, *Structural Semantics*, pp. 38–39, 98–99. We should not expect to find for all contexts exact synonyms in English for ἐπιστήμη. We should, however, cautiously seek out whatever English word approaches ἐπιστήμη most nearly in its application. For a characterization of application, see Lyons, pp. 55–56.
65 N. R. Murphy, *The Interpretation of Plato's Republic*, pp. 98–99. John Lyons, *Structural Semantics*, p. 216, n. 1, notes that in many contexts "understand" is the best translation of ἐπίστασθαι. After the manuscript for my book was submitted for publication, there appeared a wide-ranging paper by Julius Moravcsik "designed to facilitate philosophical conversations about the concept of understanding" ("Understanding and Knowledge in Plato's Philosophy," *Neue Hefte für Philosophie* 15/16 [1979]: 53–69). Moravcsik claims that "understanding is not the same as propositional knowledge" (p. 55), and that it involves "possessing the right concepts" and "intuitive insight," as well as "applying rules—based on concepts—to practice" (p. 60). He outlines Plato's theory in the formula "insight + skill = understanding" (p. 59), and devotes slightly over seven pages to the explication of Plato's epistemology from the early dialogues through the *Philebus*. This explication contains much that is promising, but it is not worked out in the detail required to be convincing. It needs arguing, e.g., that Plato was at all concerned with anything that can be adequately represented today as a concept, that he based rules on such concepts (no examples are given), and that since "for Plato understanding is tied to forms of 'know-how' and activity," "this is why he can maintain . . . that excellence ('arete') is understanding" (p. 61). It is not clear how insight plus skill provide the behavioral guarantees that Plato saw built into excellence. The physician who murders a patient for a fee has per-

fect insight and skill; indeed, this is what makes his crime so difficult to detect. Why are insight and skill incompatible with vice? On this key question, Moravcsik's account provides no illumination, for it fails to consider ἐπιστήμη as a complex state of the psyche involving conative elements and guaranteeing causally that one who is in it will act in excellent or virtuous ways. If understanding is to be construed as "the state of mind having internalized rules" (p. 67) and explicitly likened to understanding a language, as Chomsky conceives of it, then it is unclear why Plato thought that (*a*) anyone who has understanding can give an account of what he or she understands, and (*b*) the rule follower who has true opinion is in a state inferior to that of the person who understands. One can surely understand a language quite well without being able to articulate the rules one is allegedly following in speaking it.

66 The gap has been further widened by the prominence given to other-than-rational and even irrational economic motivation in the interpretations of by Adam Smith and Charles Beard (whose books, many stressing such motivation, reportedly sold over 10 million copies prior to 1956), and in popular interpretations or misinterpretations of the views of Karl Marx. (As to their being misinterpretations or not, see Erich Fromm, *Marx's Concept of Man* [New York, 1961], pp. 1–19, 24–26.)

67 That I will not object as an interpreter of Plato is no indication that I will not object as a philosopher. On this sort of distinction see Jon Moline, "On Philosophical Neutrality," *Metaphilosophy* 1 (January, 1970): 20–38.

68 The qualification "for now" is important. Plato's dialogues will never be without interest so long as the human personality works as it does. But interpretations of those dialogues, the present one not excluded, are doomed to eventual obsolescence. Plato and those who at any given time want to understand his views without mastering Attic Greek are like people on opposite banks of an unfordable river in a region subject to periodic earthquakes. The translator and interpreter bridge these banks knowing their bridges will not be passable for long.

Chapter 2: Dialectic and Ἐπιστήμη

1 If in their uses of putatively "intellectual" terms Socrates and Plato's other spokesmen make no distinction between intellectual uses or senses of these terms and nonintellectual ones, then it may even be a mistake to think that Plato had any conception of intellect or reason as distinct from passion. This point is considered more fully in Chapter 3. Arthur Adkins, in his masterful book *Merit and Responsibility* (Oxford, 1960), p. 164, adopts a similar methodology in remarking: "When a single term of value in Language A spans two situations (*a, b*) which are distinguished in Language B, it is misleading to say that Language A uses the same word to mean both *a* and *b*: it is truer to say that Language A has no word for either *a* or *b*, but rather a different system of values, with the different world-view which accompanies it."

2 The term λόγος itself is seldom used in the Homeric epics.

3 Hjalmar Frisk, *Griechisches etymologisches Wörterbuch* (Heidelberg, 1970), 2:94; J. B. Hofmann, *Etymologisches Wörterbuch des Griechischen* (Munich, 1949), p. 175.
4 Henri Fournier, *Les Verbes "Dire" en Grec Ancien* (Paris, 1946), pp. 53–54. fournier has been followed in this by Heribert Boeder, "Der frühgriechische Wortgebrauch von *Logos* und *Aletheia*," *Archiv für Begriffsgeschichte* 4 (1959): 82–84, and Gerold Prauss, *Platon und der logische Eleatismus* (Berlin, 1966), p. 84.
5 Boeder, "Der frühgriechische Wortgebrauch von *Logos* und *Aletheia*," pp. 82–86.
6 Fournier, *Les Verbes "Dire" en Grec Ancien*, p. 53.
7 Prauss, *Platon und der logische Eleatismus*, pp. 84 ff., has written as if he thought this were the case, following Boeder.
8 This will prove to be important in Chapter 6 when we consider the claim of Prauss that Plato abandoned a "selecting" or "gathering" model of λόγος in favor of a new "interweaving" model. That weaving similes were not, however, new as applied to speaking or giving accounts is clear from Pindar, *Olympian Ode* 1. 28, as Boeder, "Der frühgriechische Wortgebrauch von *Logos* und *Aletheia*," p. 90, has pointed out.
9 See esp. *Iliad* 11. 404–10; 21. 552 ff.; and 22. 98 ff. Boeder, p. 87, comments incisively upon such passages.
10 On the wide range of possible meanings for such questions see Richard Robinson, *Plato's Earlier Dialectic* (Oxford, 1953), ch. 5.
11 Ibid., p. 32.
12 R. E. Allen, *Plato's "Euthyphro" and the Earlier Theory of Forms* (London, 1970), pp. 69–70; John Burnet, *Plato's "Euthyphro," "Apology" of Socrates, and "Crito"* (Oxford, 1924), p. 32; I. M. Crombie, *Plato: The Midwife's Apprentice* (London, 1964), p. 44; P. T. Geach, "Plato's *Euthyphro*: An Analysis and Commentary," *The Monist* 50 (1966): 369–82; Alexander Nehamas, "Confusing Universals and Particulars in Plato's Early Dialogues," *Review of Metaphysics* 29 (1975): 287–306.
13 At *Theaetetus* 177E I am reading ὁ ὀνομαζόμενον θεωρεῖται with Wohlrab and B.
14 The verbal character of proceeding ἀντιλογικῶς is made apparent at *Theaetetus* 164C. One who proceeds in this way is satisfied if he seems to have got the better of the λόγος he is discussing by merely verbal agreements (πρὸς τὰς τὸν ὀνομάτον ὁμολογίας), or by abusing the author's orphan words (165E). One who proceeds in this way strives for victory by getting his opponent involved in verbal entanglements (166C), by laying too much stress on the words in the λόγος (166E), by using as his basis the ordinary meanings of verbs and nouns and perverting them haphazardly as the many do, thus causing confusion (168C). In the *Sophist*, the meaning of ἀντιλογική changed somewhat. Previously in the dialogues the distinction between ἐριστική and ἀντιλογική was evidently one between a generic form of hostile and combative argument and a species which proceeded by making purely verbal appeals as outlined above (though one could fall into such appeals, and thus indulge

in ἀντιλογική inadvertently, as *Republic* 454A–E indicates). At *Sophist* 225B, however, τὸ ἀντιλογικόν becomes the genus, and τὸ ἐριστικόν the species, the difference being that τὸ ἐριστικόν has rules of art and its genus does not.

15 Kenneth Sayre, *Plato's Analytic Method* (Chicago, 1969), p. 120, claims that Plato viewed the ability to give an account as necessary for ἐπιστήμη, as does Winifred Hicken, "Knowledge and Forms in Plato's *Theaetetus*," in R. E. Allen, ed., *Studies in Plato's Metaphysics* (London, 1965), p. 188.

16 One main issue dividing interpreters since F. M. Cornford's *Plato's Theory of Knowledge* (London, 1934) has been whether or not the *Theaetetus* is a covert attempt to show the difficulties of defining ἐπιστήμη if one is forced to do without a theory of forms. Cornford (pp. 11–21, 141–42) claims that it is such an attempt, while critics—e.g., Richard Robinson, in "Forms and Error in Plato's *Theaetetus*," *Philosophical Review* 59 (1950): 3–30—say it is not. Robinson (pp. 14–16) takes the final section, from 201E on, to be a telling critique of Plato's own view of ἐπιστήμη, a view which Plato nevertheless continued to espouse despite his having refuted it. Robinson's rejection of Cornford's position (p. 9) turns on what each of them takes a form to be.

17 Robinson, "Forms and Error in Plato's *Theaetetus*," p. 16.

18 *Republic* 534B–C. See Gregory Vlastos, "The Paradox of Socrates," in Gregory Vlastos, ed., *Socrates* (Garden City, 1971), p. 6.

19 Vision metaphors in epistemological contexts are common in many languages, and Plato frequently employs them, as at *Republic* 432A, 533C, 537C. Whether or not these are more than metaphors will be discussed in treating the forms in Chapters 4 and 6.

20 A. E. Taylor, e.g., in *Plato: The Man and His Work*, 6th ed. (New York, 1952), pp. 287–88, said: "That Socrates finds himself unable to speak of this form of the good except negatively, and that he can only characterize it positively by an imperfect analogy, is inevitable from the nature of the case. The same thing may be seen in any philosophy which does not simply deny or ignore the 'Absolute' or supreme source of all reality. Because this source is *ex hypothesi* a source of all reality, you are bound to insist that it transcends, and is thus 'wholly other' than, every particular real thing; every predicate you affirm of it belongs properly to some of its effects in contradistinction from others and can therefore only be asserted of the supreme source 'analogically' and with the warning that the analogy would mislead if pressed unduly. . . . It remains, when all is said, an unexhausted and surprising 'mystery.'" He adds (p. 289), "Neither Plato nor anyone else could tell another man what the good is, because it can only be apprehended by the most incommunicable and intimate personal insight."

21 Actually, there is room for considerable doubt that the good was among the matters referred to in *Epistle 7* at 341C when Plato says that there is no writing of his on "these matters." This doubt should arise whether or not one takes Plato to be claiming that these matters are inexpressible. Glenn Morrow, in *Plato: Epistles* (Indianapolis, 1962), p. 66, speculates that Plato's views on the good were among these matters, though he correctly takes Plato to be

claiming merely that it is inadvisable to express such matters in writing, not that they are inherently beyond expression. Yet the reference to "these matters" can only be to something mentioned previously; hence, it is not helpful to interpret it in terms of Plato's revealing later, at 344D, that Dionysius's book dealt with the first and highest things in nature, as Morrow interprets it (pp. 64–65). Even the reference to the first and highest things in nature as being the subject of Dionysius' tract should be taken in the light of Plato's claim at 341B that Dionysius' tract was on the subjects in which he had received instruction from Plato and of his characterization of those subjects at 340B–341B. He claims to have taught Dionysius merely the character of philosophy as a whole, how many preliminaries it entails and how much labor, the divine gifts necessary to pursue it, and the orderly mode of daily life conducive to it. There is no hint here of the good.

To speak of Plato's mysticism is perhaps not useful, since "mysticism" is an epistemologically promiscuous term ranging over a number of quite distinct issues. To speak more precisely, the point at issue here is whether or not Plato accepted what is now called the effability hypothesis, i.e., the view that anything that can be thought can be said. I have argued that Plato does accept it. Later philosophers who have also accepted it are J. J. Katz, *Semantic Theory* (New York, 1972), pp. 18–24, and John R. Searle, *Speech Acts* (Cambridge, 1969), pp. 19–21. Some reasons for not accepting it have been reviewed by E. Keenan, "Some Logical Problems in Translation," in F. Guenthner and M. Guenthner-Reutter, eds., *Meaning and Translation* (London, 1978), p. 159, n. 3; Keenan also develops reasons for qualifying or weakening the hypothesis (pp. 159–63) while still retaining what is central to it (pp. 166–67).

22 Following Grote, E. Meyer, Wilamowitz, Taylor, Morrow and many others, I accept the *Epistle 7* as genuine, including the passage from 342A to 344D which Constantin Ritter rejected as a spurious interpolation in an otherwise genuine Platonic Letter (*Platons Gesetze* [Leipzig, 1896], app., pp. 371 ff.). Ludwig Edelstein, *Plato's Seventh Letter* (Leiden, 1966), pp. 80–85, in rejecting the letter, overstated Plato's confessed reticence about serious matters as "deliberate deception."

23 Edelstein, *Plato's Seventh Letter*, p. 83, oddly characterizes *Epistle 7* as having asserted "the impossibility of expressing in words the last truths of Nature," though he recognizes that Plato *argues against* doing this "impossible" thing. Edelstein has overlooked the ambiguity in ῥητόν. Had he not done so, the congruity between *Phaedrus* and the letter would have been evident. Kurt von Fritz, "The Philosophical Passage in the Seventh Platonic Letter and the Problem of Plato's 'Esoteric' Philosophy," in John P. Anton and George L. Kustus, eds., *Essays in Greek Philosophy* (Albany, 1971), p. 409, notes the irony of such misunderstandings as these: "Most of the arguments commonly set forth against the authenticity of the philosophical passage present in fact a prime illustration of what the author of the letter says about the inevitable weakness of every written account of certain things." For the surprisingly persistent view that Plato had "secret doctrines" (actually not-so-secret, since

those who hold this view often claim to have discerned them), see Hans Joachim Krämer, *Arete bei Platon und Aristoteles: Zum Wesen der platonischen Ontologie* (Heidelberg, 1959), pp. 380–486, and von Fritz's compelling treatment of it ("The Philosophical Passage in the Seventh Platonic Letter," pp. 429–42, esp. p. 434).

24 How involved this answer would be on the view of the later Plato is evident from the *Timaeus* and *Philebus*. Human beings have a portion of divine νοῦς, and the function of divine νοῦς is to impose order and proportion on irrational ἀνάγκη, or necessity, by persuading it to guide most things toward the good.

25 *Meno* 85C–D, 98A. Cp. *Phaedrus* 249B–C. Recollection, on Plato's view, is achieved not by some mystical insight but by the process of hard, dialectical work carried through successfully to yield a sturdy account. He continues to hold this theory of recollection even in late dialogues. This was argued very ably by Norman Gulley, *Plato's Theory of Knowledge* (London, 1962), pp. 108–20.

26 That virtuous nonverbal behavior on a few given occasions or in a short timespan is not sufficient to distinguish ἐπιστήμη from ὀρθὴ δόξα is clear from *Meno* 97A–C. Even though it is not sufficient, it is necessary, as is clear from the fact that Plato frequently cited a person's behavior as providing a knockdown proof of a lack of σοφία or ἐπιστήμη. Even as early as *Apology* 34C, e.g., Socrates argued that one's conduct in court (bringing in one's children to weep and move the jurors, e.g.) can be a disgrace. The reason it is a disgrace is that it shows one lacks σοφία. It is unthinkable, on his view, that one who really had σοφία would pull out all the stops to postpone death. He explicitly interprets the fear of death as owing to one's thinking one understands what one does not understand (29A–B); and Socrates' own self-proclaimed wisdom consisted precisely in his not indulging in such overweening thoughts, as one can discern at 20D–21C. That one's acts can count decisively against any claim one has to ἐπιστήμη on Plato's view is borne out by Socrates' claim at *Phaedo* 79D that φρόνησις, which is simply ἐπιστήμη by another name, is a state of detachment from the body and its desires. Plainly then, one's acts can in effect refute one's claim to ἐπιστήμη as easily as one's words. This remained Plato's view throughout his life, as is indicated by *Laws* 961D–E. For similar interest in the acts of the reputedly wise see *Gorgias* 515A–B, 515D ff., 517A, and, for Socrates, Xenophon, *Memorabilia* 1. 2. 29–38. For a contrasting interpretation of Plato's interest in the acts of people as indications of their wisdom see Gregory Vlastos, "Socratic Knowledge and Platonic Pessimism," *Philosophical Review* 66 (1957): 228.

27 For a description of the process involved in such trials by fire see R. J. Forbes, *Metallurgy in Antiquity* (Leiden, 1950), pp. 157–60, 173. As a citizen of a mining town in which people of Plato's social stratum owned slaves and concessions in the digs at Laurion south of the city, and even, as in Thucydides' case, near Amphipolis (Thucydides 4. 104 ff.), Plato would have been likely to pick up some mining lore. Although the mines at Laurion evidently yielded no gold, Plato shows a familiarity with aspects of the gold-refining process at *Statesman* 303C–304A. He describes smelting at *Timaeus*

58E, the appearance of gold-bearing minerals at 59B, and the goal of the refining process at *Epistle 2*, 314A–B.

28 At our incarnation, according to *Timaeus* 42B, we are given the task of mastering pleasure, pain, fear, anger, and the like. If we do this, we live justly, and if not, unjustly. As 90B makes clear, to be mastered by these is to be filled with entirely "mortal" or transitory opinions.

29 Aristotle is not attentive to the importance of the office of the εὐθύνοι, or examiners, in Plato's state when he remarks, at *Politics* 1265a, that Plato brings the constitution of the *Laws* by degrees back to the form of the *Republic*. Strangely, Aristotle was well aware of the importance of similar offices in existing states. See, e.g., *Politics* 1322b11 ff. Modern writers have also on occasion overlooked the constitutional importance of the examiners and the check they pose upon the performance of the guardians. See, e.g., Leo Strauss, *History of Political Philosophy* (Chicago, 1963), p. 61.

30 *Laws* 691C–E at first sight seems to support this line. See E. R. Dodds, "Plato and the Irrational Soul," in G. Vlastos, ed., *Plato* (Garden City, 1971), pp. 217–18, for an unusually sensitive presentation of the standard view.

31 *Laws* 716A–B and 713C appear to support this interpretation. Cp. 874E ff.

32 *Laws* 713C is perhaps the most important passage. But compare 709C ff. Gregory Vlastos, in "Socratic Knowledge and Platonic Pessimism," p. 237, n. 27, cites 875B–C as especially important. He takes this passage to claim that "even a man who starts with 'adequate', i.e., philosophical, knowledge and then gets 'unaccountable, autocratic' power will be led to ruin by his 'mortal nature.'"

33 *Laws* 709B, perhaps. See also 712A.

34 *Epistle 7*, 324D–325C, describes Plato's youthful disillusionment.

35 Ernest Barker's widely read treatise *Greek Political Theory* (London, 1918; New York, 1960), pp. 340 ff., is perhaps the chief source of this interpretation.

36 *Laws* 710D–E must figure in the interpretation of 712A, which claims that wherever the greatest power coincides with wisdom and temperance, the seed of the best state and the best laws is planted. These are to coincide, not in one person, but in separate persons of like mind. Plato is not saying that power is not to be shared. Note the quotation from Hesiod at 690E to the effect that oftentimes the half is greater than the whole. Since writing the *Republic,* Plato has seen that a ruler need not be engaged in a zero-sum game, one in which the total quantity of power is constant and any power given another represents a net loss to the giver. As Crombie aptly put it in commenting upon the *Statesman*, "One of the things that a man knows, if he knows how to create a united community, is that he must not govern by force; and therefore the true statesman will govern with consent, not in the sense that he will exact nothing except what his subjects have already seen to be desirable, but in the sense that he will not exact anything which his subjects will be unable to consent to when he has enacted it, and which he will therefore have to impose by force" (I. M. Crombie, *An Examination of Plato's Doctrines*, 1 [London, 1962]: 167–68). Plato, however, goes even further than Crombie seems to indicate;

he sees friendliness, freedom, and amenability to persuasion both as valuable in their own right and as increasing the power of the state in which they are found.

37 The Loeb translator's reading of ἀνθρωπεία φύσις as "human being" is seriously misleading. Plato is discussing human *nature*, though that is not the only nature human beings happen to possess.

38 Barker, *Greek Political Theory*, p. 362. He bases his view on *Laws* 875C–D.

39 Plato's caution here ought to come as a surprise, given the certified divine nature of the examiners, though commentators ordinarily give it little or no attention. See, e.g., Crombie's dismissal of the examiners (*An Examination of Plato's Doctrines*, 2:175).

40 Since in the relevant sense of "evil"—i.e., evil nature—no one *becomes* evil, and since the tests prior to the election were designed to focus on evil in just this sense, the phrase translated "after his election" (ὕστερον τῆς κρίσεως) belongs with the word translated "demonstrate" (ἐπιδείξῃ), not with the phrase translated "by becoming evil" (κακὸς γενόμενος), as in the Loeb translation. R. B. England, in his excellent commentary, *The Laws of Plato*, 2 (London, 1921):584, unfortunately suggests a translation even looser than the Loeb's: ". . . lest it be seen that he has deteriorated as men may." This does not do justice to the sort of tests Plato had required, tests which, as Plato explicitly said at 650B, focus upon the natures and conditions (τὰς φύσεις τε καὶ ἕξεις) of men's psyches. Doubtless, on Plato's view it is human nature to change in surprising ways, but the examiners have been tested and certified as being divine at 945C, and whatever is divine does not change so as to do evil.

Chapter 3: Ἐπιστήμη and the Psyche

1 Constantin Ritter, *Platon*, 2 (Munich, 1923):448–50; A. E. Taylor, *Plato* (New York, 1956), p. 282; Andreas Graeser, *Probleme der platonischen Seelenteilungslehre* (Munich, 1969), p. 16.

2 Kantian faculty psychology is not in question in this study. The variety in question we owe to Aristotle, who first articulated it in opposition to Plato. Aristotle had general taxonomic scruples about having the same things (in this case the same δυνάμεις, or faculties) show up on both sides of a division (*De Anima* 432b5–8). The priority of distinct activities in the definition of δυνάμεις is clear at 415a19–20 and 416a19–20. In Plato's use, δύναμις is not narrow enough in meaning to be translated "faculty"; see, e.g., *Republic* 477C1–3, D1–6. Thomas Reid, *Essays on the Active Powers of Man* (Edinburgh, 1788), pp. 76, 187–88, is actually in Aristotle's camp, though he fancies himself a follower of Plato. He is followed in suggesting that Plato was a faculty psychologist by interpreters and translators who (1) refer to the parts of the psyche as faculties or powers, (2) term these parts "principles," or (3) describe the activity, nature, and relation of these parts to the person whose parts they are as if they were faculties or principles of Reid's sort. See, for example, F. M. Cornford, "The Division of the Soul," *Hibbert Journal* 28

(1929–30): 206–19; A. Chaignet, *De la Psychologie de Platon* (Paris, 1862), pp. 219, 231, 235; Andreas Leissner, *Die platonische Lehre von der Seelenteilung: Wesen und Stellung innerhalb der platonischen Philosophie* (Nordlingen, 1909), p. 39; N. R. Murphy, *The Interpretation of Plato's "Republic"* (Oxford, 1951), pp. 32, 34; Paul Shorey, "The Unity of Plato's Thought," *Decennial Publications*, 6 (Chicago, 1904), 1st ser.:166 ff.; R. C. Cross and A. D. Woozley, *Plato's "Republic": A Philosophical Commentary* (London, 1966), p. 124; T. M. Robinson, *Plato's Psychology* (Toronto, 1970), pp. 42–43, 51, 121, 124; W.K.C. Guthrie, "Plato's Views on the Nature of Soul," *Fondation Hardt Entretiens* (Geneva) 3 (1955):17–18; W.F.R. Hardie, *A Study in Plato* (Oxford, 1936), p. 141. For an exception, see Terry Penner, "Thought and Desire in Plato," in Gregory Vlastos, ed., *Plato*, 2 (Garden City, 1971):96, 100–101.

3 Bernard Williams's translation, in "The Analogy of City and Soul in Plato's *Republic*," in E. N. Lee, A.P.D. Mourelatos, and Richard Rorty, eds., *Exegesis and Argument: Studies in Greek Philosophy Presented to Gregory Vlastos* (Assen, 1973), p. 196.
4 Cp. Léon Robin, *La Pensée Grecque* (Paris, 1963), p. 231.
5 Such classes need not have more than a single member each (369D–E). Justice for Plato is a restriction and specialization of function which yields harmony, since the restriction automatically puts the power to rule in the right hands and secures agreement about who is to do what. Justice is not itself a harmony, as J. D. Mabbott maintains in "Is Plato's *Republic* Utilitarian?" in Vlastos, *Plato*, 2:60 and 61. To maintain this is to conflate justice with temperance. Cp. *Republic* 430D8–E4.
6 Cp. F. M. Cornford, "Psychology and Social Structure in the *Republic* of Plato," *Classical Quarterly* 6 (1912):264; A.W.H. Adkins, *Merit and Responsibility* (Oxford, 1960), p. 312, n. 1; and Robinson, *Plato's Psychology*, p. 46. Each assumes that what obtains between the polis and psyche on Plato's view is an analogy merely, and a forced one at that, as does Bernard Williams, "The Analogy of City and Soul in Plato's *Republic*," p. 197.
7 The translation follows that of G.M.A. Grube, *Plato's "Republic"* (Indianapolis, 1974), p. 96, substituting "psyche" for "soul."
8 *Laws* 626D–627B, 635D, 644D–645B, 863A–864B; see also *Timaeus* 69B–72D, *Sophist* 227E ff., 228B esp.
9 This is not a statement of the principle of noncontradiction, as is sometimes suggested. Anthony Kenny, *The Anatomy of the Soul* (Oxford, 1973), p. 4, characterizes it more appropriately as "the principle of noncontrariety."
10 Uniqueness or singularity of activity or ability must not be inferred from the use of the definite article here or in *c*, a use discussed and interpreted later in this chapter.
11 The italicized words render ἐὰν μὴ ὑπὸ κακῆς τροφῆς διαφθαρῇ, a phrase not given due emphasis by interpreters who see this passage as suggesting that the "spirited" and "calculative" are really one part, since they do not normally conflict. Plato's point is that they are two parts because they *can* conflict, and he could not have developed either the objection to timocracy he does at

547D ff. or the sort of analysis of timocratic men he does at 548D ff. had he not laid this foundation. Contrast James Adam, *The "Republic" of Plato*, 2nd ed., 1 (Cambridge, 1963), app. 4, esp. p. 271. Michael J. O'Brien, *The Socratic Paradoxes and the Greek Mind* (Chapel Hill, 1967), p. 156, overlooks the phrase above in construing the spirited part as always taking the side of the calculative.

12 Later at *Republic* 571B–572B Plato cites the evidence of psychic faction provided by the contrast between the content of dreams and the content of our waking experience.

13 *Republic* 441C–D, trans. Grube, *Plato's "Republic,"* p. 105.

14 On this point see Penner, "Thought and Desire in Plato," and J.R.S. Wilson, "The Argument of *Republic* IV," *Philosophical Quarterly* 26 (April 1976): 113.

15 The specific number of parts posited is not crucial. What is crucial for the isomorphism of the polis and psyche is the pattern of argument, which requires that polis and psyche have the same number and type of parts. Thus, it is of no major importance that bipartition is suggested as early as 375C ff., that the possibility of more than three parts is envisioned at 443E1, or that Plato sounds rather tentative and undogmatic about the number at 544D7–9. That the number of parts in the polis can be no greater than the number of psychic parts is indicated at 435E–436A. Cp. 544D7–9 and 544E3–5.

16 The objection to the seeming anthropomorphism here is taken up at the end of this chapter.

17 I. M. Crombie, *An Examination of Plato's Doctrines* 1 (London, 1962): 354–56, has denied this, as have Cross and Woozley, *Plato's "Republic,"* p. 128, and Murphy, *The Interpretation of Plato's "Republic,"* p. 69.

18 The argument in which parts are distinguished by their order of emergence at 441A7–B2 is Glaucon's, not Socrates'.

19 This is not to say that it cannot all be confined in one body, or to suggest that the complex so confined cannot be "unified" and "made one" as the good polis is when it achieves unanimity. But unanimity does not bring with it loss of distinctness in the parts. This distinctness no more warrants T. H. Martin's conclusion that Plato has posited *three souls* in each person than it would warrant the conclusion that each person has two bodies because one arm can push against another in isometric exercises (*Etudes sur le Timée de Platon* [Paris, 1841; reprinted New York, 1976], pp. 298–301).

20 Here I accept Graeser's term *Kompetenzen*, while rejecting his argument that what he terms the *Satz vom Widerspruch* or *Kontradiktionsprinzip* establishes that the competence of one part cannot overlap that of another (*Probleme*, p. 15). The conclusion is true, but for more complex reasons than Graeser's argument suggests.

21 Cp. Eduard Zeller, *Die Philosophie der Griechen*, 4th ed., 2 (Leipzig, 1889): 845.

22 See n. 2 above, and G. F. Stout and J. M. Baldwin, eds, *Dictionary of Philosophy and Psychology*, 1 (New York, 1901):369. Similar views were held in German faculty psychology. Christian Wolff, for example, in his *Vernünftige*

Gedanken von den Kräften des Menschen (Halle, 1738), characterized a faculty as a *Fertigkeit* (p. 144).

23 E.g., Cross and Woozley, *Plato's "Republic,"* pp. 123–24, and Hardie, *A Study in Plato*, p. 139.

24 Reid, *Essay on the Active Powers of Man*, pp. 47, 54, and 276, was clearly aware that a power requires an agent to use it, that agent being the person. Cp. Robinson, *Plato's Psychology*, pp. 47–48.

25 Thrasymachus's claim that virtue is the interest of the stronger may be seen as an expression of an unbridled part C; Laches' claim at *Laches* 190E that "courage is the willingness to stay at one's post, face the enemy, and not run away" seems an expression of part B; Hippias' all-too-revealing suggestion that "beauty is nothing but gold" would be a paradigmatic expression of part C.

26 Here I differ with Adam, *The "Republic" of Plato*, 2:406, who finds something new: C's opinions. Earlier Adam had recognized the internal dialogue posited at 437A (1:249). And since a dialogue involves an exchange of opinions, he had in effect recognized what he later overlooks.

27 At *Republic* 435E2–3 he says that qualities of the polis could not have got into it from any other source. The claim is repeated at 544E1–2.

28 Commentators who, like Shorey and others, see Plato through the lens of faculty psychology, fail to do justice to his insight into the normal *dis*unity of consciousness when they suggest that he was concerned to show the "synthetic unity of thought" (Shorey, "The Unity of Plato's Thought," p. 45).

29 O'Brien, *The Socratic Paradoxes and the Greek Mind*, notes the rule of reason in the psyche (pp. 178–79) and the "subjection" of lower parts to higher (p. 187) but does not account for Plato's talk of persuasion, gentleness, and friendliness in the psyche.

30 It will be readily apparent that Plato cannot conceive of the thought or opinion of a part and that of a person along precisely the same lines without generating a regress. How those lines differ is discussed below.

31 The psyche, on Plato's view, is the true self, as *Republic* 469C and 526A–B indicate.

32 This fuller Hippocratic study may be part of the longer and harder way referred to in *Republic* 435D1–5. See *Phaedrus* 272C1–2.

33 Williams, "The Analogy of City and Soul in Plato's *Republic*," pp. 202–4, overlooks this point in Plato's argument, and concludes as a result that there are grave obstacles to Plato's analogy between psyche and polis. See also p. 197, "the absurd result. . . ."

34 W. H. Thompson, *The "Phaedrus" of Plato* (London, 1869), pp. xiii–xiv, notes that diverse views as to the leading idea of the dialogue are suggested by the various subtitles affixed to it by even its Greek commentators—"Concerning Beauty," "Concerning Love," "Concerning Rhetoric," "Concerning the Good," "Concerning the Psyche," etc. R. Hackforth, *Plato's "Phaedrus"* (Cambridge, 1952), pp. 8–10, also notes ancient and modern scholars' puzzlement on the subjects and purposes of the dialogue.

35 *Meno* 80A; *Phaedo* 77E, 78A, 114D; *Charmides* 156D–157A, 176B; *Republic* 426B, 364B, 608A; *Theaetetus* 149C, 157C; *Laws* 659E, 665C, 666C, 670E, 773D, 812C, 887D, 837E, 903B, 909B, 933D, 944B.
36 Yvon Brès, *La Psychologie de Platon* (Paris, 1968), pp. 288–308; Kenny, *The Anatomy of the Soul*. See also three papers in Vlastos, *Plato,* 2: R. Demos (p. 55), G. Vlastos (p. 68), and W. J. Verdenius (p. 264).
37 P. Lain-Entralgo, "Die platonische Rationalisierung der Besprechung (ΕΠΩΙΔΗ) und die Erfindung der Psychotherapie durch das Wort," *Hermes* 86 (1958):298–323. Cp. Brès, *La Psychologie de Platon*, pp. 318–19.
38 The translation is that of W.R.M. Lamb, *Plato with an English Translation* (London and Cambridge, Mass., 1955), p. 21. This theory of "charms" is overlooked by critics such as R.H.S. Crossman, who remarked: "In politics there are no anesthetics or drugs to make the suffering easier for the patient to bear. For the good of the State the ruler must punish and banish and kill the citizen who objects to the political operation the State must undergo." ("Plato and the Perfect State," in T. L. Thorson, ed., *Plato: Totalitarian or Democrat* [Englewood Cliffs, 1963], p. 33).
39 C. W. Müller, *Gleiches zu Gleichen* (Wiesbaden, 1965), esp. pp. 69–73, is useful on such theories.
40 *Phaedrus* 270C–D provides only one of the many indications of Plato's contact with current medical ideas.
41 On the function of myth in Plato there is good reason, then, to disagree with those who regard his myths as means of expressing higher truths inaccessible to dialectical expression. G. S. Kirk, *Myth* (Cambridge, 1970), p. 259, claims that Plato "uses myth as second-best." This suggests that it is a forced alternative to dialectic, which seems misleading. Myth is the Platonic therapy of choice for parts B and C, which are as indifferent to dialectical argument as part A is to what Kirk terms "purely evocative and imagistic" tales of "lands flowing with milk and honey." Guthrie, "Plato's Views on the Nature of the Soul," p. 18, conflates the use of myth with mysticism.
42 Lamb trans.
43 Harold North Fowler, trans., *Plato with an English Translation* (London and Cambridge, Mass., 1960), p. 391.
44 E. R. Dodds ("Plato and the Irrational Soul," in Vlastos, *Plato*, 2:214) speaks of "the unitary soul of the *Phaedo*." The view that the psyche in the *Phaedo* is represented as unitary or partless is perhaps the most widely accepted interpretation. See, e.g., W.K.C. Guthrie, "Plato's Views on the Nature of the Soul," p. 233, in the same volume. The interpretation draws its apparent textual support from *Phaedo* 78B3–C5, 80B9–12. But these passages show, not that Plato here thinks the psyche has no parts, but only that *if* it has parts, it was not compounded out of them. The doubtful assumption is that whatever is complex must necessarily have been constructed or combined, and is therefore in jeopardy of dissolution. The "combination" in question is the adding of rivets to the body, i.e., excessive bodily pleasures, not the addition of parts of the psyche.

45 G.E.L. Owen, surprisingly, denies the continuity of the dialogue by remarking: "Certainly neither the tripartite soul nor the theory of paradigms which bulked so large in the mythic hymn plays the least part in the subsequent proposals for a practical psychology or rhetoric" ("Plato on the Undepictable," in Lee, Mourelatos, and Rorty, *Exegesis and Argument*, p. 350).
46 Charles Kahn, "Plato on the Unity of the Virtues," in W. H. Werkmeister, ed., *Facets of Plato's Philosophy* (Assen, 1976), p. 27.
47 For an excellent discussion of this *Gorgias* passage see Norman Gulley, "The Interpretation of "No One Does Wrong Willingly' in Plato's Dialogues," *Phronesis* 10 (1965): 82–96.
48 On occasion Plato uses ἄκων, as he does most words, in demotic or nontechnical ways, as, e.g., at *Crito* 48E and 52C. Cp. *Protagoras* 345E and *Gorgias* 509E. He even recognizes such uses of his epistemic terms at *Philebus* 55C ff., while maintaining that these terms, so used, have referents inferior to the referents they have when used of truer and purer referents. The place of these observations in Plato's overall theory will be discussed in the next chapter.
49 Stout and Baldwin, *Dictionary of Philosophy and Psychology*, 1:369; emphasis added.
50 David Hume, *A Treatise of Human Nature*, ed. L. A. Selby-Bigge (Oxford, 1928), p. 252. I am indebted to Keith Yandell at this point.
51 Richard Taylor, "Voluntarism," in Paul Edwards, ed., *The Encyclopedia of Philosophy*, 8 (New York, 1970):270.
52 As O'Brien, *The Socratic Paradoxes and the Greek Mind*, p. 211, has noted, we cannot even translate the phrase "freedom of the will" into Plato's Greek.
53 As David Keyt has remarked, "One sometimes finds a *philosophical* objection to a theory offered as an objection to a theory qua interpretation—even though it is a gross non sequitur to argue that a theory is a bad interpretation because it is a bad piece of philosophy. (But this fallacy is easily committed by Platonic scholars. One doesn't want the master to look bad.)" ("Plato on Falsity," in Lee, Mourelatos, and Rorty, *Exegesis and Argument*, p. 286.)
54 Cross and Woozley, *Plato's "Republic,"* p. 129; Crombie, *An Examination of Plato's Doctrines* 1:354–56; Hardie, *A Study in Plato*, p. 139. For a more sanguine view, see Dodds, "Plato and the Irrational Soul," pp. 215–17.
55 Aristotle, *Physics* 187b2–8. Cp. *Phaedrus* 237D–238C.
56 Leissner, *Die platonische Lehre von der Seelenteilung*, p. 46; Cross and Woozley, *Plato's "Republic"*, p. 124. See also Wright Neely, "Freedom and Desire," *Philosophical Review* 83 (January 1974): 42–43; Wilson, "The Argument of *Republic* IV," p. 122.
57 This problem was recognized by Aristotle, *De Anima* 411b5–30, but Plato himself was perhaps aware of it, for at *Phaedrus* 277B–C, where he requires of his rhetorician-psychologist the ability to divide and define by εἴδη until further division is impossible, he mentions dividing up psyches in the same way, devising elaborate and harmonious accounts for complex psyches and simple accounts for simple ones (presumably parts of the psyche). The parts

are simple—i.e., partless—on the relevant ground for recognizing parts.
58 At *Republic* 558C ff. Plato offers the psychological basis in his theory for the overt political conflict between potential oligarchs, tyrants, and democrats, all of whom love possessions. He distinguishes necessary and unnecessary ἐπιθυμίαι, and among the unnecessary ones he distinguishes those that are "terrible, fierce, and lawless" from those that are not. The oligarch is ruled by the necessary desires, inhibiting the others. The democrat makes no distinction between necessary and unnecessary desires, and is influenced by each in turn (561A–E). The tyrant is ruled by the lawless unnecessary desires, which hinder other desires (574A).
59 This confusion may be encouraged by treating the psyche itself as an Idea, without sufficient qualification, as A. J. Festugiere does in *Contemplation et Vie Contemplative selon Platon*, 2nd ed. (Paris, 1950), p. 122.
60 Another objection to conceiving of the parts as agentlike deserves mention. Hardie, *A Study in Plato*, pp. 139–40, and Cross and Woozley, *Plato's "Republic,"* p. 129, have argued that this conception would commit Plato to denying that persons could properly be held morally responsible for their actions. As Arthur Adkins has argued, however, the notion of moral responsibility has no clear counterpart in classical Greek thought, even when applied to persons themselves (*Merit and Responsibility* [Oxford, 1960], chs. 13–14). Had he wished to develop such a notion, Plato could have spoken of a notion of subpersonal responsibility, the responsibility of the wisdom-loving part for nourishing itself and for guiding the lesser parts. One can perhaps read *Republic* 619B–620D, 606A8–9, and *Timaeus* 42B–D as suggesting that he did develop this notion. Finally, it is fair to point out that we ascribe moral responsibility even to committees dominated by a strong minority.
61 For example, K. V. Wilkes, "Anthropomorphism and Analogy in Psychology," *Philosophical Quarterly* 25 (April 1975): 126–37.
62 See, e.g., Wilson, "The Argument of *Republic* IV," p. 115: "That interpretation which is most interesting and least erroneous as philosophy is likely to be right."
63 *Republic* 403A; *Symposium* 205B, 210A–212A. On Diotima's view, people mistakenly single out a certain sort of *eros* and misappropriate for it alone the name appropriate for many diverse sorts of loves—indeed, the name appropriate for any drive towards the good. This love, rightly considered, is not specific. As Cornford remarks, "Eros . . . is not to be defined in terms of any of its possible objects. The name 'Eros' is commonly misappropriated to one species of love—desire for the enjoyment of physical beauty; but properly it means 'any and every desire for good things or for happiness.'" And Cornford rightly noted that *Republic* 485D reiterates this in its hydraulic simile. See Cornford, "The Division of the Soul," 213, 215.
64 Sigmund Freud, *The Standard Edition of the Complete Psychological Works of Sigmund Freud*, 28, 22, 19, trans. L. Strachey (London, 1952–1966), 28:91; 22:209; 19:218.
65 On the psychological theory Plato held, it would be incautious to assume that

the Myth of Er at *Republic* 614A ff., and similar passages suggesting reincarnation at *Phaedrus* 249B and *Timaeus* 91A–92C, must be more than ἐπῳδαί addressed to the parts of the psyche concerned with body and perhaps with honor, though they *may* be more than this.

Chapter 4: Ἐπιστήμη and Forms in Early and Middle Dialogues

1 At the suggestion of Wittgenstein, R. S. Bluck and Peter Geach have considered the view that forms are or at least resemble standards such as the standard pound (R. S. Bluck, "Forms as Standards," *Phronesis* 2 (1956): 115–21, and Peter Geach, "The Third Man Again," *Philosophical Review* 65 (1956): 74). R. C. Cross suggested that a form in Plato functions as a logical predicate ("Logos and Forms in Plato," *Mind* 63 [1954]: 448), and not, as has often been thought, a simple nameable "known ultimately by acquaintance" (p. 446). George Brown ("The Alleged Metaphysics in the *Republic*," *Proceedings of the Aristotelian Society*, supplementary vol. 19 [1945]) claimed that "a form is nothing more subtle than that which is expressed in a definition that has been examined and found to stand up to every possible criticism. A form is the logical correlative of a definition." R. L. Nettleship, by contrast, seems to have regarded forms as laws of nature, albeit laws described in dangerous ways by Plato (*Lectures On Plato's Republic*, 2nd ed. [London, 1962], pp. 255, 275). Paul Natorp took forms to be concepts of the methodical, lawlike sort appropriate as logical foundations for science, and thus explicitly likened Plato to Kant (*Platons Ideenlehre: Eine Einfuehrung in den Idealismus*, 2nd ed. [Leipzig, 1921], p. 462). Eric Havelock (*A Preface to Plato* [New York, 1967], pp. 256–71) takes forms to be abstractions "created by an act of intellectual isolation and integration" (p. 257), though he contradicts this view by admitting that "we do not invent them" (p. 264). Plainly, not all of these characterizations of Platonic forms can be right if they are all addressed to the same dialogues, if Plato did indeed have the concepts they attribute to him, and if he had anything coherent enough to deserve the name "theory" at all. A scientific law is propositional, while a predicate appears as only one component in a proposition. Standards and paradigms such as meter-bars and pounds are neither abstractions nor concepts, but they are both arbitrary to some degree and wholly nonpropositional in character, which scientific laws are not. And if a form is nothing more subtle than the logical correlative of a definition, it is a mystery why all the above characterizations of a form have some plausibility.

2 A few interpreters have admitted their surprise—e.g., A. E. Taylor in his helpful work, *Varia Socratica* (Oxford, 1911), pp. 178–80—and have thus encouraged asking the right questions about forms. Taylor's interpretation has been much commented-on, first and perhaps still best by C. M. Gillespie, "The Use of εἶδος and ἰδέα in Hippocrates," *Classical Quarterly* 6 (1912): 179–203.

3 For mud or clay see *Theaetetus* 147A; for fishing, *Sophist* 218D ff.; for square roots, *Theaetetus* 147C–148B.
4 This is the chief thing which puzzled Taylor, though he saw the range of interlocutors as being narrower than it was. There is no evidence that Parmenides, Glaucon, Adeimantus, or Phaedrus were Pythagoreans, as on Taylor's view they would be. And Cratylus (*Cratylus* 439C–D) accepts forms though he is a Heraclitean. For other arguments on this point see H. C. Baldry, "Plato's 'Technical Terms,'" *Classical Quarterly* 31 (1934): 141–50. Like Taylor, Baldry takes Plato to be under Pythagorean influence in his theory of forms. This might be true, or part of the truth, but it is not an accessible part. W. D. Ross had what will probably be the last word on such views as Baldry and Taylor proposed: "Our ignorance about the history of Pythagoreanism, and about the dating of developments in it, is profound" (*Plato's Theory of Ideas* [Oxford, 1951], p. 14). If our interest is in shedding light on Plato's theory of forms, we can scarcely expect to get it from so dark a source as the Pythagoreans.

The range of interlocutors Plato saw fit to treat as privy to a notion of forms is wider still if we accept R. E. Allen's conclusions in *Plato's "Euthyphro" and the Earlier Theory of Forms* (London, 1970), pp. 70–74. If the arguments of the present chapter are correct, Allen's claim that even in early dialogues Plato had a theory of forms as standards or perfect paradigms is plausible, since such a theory, I argue, is grounded in pre-Socratic scientific thought known to Plato.
5 Taylor, *Varia Socratica*, p. 179.
6 *Protagoras* 318B–D, 328E–329D, 336B–D; *Euthydemus* 227C–228E; *Republic* 345B–347A.
7 *Meno* 100B; *Protagoras* 361C–D; *Republic* 354B–C; *Charmides* 175A–176A.
8 The unclarity addressed in the *Parmenides* does not concern what a form is, but rather some evidently implausible things Socrates has said about forms, as is indicated in Parmenides' questions at 130B: "Tell me, do you yourself distinguish, as you say, some forms which are themselves separate, separate from the things which share in them? And do you think there is a likeness itself apart from the likeness we possess, and indeed a one and a many and all other such things as you heard Zeno speaking of just now? . . . And also . . . a certain form of justice alone by itself and of beauty and good and of all such things? . . . And is there a form of man apart from us and from all others such as we are, a form of man itself or fire or water?"
9 The philosophical necessity of forms in Plato's philosophy of science was argued in H. F. Cherniss's article, "The Philosophical Economy of the Theory of Ideas," *American Journal of Philology* 57 (1936), reprinted in R. E. Allen, ed., *Studies in Plato's Metaphysics* (London, 1965), pp. 1–12.
10 Even in Socrates' prime, a generation before Plato wrote dialogues, medicine was already regarded as "ancient," as one can see from the late-fifth-century B.C. Hippocratic work *Ancient Medicine*. As W.H.S. Jones noted, "Medical schools first arose on the rim of the Greek world, especially in that part of the

Asiatic coast where Ionian joined Dorian and both came in contact with remains of older cultures from Crete and Caria, as well as with strangers from Egypt and the East" (*Hippocrates*, 4 vols. [London, 1923–31], 3: xiv). The sophistication of Egyptian medicine is indicated by the Edwin Smith Papyrus, which is said to date from seventeenth century B.C. or earlier. As Jones remarked, "This remarkable Papyrus indicates that the Egyptians possessed a semi-scientific surgery not much inferior to that of Hippocrates more than a thousand years before his birth."

The writer of the *Iliad* 11. 514 notes that a skilled military surgeon is worth many other men. Since the *Iliad* was widely memorized and served as something of a cultural encyclopaedia, as Havelock argues, Greek surgery if not Greek pathology must have been quite familiar. But since wounds cannot have been much more common than malaria, pathology probably was not unknown.

11 As evidence of physicians' travels we have a physician's own notebook in the Hippocratic work *Epidemics*, which describes cases encountered in various cities. Herodotus (2. 125, 131–37) tells of Democedes, who practiced in Aegina, Athens, Samos, and Susa. From the biographies of Soranus, Suidas, and Tzetzes, late as they are, one may gather that Hippocrates himself probably traveled at least to Abdera, Macedon, Persia, and perhaps to Athens. Certainly he was known in Athens, since Plato mentions him in the *Protagoras* 311B as running a medical school in Cos which it was evidently possible for Athenians to attend, and in the *Phaedrus* at 270C ff. as holding that one cannot know the nature of the body without understanding the nature of the whole person, psyche included. As evidence of medical lectures, though in this case perhaps late ones, we have *Precepts* 12, which takes a dim view of them. Eryximachus at *Symposium* 186A ff. delivers what is in effect a medical lecture as a talk about Eros.

12 Medicine, he says at *Gorgias* 510A, has an account to give of the treatment it offers, and it has investigated the nature and the cause of what it treats, a point repeated in the *Laws* passages cited above in the text. Medicine and gymnastics have some claim to rule over the body, since they know what is wholesome and what is harmful for bodily excellence, he notes at *Gorgias* 517E. In the *Symposium*, the physician Eryximachus pointedly advises Aristophanes to speak as if he were giving an account (189B) and to take care to say only what he can defend, and his own description of the role of love in medicine seems intended as an account. Plato credited the physician not with mere know-how but with a defensible understanding of whom he should treat, when he should treat them, and how much treatment they require (*Phaedrus* 268A–C). He regarded physicians with that piety he usually reserved for the gods. At *Republic* 408B ff., Socrates refuses to believe the story that Asclepias accepted a bribe to heal a man who was fated to die and was struck by lightning in retribution. He does not believe it right to treat hopeless cases (*Republic* 426A), and refuses to believe that the legendary founder of medicine would have done wrong. In *Republic* 1, even Thrasymachus is made to

maintain that the physician in respect of his art at least makes no mistake (340E–341A).

13 In treating of the medical writings, I shall make no comment on what has come to be known as the Hippocratic question—the question of which, if any, of the extant writings from the Hippocratic library Hippocrates himself actually wrote. Hence, when I cite a work as having "Hippocrates" as its author, I mean no more than that it is found in the Hippocratic corpus.

It has been necessary, however, to reach conclusions about the dates of treatises in this corpus, and this is a controversial business. The weight of scholarly opinion has always been behind a pre-Platonic, late-fifth-century dating of most of those cited. Hans Diller ("Hippokratische Medizin und Attische Philosophie," *Hermes* 80 [1952]: 385–409) has argued that the most important of these treatises—*Ancient Medicine*—was post-Platonic. He agrees with previous scholars that the work contains language and points of a substantive sort which bear close resemblance to those found in a number of Platonic dialogues. But Diller poses the question whether it might have been the writer of *Ancient Medicine* who was leaning on Plato, rather than vice-versa, and answers that it was. He details the resemblances between points in *Ancient Medicine* and those in various Platonic dialogues with great thoroughness. He regards the level of methodological sophistication shown in the work as unthinkable before Plato (p. 393).

Space does not permit a detailed refutation of this conclusion, but consider briefly the following points which have sufficed to convince most other scholars in the past and still convince me that *Ancient Medicine* is the earlier. Which is more probable: that (*a*) Plato, who mentions Hippocrates and other physicians (Eryximachus, Acumenus, Herodicus, Philistion, Acesimbrotus, Iatrocles) by name, knew the contents of two or three of the Hippocratic medical writings which have come down to us and, admiring those contents, drew on them freely as examples of the best in current science; or that (*b*) an unknown post-Platonic writer possessed and drew on more of the Platonic corpus than Aristotle seems to have known in writing *Metaphysics A* and parts of the *Nicomachean Ethics*, though in fact he disagreed with much of what he found there, never mentioned Plato's name or indeed the name of anyone after Empedocles, whom he treats as the latest thing in philosophy, and found it still possible to use the term for "sophist" in its neutral-to-honorific fifth-century sense, something no other fourth-century writer did? After Anaxogoras, Democritus, and Plato, Empedocles would have been unlikely to receive such attention. And though the literature of the fourth century is Attic, while this medical treatise is Ionic, one cannot chalk up the different use of "sophist" to that, especially since the medical writers plainly got around Greece and were very much involved in discussions with Attic sophists and philosophers. Most particularly, one cannot attribute this curious use of the term for "sophist" to the writer's being an isolated Ionic if the thrust of one's argument is that he was not isolated but was mining Plato's dialogues. Sophistry as characterized by Plato could scarcely have struck the medical writer as any more scientific than it did Plato's Socrates. It seems likely, then, that *Ancient Medicine* is pre-Platonic.

14 The fact that Alcmaeon is said to have heard Pythagoras (DK 24A1) provides an indication of the period in which Alcmaeon was at work.

15 Gregory Vlastos, "Equality and Justice in the Early Greek Cosmologies," in D. J. Furley and R. E. Allen, eds., *Studies in Presocratic Philosophy*, 1 (New York, 1970): 57–58.

16 Hippocrates, *On Breaths* 1, trans. W.H.S. Jones, *Hippocrates*, 2:229. Cp. *Sacred Disease* 2. 45, 21. 9–25.

17 F. M. Cornford, *Plato and Parmenides* (Indianapolis, n.d.), p. 47. This view of powers or quality-things seems to have been the one articulated by Parmenides in the "Doxa" section of his poem, as A.P.D. Mourelatos has pointed out in "Heraclitus, Parmenides, and the Naive Metaphysics of things," in E. N. Lee, A.P.D. Mourelatos and R. Rorty, eds., *Exegesis and Argument: Studies in Greek Philosophy Presented to Gregory Vlastos* (Assen, 1973), p. 28: "The main features of the cosmology of 'Doxa' are these: Things in our familiar sensible world are a mixture of two 'opposites' (ἀντία) or 'forms' (μορφαί), Light and Night. Each of the two opposites is cognate with a series of 'powers' (δυνάμεις), e.g., 'shining' and 'nimble' for Light, 'obscure' and 'heavy' for Night. The two forms are 'equal', in the sense that neither is more positive or real than the other. Each is self-identical (B8. 57 'in every way the same with itself', said of Light; 8. 58 'in itself', said of Night), that is, may be viewed as a complete thing in its own right. The distinction between these opposites is formulated in spatial terms (cf. B8. 55 ἐκρίναντο δέμας, 8. 55–56 ἔθεντο χωρίς; note also the spatial array of B12). Their unification, too, is envisaged in spatial terms, as a 'mixing' in which the opposites 'come together' (cf. B12. 5 πέμπουσα . . . μιγῆν) to 'fill' (B9. 3, B12. 1) as 'alotted space' (B12. 2 αἶσα)."

18 *Airs, Waters, Places* 12 illustrates the far-reaching manifestations of such "combat" on the author's view. Climate, physique, harvests, etc., are all involved.

19 This has been stated many times, but best perhaps by H. C. Baldry, "Plato's 'Technical Terms,'" pp. 141–42.

20 See, e.g., *Symposium* 189E, in Aristophanes' speech; *Timaeus* 53C; *Protagoras* 352A; *Republic* 510D–E.

21 Aetius 1. 7. 28, and 1. 3. 20 (DK A32 and 33).

22 Vlastos, "Equality and Justice," p. 63.

23 Gregory Vlastos, "The Physical Theory of Anaxagoras," *Philosophical Review* 59 (1950): 41.

24 Hippocrates, *On Breaths* 2. The work is usually thought to date from the late fifth century B.C. See Jones, *Hippocrates*, 2:221.

25 Aristotle, *Metaphysics* 991a ff., says that the theory was first stated by Anaxagoras and later by Eudoxus, though he seems to discuss mainly Plato's version of it.

26 Hippocrates, *On the Art* 6. The writer calls the substances physicians employ

in curing patients εἴδη, "forms," while in 8 he explicitly treats them as δυνάμεις, "powers."

27 See R. Hackforth, *Plato's "Phaedo"* (Cambridge, 1955), p. 152, nn. 4 and 5. Hackforth sees the "bringing up" as done by the object of the attack, but this seems confused, for it does not fit the example of threeness bringing up (i.e., bringing *with it*) oddness which Hackforth sees as involving the same point.

28 Hackforth, *Plato's "Phaedo,"* p. 162, remarked of this passage: "It seems to me beyond question that ψυχή is *at present* (i.e., down to 105E9) regarded as an immanent character or form. For only so can what is now asserted of soul be a corollary, or deduction, or application—whatever one chooses to call it—of the elaborate argument about exclusion of opposite forms." While this seems a useful remark, Hackforth appears not to appreciate that forms are character-powers or "quality-things," and hence sees Plato as having regarded the soul or psyche as a "substance" later in the argument, not seeing that the notion of a substance or subject is foreign to Plato's way of describing the relationship between forms and particulars since it suggests that attributes, predicates, or properties are dependent entities, which forms clearly are not.

29 John Burnet, *Greek Philosophy from Thales to Plato* (1914; rpt. London, 1960), p. 155.

30 See, e.g., Gregory Vlastos, "Reasons and Causes in the *Phaedo*," *Philosophical Review* 78 (1969): 291–325.

31 For a review of various positions on causality, see Richard Taylor's essay "Causality," in Paul Edwards, ed., *The Encyclopedia of Philosophy*, 2 (New York, 1967):57–66.

32 See, e.g., Bertrand Russell, "On the Notion of Cause," in *Mysticism and Logic* (New York, 1918), p. 180, reprinted in Bertrand Russell, *On the Philosophy of Science*, ed. Charles A. Fritz, Jr. (Indianapolis, 1965), p. 163.

33 Richard Taylor, "Causality," p. 66.

34 Plato describes facets of Empedocles' work at *Meno* 76C and *Theaetetus* 152E. And he was evidently acquainted with numerous physicians. He mentions Eryximachus, Philistion, and others. According to Galen, Socrates' own teacher, Prodicus, wrote a work, *On the Nature of Man*, in which he made important contributions to medical nomenclature, contributions which Plato accepted (*Timaeus* 83–86). Galen, the best-known physician of his time, some 600 years after Plato, treats Plato's medical knowledge as important enough to justify mentioning him as an expert in the same line with Hippocrates and the other great physicians of the fourth and fifth centuries. For a full discussion of Empedocles' idea of mixtures, see Carl Werner Müller, *Gleiches zu Gleichem* (Wiesbaden, 1965), pp. 26–64.

35 Gerald Frank Else, "The Terminology of the Ideas," *Harvard Studies in Classical Philology* 47 (1936): 17–55.

36 Ibid., p. 22. For a distinction between forms which impart qualities and forms which impart motions, see below in text. See also J. N. Findlay, *Plato: The Written and Unwritten Doctrines* (London, 1974), p. 34.

Notes to Pages 91–92

37 Ibid., p. 36. Else thought Plato inherited a theory of "kinds" from the Hippocratic physicians (pp. 19–20, 23), but that he gradually evolved and then later abandoned a theory of separate "ideas" (pp. 34–35, 41), the semantic marker for which was the indefinite τις as in μία τις ἰδέα. But this distinction between kinds and ideas will not survive scrutiny of the Hippocratic works which Else thinks employ εἶδος in the sense of "kind," not "idea," but nevertheless do so in conjunction with this allegedly distinctive τις. See, e.g., *Ancient Medicine* 15, with its reference to αὐτό τι ἐφ' ἑωυτοῦ θερμὸν ἢ ψυχρόν. Else's admission that in the *Phaedo* and the *Republic* ideas are only half-separated (p. 51) is also an embarrassment to his thesis. It is more plausible simply to take "separation" language as intended to serve one purpose, that of emphasizing the distinctness of forms as apprehended, and "immanence" language to serve quite another, that of emphasizing the causal role of forms as powers.

38 Suppose one, perhaps unwittingly, (*a*) accepts the Aristotelian dogma that to exist in the universe is to be confined to a place, (*b*) overlooks the difference between (i) a logical vocabulary devoid of causal or explanatory use and (ii) an ontological vocabulary having a causal or explanatory use, and (*c*) prefers to read Plato as if he had used *b*i, since this is presently the favored philosophical vocabulary. One might then construe Plato's talk of a form of largeness in terms of his using relational predicates, and interpret any difficulty in reconciling what Plato says about a form as a power at work *in* (i.e., *confined* within) a particular thing as ruling out there being a form correlating with a relational predicate, for a relational predicate *links* or *relates* two or more things and thus cannot be present in (i.e., *confined* within) only one of them. If one thought Plato saw this difficulty in there being forms for relational predicates present in things as constituents, one might then construe this as a reason for Plato to "separate" forms from particulars and abandon his talk of their being in particulars as components.

See John Brentlinger, "Incomplete Predicates and the Two-World Theory of the *Phaedo*," *Phronesis* 17 (1972): 60–79, for an argument that difficulties with incomplete predicates such as "large" led Plato to regard Simmias's largeness, not as a constituent enlarging him, but as something separate from him, something relating him to Socrates but *in* neither of them. Brentlinger's arguments will be discussed further in Chapter 6, but if the arguments advanced in the present chapter are correct, largeness is no more embarrassing to Plato's power/mixture model than beauty or oddness, for none of these were predicates as he described them. They were δυνάμεις which could not be comfortably confined to any of their perceived instances, and thus on any model of "being located in" patterned on the misguided Aristotelian one, they would appear to be quite impossibly confined in more than one place at once. There is reason to believe that Plato recognized that such a model for place or location was inappropriate for a form, or δύναμις, in which a particular has a μοῖρα, or share. In the *Parmenides*, the youthful Socrates' perfectly appropriate "one-day-in-many-places" line is ignored by the overbearing Parmenides in favor of his confining "one-sail-above-many-sailors" line. It is a mistake to take talk of a form's being *in* a thing as suggesting that it is *confined* within that thing. It would be more apt to compare a form with gravity, or with the U.S. Air Force, which is presently in the United States but also in Japan, Korea, England, and Germany. By contrast, it is simply a confusion to locate a predicate such as "large" anywhere save in the sentences in which it is used. But Plato was not discussing predicates: he was discussing εἴδη or δυνάμεις.

39 Else noted this, but then attempted to reconcile it with the familiar view that Plato thought forms ("ideas") literally separate from things. He claimed that Plato confused the natural and logical functions of forms. I am claiming, rather, that he did not confuse them, but that we are wrong to make such a distinction when interpreting Plato. We have our choice: we can take him to be doing very crudely what we do when we distinguish universals from causes, or we can take him to be doing reasonably well what his predecessors did. Plato was not trying to equal successors such as Bertrand Russell; he was trying to develop an account which would pass more stringent tests than the accounts of predecessors such as Anaxagoras and Hippocrates. On his debt to Hippocrates, and to Greek medicine generally, see Werner Jaeger, *Diokles von Karystos*, (1938; rpt. Berlin, 1963), pp. 7–11; *Paideia*, 3, trans. Gilbert Highet (Oxford, 1961): 3, 12–13, 21–24, 38.

In having arrived at an interpretation of Plato's forms as causes in almost the pre-Socratic sense of agent-powers, I am much indebted to Gregory Vlastos's seminal discussion in "Reasons and Causes in the *Phaedo*," in *Plato*, 1 (Garden City, 1971): 132–66, even though I have come to disagree with his interpretation. Vlastos's view is closer perhaps to Paul Shorey's than to others'. Shorey held forms to be "logical reasons" and in no strict sense causes. Vlastos (pp. 132–33) rejects the view of Eduard Zeller, *Philosophie der Griechen*, 2, 5th ed. (Leipzig, 1922): 687, n. 1, that Plato's forms served simultaneously the functions of formal, efficient, and final causes. Vlastos himself suggests that the forms are "logico-metaphysical conditions" (p. 153), and that the relations between them are relations of logical necessity.

Space does not permit a full discussion of Vlastos's argument, but I would suggest that at least one of the reasons he evidently had for embarking upon it is mistaken. This reason lies in the reading which Vlastos and others have suggested for Socrates' claim at 99D that having initially been attracted to the promise of Anaxagoras' views, he saw certain inadequacies in them and embarked upon a δεύτερος πλοῦς, which is widely taken to be a "second-best" method of inquiry. One's reading of this passage is fundamental for the understanding of Plato's methods and of the forms he posits, and it is misreading of it, I would suggest, which impels Vlastos to credit Plato with the views he did. We know from Menander Fr. 241 that the phrase δεύτερος πλοῦς was sometimes used of the stage in a voyage when a ship was becalmed and its crew were forced to propel it by oars at what must have seemed an excruciatingly slow pace. The suggestion of a second-best way of proceeding is unmistakable in this use. Plato, however, was fond of having Socrates use phrases in an ironic way, and when we look carefully at the argument in this section of the *Phaedo* and at what Plato subsequently does there, it seems most implausible that he meant to suggest that his second procedure was inferior to any viable alternative.

The πρότος πλοῦς, or first voyage, was an Anaxagorean disaster guaranteed to end in blindness for the one persisting in it (99D), since by treating the causes to be investigated as bodily, it suggested that one could perhaps investigate them by the use of the eyes; and to investigate the most powerful cause, the sun, in that way would clearly lead to blindness. Socrates chose thereupon his way of proceeding which he ironically terms his "second" voyage, an investigation by means of λόγοι, or accounts. On this method one lays down an hypothesis and proceeds to examine it. As is indicated by 100B and 99D, this is simply the method Socrates had always been depicted as having used, namely asking someone to posit an account and then attempt to defend it. But this method surely does not mark even the temporary abandonment of concern for "final" causes, as Vlastos suggests (p. 138, n. 15), since the causes Plato does proceed to investigate are perfect paradigms as well as powers of a sort not unfamiliar to Anaxagoras.

40 Galen (15. 9 ff.) held that Plato was referring to *The Nature of Man*, a proposal which has had few takers. Littré held that Plato was referring to chapter 20 of *Ancient Medicine*. Jones, *Hippocrates*, 1:xxxv, notes certain similarities between the views attributed to Hippocrates and those in this chapter of *Ancient Medicine*, and leaves the matter at that. W. Capelle, "Zur Hippokratischen Frage," *Hermes* 57 (1922): 252–53, saw the author of *Ancient Medicine* 20 as taking exactly the opposite position from that suggested by Plato in the *Phaedrus* passage. Plato suggested that there can be no understanding of the art of medicine without an understanding of the whole of nature, as Capelle read him, while the author of *Ancient Medicine* holds that there can be no understanding of the whole of nature without an understanding of medicine. Plainly, there is no necessary opposition between these two views, though Capelle is right, I think, in pointing out how very different in tone the almost antiphilosophical writer of the medical treatise is from Plato in the *Phaedrus*. Louis Bourgey, *Observation et Experience chez les Medecins de la Collection Hippocratique* (Paris, 1953), pp. 89, regards the whole question of which Hippocratic work Plato was referring to as badly posed. He regards the *Phaedrus* passage, not as reporting on a definite work of Hippocrates, but as reflecting the general teaching of Hippocrates as it was commonly known. Hence, he regards it as shedding light on several different works from the collection. This is, I think, the most plausible conclusion, though it can nevertheless be pointed out that Plato's remarks here bear a closer affinity with those in *Regimen* 1 than with others, particularly regarding τοῦ ὅλου.

41 These are particularly common in his characterization of the care and feeding of the three parts, or forms, of the psyche in books 4 and 9 of the *Republic*.

42 Bourgey, *Observation et Experience chez les Medecins de la Collection Hip-*

pocratique, pp. 96, n. 2, regards as incontestable the chronological anteriority of the important medical treatises such as *Ancient Medicine* and *Epidemics* to the Platonic corpus.

43 Alexander Nehamas, "Plato on the Imperfection of the Sensible World," *American Philosophical Quarterly* 12 (1975): 109, argues that the imperfection of sensible particulars on Plato's view in the middle dialogues was not a matter of their being approximately beautiful or just, but a matter of their being only accidentally so. But to be acceptable this claim would need careful qualification. The beauty in a beautiful object, on Plato's view, is a portion of the form of beauty and is perfectly beautiful. But this portion of beauty is mixed with and perhaps partially obscured by ugliness in that particular, so that the particular itself may be said to be only approximately beautiful, much as one might say that a bucket of white paint mixed with a bit of black tint is only approximately white or "off-white."

44 Ibid., p. 108; Alexander Nehamas, "Predication and Forms of Opposites in the *Phaedo*," *Review of Metaphysics* 26 (1972): 469; R. E. Allen, "The Argument from Opposites in *Republic* V," *Review of Metaphysics* 15 (1961): 325–35. This view has been disputed by F. C. White, "Plato's Middle Dialogues and the Independence of Particulars," *Philosophical Quarterly* 27 (1977): 197.

45 Vlastos, "Equality and Justice," p. 62.

46 Diogenes Laertius, *Vitae Philosophorum* 7. 67.

47 Consider, e.g., similar talk of the concentration of an acid in modern chemistry.

48 Gregory Vlastos has rightly taken exception to such conceptions of science in his review of F. M. Cornford's *Principium Sapientiae*, reprinted in Furley and Allen, eds., *Studies in Presocratic Philosophy*. Another essay in the same volume—Karl Popper's "Back to the Presocratics"—does the same. For a critique of the Humean conception of causality which leads its adherents to dismiss talk of powers too lightly, see R. Harré and E. H. Madden, *Causal Powers* (Oxford, 1975).

49 Else, "The Terminology of the Ideas," pp. 23 ff., cites the usual reasons for this with regard to the Hippocratic treatises. Numerous examples are cited in the Liddell-Scott-Jones lexicon.

50 G.M.A. Grube may have hit on the sort of transition involved in describing the shuttle passage at *Cratylus* 386E. He remarked, "In this passage of the *Cratylus* we can almost see the change of meaning taking place from 'what a thing looks like', its appearance, to the pregnant meaning of *eidos* as 'that like which the shuttle looks', and the transition is by way of a metaphor, 'to look' from a physical becomes a mental act" (*Plato's Thought* [London, 1935], p. 14). It does not, however, lose its suggestion that there is something which the relevant act of looking has one looking *at*.

51 This etymology was ignored by Taylor in *Varia Socratica*, but the omission was rectified by H. C. Baldry, "Plato's Technical Terms," p. 141. See also Findlay, Plato: *The Written and Unwritten Doctrines*, p. 30.

Notes to Pages 98–110   219

52 Heraclitus B107. Heraclitus had also remarked that observation must be checked by understanding (B107), and that nature loves to hide (B123). As W.K.C. Guthrie (*History of Greek Philosophy*, 4:37 and 2:395, n. 2) reminds us, even Plato's contemporary Democritus had called the ultimate realities ἰδέαι, and had said they were "accessible only to thought."
53 Heraclitean influence in some of the writings is readily apparent, as Jones noted in commenting upon *Regimen* 1: "The philosophic position is that of an intelligent and progressive eclectic, who combines, instead of merely adding together, the results reached by his predecessors. The perpetual flux of Heracleitus and his harmony through opposition; the four 'opposites' of Empedocles; the brilliant theory of change elaborated by Anaxagoras—all these are worked up into a system that appears like the creation of a single mind" (*Hippocrates*, 4:xliii).
54 On physique, e.g., see *Airs, Waters, Places*, chs. 3, 5, 12.
55 *On the Art* 11. The same writer also contrasts opinion with understanding, claims that medicine has a λόγος, or account, to give to justify its treatment, and reminds one of the Socratic paradoxes when he remarks of those who get ill, "If indeed they understood [ἠπίσταντο] their diseases they would never have fallen into them," all in the same chapter. One might be tempted to regard the work as post-Platonic were it not for the fact that it is so clearly a product of a great sophist and of a piece with other works in the corpus which mention Melissus and Empedocles as *the* forces in philosophy.
56 *The "Republic" of Plato*, trans. F. M. Cornford (Oxford, 1945), pp. 217–18 (6. 506).
57 See, e.g., G. H. Von Wright, "The Logic of Action: A Sketch," in Nicholas Rescher, ed., *The Logic of Decision and Action* (Pittsburgh, 1967), p. 122.
58 Willard Van Orman Quine, "Two Dogmas of Empiricism," in *From a Logical Point of View* (Cambridge, 1953), p. 42; idem, *Word and Object* (New York, 1960), pp. 18, 35.
59 See Rescher, "Semantic Foundations for the Logic of Preference," in Rescher, *The Logic of Decision and Action*, p. 43; and R. Chisholm and E. Sosa, "Intrinsic Preferability and Supererogation," *Synthese* 16 (1966): 325.
60 *Republic* 589B–C indicates that this lengthy praise of justice is from every point of view true and praise of injustice wholly false as Plato sees it.
61 Charles Kahn, "Why Existence Does Not Emerge as a Distinct Concept in Greek Philosophy," *Archiv für Geschichte der Philosophie* 58 (1976): 323–34, argues that existence is not a subject for philosophical reflection among Greek philosophers.
62 Alexander of Aphrodisias, *in Aristotelis metaphysica*, in *Commentaria in Aristotelem Graeca*, 1, ed., F. Hayduck (Berlin, 1891): 82. 11–83. 23.
63 G.E.L. Owen, "A Proof in the ΠΕΡΙ ΙΔΕΩΝ," reprinted in R. E. Allen, ed., *Studies in Plato's Metaphysics* (London, 1965), p. 295.
64 Ibid., p. 307.
65 W. D. Ross, *Plato's Theory of Ideas* (Oxford, 1951), pp. 228–230. Ross mistakenly claims that there is a trend away from "immanence" language towards

"transcendence," but he fails to consider all the evidence—e.g., uses of the verbs συγκεράνυμμι and μίγνυμι in late dialogues. This evidence will be taken up in Chapter 6.

66 Suggestive of the mixing model are such terms in Ross's list I as μετέχειν, ἰέναι εἰς, and ἐνεῖναι. Suggestive of the paradigm/copy model are terms from list II such as παράδειγμα, αὐτὸ καθ' αὐτό, μιμεῖσθαι, and the like. J. N. Findlay claims that "what these various metaphors show is that Plato does not really care how instantiation is pictured" (*Plato: The Written and Unwritten Doctrines*, p. 36).

67 Else, "The Terminology of the Ideas," p. 47.

68 R. E. Allen, "Participation and Prediction in Plato's Middle Dialogues," in Vlastos, *Plato*, 1:167.

69 Ibid., pp. 167–69. Recognizing these embarrassments for the view Plato is alleged to have held, Allen rightly tries to do justice to Plato's use of forms as paradigms for sensible objects and as the primary and only rightful bearers of names. He attempts to construe forms as universals of a special sort—ones not sullied by commutative relations with their many instances (pp. 177–79). But Plato's use of a mixture model calls for more drastic treatment of the attempt to regard forms as universals, in my judgment.

70 A. L. Peck, in "Plato Versus Parmenides," *Philosophical Review* 64 (1962): 162–63, expressed what mars any interpretation of the third-man argument (Vlastos's, e.g.) as indicating a Platonic commitment to forms as properties: "There is no mention here [*Parmenides* 130B] of 'property' or of 'instances of a property' and so on, and indeed Vlastos admits (p. 341, n. 39) that phrases such as 'the Similarity which we possess' are 'substantial in linguistic form.' Nevertheless, he claims, they must be taken as 'adjectival in sense.' This may, no doubt, be good modern practice; but to adopt it for Plato shows a complete misunderstanding of him. Plato, whether he uses adjectival or substantival formations (as he does indiscriminately) when speaking of particulars (e.g., 'the likeness in us,' 'the many large things') does not regard the 'F' of which he is speaking as a 'property' or as 'adjectival' or 'predicative': Such terminology and the outlook it expresses belong to another attitude of thought."

71 Gerold Prauss, *Platon und der logische Eleatismus* (Berlin, 1966), pp. 54–60.

72 Allen, "Participation and Predication in Plato's Middle Dialogues," p. 177.

73 Havelock, *Preface to Plato*, pp. 249–50, 256–57, seems to have taken forms in this way sometimes; and Else, "The Terminology of the Ideas," p. 52, remarks that "inductive reasoning is the very heart and soul of the Socratic dialogues, where it takes the form of searching for the μία ἰδέα of each kind."

74 For examples of the term used in this sense see *Iliad* 13. 101; Herodotus 1. 71 and 1. 77; Thucydides 1. 26, 2. 90.

75 *Republic* 588B–589B. Something like a psychic crisis is described at 553A–554E. The Hippocratic work *Prognostic* is an essay on the symptoms of crisis and on how to predict the outcome. See, e.g., *Prognostic* 23 on

"critical days," and *Prognostic* 25 on estimating the relative powers of contending opposites.
76 Gregory Vlastos, "The Third Man Argument in the *Parmenides*," reprinted in R. E. Allen, ed., *Studies in Plato's Metaphysics* (London, 1965), pp. 231–64, esp. p. 232, takes this line in interpreting Plato, a line criticized by Wilfred Sellars, "Vlastos and the Third Man," *Philosophical Review* 64 (1955): 405–37.
77 Prauss, *Platon und der logische Eleatismus*, ch. 2, sec. 8, discusses very thoroughly this line of thought in Plato.
78 Burnet, *Greek Philosophy from Thales to Plato*, p. 165.
79 Here see F. C. White's useful discussion in "Plato's Middle Dialogues and the Independence of Particulars," pp. 202–3. White takes particulars in the *Phaedo* to be "essentially characterized particulars with per se properties of their own." Hackforth, *Plato's "Phaedo"*, p. 155, argues compellingly that this passage at 102C does not distinguish essential from accidental properties of particulars. Indeed, far from having distinguished accidental from essential properties or attributes of particulars, Plato in the *Phaedo* displays what Charlotte Stough has termed "insensitivity to any relevant distinction between an attribute and that of which it is an attribute, such that to say of Simmias that he is large is not to predicate a property (relational or otherwise) of Simmias, but to assimilate to Simmias a 'thing'-component apparently of the same logical type" ("Forms and Explanation in the *Phaedo*," *Phronesis* 21 [1976]: 12). Stough goes on to describe Plato as providing a solution to such puzzles in the *Phaedo* by introducing "the new formula 'x partakes of Φ'" (p. 18), and this further part of her interpretation is not compelling. The "formula" is not new, having been used previously by Plato in the *Gorgias* at 467E ("sharing in the good") and at 448C; by Plato's Socrates at *Euthyphro* 306A, B, and C, where it appears as a variant of his "compounding" line; by Plato's Diotima at *Symposium* 208B; and by Plato's Protagoras in his myth at *Protagoras* 322D and 323A. It was used before Plato by Diogenes of Apollonia (DK 64B5) and, most significantly, by Anaxagoras in fragments DK 59B6 and DK 59B12, where Anaxagoras is expressing the very sort of view whose abandonment this allegedly new formula is supposed to mark in Plato's *Phaedo*. It seems more probable that the use of this formula in the *Phaedo* marks Plato's continued adherence to the view Stough claims he abandons.
80 It would be nearer the truth to say, with Evan Burge ("The Ideas as Aitiai in the *Phaedo*," *Phronesis* 16 [1971]: 10), that sensible phenomena are on Plato's view "simply bundles of attributes held together by law-like regularities in view of their instantiation of ideas which have definite and unchanging relations to one another." I say "nearer the truth" and not "true" because the notion of an attribute makes no sense apart from the implied contrast with the subject having the attribute, a subject which Plato did not recognize. K. W. Mills, "Some Aspects of Plato's Theory of Forms: *Timaeus* 49C ff.", *Phronesis* 13 (1968): 167, has drawn out the (for us) radical implications of Plato's not having accepted what we might call a *logos*-structured view of reality: "I

agree that Plato held that sensibles do not exist, in the sense that there are no objects at all, sensible or otherwise, apart from the Forms and space. . . . It seems to me that what is always changing is not a class of things or objects, but the answer to the question, Which of the Forms is now being reflected in this part or that part of space?"
81 Alexander Nehamas, "Plato on the Imperfection of the Sensible World," p. 110.
82 The translation is that of R. G. Bury, *Plato with an English Translation* (London and Cambridge, Mass., 1929): 145.

Chapter 5: Ἐπιστήμη, Reality, and Truth

1 The contrast continues in some of the later dialogues. See, e.g., *Theaetetus* 186D, and *Philebus* 58A, 59A–C.
2 Republic 524C–525A and 478E–479E are suggestive on this point when compared with *Phaedo* 74A–75A and 76A, and viewed in the light of the evidence that Plato continued to hold the view that our coming to understand forms is recollection even in dialogues later than *Republic* and *Phaedo*—e.g., *Philebus* 34C, and *Phaedrus* 249B–C.
3 N. R. Murphy, *The Interpretation of Plato's Republic* (Oxford, 1950), pp. 154–55, seems to have come closest of past commentators to discerning the sort of model Plato employs, but he declares that ἀλήθεια cannot mean "reality." Although he notes that ἀληθής denoted conformity to type, he does not recognize λόγος as such a type. He takes Plato to hold a correspondence theory of truth (p. 181).
4 At *Republic* 507A Plato speaks of the sun as the "offspring" of the good. At *Phaedo* 103E there is a very clear statement of one of the views central to Plato's paradigm/copy distinction: only the εἶδος, the form or paradigm, deserves the same name through all time. Other things evidently receive that name from time to time by a sort of courtesy based on momentary and partial resemblance to the paradigm. This goes far to explain Plato's alleged use of many of his more honorific terms (even ἐπιστήμη, as at *Meno* 97A–B, *Theaetetus* 201C, and *Philebus* 61D–E) in what has been called a demotic or popular sense. He is, of course, willing to call even bad copies by the name of their original, provided that in context there is no danger of confusing them with their original. If he thinks there is such a danger, he denies they deserve the name at all, or contrasts them with their enduring (βέβαιον), pure (καθαρός) and true (ἀληθής) originals, as he does even with ἐπιστήμη at *Philebus* 59C.
5 See, e.g., *Philebus* 59C. Cp. *Republic* 460C for the social implications of such a view as Plato tried to work them out.
6 See, e.g., *Republic* 507B.
7 See esp. *Theaetetus* 152D. A similar homogeneity when compared with itself is also suggested by Plato's seemingly ungrammatical absolute uses of his terms for "like" and "unlike." He means "like itself" or "unlike itself" when

he uses these of something. See, e.g., *Theaetetus* 159D. When used absolutely, his term for "one" bears a similar sense. It means "unified," or "qualitatively at one with itself."

8 It can no longer be disputed with much plausibility that the term ἀλήθεια derives from the privative ἀ and λανθάνω, "escape notice." This derivation, however, by no means suggests that truth is in any sense private or subjective, as Boeder has shown in "Der frühgriechische Wortgebrauch von *Logos* und *Aletheia*," *Archiv für Begriffsgeschichte* 4 (1959): 92–101.

9 Alan R. White, *Truth* (Garden City, 1970), pp. 4–5.

10 Gregory Vlastos, "Degrees of Reality in Plato," in Renford Bambrough, ed., *New Essays on Plato and Aristotle* (London, 1965), p. 2.

11 This passage also indicates that the term ἄλογον, often rendered "silly" or "ridiculous," derived its sense from the third sense of λόγος and the ἀ-privative. Whatever was ἄλογον was simply and obviously not a λόγος or was beyond or, more accurately, *beneath* λόγος.

12 *Gorgias* 513B ff. is typical of claims to this effect throughout the corpus.

13 This is the point of *Sophist* 268B–D. Since the sophist imitates the wise person using the medium of speech, plainly he imitates what the wise person says, and what the wise person says constitutes an account. Cp. 266C–D.

14 Cp. *Republic* 10 on Homer and other poets.

15 At *Philebus* 57E–59C Plato again makes it clear that he thought this power of discussing and giving or receiving accounts depended on there being τὰ ὄντα ἀεί, things which always *are* (59A8), perfectly stable, wholly true, or genuine eternal objects, objects to which all other things are secondary and inferior (δεύτερά τε καὶ ὕστερα) (59C).

16 Gregory Vlastos, in "A Metaphysical Paradox," *Proceedings and Addresses of the American Philosophical Association* (1966), pp. 5–19, has argued compellingly that Plato's terms for reality are seriously misunderstood when read as if he were discussing existence. John Brentlinger, "Incomplete Predicates and the Two-World Theory of the *Phaedo*," *Phronesis* 17 (1972): 60–79, rejects Vlastos's view, but does not, I think, argue sufficiently for doing so. He does not attempt to show why or how a "degree of existence" view might seem any more intelligible to a speaker of Greek or Latin than it does to a speaker of contemporary English, but simply asserts that it would. The argument of this present chapter lends additional support to Vlastos's claim that reality was not identical with existence on Plato's view. Charles Kahn, in "The Greek Verb 'To Be' and the Concept of Being," *Foundations of Language* 1 (1966): 245–65, argued convincingly that existence was not a problematic notion for Greeks. Cp. "Why Existence Does Not Emerge as a Distinct Concept in Greek Philosophy," *Archiv für Geschichte der Philosophie* (1974), pp. 323–34.

17 This is otherwise difficult or impossible to explain. For example, Francis M. Cornford, *Plato's Theory of Knowledge* (New York, 1957), pp. 321–23, is forced to regard the final treatment of the sophist as an image-maker (264D–268D) as a conscious shelving of the problem discussed in preceding sections.

18 *Republic* 596C–602C, 397D–398B; see also *Laws* 668A–B on correctness in imitation, and 669D on the principal criterion for this, coherence. One cannot tell what *worthy* original is intended by inspecting an incoherent and thus incorrect imitation. This line of argument in the *Laws* is precisely what one would predict if Plato maintained his paradigm/copy distinction to the end, as I shall argue in Chapter 6 that he did. The mention of imitation of the beautiful (τοῦ καλοῦ μιμήματι) at *Laws* 668B1, of a worthy (ἀξιολόγων) original at 669E5, and a strong indication of Plato's continued ontological realism at 668A2–5 are much as one would predict if Plato continued to conceive of these worthy originals to be imitated as forms serving as paradigms. It is of interest that Plato still favors classification κατ' εἴδη, or according to forms, at 630E.

19 In Greek as in English the term for "about" could have a concrete meaning suggesting "round about," "encircling," or the like. When Plato suggests that an account is περί τινος, or "*about* something," he is using an expression which complements his frequent description of the mind of one who can give such an account as grasping some object mentally. See, e.g., *Phaedo* 65C, *Republic* 572A.

20 Aristotle, *Topics* 106a13 ff., 107a14 ff.; a similar insight seems to underlie J. L. Austin's move in "Three Ways of Spilling Ink," *Philosophical Review* 75 (1966): 431.

21 For nondiscursive uses of κίβδηλος see *Republic* 366B, *Laws* 728D; and for a link between the verb κιβδηλεύω, "to adulterate," and the verb ψεύδεσθαι, "to lie," see *Laws* 917B. For nondiscursive uses of ἀληθής and ψευδής see *Philebus* 36C ff., 40E, and *Timaeus* 44A. For discursive uses of κίβδηλος see the text below. Note also Plato's uses of γνήσιος, "legitimate," both of accounts, as at *Phaedrus* 276A and by implication at *Republic* 496A, and of nondiscursive entities, as at *Statesman* 293E, *Republic* 535C, 587B, and *Laws* 765D.

22 Nelson Goodman in his *Languages of Art* (Indianapolis, 1968), pp. 72–73, takes a metaphor to be calculated category-mistake. But this is not to say that every calculated category-mistake is a metaphor. Some may be straightforward attempts to destroy old category lines, to deny that there are such categories at all.

23 Plato frequently used terms suggesting purity (καθαρός, εἰλικρινές, ἄκρατον, etc.) of anything good or anything which he thought was as it should be, whether the thing in question was verbal or not. See, e.g., *Philebus* 51D, 52C, 52E, 59B–C. The *real X* is purebred or legitimate, not a bastard or mongrel on his view. He leans heavily on what for us could only be figures of speech. But as was argued in the preceding chapter, these were evidently not mere figures for him.

24 Cp. *Phaedrus* 238B, 249C, 260D–E, 271C–D; *Phaedo* 85D; *Republic* 532A; *Theaetetus* 148D; *Philebus* 57E; *Republic* 532D.

25 On the principle stated at *Timaeus* 29B–C, it would follow that an account which shifted and proved refutable was necessarily an account of a shifting and unstable object, not a form. See also 51D.

26 As noted in Chapter 2, it is an important premise in the political arguments of the *Republic* that tests for ἐπιστήμη and hence for ἀρετή, or excellence, can be survived, put behind one, or passed successfully, for only this could provide the decisive guide Plato postulates in projecting the future performance of the person tested. The relevant passages are 503A, 540A, and 526B.
27 Trans. W.R.M. Lamb, *Plato with an English Translation* (London and Cambridge, Mass., 1925), p. 471.
28 The term I have rendered "stands" here, συμβαίνω, can mean "agree" or sometimes "follow." The former, though appropriate as showing the *ground* for "standing," does not show the *result* so clearly. The latter is likely to have anachronistic connotations of strict deductive sequence.
29 Trans. Harold North Fowler, *Plato with an English Translation* (London and Cambridge, Mass., 1921), p. 423.
30 At *Theaetetus* 154D, e.g., Socrates suggests that they look into themselves to see whether the things they think harmonize or not. Sadly, they do not, as emerges at 155B.
31 Such talk of warring powers Plato evidently took very seriously, and it was quite Greek of him to do so, as was argued in the preceding chapter. For Plato's view that what is perfectly real is wholly in harmony with itself, and that lesser things are not in harmony with themselves, see *Republic* 500C and *Philebus* 59B–C.
32 For ὑγιής see *Phaedo* 90C, *Republic* 603B, *Phaedrus* 242E, and *Theaetetus* 194B; for σαφής see *Laws* 921B and 965C, and for the associated noun σαφήνεια see *Republic* 478C, 509D, *Phaedrus* 277D; for βέβαιος and the associated noun βεβαιότης see *Phaedo* 90C, *Republic* 537C, *Philebus* 59B–C, *Phaedrus* 275C, 277D, *Timaeus* 29B, 37B, *Laws* 653A. For ἐρρωμενέστατον see *Phaedo* 100A.
33 See, e.g., *Gorgias* 493D, 527A; *Republic* 582A, 585B, 484C; *Phaedo* 65E; *Statesman* 300E, 301E; *Philebus* 14B, 58C, 58D, 59B, 55C.
34 See, e.g., Ernest Gowers, *The Complete Plain Words* (Harmondsworth, 1962), pp. 232–33.
35 W.V.O. Quine, e.g., once employed the term "truer" (*Word and Object* [Cambridge, Mass., 1960], p. 69), though he would be likely to regard this as simply a stylistic variant of "closer to the truth."
36 Vlastos, "Degrees of Reality in Plato," pp. 2–3.
37 One sign of superficiality for an expression E is surely the general avoidance of it in serious contexts where speakers are expected to be as accurate and literal as possible. Leslie Armour, in *The Concept of Truth* (Assen, 1969), pp. 121–25, has given a lucid statement of some of the difficulties which recent writers and speakers of English would fear if truth were treated as a matter of degree at anything but a superficial level. But serious and even reflective Greek writers gave no sign of having expected any such difficulties, and this is reflected in usage. For some pertinent examples see Herodotus 6. 69; Isocrates, *Antidosis* 132, 278, 195, 84; *Trapeziticus* 54; Thucydides 1. 23. 6, 2. 6. 1, 7. 67. 4; Xenophon, *Apologia Socrates* 13, *Oeconomicus* 16. 4, *Hellenica* 3. 3. 2; Demosthenes 8. 38, 10. 55, 18. 1 (Blass's pagination). Thucy-

38 *Meno* 97A–B on the road to Larissa suggests this, as do *Sophist* 263A–B ("Theaetetus sits," "Theaetetus flies") and *Theaetetus* 201C on the eyewitness's knowing the truth and the judge's merely having a true opinion (presumably about some physical happening). These are true only temporarily and hence to a degree.

39 On the general point see Otto Jespersen, *The Philosophy of Grammar* (London, 1924), p. 244, and Edward Sapir, "Grading: A Study in Semantics," *Philosophy of Science*, 12 (1944): 96–97. The general range of Plato's use of ἀληθής seems to indicate awareness of this point. At *Laws* 634C, e.g., he is trying to discern τό τε ἀληθὲς ἅμα καὶ τὸ βέλτιστον, "what is simultaneously true and *best*," while in the *Gorgias* passage discussed below, he is willing to call a particular claim *true* but seems not at all sure it was *best*. It was merely better than others which had been suggested to him.

40 *Gorgias* 486D. (For a description of the use of the touchstone, see Earle R. Calley and John F. C. Richards, translators and commentators, *Theophrastus on Stones* [Columbus, Ohio, 1956], pp. 151–53.) One may be uneasy about Socrates' saying, just before denying that he knows, that his views are fastened in iron and adamant (508E–509A), since this may seem a suitable figure for a claim to knowledge of the truth without qualification, particularly given the "tying down" or "fastening" simile at *Meno* 98A. But as often as he uses the language of fastening to describe really good and tight connections in the dialogues, nowhere does he demean those connections by specifying such notoriously breakable sensible materials for them save in the one place where Socrates is made to show in other ways that he is unsure of the strength of those connections—in our passage at *Gorgias* 509A. Plato often represented Socrates as having scant respect for the stability or strength of such sensible materials as iron and adamant. Where he does use fastening language for good and tight connections, as at *Meno* 98A, he is careful to keep the connections immaterial. What fastens an opinion down is extensive, repeated dialectical questioning.

41 The *Republic*'s line simile at 511E explicitly correlates degrees of certainty with degrees of reality, genuineness, or truth.

42 Jaako Hintikka, "Time, Truth, and Knowledge in Ancient Greek Philosophy," *American Philosophical Quarterly* 4 (1967): 2, 5, 8.

43 Hintikka (ibid., pp. 11–12) documents this.

44 For the intransitive of "mean," consider the criticism directed at Alice in *Through the Looking Glass*: "You should have meant!" As early as the Stoics it was explicitly recognized that what speakers mean is prior to what their sentences mean, as William and Martha Kneale have pointed out in *The Development of Logic* (Oxford, 1962), p. 157. This has also been recognized by later philosophers, such as John Hospers (*An Introduction to Philosophical Analysis* [Englewood Cliffs, 1950], p. 75), H. P. Grice, and Dennis Stampe. To recognize the primacy of speakers' meaning is not to claim the primacy of a speaker's meaning. The latter would be Humpty Dumpty's view that one can intelligibly make a sentence mean what one likes. For a novel and lucid

treatment of the social contribution to meaning, see Hilary Putnam, "Meaning, Reference, and Stereotypes," in F. Guenthner and M. Guenthner-Reutter, eds., *Meaning and Translation* (London, 1978), pp. 71–73.

45 At *Sophist* 218B–C, e.g., it is admitted that the participants use the same word, but it requires further investigation to determine whether or not they have in mind the same thing when they use it, i.e., whether they *mean* the same thing by it. As noted in Chapter 2, the dialectical questioner, on Plato's view, is to look to what the answerer means insofar as possible. This is why Socrates is made to protest quite fairly on Protagoras's part at *Theaetetus* 166D–E that one must not lay too much stress upon the words employed in an argument. This is also perhaps the reason he is made to proceed apologetically at 184C. (Cp. *Sophist* 220D.) It is in stressing Plato's sense of the tenuousness of the relation between existing words and forms that this interpretation of Plato's theory of meaning differs from the otherwise similar interpretation offered by Charles Kahn in "The Meaning of 'Justice' and the Theory of Forms," *Journal of Philosophy* 69 (1972), 567–79.

46 This belief on Plato's part may help account for his indulging in what to a modern reader appears to be the stylistic vice of elegant variation.

47 *Theaetetus* 165E. Cp. *Phaedrus* 274C–278C, esp. 278C, and *Epistle 7*, 341E–344E.

48 One of several indications of Plato's having held this view is at *Republic* 478B, in his treatment of δόξα, or opinion.

49 *Gorgias* 507C.

50 Plato would have agreed with Hilary Putnam that "the psychological state of the speaker does *not* determine the extension (*or* the 'meaning' speaking preanalytically) of the word" ("Meaning, Reference and Stereotypes," p. 65). In fact, Plato would have argued that the psychological state of the speaker was determined by the extension of the word, if by "extension" we mean the extralinguistic object to which the speaker is attending.

51 At *Theaetetus* 159C ff. Plato attempted to explain error as a purely psychic phenomenon not dependent upon the quality of what was thought *about*, and thus considered, at least, an explanation of error more congenial to modern philosophers, but this attempt foundered, as 196B–C indicates. In the sequel to the *Theaetetus*, the *Sophist*, Plato resumes with renewed energy his attempt to explain the falsity of the psychic contents reflected in one's accounts by construing it, not as the result of faulty bookkeeping, warehousing, or the like, but as the direct result of attending to faulty objects as if they could be paradigmatic.

52 Vlastos, "Degrees of Reality in Plato," and Kahn, "The Greek Verb 'To Be' and the Concept of Being."

53 Dennis Stampe, "Toward a Grammar of Meaning," *The Philosophical Review* 77 (1968): 137–74. Stampe was commenting upon the following argument by a contemporary Platonist: "For just as an opaque body may be seen, so a concept may be understood or grasped. In both cases the observation is not direct but through intermediaries—light, lens of eye, an optical instrument, and retina in the case of the visible body, linguistic expressions in the case of

the concept" (Alonzo Church, "The Need for Abstract Entities in Semantic Analysis," reprinted in J. J. Katz and J. A. Fodor, eds., *The Structure of Language* [Englewood Cliffs, 1964], p. 442). If the argument of this book is correct, however, Plato thought of our mental "vision" as turned, not on concepts, but on extralinguistic forms or powers.

54 In the *Sophist* itself the alleged sophism is expressed at 237C ff. There is also a version of it at *Euthydemus* 286C–D, and an attempt at a corollary for false names at *Cratylus* 429B. A false name falls short of the *form* of namehood (389D).

55 A massively detailed and magisterial interpretation of Plato's treatment of negation and nonbeing in the *Sophist* has been developed by Ed Lee, "Plato on Negation and Not-Being in the *Sophist*," *Philosophical Review* 81 (1972): 267–304. The argument of the present chapter is consistent with Lee's interpretation, but suggests one further way in which Lee's interpretation can illuminate what is going on in the *Sophist*. Lee remarked: "One particularly enigmatic aspect of the dialogue ought to be mentioned here: it is that this carefully constructed doctrine of the Parts of Otherness—its entire apparatus of determinations and antitheses—is left totally unused in Plato's subsequent account of falsity (263b–d): one of his major 'analytic' achievements is thus *not* applied to one of his major 'analytic' problems!" On the interpretation offered thus far this is no longer, I think, an enigma. The achievement is applied to the problem. Given that Plato operated on a paradigm/copy model and treated particular accounts as either quite like their form and hence true, or "other" than their form and hence false, Plato's treatment of otherness and its "parts" was evidently developed for the sake of application to the problem of falsity in accounts.

56 This is indicated at *Sophist* 263D. Plato no sooner establishes to his satisfaction that there is such a thing as a false account than he introduces lesser entities for such an account to be about, things which are other than those that truly *are*.

Chapter 6: Eleaticism, Division, and Ἐπιστήμη in the Late Dialogues

1 John Brentlinger, "Incomplete Predicates and the Two-World Theory of the *Phaedo*," *Phronesis* 17 (1972): 66. (Subsequent page references to this article appear parenthetically in the text.) See also Paul Woodruff, "The Socratic Approach to Semantic Incompleteness," *Philosophy and Phenomenological Research* 38 (1978): 458–59.

2 Plato, *Phaedo*, trans. Hugh Tredennick, in *Plato: The Collected Dialogues*, Edith Hamilton and Huntington Cairns, eds. (New York, 1961), p. 84.

3 G.E.L. Owen, "A Proof in the Περὶ Ἰδεῶν," in R. E. Allen, ed., *Studies in Plato's Metaphysics* (New York, 1965), popularized the expression. Brentlinger (p. 70, n. 12) explains that he himself uses the expression "to describe two sorts of terms: attributive predicates, and relations. . . . We must assume

that all statements have one and only one subject term which indicates one thing or group of things the statement is about or refers to. A predicate is incomplete if, when joined to a subject term, it does not make a complete statement unless a completing substantive is understood from the context."

4 Alexander Nehamas, "Plato on the Imperfection of the Sensible World," *American Philosophical Quarterly* 12 (1975): 108, 116, claims that the forms Plato postulates in the *Phaedo* and in the middle books of the *Republic* all correspond to incomplete predicates. This cannot be correct, for in the *Phaedo*, at 103E2, Plato indicates that the examples which follow are examples of forms, as they must be if his conclusion at 107A is to follow. Among these forms are life, death, illness, fever, music, and psyche. The corresponding predicates are neither relatives nor attributives, and hence are not themselves incomplete in the required sense. As for the *Republic*, Nehamas in his "Predication and Forms of Opposites in the *Phaedo*," *Review of Metaphysics* 26 (1972): 467, has said that "when Socrates generalizes to 'the beautiful, the good, and all such being' at 74D8–9 (or to 'all the Forms' at *Rep.* 476A5) we have no license to infer that any Forms have been generated other than those corresponding to those properties which are instantiated along with their opposites." The context at 476B does not warrant this restriction. Glaucon has confused lovers of wisdom, not with their opposites (assuming this makes any sense), but with people who happen to resemble them in their love of learning—the lovers of artistic spectacles who want to witness and "learn" the latest in that area, and can't get enough of such learning. In general, when Plato says "all forms," the burden of proof is on those who want to restrict the range of the expression, not on those who take him to mean what he says, especially when the weight of textual evidence is in favor of a wide range of forms. See, e.g., *Phaedo* 65D13–E1, 75D1–2, 76D8–E1, 100B5–7, and *Republic* 596A6–7.

5 On the account of Christopher Kirwan, "Plato and Relativity," *Phronesis* 19 (1974): 115, Plato may have worse problems with "complete" predicates than with the allegedly troublesome "incomplete" ones.

6 G.E.L. Owen, "The Place of the *Timaeus* in Plato's Dialogues," *Classical Quarterly*, n.s. 3 (1953): 79–95; Gerold Prauss, *Platon und der logische Eleatismus* (Berlin, 1966), pp. 187–88, 197, 201.

7 H. F. Cherniss, "The Relation of the *Timaeus* to Plato's Later Dialogues," *American Journal of Philology* 77 (1957): 284 ff. Owen's rejoinder to Cherniss, "Plato on the Undepictable," in E. N. Lee, A.P.D. Mourelatos, and R. Rorty, eds., *Exegesis and Argument* (Assen, 1973), pp. 349–61, is not convincing, for it does not meet the attack on his use of stylometry and attempts, rather, to show that one passage in the *Statesman* can be read other than as a reference to paradigmatic forms. W.K.C. Guthrie's discussion of this disagreement (*A History of Greek Philosophy*, 5 [Cambridge, 1978]: 178 ff.) is illuminating apart from what he says about myth and poetry as vehicles of truth on Plato's view. He remarks on *Statesman* 269D, "If this occurred in a 'middle' dialogue it would be taken for granted that it described the divine (*Phd.* 80b etc.) and unchanging realm of Forms, and its relation to the physi-

cal world, so why not now?" (pp. 179–80). This goes to the heart of the methodological issue. Herwig Görgemanns, *Beiträge zur Interpretation von Platons Nomoi* (Munich, 1960), pp. 218–26, saw possible traces of the theory of forms even in *Laws* 12. And Cherniss, in his review of Gerhard Müller, *Studien zu den platonischen Nomoi* (Munich, 1951), in *Gnomon* 25 (1953): 367–79, was even more positive than Görgemanns, rightly, I think. Cherniss argues plausibly (pp. 375–79) against Müller's suggestion that in the *Laws* the theory of forms has disappeared. He is supported in this by Guthrie (5:378).

8 Nehamas, "Predication and Forms of Opposites in the *Phaedo*," p. 469, claims that "in order to derive the (partially) contradictory aspect of sensible particulars, something must remain constant for the contrary properties to apply to." These constant or essential properties are the ones marked by complete predicates, such as "man" as applied to Simmias (ibid., p. 471). It is only because Simmias has complete properties that we can identify him as having incomplete ones. The claim is plausible. It is good Aristotle, and good philosophy. But there is no evidence that Plato accepted it, and good evidence that he did not. Had he accepted the view that Simmias' "identity is grounded in his manhood," Plato could not have regarded an individual's reincarnation in nonhuman life forms as intelligible. But he did regard this as intelligible, as we know from *Republic* 620A–B, *Phaedrus* 249B, and *Timaeus* 90E–92C. That the above passages are myths and ἐπῳδαί is not to the point, for even myths and charming stories must be intelligible, and speaking of what has lost its alleged essence as having maintained it is simply not intelligible.

9 Norman Malcolm, *Dreaming* (London and New York, 1959), pp. 78–81. The philosophical issues involved in Malcolm's discussion were illuminated in Hilary Putnam's "Dreaming and Depth Grammar," originally published in R. Butler, ed., *Analytical Philosophy*, 1st ser. (Oxford, 1962), and reprinted in Hilary Putnam, *Mind, Language, and Reality* (Cambridge, 1975): pp. 304–24. These issues were also discussed usefully in C. S. Chihara and J. A. Fodor, "Operationalism and Ordinary Language: A Critique of Wittgenstein," *American Philosophical Quarterly* 2 (1965): 281–95, esp. 289–90. For an interpreter of Plato the chief issue here is perhaps not what counts as meaning or as change of meaning, but rather—given that a wide range of interpretations have been given to the notions of meaning and change of meaning, and given that Plato is concerned with meaning in some sense—whether we are to approach the text of Plato with the unstated and unexamined orthodox assumption that he adhered to some fashionable one of these interpretations, or whether we are to lay down hypotheses about the interpretation he gave to meaning and allow the full range of textual evidence to be invoked against these as tests.

10 This difficulty figures in Brentlinger's argument when he invokes as if its meaning were clear Plato's distinction between the "absolute" (καθ' αὐτό) and the "relative" (πρός τι). As Alexander of Aphrodisias reports a series of rapid-fire Aristotelian shots at the theory of forms in the Περὶ Ἰδεῶν (Alexander, *in Metaphysica* 97. 27–98), Aristotle capitalized on this same difficulty, treating αὐταὶ καθ' αὐτάς as if it suggested freedom from relation

achieved by spatial separation, not self-consistency or freedom from opposites.

There are other difficulties with Brentlinger's argument. If it were to be compelling that attention to incomplete predicates in the *Phaedo* gave Plato a motive for "separating" the forms, then one would not expect to see in dialogues earlier than the *Phaedo* either evidence of Platonic awareness of the difficulties posed by what Brentlinger terms incomplete predicates or evidence of the "separation" of the forms. In fact one finds evidence of both. *Euthydemus* 293B7–E10 depicts Socrates as being wary of contentious uses of ἐπιστήμων ("knowledgeable," but about what?), and at 297E1–299A1 he is equally wary about what one might construe as "incompleteness" in the Greek term for "father" (of whom?). Moreover, as R. E. Allen has argued in *Plato's "Euthyphro" and the Earlier Theory of Forms* (London, 1970), pp. 130–36, forms were "separate" in early dialogues in precisely the ways they were in middle ones such as *Phaedo*.

11 See, e.g., I. M. Crombie, *An Examination of Plato's Doctrines*, 2 (London, 1963): 437–40.
12 *Philebus* 23D10, 24C4, 25E1–2, 26A7–10, 26D9–10, 26E8–9, 27B1–3. This is not to say that each is reduced to what it can do. That would be to attribute to Plato a faculty ontology.
13 Here see Carl Werner Müller, *Gleiches zu Gleichem* (Wiesbaden, 1965), pp. 65–72.
14 Gisela Striker, *Peras und Apeiron: Das Problem der Formen in Platons "Philebos,"* Hypomnemata, no. 30 (Göttingen, 1970).
15 For expressions suggesting Plato's continued interest in the causal influence of forms as powers, see *Philebus* 24D, 25E, 26A, 26B, 26E, 27B, 27D, 28E, 29B, 31A, 58D, and 64D–E.
16 Prauss, *Platon und der logische Eleatismus*, p. 201.
17 A.P.D. Mourelatos, "Heraclitus, Parmenides, and the Naive Metaphysics of Things," in Lee, Mourelatos and Rorty, *Exegesis and Argument*, p. 17, n. 2, appears to agree with Prauss's interpretation and accordingly, characterized the late Plato's world as *logos*-textured.
18 J. Moravscik, "ΣΥΜΠΛΟΚΗ ΕΙΔΩΝ and the Genesis of ΛΟΓΟΣ," *Archiv für Geschichte der Philosophie* 42 (1960): 117–29, has argued that συμπλοκή should be taken as "interwovenness" on the ground that "a plurality of Forms, woven into a pattern, underlies each meaningful sentence" (p. 117), and that "the text does not say that we human beings do the interweaving of the Forms. It says, rather, that discourse becomes possible for us on account of the interwovenness of the Forms. What we human beings do is the interweaving of speech-elements. The interwovenness of Forms is hardly the result of our efforts; it is rather a condition which makes our efforts possible." This is a helpful description. But the situation is even more complex than it suggests. As *Statesman* 309A–B indicates, we *do* accomplish the interweaving of sensible or perceivable εἴδη whenever we create any lasting particular. Our being able to do so, however, depends upon a network of antecedent relationships among νοητὰ εἴδη, or intelligible forms, a network we do not bring

about but merely characterize dialectically by the process of division. This network is described below.

19 The suggestion that a particular such as a person's psyche is a synthesis or compound of elements put together but not in the best way was mentioned again at *Republic* 611B. Cp. *Phaedo* 92E. Plato seems to be speaking of sensible particulars at *Republic* 533B when he speaks of the sorts of things which the ordinary technical skills are concerned with as γένεσις τε καὶ σύνθεσις, "generation and composition," and contrasts this with dialectic, which is concerned with ὃ ἔστιν ἕκαστον, "what each thing really is." At *Cratylus* 431B Plato referred to a λόγος as a σύνθεσις of ῥημάτων καὶ ὀνομάτων, "a putting together of verbs and nouns."

20 Trans. W.R.M. Lamb, *Plato: Lysis, Symposium, Gorgias* (London, 1925), p. 207.

21 Prauss, *Platon und der logische Eleatismus*, pp. 41, 180, 194–97.

22 D. W. Hamlyn, "The Communion of Forms and the Development of Plato's Logic," *Philosophical Quarterly* 5 (1955): 289. Alexander Nehamas, "Predication and Forms of Opposites in the *Phaedo*," p. 461, n. 2, appears to deny this. But to deny it is to force an implausible sense on καὶ ἀλλήλων κοινωνίᾳ at 476A, for Plato would have to be read as equivocating on κοινωνίᾳ here by listing, in a single series, entities which are not in the same sense in community with forms. Such a reading would require argument.

23 W. D. Ross, *Plato's Theory of Ideas* (Oxford, 1951), p. 32.

24 Hamlyn, "The Communion of Forms and the Development of Plato's Logic," is, I think, right in defending the traditional view that Antisthenes was the "bogey" who haunted Plato with the specter of not being able to say anything instructive about forms. Prauss, *Platon und der logische Eleatismus*, pp. 174, argues that the Antisthenes hypothesis is superfluous as an answer to the question, Whose view is in question in Socrates' dream in the *Theaetetus*? As will emerge in the following section, this is, I think, half-right in that (*a*) Plato had himself said things all too suggestive of Eleaticism in his exaggerated emphasis upon the "purity" or "singularity" of forms, but only half-right in that (*b*) these suggestions of Eleaticism could not have been reconciled with the rest of Plato's epistemology and ontology, and hence are not likely to have been intended as Antisthenes evidently would have intended them.

25 James Adam, *The Republic of Plato*, 1 (Cambridge, 1963): p. 168, denies that the εἴδη spoken of here are the full-blown Platonic forms, since he agrees with the view that these are nowhere introduced before book 7. His reasons rest on the belief that such forms must be "transcendent," while these are "immanent." Interpreting terms for the distinctness and purity of forms as apprehended by the mind as if the effect of these terms was to claim that forms are removed from our world was criticized earlier, in Chapter 5.

26 Winifred Hicken, "The Character and Provenance of Socrates' 'Dream' in the *Theaetetus*," *Phronesis* 3 (1958): 126. Prauss, *Platon und der logische Eleatismus*, p. 164, complains that this makes Socrates' enterprise here into a mere contest, while he sees it as suggesting a much more hostile conflict, one

which undermines ultimately the extreme Eleaticism which Prauss sees as presupposed in the "dream" passage of the *Cratylus*. I agree that extreme Eleaticism is undermined in the *Theaetetus* and *Sophist*, but deny that Plato was ever a party to it save inadvertently, owing to confusion in his less-than-clear use of such terms as μονοειδές, εἰλικρινές, and the like. For a treatment of error and truth in Platonic dreams, see David Gallup, "Dreaming and Waking in Plato," in John P. Anton and George L. Kustus, eds., *Essays in Ancient Greek Philosophy* (Albany, 1971), p. 18. M. F. Burnyeat, "The Material and Sources of Plato's Dream," *Phronesis* 15 (1970): 104–5, rightly remarks that for Plato, "Epistemologically, a dream is something to look back on as dim and doubtful."

27 Prauss, *Platon und der logische Eleatismus*, p. 163, appears to overestimate the epistemic reliability of dreams on Plato's view.

28 Gilbert Ryle, "Plato's *Parmenides*," in R. E. Allen, ed., *Studies in Plato's Metaphysics* (London, 1965), pp. 139–41; Crombie, *An Examination of Plato's Doctrines*, 2:14; John Cooper, "Plato on Sense-Perception and Knowledge," *Phronesis* 15 (1970): 123–46. The most nearly convincing of these arguments is that of Cooper (pp. 126–27), but even it founders on a false contrast between the roles assigned to the senses and to the mind in *Republic* 7 and the roles assigned them in the *Theaetetus*. Cooper makes much of what I take to be a Platonic *façon de parler* at *Republic* 523B, where Plato speaks of the senses as if they see or discriminate, contrasting this with *Theaetetus* 185B and E, where Plato insists that it is the psyche which views some things through (διά) the powers of the body and the sense organs and others through its own powers. Cooper regards this as a new doctrine in the *Theaetetus*, but it is not; it paraphrases *Republic* 529B–D, where Plato first contrasts the psyche's looking "downwards" at sensible things with its looking "upward" at true realities, using the instrumental dative (not the equivalent διά) to claim that it looks "downward" by using sight (ὄψει) and upward by using an account (λόγῳ) and thought (διανοίᾳ).

29 F. M. Cornford, *Plato's Theory of Knowledge* (New York, 1957), pp. 141–42, 144, 146, 154, 162–63, argues that the *Theaetetus* makes as little mention as possible of forms, but concedes rightly (pp. 105–6) that the passage at 185C–186E has to do with forms.

30 With Crombie, *An Examination of Plato's Doctrines*, 2:115, I would hold that "it cannot be denied that the theory speaks of its elements as if they were physical elements (they are said to be sensible at 202B6); but of course what applies to physical elements in so far as they are elementary will apply to any other elements there may be." This is, I think, the key to the understanding of *Theaetetus* 200 ff.

31 Kenneth M. Sayre, *Plato's Analytic Method* (Chicago, 1969), pp. 120–21, 132–37. Earlier, Cornford made a suggestion along similar lines in *Plato's Theory of Knowledge*, p. 162. On the difficulties with this suggestion see John McDowell, *Plato: Theaetetus* (Oxford, 1973), pp. 257–59.

32 Sayre, *Plato's Analytic Method*, p. 121. Sayre claims that no argument or

counterexample is provided in the *Theaetetus* to show that true opinion with an account is insufficient for ἐπιστήμη, and that all Plato needs to do is supply an adequate sense of λόγος. He admits, however, that Plato rejects this final account of ἐπιστήμη along with the other two Theaetetus has presented (p. 136), though he thinks Plato has done this prematurely.

33 See, e.g., *Cratylus* 397B–C. There is really no good English translation of εἰκός. "Probable" or "likely" will not suffice, for they do not suggest, as the Greek does, a link with mere seeming, and hence do not arouse the reader's memory of Plato's paradigm/copy model, according to which νοῦς apprehends originals and the senses apprehend mere εἰκόνες, or crude likenesses, which prove ultimately to be unlike their originals in crucial ways.

34 *Theaetetus* 210C, trans. Harold North Fowler, *Plato With An English Translation* (London and Cambridge, Mass., 1921), p. 257.

35 C. M. Gillespie, "The Logic of Antisthenes," *Archiv für Geschichte der Philosophie* 26 (1913): 483–84, argues persuasively that *Theaetetus* 201C ff. refers to Antisthenes. He points out the close verbal correspondences of 201E and 202A with *Sophist* 251A ff. Gillespie is supported in this view by W. D. Ross, *Aristotle: Metaphysics*, 1 (Oxford, 1924): 346–47.

36 He was quite capable of admitting, as at *Hippias Major* 289C–E, that the beautiful is beautiful, while still pressing for an account of what the beautiful is.

37 Plato could have given up the view that forms are pure or unmixed, but he did not choose to do so, as is clear from *Philebus* 59B–C. The issue, then, is not whether he should say that the forms are pure or unmixed, but rather what is to be understood by his saying this.

38 Crombie, *An Examination of Plato's Doctrines*, 2:382, claims that when Plato wants to get down to serious business, he drops the technique of division. Since Plato has been occupied with elaborating and employing that technique since very nearly the beginning of the work, everything down to 232B would, on Crombie's view, seem to be less than serious business or only a prolegomenon to serious business. But then it would be difficult to explain why Socrates is made to speak so highly of the method at *Phaedrus* 265E and 277B–C and at *Statesman* 287C, or why he employs it again from *Sophist* 264D to the end, stating his final account of the sophist in terms suggestive of the method at 268C–D.

39 A. E. Taylor, *Plato: The Man and His Work* (New York, 1956), p. 376, not only accepts Theodorus' reading but constructs an elaborate story around it, one which evidently encourages Taylor to translate Socrates' θεὸς ἐλεγκτικός, "refutative divinity," as "a 'fiend' in constructing dilemmas." Cornford, in *Plato's Theory of Knowledge*, p. 169, spoke of Socrates' fearing "a very spirit of refutation," and took this refutation to be Eleatic, as Taylor did. Plato is less likely to suffer refutation by Eleatics, however, than he is to suffer it for adopting Eleatic or, more exactly, Antisthenean language in which his views about giving accounts and about the entities of which he wished accounts to be given would emerge as incoherent.

Notes to Pages 166–174

40 With R. E. Allen, "The Interpretation of Plato's *Parmenides,*" *Journal of the History of Philosophy* 2 (1957): 143, and R. S. Bluck, "The *Parmenides* and the Third Man," *Classical Quarterly* 50 (1956): 36–37, I take the *Parmenides* to be chiefly an exploration of the ridiculous consequences of taking Plato's forms in ways other than they were intended, but ways his language had not ruled out. This is not to say, however, that Plato was quite clear about what precisely was wrong with his language when he wrote the *Parmenides,* far less that he saw as yet any way to improve upon it. As Hamlyn remarked in "The Communion of Forms and the Development of Plato's Logic," p. 296, Plato gives the impression that he is groping for the solution to a problem he had not yet succeeded in formulating clearly.

41 This begins to emerge at *Sophist* 246A ff., and is quite clear by 258E ff., where the stranger contrasts what he now says with what he long ago gave up saying—that negation bears a certain ontologically embarrassing interpretation.

42 By speaking here of "complements" I do not wish to suggest that forms can be interpreted extensionally as classes or sets. A form is a class or set only in the remote sense of the meaning, i.e., as the intended referent of a class name, where that name is thought to apply without qualifications only to a perfect paradigm for a class, not to the members of it. I am indebted to Jack Temkin on this point. For a forceful argument that no extensional interpretation of forms can be adequate, see J. Moravscik, "The Anatomy of Plato's Divisions," in Lee, Mourelatos, and Rorty, *Exegesis and Argument,* pp. 324–48.

43 On dialectic as division see Julius Stenzel *Studien zur Entwicklung der Platonischen Dialektik von Sokrates zu Aristoteles,* 3rd ed. (Stuttgart, 1961), pp. 94–105.

44 What, e.g., is the distinction, if any, between ἡ ποιητική, "the productive art," divided in two at *Sophist* 265A–B, and ἡ πρακτική or χειροτεχνική mentioned at *Statesman* 259C–D in a process of division aimed at tracking down quite a different quarry? There are indefinitely many such questions any potential dialectician would have to ask concerning even one attempt at tracking a single "quarry" by division.

45 *Sophist* 233C. The conclusion here seems to be anticipated at *Republic* 598C–D, which shows as many signs of having been composed later than the rest of the *Republic* as book 1 does of having been composed earlier than the rest.

46 See Chapter 2, above, for the evidence of Plato's having believed that such tests are not sufficient.

47 *Laws* 653A, 689B; *Philebus* 11D, 21C, 60D. The latter passages, especially, verge on being cavalier regarding Plato's earlier emphasis on the importance of the distinction between ἐπιστήμη and ἀληθὴς δόξα. This can scarcely be an accident, and demands explanation in terms of Plato's developing views.

48 Certainly the *Timaeus* is clear on this at 51D–E. And *Laws* 632C suggests that those who have understanding or wisdom and those who have true opinion are distinct persons, and hence that they are in distinct states or conditions,

though it does not, of course, suggest that we have any sufficient means for certifying that a person is in the better of the two. The person's own feeling of ἔκλαμψις, or "illumination," is worthless to others, and perhaps to himself. The dawning of a true opinion (or even a false one) may seem immensely illuminating.

49 *Statesman* 275C, trans. Harold North Fowler, *Plato With An English Translation* (London and Cambridge, Mass., 1962), p. 69.
50 Plato's final position in epistemology resembles that of Xenophanes, who long before had remarked, "For even if he were to hit by chance upon the whole truth, he himself would not be aware of having done so, but each forms his own opinion" (DK B34, trans. J. M. Robinson, *An Introduction to Early Greek Philosophy* [Boston, 1968], p. 56.
51 *Crito* 46B, trans. Harold North Fowler, *Plato With An English Translation* (London and Cambridge, Mass., 1960), p. 161.
52 *Laws* 950B–C.

Conclusion

1 A. K. Sen, "Rational Fools: A Critique of the Behavioral Foundations of Economic Theory," *Philosophy and Public Affairs* 6 (1977): 337–41, has commented usefully on the importance of preferences ranging over preferences. See also his "Choice, Orderings, and Morality," in S. Körner, ed., *Practical Reason* (Oxford, 1974).
2 Here I am conscious of a debt to John Ciardi.
3 For Plato's treatment of misology, see *Phaedo* 89C–90E.
4 A rough reconstruction of some of the rules of this art was undertaken in Chapter 2, above.
5 Gilbert Ryle, *The Concept of Mind* (Oxford, 1949).
6 Hilary Putnam, *Meaning and the Moral Sciences* (London, 1978), p. 115.
7 Ibid., pp. 115–16.
8 Such talk of turning attention from one sort of object to another is best understood not as committing Plato to two "separate" worlds, as was argued in Chapter 4. It is best construed, rather, as one of his ways of trying to make vivid a distinction between two distinct ways of attending to the world.

Glossary

This glossary is intended for the use of readers who do not know Greek, but do know the Greek alphabet well enough to find words in the series below. The order of entries, reading across the page from left to right, is as follows: Greek word, transliteration of the Greek word into the Roman alphabet, approximate pronunciation, variant Greek forms appearing in the text (if any), and meanings. Where meanings have been explained in the text, the entries here in the glossary will generally be more conventional, and will give one some idea of the range of possible readings. A number of terms normally occurring in Greek as adjectives are given here as nouns if Plato so employed them.

αἴσθησις. *aisthesis*, ICE-thay-sees, "sense perception," "sensation."
αἰσθητά. *aistheta*, ice-thay-TAH, "sensible entities," "objects of perception."
αἰτία. *aitia*, eye-TEE-ah (Ionic αἰτίη, pl. αἰτίαι), "cause," "responsibility."
ἀκρασία. *akrasia*, ah-krah-SEE-ah, "weakness of will," "moral weakness," "lack of self-control."
ἄκων. *akon*, AH-cone, "involuntary," "constrained."
ἀλήθεια. *aletheia*, ah-LAY-thay-ah, "truth," "reality."
ἀληθής. *alethes*, ah-lay-THACE (neuter ἀληθές), "true," "real."
ἀντιλογική. *antilogike*, ahn-tee-lo-ghee-KAY, "the art of disputation."
ἄπειρον. *apeiron*, AH-pay-ron (pl. ἄπειρα), "boundless," "infinite," "unlimited."
ἀρετή. *arete*, ah-rey-TAY, "excellence," "virtue."
ἀρχή. *arche*, ahr-KHAY, "beginning," "origin," "source."
ἀσυνεσία. *asynesia*, ah-syn-eh-SEE-ah (Ionic ἀσυνεσίη), "want of understanding," "stupidity."
ἀτραπός. *atrapos*, ah-trah-POSS, "path."
αὐτὸ καθ' αὑτό. *auto kath hauto*, ow-TOW kath how-TOW, "itself throughout itself," "itself in relation to itself," "absolute."
βάσανος. *basanos*, BAH-sah-noss, "test," "trial of genuineness," "inquiry by torture."
βέβαιος. *bebaios*, BEH-bye-oss (neuter βέβαιον), "firm," "steady," "steadfast," "enduring."
βεβαιότης. *babaiotes*, beh-bye-OTT-ace, "steadfastness," "stability."
γιγνόμενα. *gignomena*, gig-NO-meh-nah, "things which become," "things which change."
γιγνώσκω. *gignosko*, gig-NOH-skoh (infinitive γιγνώσκειν), "know," "come to know," "understand."
γνῶσις. *gnosis*, GNOH-sees, "knowledge," "understanding."

διαλέγομαι. *dialegomai*, dee-ah-LEG-oh-my (infinitive διαλέγεσθαι), "discuss," "carry on discourse with," "practice dialectic."
διαλεκτική. *dialektike*, dee-ah-lek-tee-KAY, "dialectic," "discussion by question and answer."
δίκαιος. *dikaios*, DEE-kye-oss, "observant of custom or rule," "lawful," "just," "right."
δικαιοσύνη. *dikaiosyne*, dee-kye-oh-SYN-eh, "justice," "rightness."
δόξα. *doxa*, DOCK-sah, "opinion," "belief."
δοξάζω. *doxazo*, dock-SAH-dzoh (infinitive δοξάζειν), "think," "imagine," "form or hold an opinion," "believe."
δύναμις. *dynamis*, DYN-ah-mees (pl. δυνάμεις), "power," "capacity."
δυσεξελεγκτότατον. *dysexelengtotaton*, dys-eks-eh-lenk-TOW-tah-ton, "most difficult to refute."
εἰδέναι. *eidenai*, eh-DEN-eye (infinitive form of οἶδα), "know," "understand."
εἶδος. *eidos*, EH-doss (pl. εἴδη, *eide*, EH-day), "form," "that which is seen," "shape," "figure."
εἰκών. *eikon*, eh-CONE (pl. εἰκόνες, *eikones*, eh-CON-ess), "likeness," "image."
ἑκών. *hekon*, heh-CONE, "readily," "willingly," "purposely."
ἔλεγχος. *elenchus*, ELL-eng-koss, "test," "refutation."
ἐπιθυμητικόν. *epithymetikon*, eh-pee-thy-may-tee-CON, "desiderative," "that part of the psyche characterized above all by sensual desire."
ἐπιθυμία. *epithymia*, eh-pee-thy-MEE-ah, "desire," "yearning," "passion."
ἐπίσταμαι. *epistamai*, eh-PEE-stah-my (infinitive ἐπίστασθαι, *epistasthai*, eh-PEE-stas-thigh), "know," "understand." ·
ἐπιστήμη. *episteme*, eh-pee-STAY-may, "knowledge," "understanding."
ἐπωδή. *epode*, eh-poh-DAY (pl. ἐπῳδαί, *epodai*, eh-poh-DYE), "incantation," "spell," "charm."
ἐριστική. *eristike*, eh-rees-tee-KAY, "the art of wrangling," "sophistry."
εὐβουλία. *euboulia*, eh-oo-boo-LEE-ah, "good counsel," "soundness of judgment."
εὔθυνοι. *euthynoi*, eh-oo-THYN-oy (pl. of εὔθυνος), "public examiner."
θεῖος. *theios*, THAY-oss, "divine."
θεός. *theos*, thay-OSS, "god."
θυμοειδές. *thymoeides*, thym-oh-eh-DESS, "spirited," "that part of the psyche characterized above all by spiritedness."
θυμός. *thymos*, thym-OSS, "soul," "spirit," "that part of the psyche characterized above all by spiritedness."
ἰδέα. *idea*, ee-DEH-ah (pl. ἰδέαι, Ionic sing. ἰδέη), "form," "shape," "outward appearance."
ἰσονομία. *isonomia*, ee-so-no-MEE-ah, "equal balance," "equilibrum."
καθ᾽ αὑτόν. *kath hauton*, kath how-TON, "throughout itself," "in accordance with itself," "absolute."
καθαρός. *katharos*, kah-thah-ROSS, "pure."
κατ᾽ εἴδη. *kat eide*, kaht EH-day, "according to forms," "in accordance with forms."
κατὰ τὸ ὄνομα. *kata to onoma*, kah-TAH tow OH-no-mah, "according to name."

καλός. *kalos*, kah-LOSS, "beautiful," "fine," "noble."
κιβδηλεία. *kibdeleia*, keeb-day-LAY-ah, "adulteration."
κίβδηλος. *kibdelos*, KEEB-day-loss, "counterfeit," "fraudulent," "base," "false."
κοινωνία. *koinonia*, koy-noh-NEE-ah, "community," "communion," "association."
κολακεία. *kolakeia*, ko-lah-KAY-ah, "flattery."
κρᾶσις. *krasis*, KRAH-sees, "mixture," "blend," "combination."
κυβερνήτης. *kybernetes*, kyb-ehr-NAY-tace, "helmsman."
λανθάνω. *lanthano*, lahn-THAH-noh, "escape notice."
λέγω. *lego*, LEGG-oh, "pick up," "gather," "pick out," "select," "recount," "say."
λογισμός. *logismos*, lo-ghees-MOSS, "calculation," "reckoning," "reasoning," "argument."
λόγος. *logos*, LOG-oss (pl. λόγοι, *logoi*, LOG-oy), "word," "statement," "account."
μετέχω. *metexo*, met-ECH-oh (infinitive μετέχειν), "share in," "partake of," "participate in."
μίμησις. *mimesis*, MEE-may-sees, "imitation," "representation."
μοῖρα. *moira*, MOY-rah, "portion," "share," "lot," "destiny."
μοναρχία. *monarchia*, mon-ahr-KEY-ah, "monarchy."
μονοειδής. *monoeides*, mo-no-eh-DACE (neuter μονοειδές), "one in kind," "simple."
μουσική. *mousike*, moo-see-KAY, "any art over which the Muses presided."
νοέω. *noeo*, no-EH-oh (infinitive νοεῖν), "perceive by the mind," "apprehend," "think," "consider," "reflect."
νόησις. *noesis*, NO-eh-sees, "intelligence," "thought," "understanding."
νοητά. *noeta*, no-eh-TAH, "intelligible things."
νοῦς. *nous*, NOOSE (in Homer, νόος), "mind," "sense," "wit," "intellect"; sometimes used by Plato of a condition or state of mind.
οἶδα. *oida*, OY-dah, "see with the mind's eye," "know," "understand."
ὄνομα. *onoma*, OH-no-mah, "name," "noun," "word."
ὄντα. *onta*, ON-tah, "things that are," "realities."
ὀρθός. *orthos*, or-THOSS (feminine ὀρθή, neuter ὀρθόν), "correct," "right."
οὐρανός. *ouranos*, oo-rah-NOSS, "vault of heaven," "sky."
οὐσία. *ousia*, oo-SEE-ah, "personal property," "stable being," "reality."
παράδειγμα. *paradeigma*, pah-RAH-daig-mah (pl. παραδείγματα), "pattern," "model," "paradigm," "exemplar."
ποιέω. *poieo*, poy-EH-oh (infinitive ποιεῖν), "make," "create."
ποιητική. *poietike*, poy-eh-tee-KAY, "productive art."
ποιοῦν. *poioun*, poy-OON, "maker," "creator."
πολυειδής. *polyeides*, po-ly-eh-DACE (neuter πολυειδές), "multiple in form."
πρός τι. *pros ti*, PROSS tee, "relative," "in relation to something."
ῥῆμα. *rhema*, HRAY-mah, "that which is said," "word," "saying," "verb."
ῥητόν. *rheton*, hray-TON, "expressible," either in the sense of "capable of being expressed" or in the sense of "right to express."
σαφήνεια. *sapheneia*, sah-FAY-nay-ah, "clearness," "distinctness."
σαφής. *saphes*, sah-FACE (neuter σαφές), "clear," "distinct."
σοφία. *sophia*, so-FEE-ah (Ionic σοφίη), "sound judgment," "wisdom."

σοφός. *sophos*, so-FOSS, "wise."
στάσις. *stasis*, STAH-sees, "faction," "civil war."
συγκεράνυμμι. *syngkeranymmi*, syn-keh-RAH-nym-mee, "mix," "blend with."
σύμμιξις. *symmixis*. SYM-meek-sees, "commingling," "commixture," "sexual intercourse."
συμπλοκή. *symploke*, sym-plo-KAY, "weaving," "intertwining."
συναιτία. *synaitia*, syn-eye-TEE-ah, "auxiliary cause."
σύνθεσις. *synthesis*, SYN-theh-sees, "putting together," "combination."
συνοπτικός. *synoptikos*, syn-op-tee-KOSS, "seeing the whole together," "taking a comprehensive view."
σωφροσύνη. *sophrosyne*, soh-phro-SYN-eh, "discretion," "temperance," "moderation."
τέχνη. *techne*, TEK-nay, "art," "craft," "skill," "discipline," "method."
τί ἐστι. *ti esti*, TEE es-tee, "What is . . .?"
τιμή. *time*, tee-MAY, "honor," "esteem."
τόπος. *topos*, TOP-oss, "place."
ὑγιής. *hygies*, hy-ghee-ACE, "healthy," "sound."
ὑπόθεσις. *hypothesis*, hy-PO-theh-sees, "proposal," "suggestion," "assumption," "hypothesis."
φάρμακον. *pharmakon*, FAR-mah-kon (pl. φάρμακα), "drugs."
φαῦλος. *phaulos*, FOW-loss, "worthless," "vulgar," "common."
φιλοκερδές. *philokerdes*, fee-lo-ker-DESS, "lover of gain."
φιλομαθές. *philomathes*, fee-lo-mah-THESS, "lover of learning."
φιλόνικον. *philonikon*, fee-LO-nee-kon, "lover of victory."
φιλοσοφία. *philosophia*, fee-lo-so-FEE-ah, "love of wisdom," "philosophy."
φιλόσοφος. *philosophos*, fee-LO-so-foss (neuter, used of part of the psyche, φιλόσοφον), "lover of wisdom," "philosopher."
φιλότιμον. *philotimon*, fee-LO-tee-mon, "lover of honor."
φιλοχρήματον. *philochrematon*, fee-lo-CHRAY-mah-ton, "lover of money," "lover of possessions."
φρήν. *phren*, FRANE, "midriff," "mind" as seat of mental activities.
φρόνησις. *phronesis*, PHRON-eh-sees, "judgment," "practical wisdom."
φύσις. *physis*, PHY-sees, "nature."
χάρις. *charis*, CHAH-rees, "grace," "favor."
ψευδής. *pseudes*, psew-DACE (neuter ψευδές), "false."
ψεῦδος. *pseudos*, PSEW-doss, "lie."
ψυχή. *psyche*, psew-CHAY (pl. ψυχαί, *psychai*, psew-CHIGH), "soul," "psyche."
ὠφέλιμον. *ophelimon*, oh-FELL-ee-mon, "beneficial."

Index

Ability, abilities, 36, 94, 178–79
Absolute, absolutes, 123, 148, 222n7, 230n10
Account: ability to give and defend necessary for ἐπιστήμη, 7–8, 12–14, 33–34, 163, 190n14; and apprehension of forms, 143; and cause, 56; as list of selected things, 34–35; as particular having a form, 126; as particular tailored to questioner and to current conditions, 135–36; form of, 126–30; function of, 129; image of thought, 136; in paradigm-fancier's sense, 125; interpretations of in *Theaetetus*, 159–65; judged by paradigm, 129; "midwife's" ability to elicit and assess, 130; object of, 223n15; objects of false accounts, 228n56; possibility of, 156–57, 164–65; senses of, 139–40; starting point for in division, 171–73; success under test certifies understanding in *Republic*, 143; sufficiency conditions for, 172; testing of in ancient medicine, 99; truth of varies with degree of reality of object, 136n25; understanding of form of necessary for dialectical testing, 132; written ones fared badly, 136
Accuracy, in dialectic, 40
Achilles, 14, 16, 34
Acquaintance, knowledge by, 8–9, 190n18, 191n19
Actions, causes of, 56–57
Acts: involuntary, 72–73; voluntary, 71
Adam, James, 204n11, 205n26, 232n25
Adamant, 226n40
Adeimantus, 210n4
Adjectives, degrees of, 133, 226n39
Adkins, Arthur W. H., 196n1, 203n6, 208n60
Adulteration, 128–29, 224n21
Aeneas, 16
Aeschines, 101
Aeschylus, 19, 22, 193n39
Aetius, 85, 213n21
Affirming the consequent, fallacy of, 175
Agamemnon, 16, 159

Agents, 87, 88
Αἴσθησις, 106
Αἰσθητική, 27
Αἰτία, "cause", 89–90
Αἰτίας λογισμός, 45
'Ακρασία, 26–27, 28, 72–73
"Ακων, 72–73, 207n48
Alcibiades, 48, 134
Alcmaeon, physician, 84, 85, 86, 87, 95, 100, 114, 213n14
'Αλήθεια: degrees of, 106, 121, 132–34, 158; derivation from privative ἀ and λανθάνω, 223n8; no discursive/non-discursive distinction, 140. *See also* Truth, Reality
'Αληθής: alleged discursive/non-discursive distinction, 128–29; alternative expressions for, 132; conformity to type, 222n3; degree constructions with, 132–33, 226n39; "unhidden", 123; used of forms, 105, 222n4
Alexander of Aphrodisias, 106, 195n59, 219n62, 230n10
Allen, R. E., 40, 94, 113, 197n12, 210n4, 210n9, 213n15, 218n44, 218n48, 219n63, 220n68, 220n69, 220n72, 221n76, 230–31n10, 233n28, 235n40
"Αλογον, 223n11
Analysis into parts, 169
Anaxagoras, 19, 74, 83, 85, 87, 99, 108, 143, 144, 145, 150, 212n13, 213n25, 216n39, 219n53, 221n79
Anger, 55
Anthropomorphism, 74–75, 86, 204n16, 208n61
'Αντί, 159
Antilogic, 114–15
'Αντιλογική, 41, 114–15, 197n14
Antisthenes, 157, 163, 168, 232n24, 234n35, 234n39
Anton, John P., 199n23, 232–33n26
Anytus, 8
"Απειρον, 149
Appearances, explanation of, 92
Appetite, 55, 58–59, 68

241

Arcadians, 15
'Αρετή: and ἐπιστήμη, 9–12, 20, 21, 27–31, 45, 46, 73–74, 143; and power, 45; and self-discipline, 24; completion of tests for in *Republic*, 225n26; condition of health in psyche, 69; in Thucydides, 20
Aristophanes, 194n54, 211n12, 213n20
Aristotle: bifurcation of theory and practice, 28; conditions for sameness of meaning, 15; on forms, xiii–xiv, 106; on place, 102–3; remarks about Plato and Platonists, xiii–xv; Socratic paradox, 26–27; mentioned, 101, 112, 128, 137, 148, 157, 173, 194n57, 195n59, 201n29, 202n2, 207n55, 207n57, 212n13, 213n25, 215n38, 224n20, 230n8, 230n10
Armour, Leslie, 225n37
Army, 57
Article, definite, 59, 203n10
Asclepias, legendary founder of medicine, 211n12
Atheist, 131
'Ατραπός, 172
Austin, J. L., 4, 21, 188n2, 194n46, 224n21
Αὐτὰ καθ' αὑτά, 106, 108
Authorities, appeal to, 39
Autonomy, prerequisite for, 179
Αὐτὸ τὸ ἴσον, 105
Auxiliaries, 57
Ayer, A. J., 189n8

Bacon, Francis, 15
Baldry, H. C., 210n4, 213n19, 218n51
Baldwin, J. M., 73, 204n22, 207n49
Bambrough, Renford, 223n10
Barbarians, 167–68
Barber, Ernest, 201n35, 202n39
Βάσανος, 130
Beard, Charles, 196n66
Beast similes, 49, 63
Beauty, 123, 189n10, 205n25, 218n43
Βέβαιος, βέβαιον, βεβαιότης, 132, 134, 222n4, 225n32
Bed, form of, 126
Begriffe, 151
Bluck, R. S., 29, 187n1, 195n63, 209n1, 235n40
Boeder, Heribert, 34, 197n5, 197n8, 197n9, 223n8

Boehme, Joachim, 17–18
Boundaries, disciplinary, ix, 183
Bourgey, Louis, 217n40, 217–18n42
Brasidas, Spartan general, 20
Bravery, 55
Brentlinger, John, 143–48, 215n38, 223n16, 228n1, 228n3, 230n10
Brès, Yvon, 66, 206n36, 206n37
Brown, George, 209n1
Buddhists, Thai, 188n6
Builder, art of, 117
Burge, Evan, 221n80
Burnet, John, 40, 89, 116, 197n12, 214n29, 221n78
Burnyeat, M. F., 232–33n26

Cairns, Huntington, 191n21
Calculative, the, 55
Calley, Earle R., 226n40
Callicles, 48, 131, 133
Capacity, distinct from competence, 57. *See also* Ability
Capelle, W., 217n40
Cartography, 169–70, 176
Category-mistakes, 85, 224n22
Cause: distinguished from auxiliary cause, 93; Humean conception of, 218n48; recent disagreements about, 89–90
Cave simile, 106, 128, 171, 182
Cebes, 69, 81
Censorship, 67
Certainty, x, 134, 190n12
Chaignet, A., 203n2
Character-powers, 93, 100, 115, 214n28. *See also* Powers, Quality-things, Δυνάμεις
Charioteer, myth of, 65, 81
Charmides, 48
Charms, 64, 66, 69, 206n38
Cherniss, Harold F., 146, 191n24, 210n9, 229n7
Chihara, C. S., 230n9
Children, control of, 67
Chisholm, R., 189n8, 219n59
Chomsky, Noam, 196n65
Church, Alonzo, 228n53
Clarity, 39
Class, 98
Classes, 235n42
Classification, according to forms in *Laws*, 224n18

Index

Clay, analysis of as model for account, 167, 210n3
Cleon, the tanner, 20, 25, 26, 27, 194n54
Clinias, 42
Coherence: criterion for correctness in imitation, 224n18; test for truth, 132, 134
Communication: basis for, 182; between parts of the psyche, 61–62, 64, 66; between persons, 66
Community, 181, 201n36
Complex question, fallacy of, 3, 40
Concepts: analysis of, 56; contrasted with forms, 151, 228n53; how differentiated, 6
Conditions: logically necessary, 148; logico-metaphysical, 216n39
Conflict: basis for distinguishing parts of psyche and polis, 61, 203–4n11; political, 208n58; psychic, 57
Connotation, 148
Constancy, 106. See also Endurance, Βεβαιότης
Constitution: of the polis, 49; Laws vs. Republic, 201n29
Conventions, variability of linguistic, 135
Cooper, John, 233n28
Copies, and originals, 222n4. See also Imitation, Paradigms
Cornford, F. M., 42, 85, 198n16, 202n2, 203n6, 208n63, 213n17, 218n48, 223n16, 233n29, 233n31, 234n39
Correspondence, and truth, 127, 132, 222n4
Cos, medical school at, 211n11
Counterexamples, discussed in medicine, 99
Counterfeits, 124, 125, 128
Coupelation, cementation, 130–31
Courage, 205n25
Cowardice, 10
Craftsmen, 57, 59
Cratylus, 210n4
Crisis, 114, 220n75
Critias, 48
Crombie, I. M., 40, 197n12, 201n36, 202n39, 204n17, 207n54, 231n11, 233n28, 233n30, 234n38
Cross, R. C., 9, 189n10, 190n16, 191n19, 203n2, 204n17, 205n23, 207n54, 207n56, 208n60, 209n1
Crossman, R. H. S., 206n38

Culture, oral, 13

Data, fitting hypotheses to, xii
Day simile, 215–16n38
Death: conception of, 89, 145; fear of, 69–70, 200n26
Deduction, 225n28
Degree, positive, 133
Demiurge, 110
Democedes, physician, 211n11
Democracy: direct, 14; element of in Laws, 49; epistemic foundations for, 177; restoration of Athenian, 48
Democrat, 208n58
Democritus, 20, 21, 212n13, 219n52
Demos, R., 206n36
Demosthenes, 225n37
Denniston, J. D., 192n30
Denotation, 147. See also Reference
Description, knowledge by, 8–9, 190n18, 191n19
Desires: necessary, 208n58; predominant, 57; unnecessary, 208n58
Δεύτερος πλοῦς, 216–17n39
Διά, 233n28
Dialectic: and decision, 35; and division of objects of ἐπιστήμη, x, 235n43; and myth, 206n41; and opinions of parts of psyche, 61; Aristotle's assessment of, xiv; constraints upon answerer in, 39–40, 40–41; constraints upon questioner in, 40–41; coping stone of philosophy, xiv; division by forms, 115, 168–70; forms necessary for, 126; power of, 101; tests for ἐπιστήμη, ix, x
Dialectical testing: and wrongdoing in Laws, 50–51; distinguishes ἐπιστήμη from ὀρθὴ δόξα, 44–45; epistemological insufficiency of in late dialogues, 171–77; of officials, 50–51; removes all but truth, 46, 131; structure of, 38; success in does not preclude wrongdoing in Laws, 47; success in precludes wrongdoing in Republic, 46–47; survival of account in, 44–45
Dialectician: ability of, 170; can give and defend account, 33–34; other names for, 70
Διαλεκτική, 35, 115
Diet, 86
Diller, Hans, 212n13

Diogenes Laertius, 218n46
Diogenes of Apollonia, 221n79
Dionysius of Syracuse, 199n21
Diotima, 41, 102, 189n10, 208n63, 221n79
Disciplines, boundaries between, ix, 183
Discursive/non-discursive distinction, 224n21
Discussion: ability to carry on, 178–83; and democracy, 14; as discipline, 180; basis for, 182–83; depends on stable reality, 223n15; dialectical, 180; function of, 65; objects of, 223n15; of discussion, 178–79; practical, 183; requirements for, 180
Disease: owing to lack of understanding, 20; treatment of, 96–97
Distinctness, as interpretation of χωρισμός, 96–97
Divine: element in our nature, 48–49; stability of, 202n40
Division: according to forms, 115, 207n57; and interwovenness, 231–32n18; and "tracking", 235n44; Aristotle's taxonomic scruples regarding, 202n2; of lives in *Philebus*, 168; of psyche, 207n57; use of, 234n38
Doctrines, Plato's alleged secret, 199–200n23
Dodds, E. R., 21–22, 23, 194n45, 194n49, 201n30, 206n44, 207n54
Dog-breeding similes, 111, 114
Δόξα: dependent on forms, 161; differs from ἐπιστήμη, 45; in Hippocratic corpus, 20
Dreams, 61, 63, 159–60, 204n12, 232–33n26
Dretske, Fred, 189n8
Droughts, genetic, 50
Δύναμις, δυνάμεις: and cause, 91, 115; and places, 103; and problem of one and many, 109; as Aristotelian faculty, 202n2; as bearer and imparter of qualities, 90; as "quality-thing" in philosophy, 144; as substance which is a power, 94; how distinguished, 91; in medicine, 84–88, 214n26; in *Philebus*, 149; meaning of in Plato, 202n2. *See also* Power, Character-power, Quality-things
Düring, I., xiii, xiiin2

Edelstein, Ludwig, 199n22, 199n23

Edwards, Paul, 207n51, 214n31
Effability hypothesis, 199n21
Εἶδος, εἴδη: and δύναμις, 87, 88, 90, 92; causal influence of, 91, 115; in medicine, 214n26; in *Philebus*, 149; mixed in food and drink, 108; no account of in dialogues, 79–81; objects of ἐπιστήμη, x; Plato's psychological use of, 75–76; root meaning of, 87, 97, 108; sensed vs. apprehended by the mind, 108. *See also* Forms
Εἰκόνες, 234n33
Εἰκός, 162, 234n33
Εἰλικρινής, 105, 122, 168, 224n23, 232–33n26
Ἔκλαμψις, 235–36n48
Ἑκών, 71–72
Ἔλεγχος: as refutation, 37; as test for incoherence, 37
Eleaticism, 148–59, 155, 156–58, 166, 232n24, 232–33n26
Eleatics, 234n39
Elements, 95, 233n30
Else, Gerald Frank, 91, 214n35, 215n37, 216n39, 218n49, 220n67, 220n73
Emotion, and intellect, 32–33
Empedocles, 19, 83, 87, 90, 95–97, 100, 108, 192n25, 212n13, 214n34, 219n53, 219n55
Endurance, as test of reality or truth, 132
Ἕν ἐπὶ πολλά, 112–15
England, R. B., 202n40
Ἐπί, alternative readings of, 113–14
Epicharmus, 24
Ἐπικρατέω, 114
Ἐπιφερέω, 114
Ἐπίσταμαι, meaning of, 14–16, 29
Ἐπιστήμη: alternative terms for, 13, 32, 191n22, 191n36; and ability to give an account, 28–31, 36–37, 41–43, 130, 172–77, 190n17; and ἀρετή, 20–21, 27–31, 46, 73–74; and behavior, 12, 46, 50, 200n26; and motivation, 14, 20, 21, 26–27, 28–31, 32; and opinion, 135; and pleasure, 26; and self-understanding, 24; and true account, 42, 200n26, 235n47; as condition of the psyche, ix, x, 51, 52, 53, 78; as psychic harmony, 78; as relation between psyche and forms, 79; as true opinion with an account, 158–65, 233–

34n32; as understanding of reality, x, 119; best rendered as "understanding", 29–31; central integrating concept, ix; claim to refutable by nonverbal behavior, 200n26; completion of tests for in *Republic*, 225n26; dialectical tests for, ix; differs from true opinion, 38; each object thereof amenable to an account, 42–43; ἡ κυρίως, 27; inadequately rendered as "know-how", 195n61; infallible, of the truth, 135; insufficiency of later dialectical tests for, 173–77; likened to ability to spell, 161; objects of, 180; of everything, 173; of guardians, 55; philosophers', 153; popular uses of term for, 222n4; problem of necessary and sufficient conditions for, 51; sufficiency of ability to give and defend an account for prior to *Laws*, 43–46, 132
Epistemology: applied in politics, 176–77; Plato's not an account of knowledge, 5
Ἐπιθυμητικόν, 59
Ἐπιθυμίαι. *See* Desires
Ἐπωδαί, 66, 69, 209n65, 230n8
Epistle 7, genuineness of, 199n22, 199n23
Equal, the, 105
Equivalence, functional, 4
Er, myth of, 68, 209n65
Ἐριστική, 197n14
Eros, 77, 208n63, 211n11
Ἐρρωμενέστατον, 132, 225n32
Error, 137, 227n51
Eryximachus, physician, 211n11, 211n12, 211n34, 212n13
Ethnocentrism, 27
Εὐβουλία, 45, 73–74
Eudoxus, 213n25
Euripides, 22–25, 90, 194n51
Εὔθυνοι, 201n29
Euthyphro, 38, 44, 133
Examiners: importance of, 201n29; nature of, 202n39; of officials in the *Laws*, 47–48; selection of, 50; virtue of, 50
Excellence, 143
Ἕξις, 202n40
Existence, 219n61, 223n16
Explanation, pattern of in Plato's psychology, 74–75
Expressibility, 43, 198–99n21
Extension, 227n50

Fables, use of, 62
Factions: in polis and psyche, 54–55; in psyche, 76, 204n12
Faculties: defined, 58; psychic, 53, 72–73
Falsity: as deviance from paradigm, 127; as otherness, 127, 142; Plato's account of, 228n55; possibility of, 124–29, 138–40
Families, guardians', 47
Fear, amenable to charm, 70
Festugiere, A. J., 208n59
Fever, 99
Findlay, J. N., 214n36, 218n51, 220n66
Finger, 107
Fishing, 170, 210n3
Flattery, 125
Fodor, J. A., 228n53, 230n9
Force, 70–71, 201n36
Forms: "absolutes", 105, 118; alleged arguments for existence of, 105–8; alleged logical functions of, 216n39; and division, 169–70; and opposites, 94; and universals, 220n69; apprehended by thought, 120, 170; Aristotle's criticisms of, xiii–xiv; causal role of, 80, 87, 88–95, 101, 112, 115, 216–17n39, 221n79, 231n15; causal role of in Empedocles, 95; changeless, simple, and good, 122; character-powers, 214n28; community of, 156–57, 232n22; complexity of, 168–70; epistemic role of, 120–21, 140; examples of in *Phaedo*, 229n4; explanatory role, 114; familiar to Socrates' interlocutors, 81–82, 88, 89; friends of, 160, 166–67; grasped by the psyche, 163–64; immanence of, 109–12, 219–20n65, 232n25; in later dialogues, 229–30n7; interwovenness of, 231n18; in *Theaetetus*, 161–62, 198n16, 233n29; location of, 100–105; models of imitation, 140; natural, not conventional, 115; no account of in dialogues, 79–81; not compounded of opposites, 155; objects of λόγος, 161; objects of thought, 80; objects of truest accounts, 140; of psyche, 75–76, 214n28; ontological role of, 92, 121; paradigms, 210n4, 220n69; philosophical necessity of, 210n9; Plato does not ask "What is a . . . ", 79–80; Plato's contribution to a theory of, 89; powers, 88, 91; provide identity of all particulars, 126–29; "quality-things",

214n28; range of, 210n8, 229n4; relations among, 80, 155–57, 168–70; relation to names, 114–15; relation to particulars, 142; reputed self-predictability of, 80; sensed in particulars, 117–18; separation and χωρισμός, 80, 95, 117, 144, 210n8, 215n37, 215n38, 216n39, 230–31n10; shares of, 119–21; simplicity and purity of, 120, 155–57, 163, 164, 168, 232n24, 234n37; stability of, 150; stereotypes, 75–76; subforms, 170; theory of as philosophy of science, 83–84; transcendence of, 219–20n65, 232n25; varying roles in mixtures, 152–54; visible vs. intelligible, 97–98; χωρισμός discussed in pre-Socratic medicine, 96–97
Fournier, Henri, 34, 197n4, 197n6
Frank, E., xiiin2
Freedom, 50, 202n36
Freud, Sigmund, 15, 20, 27, 29, 30, 77, 160, 192n33, 208n64
Friendliness, 50, 202n36, 205n29
Frisk, Hjalmar, 197n3
Fritz, Kurt von, xiiin2, 17–18, 193n37, 199n23
Fromm, Erich, 196n66
Frostbite, 99
Furley, D. J., 213n15, 218n48

Gain, lover of, 59
Galen, physician, 99, 214n34, 217n40
Galis, L., 189n8
Gallup, David, 232–33n26
Game, zero-sum, 201n36
Geach, Peter T., 40, 197n12, 209n1
Genealogy, and later dialectic, 169
Γένος, 127
Genuineness. See Truth, Reality
Gettier, Edmund, 189n8
Giants, 160, 167
Γιγνόμενα, 150
Γιγνώσκω, 191n18
Gillespie, C. M., 163, 209n1, 234n35
Glaucon, 33, 91, 131, 204n18, 210n4, 229n4
Γνῶσις, 107, 187n1, 190–91n18
Gold: adulteration of likened to false account, 129; certification of, 130–31; purification and testing of, 46, 130–31, 200n27

Gomme, A. W., 25, 194n53
Gomperz, Theodor, 193n43
Good, the: in *Epistle 7*, 198n21; must be understood by guardians, 43; possible object of account, 43, 189n10
Goodman, Nelson, 224n22
Görgemanns, Herwig, 229–30n7
Gorgias, 125
Gould, John, 187n1, 195n61
Gowers, Ernest, 225n34
Graeser, Andreas, 202n1, 204n20
Grammar, xiv, 116
Grammar, surface, 132, 138, 225n37
Grant, A., 195n58
Grice, H. P., 188n4, 226n44
Griffiths, A. Phillips, 8, 190n13
Grote, G. M. A., 199n22
Grube, G., 203n7, 204n13, 218n50
Guardians: must understand the good, 43, 45; not impossible, 43; power of, 171; tests for, 45–46
Guenthner, F., 188n3, 199n21, 227n44
Guenthner-Reutter, M., 188n3, 199n21, 227n44
Gulley, Norman, 200n25, 207n47
Guthrie, W. K. C., 195n60, 203n2, 206n41, 219n52, 229n7
Gymnastics, 211n12

Hackforth, R., 205n34, 214n27, 214n28, 221n79
Hamilton, Edith, 191n21
Hamlyn, D. W., 156, 190n18, 232n22, 235n40
Hardie, W. F. R., 203n2, 205n23, 207n54, 208n60
Harmony: and justice, 203n5; and reality, 225n31; psychic, 62–71, 78, 225n30
Harré, R., 218n48
Havelock, Eric, 13, 192n29, 209n1, 211n10, 220n73
Health: as conceived in medicine, 84–85; as goal for psyche, 66–67; disturbances of, 114; how produced, 150; psychic, 66, 69, 74
Hector, 34
Hedonism: alleged Socratic, 194n55; psychological, 26
Heitsch, Ernst, 192n28

Heraclitus, 20, 21, 51, 98, 108, 193n42, 219n52, 219n53
Hermocrates, Syracusan leader, 20
Herodotus, 19, 87, 193n38, 193n39, 211n11, 220n74, 225n37
Hesiod, 19, 22, 24, 192n31, 201n36
Hicken, Winifred, 159, 198n15, 232n26
Hintikka, Jaako, 134–35, 226n42, 226n43
Hippias, 121, 205n25
Hippocrates: ability to give and defend an account, 12; and δυνάμεις, 213–14n26; and εἴδη, 213–14n26; authorship of works in corpus, 192–93n25, 212n13; dating of works, 193n43, 217–18n42, 219n55; friend of the forms, 167; nutritional model, 67; Plato extended notions of, 100; Plato's model for thorough study, 65, 92–93, 205n32; mentioned, 126, 192n26, 214n34. Works: *Airs, Waters, Places*, 213n18, 219n54; *Ancient Medicine*, 83, 95, 96, 97, 98, 108, 210n10, 212n13, 215n37, 217n40, 217–18n42; *Epidemics*, 211n11, 217–18n42; *On Breaths*, 85, 88, 213n16, 213n24; *On Regimen* 83, 86, 92, 99, 114, 217n40, 219n53; *On the Art*, 20, 83, 88, 97, 98, 115, 193n43, 213n26, 219n55; *Precepts*, 211n11; *Prognostic*, 220–21n75; *The Nature of Man*, 12–13, 99, 217n40; *The Sacred Disease*, 83, 213n16
Hofmann, J. B., 197n3
Homer: educational role of, 14, 34; epistemic terms in, 14–22 *passim*; importance of λόγος in, 13, 192n27; on value of surgeon, 211n10; Plato's assessment of, 233n14; translations of, 192n32; works mentioned, 192n31, 193n34, 197n9, 220n74
Homunculi, 74, 77
Honor: appeals to love of, 68; lover of, 59, 60, 75
Horse, Trojan, 98
Hospers, John, 226n44
Hostage simile, 134, 163
Hume, David, 15, 19, 20, 27, 29, 30, 73, 192n35, 207n50, 218n48
Humpty-Dumpty, 226n44
Hunting, 170
Hydra, 63
Hydraulic simile, 77–78

Hypotheses: in dialectic, 169, 177; interpretive, xi; must not go unexamined, 80

Id, the, 192n33
Ἰδέα, ἰδέαι, 87, 219n52. See also Εἶδος, εἴδη, Forms
Ideas. See Forms
Idomeneus, 16
Illumination, 235–36n48
Imitation: and separation of forms, 144; correctness in, 224n18; in accounts, 124
Immanence, of forms, 109. See also Mixture model, Sharing, Μοῖρα
Immortality, 69, 71, 81, 89, 145
Incarnation, 201n28
Incoherence, inconsistency, in dialectic, 38, 40, 131, 170
Indo-European, grammatical structure of, xiv, 116
Induction, and forms, 113
Injustice: and discord, 91; and usurpation of function, 58; no one commits willingly, 71–73
Inquiry, paradigms of, x
Instability, 176
Intellectualism, 10–11, 19, 21–22, 33, 62–63, 193–94n44
Intellectual/non-intellectual distinction, 196n1
Intentions, and meaning, 4, 188n5
Interpretation: principles of, 3; problems in, 191n24. See also Methodology, interpretive
Interwovenness, 139, 152–54, 231n18
Iron, 226n40
Is, alleged ambiguity of Greek word for, 138
Isocrates, 101, 193n38, 225n37
Isomorphism, of polis and psyche, 54–55, 58, 63, 76, 204n15
Ἰσονομία, 84–85, 96

Jaeger, Werner, 216n39
Jespersen, Otto, 226n39
Joachim, H. H., 195n58
John, Saint, 179
Jones, W. H. S., 20, 210n10, 219n53
Justice: and harmony, 91, 203n5; and temperance, 203n5; civic, defined, 54; defined, 203n5; how achieved, 62–71;

psychic source of political, 63; same in polis and psyche, 53–54, 115

Kahn, Charles, 70, 138, 207n46, 219n61, 223n16, 227n45, 227n52
Kant, Immanuel, 146, 192n33, 202n2, 209n1
Καθαρός, 122, 222n4, 224n23
Καθ' αύτόν, meaning of, 105, 123, 230–31n10
Katz, J. J., 199n21, 228n53
Keenan, E., 188n3, 189n7, 199n21
Kenny, Anthony, 66, 203n9, 206n36
Keyt, David, 207n53
Κίβδηλος, κιβδηλεία, 128–29, 224n21
Kimball, John P., 188n2
Kirk, G. S., 193n40, 206n41
Kirwan, Christopher, 229n5
Kneale, Martha, 226n44
Kneale, William, 226n44
Know-how, 195n61
Knowledge: and ability to give and defend an account, 8–9; and justified true belief, 189n8; and motivation, 15; and skepticism, 190n12; by acquaintance, 8–9, 190n18, 191n19; by description, 8–9, 190n18, 190n19; compatible with vice, 10–11; inadequate as translation of ἐπιστήμη, ix, 6–7, 32, 33; insufficient to meet demands of dialectic, 41; on authority, 190n14; Plato's alleged account of, 3. *See also* Ἐπιστήμη
Κοινωνία, 232n22
Κολακεία, 125
Krämer, Hans Joachim, 200n23
Κυβερνήτης, 179
Kustus, George L., 199n23, 232–33n26

Laches, 205n25
Lain-Entralgo, P., 66, 206n37
Lakoff, Robin, 188n6
Language, poetic, 128
Largeness, 215–16n38
Larissa, road to, 226n38
Lattimore, Richard, 23, 194n49
Learning, lover of, 59, 229n4
Lee, E. N., 203n3, 207n46, 207n53, 228n55, 229n7, 231n17, 235n42
Λέγω, earliest uses non-discursive, 34
Leissner, Andreas, 203n2, 207n56

Leontius, 55, 57, 61, 75, 77
Lesky, A., 23, 194n49
Libido, 77
Likeness, 111, 222n7
Limit, 149, 168
Line simile, 128, 190n17, 226n41
Linguistics, method of contrasted with philosophy, 187n1, 191n18
Linnaeus, Carolus, 179
Lion, 63
Location, distinct from confinement, 103, 109
Logic, philosophical, 90–91, 147, 148
Λογισμός, 55, 106
Λογιστικόν, 59
Λόγον διδόναι, 36–37
Λόγος: ability to give and defend necessary for ἐπιστήμη, 12–13, 29, 34; and sorting, 129; as answer to Τί ἐστι . . . , 36–37; as catalog, 35; as particular having a form, 127, 135; as σύνθεσις ῥημάτων καὶ ὀνομάτων, 232n19; form of, 126–29, 222n3; function of, 129; importance of, 13; interpretations of in *Theaetetus*, 159–65; investigation by, 217n39; main uses of term, 36; meaning of in Theaetetus' third account of ἐπιστήμη, 82, 233–34n32; paradigm of, 129; proceeds from and to a certain part of the psyche, 67; provided for oneself and others, 70; relation to paradigm of, 140; senses of, 139–40
Logos-structure, logos-texture, xiv, 152–54, 221–222n80, 231n17
Love of wisdom, 67
Lover of wisdom, 70
Lovers, stereotypical, 76
Loves: multiple for each part of psyche, 59–60; predominant, 59
Lying, 224n21
Lyons, John, 15, 187n1, 189n9, 190n17, 191n18, 191n22, 195n64, 195n65
Lysander, 48
Lysias, 193n38

Mabbott, J. D., 203n5
McDowell, John, 233n31
MacIntyre, Alisdair, xv
Madden, E. H., 218n48
Magnetism model, 90
Malcolm, Norman, 148, 230n9

Many questions, fallacy of, 105
Mapping, 101, 172–73
Martin, T. H., 204*n*19
Meaning: and author's intentions, 4, 188*n*5; and dialectical questioning, 227*n*45; and reference, 139, 142; differences of, 194*n*46; Plato's concept of, 135, 147–48, 227*n*45; Putnam's view of, 181–82, 227*n*50, 230*n*9; social contribution to, 226–27*n*44; speaker's, 226*n*44
Means/end relationships, 60, 76
Meddlesomeness, 57, 58
Medea, 22–24
Medicine: and accounts, 211*n*12, 219*n*55; and forms, 93, 117; and philosophy, 84–88, 95–97, 212*n*13; and the Socratic paradoxes, 20; and understanding of whole of nature, 217*n*40; as addition and subtraction, 85; chief pattern for explanation in, 84–88; Egyptian, 211*n*10; most advanced of ancient sciences, 83–84; origin of, 210*n*10; Plato's familiarity with, 206*n*40
Μεικτά, 149–50
Meinong, Alexius, 124
Melden, A. I., 191*n*23
Melians, 13
Melissus, 83, 192*n*25, 219*n*55
Menander, 216*n*39
Meno, 26
Metallurgical similes, 154
Metallurgy, 130–31, 200*n*27
Metaphor, 151, 224*n*22
Methodology: interpretive, x–xiii, 76–77, 80–81, 113, 151, 191*n*24, 196*n*1, 207*n*53, 208*n*62, 216*n*39, 229*n*4, 230*n*9; linguistic vs. philosophical, 187*n*1, 191*n*18; Plato's, xi, 107–8
Meyer, E., 199*n*22
Midwife, dialectical, 130, 162
Mills, K. W., 221*n*80
Mining, 200*n*27
Misology, 180
Mixture model: and beauty, 218*n*43; clarified in *Sophist*, 168; in Anaxagoras, 143; in late dialogues, 216*n*66; in medicine, 84–88, 96; in Parmenides' poem, 213*n*17; in *Philebus*, 149; in *Republic*, 109–10; in *Sophist*, 151–55; ontological and explanatory role of, 118; Plato's medical precedent for, 115; use of, 111–12; vs. paradigm/copy model, 109–12
Modus tollens, 180
Μοῖρα, 119–20, 143–44, 150
Moline, Jon, 194*n*49, 196*n*67
Monarchy, medical use of notion, 85, 114
Μοναρχία. *See* Monarchy
Money, love of, 59, 60
Μονοειδής, 123, 155, 163, 232–33*n*26
Moore, G. E., 102, 125, 189*n*10
Moravscik, Julius M. E., 195*n*58, 195–96*n*65, 231*n*18, 235*n*42
Morrow, Glenn, 198*n*21, 199*n*22
Μουσική, 62
Mourelatos, A. P. D., 203*n*3, 207*n*53, 213*n*17, 229*n*7, 231*n*17, 235*n*42
Müller, Carl Werner, 206*n*39, 214*n*34, 231*n*13
Müller, Gerhard, 230*n*7
Multitude, the: Plato's changing assessment of, 49; share of power in *Laws*, 49
Murphy, N. R., 187*n*1, 195*n*65, 203*n*2, 204*n*17, 222*n*3
Murray, Gilbert, 16
Muses, 35, 90, 192*n*28
Music: choice of, 69; need of psyche for, 62; psychological sophistication in, 67
Musical similes, Plato's use of, 53
Mysticism, 42–43, 206*n*41, 199*n*21
Mystics, 14
Mytelenaeans, 25
Mythology, 65
Myths: function of in dialogues, 68–70, 206*n*41; intelligibility of, 230*n*8

Names: conventionality of, 135; false, 228*n*54; form of, 228*n*54
Natorp, Paul, 209*n*1
Nature, divine: basis for good judgment, 49, 71, 177; does not change, 202*n*40; in examiners, 202*n*39; unfailing supply of in *Laws*, 50
Nature, human: and changing behavior, 202*n*40; and human efforts in epistemology, 176; interweaving of elements in, 154; not the only nature humans possess, 202*n*37; weakness of, 47–49
Nature, inborn, 50–51
Nature, mortal, 201*n*32

Neely, Wright, 207n56
Negation: and ontology, 235n41; and oppositeness, 139; as otherness, 139, 168; Plato's late treatment of, 139
Nehamas, Alexander, 40, 94, 116, 197n12, 218n43, 218n44, 222n81, 229n4, 230n8, 232n22
Nestor, 13
Nettleship, R. L., 209n1
Nida, E. A., 4, 188n3, 188n6
Νόησις, 52
Νοητά, 153
Noetic "world", 100–105
Νοητὸς τόπος, 100–105
Nomenclature: conventional, 41, 115; medical, 214n34
Nonbeing: not identical with non-existence, 127; otherness, 127, 142
Noncontradiction, principle of, 203n9
Noncontrariety, principle of, 203n9
Νοῦς : always associated with true account, 42; and emotion, 193n39; apprehends forms as distinct and pure, 108; cause of mixtures, 149; cause of motion, 117; cosmic, 94, 150; divine, 200n24; meaning of, 16–19; mixed with ἀνάγκη in *Timaeus*, 110
Nutrition: medical theories of, 67; Plato's use of as model, 92, 150, 217n41

O'Brien, Michael J., 193n44, 195n62, 204n11, 205n29, 207n52
Obscurantism, 80
Occam's eraser, 194n46
Oddness, 214n7
Odysseus, 17, 35
Officials, mistrust of in *Laws*, 174–77
Οἶδα, 14–15, 19
Oligarch, 208n58
One, 222–23n7
One over many, 112–15
Onians, R. B., 194n47
Ὄντα, 92, 223n15
Ontology: faculty, 231n12; link to dialectic, 168–70; of forms, 99, 112–13; Plato's later, 149
Opinion: contrasted with understanding, 38; dependent on forms, 161; in later dialogues, 174; in medical writings, 20; in *Republic*, 227n48; mortal, 201n28; objects of, 135; of each part of psyche, 61–62; tying down, 135
Opposites: and forms, 94–95, 148–49; and negation, 139; approach and retreat of, 89; as cures for opposites in medicine, 85; behavior of on juxtaposition, 145; compatible in particulars, 111; conflict between, 114; distinguished from "others", 167–68; doing and suffering, 54–55, 61–62; in medicine, 220–21n75; in Parmenides' poem, 213n17; in sensible particulars, 94, 119; semantic significance of, 128–29
Orthodoxy, interpretive, x–xi
Ostwald, Martin, 194n58
Otherness, 139, 142, 228n55
Οὐρανός, 104
Owen, G. E. L., 106, 146, 195n58, 207n45, 219n63, 219n64, 228n3, 229n6, 229n7

Page, D. L., 192n26
Παραδείγματα, xiv, 100. *See also* Paradigms, Paradigm/copy model
Paradigm/copy model: and naming, 224n4; complementary to mixture model, 119–21; employed in judging truth of accounts, 128–29; epistemological and moral role of, 118; evidence of, 220n66; in characterizing accounts, 139, 228n55; influence on Plato's view of truth and reality, 121; in *Laws*, 224n18; in *Phaedo*, 144–46; use of, 110–12; wide range of, 138
Paradigms, 60, 75, 76, 77, 109–12, 121, 224n18
Paradoxes, Socratic, 9–12, 20–21, 22, 25–27, 32, 71–74, 195n61, 219n55
Paraphrase, criteria for, 188n3
Parmenides, 81, 108, 109, 126, 166, 167, 210n4, 213n17
Participation: degrees of, 116–17; in dialogues prior to *Phaedo*, 221n79. *See also* Shares, Sharing, Mixture model
Particulars: as imitations, 125–29; bare, 116; epistemic unreliability of, 119; imperfection of, 218n43; mixtures in *Philebus*, 150; mixtures of opposites, 106, 122, 155; mixtures of portions of forms,

115, 143, 155, 214n28, 220n79; participation in opposites, 155; structure of, 116–17
Pathology, 211n10
Patient, ancient physician's view of, 85–87
Patroclus, 34
Pausanias, 194n51
Peck, A. L., 220n70
Pei, Mario, 188n6
Penelope, 16
Penner, Terry, 203n2, 204n14
Πέρας, 149
Persuasion: amenability to, 202n36; and the complexity of the psyche, 65; business of the wisdom-loving part, 65; in Homer, 192n28; internal, 63–64, 66, 68, 69, 73–74; not used by lover of honor, 71; rhetorical, 37
Phaedra, 24–25
Phaedrus, 81, 210n4
Φάρμακα, 66
Φαῦλος, 166
Φιλοχρήματον, 59, 60
Φιλοκερδές, 59
Φιλομαθές, 59
Φιλόνικον, 59
Φιλότιμον, 59
Philosopher-kings, 45, 59
Philosophers, true, 107–8
Φιλόσοφον, 59
Philosophy of science, 100
Φρήν, 22
Φρενο–, 22
Physicians: didactic manner with patients, 83; have ability to give and defend account, 211n12; many named by Plato, 212n13, 212n34; Thracian, 66; travels and lectures of, 83–84, 211n10; true, 66
Φύσις: and conceptual operations, 151; human, 202n40; inborn, 50–51
Piety, 44
Pigment-mixing model, 87, 90, 144
Pigs, and statesmen, 170
Pindar, 19, 154, 193n39, 197n8
Place: Aristotle's view on, 215n38; metaphor for condition, 102
Plague, at Athens, 192n26
Plato, listed with physicians by Galen, 214n39
Platonist, two senses of, 76–77

Pleasure: some approved by best part of psyche, 60; to be mastered, 201n28
Poetry: choice of, 69; psychologically sophisticated, 67–68
Poets, mimetic, 67
Polemics, purpose of, 23–25
Polis, isomorphic to psyche, 53–54, 204n15
Politicians: Plato's assessment of, 62; Plato's experience with, 47–48
Politics: and dialectic, 37, 45; and epistemology, x, 51; and ontology, x; and tests for ἐπιστήμη and ἀρετή, 225n26; conflict in, 208n58; ideals for organization of, 45; in Laws, 149, 175; links to dialectic, epistemology and ontology, x, 47, 143, 149, 176–77; practicality of Plato's, 45, 48
Πολυειδής, 123, 155
Polyphemus, 14
Popper, Karl, xi, xin1, 218n48
Positivism, logical, xi
Power: and ἀρετή, 45; distribution of in Republic, 45–46; explanatory, 74, 76. See also Character-powers, Quality-things, Δύναμις
Power/mixture model: alleged difficulties with, 143–49; influence on Plato's view of truth and reality, 121; more suggestive than paradigm/copy, 142
Powers: causal role of, 87, 144; equal balance of in health, 84–85; in contention, 225n31; in medicine, 84–88
Prauss, Gerold, 113, 146, 159, 197n4, 197n7, 197n8, 220n71, 221n77, 229n6, 231n17, 232n21, 232n26, 233n27
Predicates: attributive, 228–29n3, 229n4; "complete", 229n5, 230n8; incomplete, 145–48, 215–16n38, 228–29n3, 229n4, 230n8, 230–31n10; relational, 215n38, 228–29n3, 229n4
Predication, Plato's alleged theory of, 115–16, 146–48
Premises, agreed, 88
Prodicus, teacher of Socrates, 214n34
Properties: and forms, 220n70; essential and accidental, 221n79; immanent, 143
Propositions, 134–37
Πρός τι, 106, 147–48, 230n10
Protagoras, 26, 165–66
Ψευδός, 128

Psyche: adjustment of parts, x; and life, 145; as true self, 205n31; causes motion, 92, 93, 117; complexity of, 232n19; division of, 203–4n11, 207n57; health of, 78; mixed with bodies, 92; number of parts thereof, 204n15; parts like agents, 64; parts of, 48, 53, 76; parts of in *Phaedo*, 206n44; parts overlap in capacities, 74; parts responsible for one's movements, 56; parts termed εἴδη, 75–76; relation to the senses, 233n28; unity of, 54, 77–78
Psyches, and form, 75–76
Psychologist, equivalent to dialectician, etc., 70
Psychology: as self-study, 65; faculty, 59, 202n2, 205n28
Psychotherapy, 66, 206n37
Purification, dialectical, 46
Purity, 75–76, 106, 122–23, 140, 148–49, 155–57, 224n2, 232
Putnam, Hilary, xi, xi$n$1, 181, 226–27n44, 227n50, 230n9
Pythagoras, 85, 213n14
Pythagoreans, 210n4

Quality-things, 87, 93, 115, 144, 214n28
Quarry simile, 171, 235n44
Questions, order of, 39–40
Quine, Willard van Orman, xi, xi$n$1, 101, 187n1, 219n58, 225n35

Rackham, H., 26, 194n58
Raven, J. E., 193n40
Realism, Plato's ontological, 224n18
Realities, forms the only, 92
Reality: and existence, 223n16; as approximation to paradigm, 127; as genuineness, 137; degrees of, 121–23, 226n41. *See also* Truth
Reason: and passion, 29–30; as ability, 36; as faculty, 58–59; practical, 192n33
Recollection: and dialectic, 45, 200n25; apprehension of forms, 106; basis for account, 35; basis for discussion, 182; doctrine holds truth is in us, 132; in later dialogues, 222n2; Socrates' description of, 190n14
Reduction: of polis to parts, 55; of psyche to parts, 55, 56

Reference: and falsity, 139; and forms, 181; and meaning, 136, 182, 188n5. *See also* Denotation, Meaning
Referring, as psychological activity, 136
Refutation: dialectical, 40, 165; rhetorical, 165; rhetorical and dialectical distinguished, 37–38
Regimen, control of mixture, 86
Regress, 74–76, 205n30
Reid, Thomas, 202n2, 205n24
Reincarnation, 209n65, 230n8
Reputation: appeals to love of, 68; lover of, 76
Rescher, Nicholas, 219n57, 219n59
Resemblance, 222n4
Responsibility, moral, 208n60
'Ρητόν, 43, 189n10
Rhetoric: internal use of, 69; ordinary, 125; psychological sophistication in, 65, 67–68
Rhetorician, 66, 207n57
Richards, John F. C., 226n40
Risks, political, 143
Ritter, Constantin, 199n22, 202n1
Robin, Léon, 203n4
Robinson, Richard, 36, 197n10, 197n11, 198n16, 198n17
Robinson, T. M., 203n2, 203n6, 205n24, 236n50
Romilly, J. de, 193n41
Roots, 95
Rorty, Richard, 203n3, 207n45, 229n7, 231n17, 235n42
Ross, W. D., 110, 156, 194n58, 210n4, 219n65, 232n23, 234n35
Roth, M., 189n8
Russell, Bertrand, 190n15, 214n32, 216n39
Ryle, Gilbert, 181, 191n23, 233n28

Sail simile, 109, 215–16n38
Sambursky, S., 193n40
Σαφήνεια, 225n32
Σαφής, 132, 225n32
Sapir, Edward, 226n39
Sayre, Kenneth, 198n15, 233n31, 233n32
Science, Greek, 83
Searle, J. R., 188n2, 199n21
Self-contradiction, 38
Self-control, 54, 65, 74
Self-inferiority, 72

Self-predication, 112
Self-study, 65
Self-understanding, 24
Sellars, Wilfred, 220n76
Sense-perception: and perfection, 113; fails to apprehend what is most real, 106; used to provoke reasoning, 106–7
Senses, and psyche, 233n28
Sensible things: and their attributes, 221–22n80; as copies, 109–12; as mixtures, 109–12; deficiency of, 111–12; impossible to conceive firmly, 136–37
Separation, of forms, 95–97, 117, 144, 230–31n10
Shares, 143
Sharing, in form, 116–17, 119
Shepherd, divine, 175
Shorey, Paul, 203n2, 205n28, 216n39
Shuttle, function of, 129
Simmias, 7, 69, 105, 126, 221n79, 230n8
Simplicity, 106, 140
Skepticism, 176
Skeptics, 190n12
Skill, inadequate as rendering of ἐπιστήμη, 15–16
Slavery, internal, 71
Smelting, 131, 200–201n27
Smith, Adam, 196n66
Smith, Edwin, papyrus, 211n10
Snell, Bruno, 22, 191n22, 194n48
Socrates: activities of, 178; futility of answers to the "Socratic Question", xiii; positive views indistinguishable from Plato's, xiii, 178; skill in discussion, 180
Solmsen, Friedrich, xiv, xivn3, 192n27, 192n28
Σοφία, 10, 20, 44
Sophist: account of by division, 173–74, 234n38; as image-maker, imitator, 125, 172, 223n13, 223n17
Sophistry, 125, 170
Sophocles, 22
Σοφός, 13
Soranus, 211n11
Sorting, 129
Sosa, E., 219n59
Soul. See Psyche
Space, 221–22n80
Space, logical, 101
Speaking, object of, 68–69

Specialization, principle of, 58
Spelling simile, 157–58, 161, 166, 171
Spirit, 55, 59
Square roots, 167
Stampe, Dennis, 138, 188n2, 188n4, 226n44, 227n53
Στάσις, 55
State: ideal, 49; second-best, 48–49
Statesman, 143, 172, 175, 201n36
Stenzel, Julius, 235n43
Stereotypes, 76, 77, 182
Stewart, J. A., 195n58
Stough, Charlotte, 221n79
Stout, G. F., 73, 204n22, 207n49
Strachey, L., 208n64
Stranger, Eleatic, 131, 165
Strauss, Leo, 201n29
Striker, Gisela, 150–51, 231n14
Stylometry, 146, 229n7
Subject, 115, 214n28
Subject-predicate structure, xiv, 113, 152–54. See also Logos-structure
Substance, 115, 214n28
Succinctness, 39
Suidas, 211n11
Συμπλοκή, 153, 231n18
Sun simile, 100, 128, 190n17, 222n4
Συναιτίαι, 93
Σύνεσις, 20
Συνοπτικός, xi, 151
Σύνθεσις, 153
Surgeon, 211n10
Symptoms, in medicine, 96
Syracuse, Plato's experiences in, 47

Taber, C., 199n3, 188n6
Taylor, A. E., 81, 198n20, 199n22, 202n1, 209n1, 210n4, 210n5, 218n51, 234n39
Taylor, Richard, 73, 207n51, 214n31, 214n33
Τέχνη, and ἐπιστήμη, 46
Temkin, Jack, 235n42
Temperance, 91, 203n5
Terminology: not our major concern, 6–7, 33; problem of instability in, 173
Testing: behavioral, 45, 47; destructive, 130–31. See also Dialectical testing
Theaetetus, 82, 158–59
Theodorus, 165

Θεός, 166
Therapy, by words, 66–69
Thersites, 192n27
Thinking, likened to sensing, 138
Third man argument, 113, 220n70, 221n76
Thompson, W. H., 205n34
Thorson, T. L., 206n38
Thought, discursive view of, 63–64, 136–37
Thrasymachus, 134, 205n25, 211–12n12
Threeness, 214n27
Thucydides, 13, 20, 21, 101, 193n41, 194n52, 200n27, 220n74, 225n37
Θυμοειδές, 59, 62
Θυμός, 21
Τί ἐστι questions: accounts are answers to, 36, 38; in medicine, 99; Plato's clarification procedure, 80
Timaeus, 81
Time, 135, 226n42
Timocracy, 203–4n11
Τις, 215n37
Τόπος, 101–2
Touchstone, 133, 226n40
Tracking simile, 171
Transcendence, of forms, 109
Translation: aim of, 4; conditions, standards for, 4–5, 188n3, 196n1; exact translation hypothesis, 188–89n27; principles of, 3; problems in, xv, 4, 33, 187n1, 188n6, 190–91n18, 191n19; requires sameness of semantic properties, 189n7
True opinion, 235n48
Trust: grounds for, ix; of officials, 175–77
Truth: and falsity, 138–40; and quality of referent, 140; and reality, 141–42; as approximation to paradigm, 121–22, 126; as qualitative perfection, 121–23; conceived on paradigm/copy model, 125–29; correspondence theory of, 222n3; criterion for, 131–32; degrees of, 132–33, 225n35, 226n41; difficulties in applying paradigm/copy model to, 123–25; never refuted, 137; object of dialectic, 41; sufficiency of coherence tests for prior to *Laws*, 132; tested destructively, 130–34
Truths, conceptual, x
Tying-down simile, 174, 226n40
Tyrant, 56, 61, 74, 208n58
Tzetzes, 211n11

Ὑγιής, 132, 225n32
Unanimity, 66, 204n18. *See also* Harmony
Understanding: and true opinion, 235n48; as translation of ἐπιστήμη, 29–31, 187n1, 195n65; conditions for, 41; encouraged in *Laws*, 50; medical, 211n12; objects of, 158; on mixture model, 110; requires highest degree of truth, 133
Unger, Peter, 190n12
Universals, 40, 112–15, 216n39, 220n69
Ὑπό, 90–91
Usage, demotic or popular, 26–27, 194n56, 207n48, 222n4
Usurpation, 57, 58, 60–61

Variation, elegant, 227n46
Verdenius, W. J., 206n36
Verificationism, x–xi
Victory: in eristic disputes, 197n14; lover of, 59, 60
Virtue: and knowledge, 9–11; and wisdom, 73–74; lacking if dialectical tests failed, 143; problems in locating, 50; Thrasymachus' account of, 205n25
Vision, mental, 42, 97, 99, 198n19, 228n53
Vlastos, Gregory, 10, 84, 87, 95, 124, 133, 138, 191n20, 195n61, 198n18, 200n26, 201n30, 201n32, 203n2, 203n5, 206n36, 213n15, 213n22, 213n23, 214n30, 216n39, 218n45, 218n48, 220n68, 220n70, 221n76, 223n10, 223n16, 225n36, 227n52
Von Fritz, Kurt. *See* Fritz, Kurt von
Von Wright, G. H. *See* Wright, G. H. von

Wants, claimed vs. real, 71–74
War, civil, 55, 58
Way, longer and harder, 205n32
Weaving simile, 152–54
Werkmeister, W. H., 207n46
"What is . . . " questions: in medicine, 99; Plato's use of, 80
White, Alan R., 123–24, 223n9
White, F. C., 218n44, 221n79
Wilamowitz-Moellendorff, Ulrich von, 23, 194n49, 199n22
Wilkes, K. V., 208n61
Will: and Platonic psychology, 73; freedom of, 207n52; weakness of, 26–27, 28, 72–73

Index

Williams, Bernard, 203*n*3, 203*n*6, 205*n*33
Wilson, J. R. S., 204*n*14, 207*n*56, 208*n*62
Wine: lover of, 63; use of in testing candidates, 47
Winnington-Ingram, R. P., 23, 194*n*49
Wisdom: and virtue, 73–74; inadequate translation of ἐπιστήμη, 28; in polis owing to guardians, 55–56; love of, lover of, xv, 59, 64–65, 71, 72, 229*n*4; of Socrates, 42–43; pretenders to, 45
Wittgenstein, Ludwig, 209*n*1
Wolff, Christian, 204*n*22
Woodruff, Paul, 228*n*1
Woozley, A. D., 189*n*8, 190*n*16, 191*n*19, 203*n*2, 204*n*17, 205*n*23, 207*n*54, 207*n*56, 208*n*60

Words, power of, 66–67
Worlds, 117
Worlds, possible, 101
Wright, G. H. von, 219*n*57

Xenophon, 13, 14, 24, 83, 192*n*28, 193*n*38, 200*n*26, 225*n*37, 236*n*50

Yandell, Keith, 207*n*50

Zalmoxis, Thracian physician, 66
Zeller, Eduard, 204*n*21
Zeno, 108, 210*n*8
Zeus, 19–20, 159
Ziff, Paul, 194*n*46

JACKET DESIGNED BY CAROLINE BECKETT
COMPOSED BY GRAPHIC COMPOSITION, INC., ATHENS, GEORGIA
MANUFACTURED BY THOMSON-SHORE, INC., DEXTER, MICHIGAN
TEXT AND DISPLAY LINES ARE SET IN TIMES ROMAN

Library of Congress Cataloging in Publication Data
Moline, Jon, 1937–
Plato's theory of understanding.
Includes bibliographical references and index.
1. Plato–Knowledge, Theory of. 2. Knowledge,
Theory of. 3. Comprehension. I. Title.
B398.K7M64   121   81–50826
ISBN 0–299–08660–7   AACR2